URBAN'S WAY

Urban Meyer, the Florida Gators, and His Plan to Win

BUDDY MARTIN

Thomas Dunne Books
St. Martin's Griffin ⚇ New York

To

Lori Gregory,

Christy Martin,

Rebecca Simmons,

and

Brenden Martin,

Who taught me to be a father

THOMAS DUNNE BOOKS.
An imprint of St. Martin's Press.

URBAN'S WAY. Copyright © 2008, 2009 by Buddy Martin. All rights reserved. Printed in the United States of America. For information, address St. Martin's Press, 175 Fifth Avenue, New York, N.Y. 10010.

www.thomasdunnebooks.com
www.stmartins.com

Design by Sarah Maya Gubkin

The Library of Congress has catalogued the hardcover edition as follows:

Martin, Buddy.
    Urban's way : Urban Meyer, the Florida Gators, and his plan to win / Buddy Martin.—1st ed.
        p. cm.
    Includes index.
    ISBN 978-0-312-38407-4
1. Meyer, Urban.   2. Football coaches—Florida—Biography.   3. Florida Gators (Football team)—History.   4. University of Florida—Football—History.   I. Title.
    GV939.M48M37   2008
    796.332092—dc22
    [B]
                                                                2008030792

ISBN 978-0-312-60494-3 (trade paperback)

First St. Martin's Griffin Edition: November 2009

10 9 8 7 6 5 4 3 2 1

PRAISE FOR *U*

"Everyone knows Urban Meyer is a great coach, an outstanding person, a proven leader, and an excellent husband and father. Now, in *Urban's Way*, he reveals why he is successful in every facet of his life."

—Lou Holtz, ESPN

"Urban actively coaches on the field and has supreme game-day leadership qualities—calling the right play at the right time. We all know it takes great players to win and Urban and his staff are doing a super job of coaching and recruiting. They also get the best athletes."

—Earle Bruce, former head coach of Ohio
State, Colorado State, and Iowa State

"Urban Meyer keeps proving he's the best college football coach in the nation—and not just the 'Gator Nation.' Now comes one of the best writers in the nation, Buddy Martin, to tell you a lot more about Meyer and the Florida Gators, and keep you entertained along the way."

—Dan Jenkins, author and sportswriter

"Few journalists gain such access and fewer still are Martin's equal as historian, reporter, writer, and fan of football excellence. Through Martin's work, readers will learn and understand how Urban Meyer became the newest legend in college football."

—Dave Kindred, author and columnist

"Every once in a while a coach comes along who seems to have the key to the secrets of the universe hidden somewhere in the 300-plus pages of his playbook. Urban Meyer seems to that guy for college football. I know no one better than Buddy Martin to deconstruct the inner workings of the current 'It' Coach."   —Jack McCallum, senior writer, *Sports Illustrated*

"Martin, a longtime chronicler of the UF program, does fine research and . . . reveals the coach's 'Plan to Win.'"   —*The Tampa Tribune-Times*

"Florida football fans wanting an inside look at the Gators' program will be appeased by *Urban's Way*."   —*The Florida Times-Union*

Also By Buddy Martin

The Boys from Old Florida: Inside Gator Nation

Down Where the Old Gators Play, Volume II

Down Where the Old Gators Play, Volume I

Looking Deep (with Terry Bradshaw)

Parting Shots (with Dan Issel)

The Denver Broncos: That Championship Season

CONTENTS

ACKNOWLEDGMENTS

This book takes the reader places he or she has never been for a close-up look at the innermost workings of a major college football program with a dynamic young coach. Any writer would have relished this opportunity, as did I, but the real payoff was the freedom with which I was allowed to lurk about on the football premises.

I'm grateful for the trust placed in me for that assignment. And to Coach Urban Meyer and his staff—especially my project coordinator, Hiram de Fries, whose original idea it was to write this book. Hiram opened doors never made accessible to me in more than forty years of covering college athletics. Anything in this book with a ring of authenticity is due to his providing that access. Hiram worked through every process, including learning how to "blog" so as to provide additional insight to the book.

I also greatly appreciated and admired the candor of Urban and his wife Shelley, whose willingness to speak openly, without sugarcoating their life experiences, enriched the story lines greatly. Urban's coaching staff was most cooperative. And Urban's father, Bud Meyer, and sisters Gigi Escoe and Erika Jones were very helpful in providing information on Urban's early years.

A special thanks to the Florida sports information department: Steve McClain, John Hines, Denver Parler, and Jennifer Wagner. Also the help of Urban's director of football administration, Jon Clark, and of executive assistant Nancy Scarborough; retired Florida Highway Patrol major Malcom Jowers; Lt. Stacy Ettel of University of Florida Police Department; Johnny Horn of the Gainesville Police Department; and assistant director of video Wayne Cederholm.

There was also the great support of my friends and associates—Gator Country colleague John Fineran edited and proofed every word; managing editor Franz Beard and friend Augie Greiner played the roles of cheerleader and adviser. *Gator Country* photographer Tim Casey's excellent photographs enhanced this book. And Ballyhoo Grill's owner, Chris Fragale, often provided the food and the table for our planning meetings.

A special bouquet to our wives, Joan Martin and Trudi de Fries.

And finally, thanks to the players at Florida, Utah, and Bowling Green for their cooperation in telling the real story of Urban Meyer, whom I found to be a unique person and remarkable football coach.

FOREWORD

The Real Story of Gator Football

Coaching football is not what people see on TV or read in the newspapers. In reality it is a very different story and daily challenge that cannot be met without quality people around you—both in the home and on the job. For the Meyer family, they are almost one and the same.

When I proposed marriage to Shelley, she had somehow already determined this challenge would be met as our team effort. Without her commitment and own vision of her husband's true calling, I'd never have been the head coach at the University of Florida today. Or maybe even been in coaching at all. Shelley knew this was really a people business, and there could be no separation of the two. The only choice for us, then, was inclusion and total immersion.

So at Florida, when we talk about "the Gator Football Family," it reaches far beyond just the huddle to include parents, children, spouses, girlfriends, brothers, sisters, and grandparents of players, coaches, and administrators. As coaches, our responsibility extends into every facet of our players' lives. Education is uppermost. And even after the players graduate, they remain part of our extended family.

I agreed to do this book because of my desire to pull back the curtain and allow members of "the Gator Nation," former players, future players, and just plain football fans to see what our program is all about. What you will be reading on these pages is an unvarnished version of how it really looks and works inside Florida Gator football.

That is why we granted veteran journalist Buddy Martin access to the inner workings of Gator football without censoring his work or telling him what to write or how to portray anybody.

I have been blessed to serve as a head football coach at three schools. All have been rewarding to me, and I am especially honored and proud to be the head football coach of the University of Florida.

The players, coaches, and support staff at Florida are dedicated and aligned to the philosophy that football is coached and played with maximum effort and competitive excellence. If our players carry that theory forward into their future lives as a part of the great Gator Nation and become the best husbands and fathers they can be, then we have won at the game of life.

As a young player, position coach, and now a head coach, I've always enjoyed the stories about people's journeys and the accomplishments both expected and unexpected. This is the story of our journey. We hope you enjoy it.

Urban Meyer

Head Football Coach, University of Florida

PREFACE

Lunch with Urban by the Lake

My cell phone rang and the name URBAN popped up on it as I was driving east on a lightly traveled north Florida road Saturday, December 22, 2007, about half past noon.

"I'm at the deli," the voice said. "What kind of sandwich do you want?"

No sandwich, I said, I'll just take a salad. No salads, he replied, so he'd bring chili instead.

Florida's national championship coach—he with the football blinders and the high-octane metabolism—was finally ready to tell his story.

And Urban Meyer was even bringing lunch.

After more than three hundred days of contemplation and observation of the Florida Gator football program from the inside, my interview with Meyer was about to take place at his lake home in a remote setting—Old Florida, Deep South, with cypress trees sprouting from a clear-water lake and sunrises that stir the soul.

This was a culmination of nearly a year's worth of research, interviews, and discussion about Florida football in one of the most intensive inside looks at a college football program ever afforded a working journalist. I had been granted access to almost any venue requested and to any person I needed to interview.

What was this conversation with Meyer going to reveal? How candid would he be about his professional and personal life? In three years at Florida, nobody had ever really got inside the head or beneath the public persona of this enigmatic Ohioan. Though I had followed him and his team closely from the start of his regime and done a couple of personal interviews over those thirty-seven months, I didn't really know much about Urban Meyer the man.

Those of us who had covered Gator football for a long time and had a personal relationship with Steve Spurrier wanted him to return to his old job and succeed Ron Zook. Meyer had been a compromise candidate for Spurrier fans. However, something different about Meyer intrigued me as I began tracking him over the next three years, regularly covering Gator games, attending his press conferences, grabbing an occasional one-on-one. He was harder to catch than Percy Harvin, more difficult to stop than Tim Tebow.

Our first private talk had come in August of 2005 when he spared me a fifteen-minute interview in an upper room at Central Florida Community College in Ocala, Florida, carving out his answers in between bites of barbecued chicken dinner just before his Marion County Gator Club talk.

In January of 2007, a few weeks after Florida's national championship win, one of Urban's associates telephoned me about possibly writing the coach's autobiography. I accepted. However, Meyer would eventually pull the plug on that first project in the spring after becoming extremely upset about the off-the-field conduct of a player. "Right now," he told me several days later, "we're a train wreck." That was my first clue about the burden Meyer carries for players who go astray.

Meyer would later reconsider and cooperate for the writing of this book in a different format, agreeing to an authorized biography instead of an autobiography. I wanted the book to be a portrait of the real Urban Meyer. He wanted this book to offer an honest portrayal of his program, hopefully providing insight and career advice for young coaches, and couldn't see why people would really be interested in "all that personal stuff about me." We wound up doing both.

In late summer of 2007, I was about to become "the fly on the wall," a sort of an invisible extra without a speaking part in the documentation of Florida Gator football.

As a prelude to writing this book, I had been in Meyer's presence for several hours at a time over fourteen weeks, but until now our dialogue had been limited to questions asked by me in group settings at his weekly postgame press conferences, or after the Heisman Trophy announcement, or following an occasional practice. Our agreement was that he would coach his football team, and I would be granted access to an occasional private coaches' meeting; locker room gatherings on game day for pregame countdowns, halftime meetings, and post-game settings; a trip to the stadium on the team bus for the "Gator Walk" behind Tim Tebow; Friday-night dinners at the hotel with the team; rides on the team bus—even one in a police cruiser; and visits to the coaching booth, where I witnessed staff discussions of game strategy on the headsets, watching and listening in fascination.

Along the way, I held extensive interviews with each of Meyer's assistant coaches and had numerous informal chats with support personnel. I was also provided regular weekly advisories by staff member Hiram de Fries about the inner workings of the program.

I even ran on the field in "the Swamp" with the team before the Tennessee game to experience what it would be like for any Gator fan willing to make the $1 million contribution to the school for that privilege.

I was there in New York for the jubilant occasion at the Hard Rock Cafe and on Times Square as Meyer and Tebow strolled up Broadway like two teenage boys who had just been invited to the prom by their best girlfriends.

During this time I found out that when football is on the mind of Urban Meyer—especially when it concerns his staff or players—other things are invisible and inaudible to him.

During the season, I had no private conversations with Meyer. I had spoken to him only when spoken to, maybe a half dozen times—then usually just a simple "Hello." I had agreed to keep the material for this book confidential until it was published.

When the 2007 season ended we would talk, which was now going to happen in about fifteen minutes. I was about to walk into the front door of his then empty lake home for an interview that would determine the course of all that work.

"The door is open," Meyer had said on his cell from the deli. "Just go on in and I'll be there shortly."

This was my first of two trips to Meyer's lake house in four days during a break before the Capital One Bowl game. All the players and assistant coaches were off for the holidays. Meyer had decided that now—three days before Christmas 2007 and nine days before Florida's bowl game against Michigan—was the best time.

There were no rules for the interview, no attempts to dodge issues or the least bit of resistance to any of my questions. There would be two sessions. At the end of the first, which lasted just under four hours, he wanted to do one more session on Christmas Eve morning at seven thirty, which would require a wake-up call of 5:00 A.M. for my trip from Ocala. It was so dark on the drive north up U.S. 301 that you could almost slice off a piece of the night with your hand. By 6:30 A.M. on Christmas Eve, I was parked at the corner gas station, plying myself with coffee, going over pre-interview notes and making small talk with the help while waiting for sunrise.

"Urban Meyer got a home around here?" I said to a man behind the counter, asking a question to which I already knew the answer.

"Sure does, right down on the lake," the employee replied. "Comes in here all the time. Speaks to everybody. He's not stuck-up like Steve Spurrier!"

Before driving off, I phoned Meyer to inquire about his need for caffeine.

"I'm putting coffee on right now," he said. His wife, Shelley, was back in Gainesville with their two daughters, and he was at the lake home with their son, Nate.

In a moment, Urban called back to say that he couldn't find the coffee, so I should bring some. (It was hiding in the freezer.) Making a U-turn, I backtracked two miles to pick it up at the gas station. Meyer then provided the breakfast: homemade German Christmas stollen bread made by the mother of defensive back Kyle Jackson.

When we did finally sit down following Florida's 9-3 regular season, Meyer revealed the most intimate details of his program, his coaching philosophy, his convictions, his joys, his vision, his disappointments, his fears, and his evolution as a coach.

Meyer was honest, open, and forthcoming in revealing a side previously unseen in public settings. Surprisingly, the next four hours produced frank and candid responses from the forty-three-year-old coach. There was almost an eagerness now to talk about his personal journey along Urban's Way.

Finally, in the aftermath of Meyer's second national championship, we sat down once again in the spring of 2009 for a lengthy interview in his stadium office, where he recounted the 2008 title run. This time he seemed calm, reassured, optimistic, and very comfortable in what he called "the best job in America."

PROLOGUE

A streak of first light tumbled softly across the northern sky and bounced gently off the lake. Then the sun suddenly illuminated the semicloudy Christmas Eve morning to reveal the near ancient and rare cypress trees that had grown from the shallows, one of the last vestiges of north-central Florida's virgin woodland. Urban Meyer, locked deep in thought about all things Gator football, was temporarily disrupted by God's handiwork. "Look at the sun out there, hitting the trees," said Meyer, almost in awe.

The man whose consumption by the game once justifiably earned him the nickname Captain Emergency temporarily put his football thoughts on a kind of TV time-out to connect with the universe. Maybe he wasn't coming to a complete stop to smell the roses, but he was at least yielding the right of way to nature's awesome beauty. This was a Kodak moment, if not a Meyer family Rembrandt, because it captured an Urban rarely seen by the public. It validated the possibility that, beyond the almost ludicrous expectations placed on him and his football associates by himself and others, his maniacal obsession with detail and zealous quest of winning, there could possibly be a flea-flicker of real life for Urban Meyer.

Turns out there are more portraits of him like this in captivity than first thought. The lake home is a safe harbor of freshwater and a natural fortress carved out of a pristine southland forest where he can decompress and rediscover himself. Here he can find a semblance of balance in an otherwise lopsided, upside-down world that requires every ounce of his energy and being for winning games and changing young men's lives.

When his team is losing or falling short of expectations, or his players are acting badly, Meyer's body and soul are so profoundly tormented that he can barely perform the normal functions of everyday living—such as eating, sleeping, shaving and, sometimes, just breathing.

Otherwise, whatever peace he can find starts in his home with his wife, Shelley, and three children, where he can also mix with his extended football family. Without these elements of comfort and security, Urban Meyer truly might not survive the trials of his self-torture, because he does not endure failure well at all.

In fact, while on the set for Fox TV in the Superdome at the BCS Championship Game between LSU and Ohio State in January 2008, Urban became physically ill—sick to his stomach—because his Florida Gators missed out on a chance to play in it. "We should be here," he told a TV associate.

Meyer not only has emotions at least as deep as the lake right out there through the sliding glass doors—a favorite docking place where he goes to plumb for cosmic insight and perspective—but a spiritual depth as well.

Out on that lake today, the morning sun on the trees had inspired that spiritual side, triggering flashbacks of last summer and the intimacy of a father-son experience that he has come to hold sacred. In the predawn darkness, around 6:00 A.M., sometimes Urban will grab his cup of coffee and a box of Corn Pops for his young son, Nate, soon to be awakened, then head down to the boat just a couple of first downs away. They will launch their Ski Nautique boat—occasionally Nate even gets to drive—and navigate toward a special vantage point where a boy and his dad can catch the morning sun peeping over the trees from the east. This is truly the Breakfast of Champions for Florida's national champion football coach. "It's unbelievable," Meyer said.

Out on the still waters, the boat is anchored, and so is the soul of Urban Meyer. But he knows more storms will be coming.

PART ONE

The Road to Gainesville

I

The Cul-de-Sac of Champions

Three men sat looking at each other in an empty University of Phoenix locker room, pondering the impact of what had just happened. Florida's national championship football coach glanced up at his father, Bud, and his mentor Earle Bruce, digging deep for some profound declaration. Urban Meyer's lifetime dream was now a reality, and the magnitude of the accomplishment began to seep into his consciousness.

All week long, Meyer had tried to trick himself into thinking his opponent was just another team in red and gray. Just once during practice, when he had heard the sound of the Ohio State band playing "Hang On Sloopy," it hit home so hard that he doubled-clutched his emotions at the realization that he was coaching against the *The* team.

Honestly, Urban's biggest dream could never have been this big: a complete annihilation of *The* Ohio State, 41–14. The Ohio State of his boyhood affection, The Ohio State where he cut his coaching teeth, The Ohio State that had also once fired his mentor Earle Bruce, and, by the way, The No. 1 team in America.

The joy—even more so the relief—was making him feel almost giddy and light of body. "I've never felt that way in my life," Meyer said later. "It was like somebody had drilled holes in the bottoms of my feet and drained out all the pressure."

Football coaches rarely have time to stop and reflect on their success as it is unfolding. There is always the next season, next game, or next down to spoil the mood. But tonight, Meyer would briefly suspend that obligation. The events of January 8, 2007, had set the college football galaxy on its ear. However, even if he was contemplating one tiny taste of gloating, his two companions would probably not have tolerated it.

Turning to the two men who always seemed to have the answers in his life, Meyer was hoping for some sort of affirmation when he proclaimed:

"And now I get to do this for fun. It's over! We won the national championship!" Now that the monkey was finally off Urban's back, it was time to celebrate, have some fun and enjoy coaching football the next season—wasn't it?

To his credit, the no-nonsense, down-and-dirty, hard-boiled Earle Bruce didn't laugh out loud. And since they weren't the kind of guys given to breaking out in table-dancing or backflipping, the coldly logical Bruce and iconoclastic Bud Meyer merely smiled and nodded.

Bud says he was already thinking that his son should have been out recruiting for the next season. Nobody knows for sure what Earle was thinking, but Urban figures he was just being humored by his old boss. "Coach Bruce was probably looking at me and really thinking, *'yeah, rrriight!'*" Urban would say.

Then—poof!—that elusive moment was gone. No champagne toasts. No victory laps. No ticker-tape parades. No flights to Bermuda to lie on the beach and toast the ultimate victory with little umbrella drinks. The next morning in Gainesville it was back to school, back to recruiting, and back to babysitting one hundred or so football players. Urban had to pinch himself to make sure this had really happened the night before.

Almost like a Blockbuster rental movie, Urban Meyer's Marvelous Adventure was over and felt as if it were due back Wednesday at five.

The dream had come true, however, and was, indeed, truly remarkable.

This former over-the-top, semi-out-of-control, control freak had hit the college football lottery. All those years as an assistant coach siphoning off the knowledge from his bosses, squirreling it away in diary form, and then field-testing his pilfered ideas—all that had come together like Harry Potter magic.

If there was a football god, he was probably repaying Urban Meyer as a responsible caretaker of the game and for being straight up with his players and fellow coaches for twenty-one years. There was no extended warranty on the honeymoon because he was back to work coaching that next morning. Even if there was a new college football sheriff, he was going to have to run for reelection.

Bud and Earle knew that the afterglow would soon be dimmed. Not even they could have predicted the ensuing struggle for the Florida Gator coaches, players, and fans in the 2007 season.

The history of Florida's incredible run in football and basketball programs, however, was still being written. Nobody quite realized that maybe a college football dynasty could be unfolding right before their eyes.

Coming when it did—just four years after Steve Spurrier had suddenly departed and the football program had taken a dip under Ron Zook—this national championship and football resurgence would revitalize the Gator Nation. It also validated the choice of Director of Athletics Jeremy Foley and President Bernie Machen, who had received some criticism for taking the guy from Utah over the return of the favorite son, Steve Spurrier. Now they looked like geniuses.

Schools such as Notre Dame suddenly had Urban Meyer envy. In just two years at Florida—only his sixth overall as head coach—the guy with the "gimmicky" offense that critics said wouldn't fly in the Southeastern Conference had possession of the crystal football. But was he a onetime wonder, or had Urban Meyer restored the Gators' glory of the nineties?

For sure, Meyer had become the brightest star in the coaching constellation as a sort of Bob Vila fixer-upper of college football. Eventually, after his fourth season at Florida, his success rate of three programs over eight seasons as a head coach was off the charts: 83 wins and only 17 losses for a whopping .830 winning percentage.

In his third consecutive season as a head coach at the same school for the first time ever, Meyer knew he would have to prove he could win with his own material.

I would have a chance to find out for myself, becoming virtually embedded with the Gator team. I amassed a large amount of information and began studying the human dynamics of his program to try to crack the code.

This was a great vantage point and a choice assignment for a columnist/author whose roots tapped into that north-central Florida dirt . . . who grew up listening to Florida football on the radio before there were live telecasts . . . and who spent a large chunk of his forty-year journalism career observing and writing about these Gators.

This is not to say that Meyer's magic formula was uncovered or that company secrets were revealed. However, after several tutorials on Meyer's "Plan to Win," I began to understand this was the matrix for everything and Urban's blueprint for success. Understanding of the Plan gave considerable enlightenment about the amount of time, money, and energy that Meyer and his staff put in to the care and feeding of players. At the same time, much is expected from those athletes as willing participants in Meyer's "competitive excellence."

All his former players admit playing for Meyer "is hard!" Those who survive the rigors of mat drills and early-morning running punishment for missed class or misbehaving badly, however, have a sense of accomplishment, although, admittedly, maybe not at the time they were retching over a trash can or laboring to get up the stadium stairs.

He promises each player: "I will not quit on you." Much of Meyer's approach stems from his conviction that he owes a player every chance to play, to graduate, and to achieve a normal, happy life by sorting out whatever demons haunt him.

Our close-up examination of Urban's Way during the 2007 season also revealed an unusual approach to dealing with players that defies conventional coaching wisdom. And Meyer is never the least bit hesitant to challenge some of college football's archaic methodology.

To wit:

- Some coaches talk about "family," but at Florida the families and children of all coaches and players are encouraged to attend Thursday's "Family-Night Dinners" to hang out at their position coach's home; parents of players also have direct access to Meyer and his staff at all times.

- Wives and children of those assistant coaches are invited on the field after the game and are escorted to the locker room by their husbands/fathers.

- Meyer requires his coaches and their wives to "babysit" players and provide a family atmosphere for them as they are mentored through football, academics, and social responsibilities.

- Through disciplinary action, players are given every opportunity to redeem themselves for mistakes made on and off the field. They are automatically suspended for major team or school violations—or eventually even terminated for breaking the law—but Meyer will continue to help them in their pursuit of their degree. These incidents are rarely, if ever, announced to the media.

- Special teams players are treated "special" since Meyer, himself, is their hands-on coach.

- Instead of constantly hammering on his players to get results on the field and in the classroom, he "bribes" them with the privileges of a "Champions Club," almost like a frequent-flier program.

- Meyer runs an offense that he mostly made up, borrowing parts from here or there, but producing a new edition or version every couple of years and adapting it to personnel.

- In what might look reckless and almost crazy at the time—but is actually calculated and well thought out—Meyer has been known to call trick plays (he calls them "special plays") in big games when the odds look heavily stacked against him. And they usually work. He doesn't think of it as chance, but rather "calculated risks." Meyer doesn't believe in "fate" or "luck," but thinks good execution in practice is the key.

Meyer's coaching technique is compartmentalized by the two sides of his brain.

With his left brain, the one associated with logic, analysis, and orderly thinking, he organizes and verbalizes his approaches to the game. This accounts for his one-two-three sequential thinking and keeps the cadence for practice and preparation. Most coaches seem to lean heavily on their left brains and Meyer is no exception. This left brain, perhaps, inspired "the Plan to Win" and his coaching manual, and it also contains the schematic for all the moving parts.

What sets the Florida coach apart from others, however, appears to be an equally strong dependence on his right brain, where the synapses of creativity drive his intuition and provide a big-picture solution. It's what inspires the fourth down fake punts, "the Spread," and "the Champions Club." It is also the side that motivates him to mentor and nurture players beyond what is necessary in his job description and coaching manual. The right side makes Urban Meyer unique.

Some of his most unorthodox approaches have not only raised eyebrows in his profession, but sometimes ruffled feathers and caused ripples in the media.

When Meyer won the Mountain West Conference title by deploying his newfangled offense, some of his critics labeled it as "gimmicky." When he brought the Spread to the SEC, naysayers laughed behind his back and predicted it would never work against all the speedy linebackers and linemen. They poked fun at his Champions Club, calling some of his psychological antics "high schoolish." It was a different kind of athlete at Florida, they said, who just wouldn't go for that cheesy stuff.

He was called "Urban Liar" by former Jacksonville columnist Mike Freeman for refusing to reveal injuries of a player; dubbed "Urban Crier" for shedding tears after a loss at Baton Rouge; and vilified as an unwelcome interloper by his enemies for preventing Steve Spurrier's return as coach of the Gators.

Some couldn't wait to find the first major glitch in Meyer's program. After Meyer stated that Florida would only recruit "the top one percent of the one percent," he was chided by critics who chirped on message boards when one of those high-profile players got into trouble off the field.

Many of those perceptions were changed that night in Phoenix when Urban's Way was validated and critics were silenced by his bringing the University of Florida its second national collegiate football championship.

For those who would say that Meyer did it mostly with the players in Zook's cupboard, the truth was that forty-three members of the national championship squad were Urban-era recruits.

When that rap could no longer hold water and he had won two national titles in three years, his critics began to pick at him as if he were a carpetbagger coach about to flee to the next college, and sometimes there were so many false reports floating out there about him leaving for Notre Dame that it came across as conspiratorial.

Meyer truly didn't care what most people said about him and was impervious to just about all criticism of him or his program. He rarely complained about the intense coverage of the media and said he only cared about his players and staff members.

"I think everybody's got a job to do," Meyer said. "People sell books. People try to say things to get the viewers intrigued. I'm OK with that. People print that Florida is 'a gimmick team' and doesn't belong. Like everyone else, I'm a competitor. But it doesn't change the way I approach the game.

"When people say, 'You can't do that'—first of all, I don't know who said it, because I don't listen. But that's kind of the way we run our program. Same thing when our special team runs a fake punt, or we do a variety of things. If I think it's going to help us win a game or help a young person out, I'm going to do it."

Ron Zook, it is said, felt the media were all against his Gators. Others say Steve Spurrier felt the media were either for or against his team. Meyer doesn't really care either way.

Meyer's handling of players has come under scrutiny. Urban majored in psychology at the University of Cincinnati, and his diploma has been put to good use. He believes in conditioning the behavioral system with rewards and extraction. It's a little trick Meyer learned by the reading of Ivan Petrovich Pavlov via John Wooden. So there is a little bit of Pavlovian/Wooden theory in Florida Gator football.

There is a good bit of basketball in Meyer's game, too—Billy Donovan style.

Urban Meyer and Billy Donovan were on a roll, with two national titles in the bank as the year 2007 began—a college sports precedent labeled the Gator Slam by fans.

Following the Gator football team's victory over Ohio State in January, the Bling Brothers on the Cul-de-Sac of Champions had their bookend national championship trophies in football and basketball. In four months, Donovan would have yet another.

This meant the best college football and basketball in the land was played out of Gainesville over a 366-day period from the spring of 2006 to the spring of 2007. It took a century, but by the time one hundred years of intercollegiate athletics rolled around, the University of Florida sports program got it right, and the nickname Titletown was not inappropriate, even if it was almost a cliché.

Now though, as Earle Bruce and Bud Meyer might have facetiously said to Urban before the start of the 2007 season, what has he done for us lately?

The challenge at hand for Meyer was going to be establishing consistency at Florida. Tim Tebow and Percy Harvin would return for 2007, but most of his Florida defense would not.

Life for the Florida football coach, contrary to his postmortem immediately after the BCS title game, was not going to be all that much fun. Meyer was about to discover he'd made one of the worst predictions of his life about the upcoming 2007 season. He knew his team was too talented to call for a "rebuilding" season, but also too green to make a championship run. With that youth came some off-season behavior problems that preoccupied the coaching staff. Urban was aware of the myriad problems players face today, including drugs.

Inside the culture of the defending champions there would be some disappointment and discordance caused by player disobedience, leading to arrests, suspensions, and demotions. These kinds of problems are not enough to make Urban Meyer cut and run, because as much as he wants to win football games and championships, he is even more committed to rescuing young athletes from the predicaments of their poor judgment. And so is his staff. That is why the job description of each position coach mandates that he keep a close eye on players. That's also why players are often guests of Shelley and Urban Meyer for cookouts and other family occasions.

Meyer and Donovan are both actively involved in the lives of their athletes. That Meyer can seek counsel on such off-the-field problems simply by walking out the front door of his home and making a hard left toward Billy Donovan's house is a big advantage to living in his Gainesville neighborhood.

Meyer's and Donovan's homes are maybe half a football field apart in a neighborhood too exclusive to be called a subdivision because there are only five houses on large, expansive lots, all two-story, some with circle drives and most with white columns.

To reach the Cul-de-Sac of Champions, one must travel through contiguous traffic roundabouts in southwest Gainesville on a narrow, two-lane road framed by moss-draped oaks. Inside the ten-foot-tall iron gate, the Meyer home sits off to the left, painted olive green with stone elevations. A basketball backboard is in the driveway, with a volleyball net and batting cage in the back, a screened-in kidney-shaped pool, plus an air hockey table and pool table in the rec room. The house has a distinct Florida-style garden decor with a country flavor— though the area outside the gate is well-populated and a grocery market and strip mall are down the street.

The expansive, gray and white home with the stone and wood facade at the end of the Cul-de-Sac of Champions belongs to Billy and

Christine Donovan, who helped recruit the Meyer family to Florida and to their neighborhood—and their school.

This world is ruled mostly by Shelley Meyer and Christine Donovan, who are friends, but don't often socialize because of their busy schedules. The Donovans were there first and Christine guided, advised, and assisted the Meyer family even before they moved from Salt Lake City in 2005. After a long negotiation with the owner of the lot, a not-so-happy Notre Dame alumnus who was still ticked about Urban's spurning the Irish, the owner finally relented and sold to the Meyers.

Gainesville is a city of definitive seasons, occasionally frosted by sub-freezing temperatures in the winter and often toasted by 95-degree summer days with 100 percent humidity—but mostly right in the middle and pleasant.

The seasons are not just defined by the equinoxes, however, but the kind of ball that is being played on campus: round or oblong.

A sign that hangs on Meyer's lake home wall proclaims: THERE ARE FOUR SEASONS—WINTER, SPRING, SUMMER, AND FOOTBALL. In Billy Donovan's house, that sign would have a fifth season added—basketball—and Urban Meyer wouldn't even mind.

They don't fraternize as much as they would probably like. "With our schedules, it's insanity," said Meyer, noting that only a few times a year do they ever get together for dinner. While they may not invite each other over for weekly fondue parties or beer and pretzels, they do occasionally share an adult beverage and indulge in coaching brainteasers.

To say Billy Donovan and Urban Meyer collaborated on winning championships would not, however, be a stretch.

On a late-night ride through the neighborhood, Donovan will notice that Meyer's car still isn't parked at his house. Their sons often play with each other, but the dads not so much. On Fridays during the off-season, Urban walks son Nate down to the bus stop, where they play a game with Bryan Donovan, rewarding the first to spot the bus with $1. "Bryan has a lot of my money," Urban said.

Billy and Urban are good friends—maybe not best pals, but better than just mere acquaintances and neighbors—and by-products of strong Catholic upbringing, which Donovan feels has shaped both family environments and their values. Urban Meyer totally gets Billy Donovan and vice versa.

"I talk to Billy all the time because he's a great motivator," said Meyer. He has borrowed several themes from Donovan, including how to prevent the "poison" from contaminating a team's attitude. Meyer remembers his basketball counterpart "pulling up the ropes after a championship win" to ward off the evil spirits of self-adulation.

Meyer wound up living on the Cul-de-Sac of Champions quite by accident. He had tried to buy the home of Spurrier, but the Ol' Ball Coach didn't want to sell. Meyer's admiration for Spurrier and his ac- complishments at Florida—which, by the way, are considerable—were not the motivation behind his request, he says. It was more a case of needing a prebuilt house right away. Steve and Urban have become pretty good friends off the field and away from the cameras, but they keep their relationship private.

Without the help of the Donovans, getting located and building a new house would have been far more difficult.

"Christine and Shelley were really involved in the whole deal," Urban said. "I just said, 'Just do what you have to do.' So we bought that lot and built a home." The Donovans' mentoring didn't end there. Impeccable timing allowed Meyer to peek inside Billy's laboratory for a clinic on team chemistry at the group affectionately known as the Gator Boyz, who were crafting a blueprint for champions. Donovan's success became the business model for Meyer's 2006 national championship football team.

"I still think a lot of our success of that whole '06 team was be- cause we got to experience witnessing one of the greatest basketball teams ever to play the game—the most unselfish, probably, I've ever seen," Meyer said. "I became a better coach watching that team. I bent Billy's ear to death."

They are as different as they are similar, virtually the same age, with Meyer eleven months and twenty-nine days older. This prized perfecta of coaches picked by Director of Athletics Foley is also the highest paid duo in college sports. Florida has to be the only place where a national championship football coach makes less money than the basketball coach—but, hey, Donovan *did* win back-to-back NCAA hoop championships. And he was retrieved from halfway down I-75 to Orlando's Not-So-Magic Kingdom when he had a change of heart about coaching the NBA's Magic and did a U-turn. So the price of poker, basketball, and football went up in Gainesville. It cost Florida just under $8 million a year for the Bling Brothers, with Donovan making an extra quarter million.

One is an overachieving gym rat from Rhode Island via Long Island who became a boy-coach with a baby face that looks as if it belongs inside a uniform instead of a Jack Victor suit; a Rick Pitino protégé who soon transformed his on-the-job training skills into championship basketball.

The other is the wunderkind from the Woody Hayes/Earle Bruce coaching tree; a hard-charging young assistant who paid attention and took copious notes, then collated them into a manual of innovative techniques as he moved up on the coaching ladder toward his dream. Meyer is still tethered to father-figure coaches such as Bruce and Lou Holtz, both of whom he calls regularly.

During the fall of 2005, in his first season at Florida, Urban suddenly became distressed by some issues that he felt might be less common for those two wiser, older coaches. That day he was overwhelmed by the lifestyle problems of his players—drugs, alcohol abuse, etc.—when he remembered that his basketball coaching friend had a file on behavioral problems thickened by more than a decade of experience.

"I was so upset that I got out of my office and called Billy and said, 'You got a minute?' He said, 'Yeah, what's wrong?' And I said, 'I need to talk to you.' I went over [to Donovan's office]. I didn't know how to handle it. So I had a heart-to-heart with Billy for about an hour and a half, and Larry Shyatt [Donovan's assistant head coach], who had to deal with that when he was a head coach as well.

"You sometimes have to fly somewhere and spend thousands of dollars and try to get meeting time with someone [like that] . . . I get out of my office, walk down the street, and visit with the best basketball coach in the game."

After the spring of 2006, as Meyer was prepping his team for what would be a championship run, he tapped into the excitement on campus about the basketball team's success. Billy made what Urban called "an extremely passionate speech" to the football team. That day Meyer learned the importance of breaking down seasons by segments.

"He talked about total commitment for the one hundred and seven days leading up to the SEC Championship game," Meyer said. "I use that all the time now. I try to break it down. On our bowl preparations, I don't go anything beyond four- or five-day segments because you lose the players."

Meyer adopted Donovan's idea of a new psychological approach on a season schedule—"It's only a hundred and seven days"—as opposed to twelve games or six months.

"A hundred and seven days! We used that big-time, even on our highlight videos," Meyer said. "I'll never forget, later in the season, 'Only thirty-seven days left.' That's when you get the guys' attention. That all came from Billy.

"And then they woke up on the morning of the game and we had a big sign made: 'Zero days left! It's time to go play the game.'"

Now the two teams were feeding off each other.

To reciprocate, as March Madness 2007 approached, Meyer, his staff, and players signed a poster, GO GET 'EM, WE'RE BEHIND YOU and sent it to Donovan's Gator Boyz. The poster counted down the seventeen days to the title game and each time the basketball players left the room they touched it for good luck.

Donovan says he learned something about organization and structure from Meyer, who has to govern a 105-man squad versus his 13.

They have similar coaching styles. Both believe in directly challenging players, Meyer perhaps even more so. Life as a Gator football player begins with throwing your press clippings away and taking a quick inventory of your shortcomings. Billy Donovan can respect that and agrees that Meyer's way is a quick primer on learning how to compete.

"One of the biggest misconceptions for these kids is that they think they understand competition," Donovan said. "And what happens is that when they are highly touted—and they've been billed or dubbed as the next NFL star or next NBA star—there can be a lot of easy ways of going through and they've never faced adversity.

"I think what Urban is doing every day is creating [competitive] confrontation out on the football field to show these guys, 'When you leave this place, you're not going to have somebody walking you to your job. There's not going to be somebody checking to see if you're on time. If you don't do what you're supposed to do, you get a pink slip and you're being fired.' I don't want to say it's tough love—it's reality of the way it is."

Donovan praises Urban for making his athletes earn their place, such as achieving the Champions Club, and for the freshmen's indoctrination of their stripe. (All incoming freshman start with a black piece of tape on their helmets, which is removed in a battlefield promotion.)

"Just because you're 'here' doesn't really mean you are 'here,'" said Donovan. "You need to earn your way into this core group of guys, and I think there's merit in that." Given their similar philosophies about coaching, they make excellent sounding boards for each other. Donovan and Meyer have developed the verbal "bounce" pass into an art form, whether it's a conversation about how to be a better dad or how to be a better coach. So while there is a good bit of basketball in Florida's football these days, there is also some football in the basketball program.

In Meyer's now celebrated and oft-copied offense, the Spread, Urban even invokes roundball principles, because it's all based on matchup strategies.

"Remember with Michael Jordan, when they put four guys over here and he'd stand over here?" Meyer said, scrawling on a piece of paper. "That's all we do.

"That's the Spread offense.

"It's matchups.

"It's basketball."

Though he says he didn't offer any counsel to Donovan during his NBA negotiations, Meyer had more than a passing interest in keeping his friend, neighbor, and coaching colleague in place.

Once Donovan said no after saying yes to the Orlando Magic and stayed at Florida, things were almost back to normal on the Cul-de-Sac of Champions.

This kind of camaraderie between football and basketball coaches would once have been unimaginable in the football-driven athletic programs of the SEC. The most difficult challenge is not in the arena, but rather in the home. In a world of time constraints and challenged priorities, they stay grounded because of their rock-solid marriages.

Their lives are different from those Ozzie-and-Harriet days of their fathers; they don't arrive home for dinner promptly at 5:00 P.M. and sit around the dinner table quizzing their kids on state capitals. It usually is ten thirty at night before Meyer gets home during the season, but the next thirty minutes are "the best part of my day" because he and his wife talk about everything nonfootball.

"In August, we kiss our wives good-bye every year," said Meyer. For Donovan, only the month differs. During a 2007 winter practice break, the Gator basketball coach said: "You've obviously got a job to do, but you've also got kids and a wife at the house, too . . . trying to balance all that stuff."

Meyer was reminded about the challenges of "being a good dad" during his initial season at Florida. It was Friday night before his first Southeastern Conference game as a coach—the Tennessee game at Ben Hill Griffin Stadium—"and I'm nervous," said Meyer.

The team meal was just over when he received a text message from Shelley, saying Nate was upset because his father, at a local Gainesville hotel with the team, wasn't there to see his first Tee Ball game. Deciding that it was important to Nate and "I'm going to go do it," Meyer inquired about having security drive him out to Nate's game. Urban didn't yet realize the celebrity that went with his new job, because he had only coached two games.

Meyer even relied on a resource that he didn't know was at his disposal until three weeks prior. Retired Florida Highway Patrol major Malcom Jowers showed up for the opening game with Wyoming as his personal protector. Urban asked Jowers if someone could drive him out to the baseball park so that he might "sneak in." Jowers held back from snickering and quickly responded that Meyer would have difficulty "sneaking in" anywhere, "but we'll do what you've got to do."

Meyer remembers getting into Johnny Horn's Gainesville Police Department car and speeding to the game, sirens blaring. He was escorted through the crowd—"because people are kind of revved up for the Tennessee weekend and they can't believe I'm there"—and stood off to the side to watch Nate hit twice, then got back in the car.

"People thought that was real neat. Nate obviously thought it was pretty neat. We go back to the hotel and get ready to go play Tennessee."

Sometimes being Captain Emergency has its rewards. Whether at home or on the field.

Those same qualities apply in both places. Meyer often tells his assistant coaches that being a father will make them better coaches. Under their watchful eyes, the players are carefully shepherded like a flock. As passionate as he is about winning, Meyer is even more committed to keeping young men out of jail, off drugs, sober, alive, in class, and educated.

Meyer is one part football coach and one part Father Flanagan, the priest of Boys Town who was the inspiration for the Oscar-winning movie starring Spencer Tracy.

"Winning football games is important to Coach Meyer," quarterback Tim Tebow said. "But getting young men on the right road in life is even more important to him."

This means that when he fails, when a wandering soul is lost from the flock, he counts it almost as a personal failure.

The day he received a call from a parent of former cornerback Avery Atkins saying he had overdosed and died was one of those times when Meyer felt terribly inadequate. But then there was Meyer's joy of watching the turnarounds in the lives of Dallas Baker, Ray McDonald, Louis Murphy, Steve Harris, etc. at Florida—plus Marty Johnson at Utah. For Urban, this is like that one good shot in a round of 98 that brings a golfer back for another day.

So was Tebow right in saying Urban would rather change a person's life than win a football game? "Tough choice," said Meyer, pondering the dilemma.

"I'd probably agree with that. But it's all changed. Twenty-five years ago, guys drank a little bit and I got them back in line. The day I got that call about Avery Atkins . . . I'll never be the same person or the same coach. Because it's real now, it's not a game. So that statement's more true now than it's ever been. I don't believe that was as true ten years ago with me. Because the stakes weren't the same."

A player flunking a class or getting a DUI was as bad as it used to get.

"There were no weapons," Meyer said of his early days as an assistant. "You heard about bar fights. OK, but there weren't six shots being fired in a bar. Drugs weren't like they are today. And I'll never forget that phone call. I was at my house when I got that phone call from his dad in the morning and he said, 'Avery's dead.' The only thing I could think about was that poor family and that lost soul that was a good soul. And what could we have done differently, when deep down, knowing everybody knows that we did so much trying to help that guy out.

"And what came to mind was, 'It's not a game—you're talking about life and death now.' And he got around people who took him . . . down. Not financially, or spiritually. They took him *down*."

Meyer will forever be haunted by the death of Avery Atkins, but that only drives him harder to keep looking for solutions.

The inevitability of failure to reach certain young players doesn't dissuade either coach on the Cul-de-Sac of Champions from taking on tomorrow's challenges—a championship to be won, or a young athlete's pathway to be altered toward a better life.

From the beginning of his relationship with players, Urban gets to know them through their mom or dad, or both.

When parents send him their son, Meyer treats him like one of his own. "And if their mother wants them to go to church on Sunday, then it's our job to see to it that he goes to church on Sunday," he says.

Sometimes the nurturing of players becomes almost parental in nature, and Urban is not above taking away privileges—the way a mom or dad would take away the car keys from Little Johnny.

Urban, named after a pope, has been known to withhold the sacraments from his flock.

Before the 2005 season, Meyer removed the Gator head from the rotunda of the Florida locker room, which was akin to taking Touchdown Jesus away from Notre Dame or Howard's Rock away from Clemson's Death Valley. Touched for good luck by each Gator player before exiting the door and running the tunnel into the Swamp, the

Gator head was a treasured tradition begun by Steve Spurrier. Then one day before the 2005 season started, the Gator head reappeared.

Meyer employed these same tactics in his two previous head-coaching jobs. He built up head-coaching equity and momentum before coming to Gainesville with a 39-8 record: a two-year mark of 22-2 at Utah (10-2 in 2003 and 12-0 with a BCS Fiesta Bowl victory in 2004) and 17-6 as a rookie head coach at Bowling Green.

"You touch that Gator head," said Florida strength and conditioning coach Mickey Marotti, whose job it is to instill discipline and work ethic in the minds and bodies of Meyer's players through weight training and mat drills, "that's investment. That's the long runs, that's the hard lifts, that's the hard practices, that's the meeting sessions, that's living your life right—all that stuff."

Urban Meyer taketh away, Urban Meyer giveth back.

Meyer's two-year start at Florida, with a record of 22-4, was better than

- **Bear Bryant's first two years at Alabama (5-4-1 in 1958 and 7-2-2 in 1959)**

- **Joe Paterno's first two years at Penn State (5-5 in 1966 and 8-2-1 in 1967)**

- **Bobby Bowden's first two years at Florida State (5-6 in 1976 and 10-2 in 1977)**

- **Steve Spurrier's first two at Florida (9-2 in 1990 and 10-2 in 1991)**

Of course some coaches had better starts than that, including the 24-1 of Miami's Larry Coker in his first two campaigns, which he later stretched to 31-1, the all-time best. Coker took over a winning program, but few coaches produced better turnarounds than Meyer, with his success coming on the heels of Ron Zook's 7-5 and a three-year slump of 23-15.

There was really no reason to expect a major letdown in 2007, but Meyer had no way of knowing what he and his staff were about to encounter with young players not yet indoctrinated into doing things the right way—Urban's Way.

On Friday night, August 31, at the Holiday Inn on Newberry Road in Gainesville, preparation for the 2007 season opener is under way.

A little before seven o'clock, the players walk into the large private dining room. They are seated in groups by position with their coaches at various round tables—offensive line, defensive line, wide receivers, punt team, etc.

On one wall is a sign in big letters: DO YOUR JOB!—one of Meyer's favorite slogans. Off to the side, toward the corner, there is a table reserved for the support staff—security, law enforcement, Florida Highway Patrol escort, chaplain, etc. In another corner is the group of young aspiring coaches called GAs, for "graduate assistants," who make up the second tier of coaches. At that table are a writer and a relative, Urban's brother-in-law Jim Escoe of Cincinnati. Later, Meyer will come over to shake the hands of the visitors. But for the most part, that's the only interaction the Florida coach will have with anybody who's not a player or a coach.

It has been a long and trying week for Meyer, who sits alone at a table toward the back. Occasionally he checks his phone for a text message or call, but for the most part he is not talkative. Wearing shorts and sneakers, his left leg rests on a chair as he partakes of an ice cream sundae from the nearby dessert bar—always a Friday-night favorite for coaches and players. Clearly he is settling in with a few private thoughts.

Some players had off-field problems during the week, but matters were cleared up. Monday's press conference was followed by a ragged practice, but the sessions got better as the week progressed. Now Mayer is observing his players like a watchful parent, but he wants them to unwind.

At first there is little frivolity, but the players do play card games and laugh. The mood eventually lightens—becomes so light, that Meyer's law enforcement escort, Malcom Jowers, is almost amazed. "I can tell you this—Charley Pell and Steve Spurrier wouldn't have allowed this because their players were told to be totally serious the night before game," he said. Jowers would know. He's escorted every coach at Florida from the field to the locker room since the late 1970s.

Urban Meyer does a lot of things by the book, but his manual is written differently. One small part of that manual is the "Plan to Win," which will be followed by the Florida Gator coaches as if it were the Holy Grail. To Meyer, that's exactly what it is. Tomorrow at the Swamp begins another season of testing the Plan.

2

The Man with the Plan

The street that passes north and south in front of Ben Hill Griffin Stadium is a two-way road named Lemerand Drive, after Florida Gator booster, philanthropist, restaurateur, and prominent Gainesville businessman Gale Lemerand. With all due respect to Urban's friend, who has contributed millions to the university, that road might have also been dubbed Urban's Way. Because that's how things run around the University of Florida football program these days.

There's a blueprint of success for the Gators, and it's all right there on Urban's virtual stone tablets. The life of Urban Meyer is metered out on the expanded version of a day planner, parts of which are given to all coaches and players. Tucked inside the 129-page document is the Plan to Win. It's only one page. While Meyer will admit to changing or tweaking his offense, or even learning to listen, and growing as a coach, Urban's organizational philosophy is the same as it was yesterday—and will be tomorrow.

Don't mistake the Plan to Win as a trumped-up bunch of football clichés and homilies that Urban Meyer writes up on the dry-erase board in halftime speeches, because it is a definitive manifesto of philosophy and intent. He says it drives every player personnel issue, every game plan, and every decision that he makes in football.

Visiting coaches who make the mistake of probing for all his secrets about the Spread offense but don't ask about what he considers the most important aspect of his program aren't going to get much of his time, or his respect.

"If a coach asks me about the Spread offense," Meyer said, "then I just give him a GA [graduate assistant coach] and let him watch a tape. If he wants to know about the Plan to Win, I'll take up some time with him."

Every coach has his own "bible," one of the most famous being Gen. Bob Neyland's "Seven Maxims," which have been copied and recycled for more than eighty years. These bibles are not dissimilar in nature, usually espousing need for attention to such details as defense, the kicking game, and turnovers—not industry secrets, nor are they just coaching platitudes.

The four main staples of Urban's mandate for success and his organizational schematic—his bible of football coaching—are:

1. **Play great defense**
2. **Turnovers (all coaches are required to teach ball security the same way)**
3. **Score in the red zone**
4. **Win the kicking game**

Not exactly the Da Vinci Code, but, as with Neyland's Maxims, it's how these principles are applied. The No. 1 item, "play great defense," can be invoked when recruiting talented athletes who can play on either side of the ball.

The real secret, says Meyer, is realizing the infallibility of the Plan. If it is followed, he says, "It is a hundred percent guaranteed" to work.

An overview of The-Plan-to-Win philosophy was given by a member of Meyer's staff:

The base philosophy of the Plan to Win is to articulate to the entire team an understandable plan that aligns team goals and balances effort and talent to give them the best chance of winning the football game by tilting the field in our favor.

Play great defense: *This means not putting the defense in a difficult field position. Make the opposing team go uphill by having to drive the length of the field. The defense can play aggressively and the entire defensive game plan is intact and available.*

Football statistics reflect the mathematical probability of scoring. It's less than 3 percent when a team starts inside its own 10-yard line. The percentage increases to 75 percent from the red zone. The longer the field position, the greater the propensity by the offensive team to make mistakes.

Take care of the football: *Again, an offense that takes care of the football will not compromise the defense. When the offense starts on the minus-20 (its own 20-yard line), the entire goal is to get two first downs. Failure dictates a punt from inside the minus-30, hence a 40-yard change of field position gives the opponent the ball at their minus-30, better field position. If successful at gaining two first downs, the goal remains to get another first down. Now a punt probably puts the opponent inside the minus-30 and the field starts to tilt. Two first downs and the entire playbook opens for the offense, and it is all downhill as long as players take care of the football.*

Score in the red zone: *Take full advantage of a downhill field. Failure gives the defense an emotional lift. Success drives more nails into the coffin of the opponent and lifts the entire team.*

Win the kicking game: *This is all based on tilting the field, does not require extraordinary talent, but does require great effort. This is truly when great effort can win. Starting with the kickoff, we try to pin the opponent inside the minus-20 by coverage and squeezing the field. It requires great effort to run downfield, be disciplined enough to stay on your landmark, and make the tackle. Beating your man with speed or by making a move is key. The kickoff return goal is to reach the minus-35. The punt team goal is to change the field position by 40 yards and zero return yards.*

This is done by having more gunners versus the standard, line splits, and directional kicks. The ability to have fake plays that can gain a first down has a greater success ratio with our spread punt because it changes every week but the principles are the same. The goal of the punt return team is either to block or return. Blocked punts lead directly to scoring and winning as it puts you in the red zone 75 percent of the time. The return team's goal is 15 yards and much easier to attain if a punt has been blocked early in the season. Because this places a greater emphasis on effort versus talent, allowing more players on the field, and as they develop, the team improves. By changing the personnel and schemes weekly, depending on the opponent, the players continually learn to grasp the concept of the game.

That's it. No trade secrets. No magic coaching dust. No trick plays. No freaky formations. And if it were all that secretive, Meyer wouldn't let visiting coaches see it or talk to them about it.

How it is applied and executed is the difference. That's where the rest of the manifesto comes into play. Meyer's policies are framed and explained in that 129-page document, part of which goes to players, part to coaches. There is also a section in the manual called "National Championship, How We WIN = Defeat the Enemy." Ironically, Meyer doesn't start out each season talking about winning the national title, but it is implied. The immediate goal is to win each game on a path to the Southeastern Conference championship. Unless Florida wins the SEC, he says, there can be no national championship.

Included in the 129-page manual is a set of core values for players:

1. **Honesty**
2. **Respect women**
3. **No drugs**
4. **No stealing**
5. **No weapons**

Also included are the guides on how assistant coaches should coach, expectations about player academics, proper player nutrition, acceptable behavior while on a date, and a day planner that covers August through November.

Built around those principles is the schedule, which designates times for such things as "summer brunch/church" to "kicking meetings" to "speed training/upper lifting" and "speed training/lower lifting."

The magic potion is simply "Do your job." That includes the following for coaches:

1. **Take care of your family and your health.**
2. **Take care of your players (academic, social, spiritual, family).**
3. **Be an expert at your position and excel as a teacher.**
4. **Recruit every day (expect to sign two to three players per year).**
5. **Be passionate about coaching and football.**

The Plan was conceived and written with a purpose, out of the need for some kind of blueprint as a new head coach. Perhaps it began with the teaching of Bud Meyer, who always told his son he had to be prepared for this moment. Urban hammered the document out in a week as he was about to leave Notre Dame for Bowling Green.

"When I took the job, I remember sitting on the phone with coach Lou Holtz for hours. That's when I came up with the Plan to Win," Meyer said. "Just sitting there in my little den at Notre Dame. How are we going to approach this thing? That's when the core values came up. That was done over a one-week period sitting at my house—early in the morning, until late at night, putting that book together. How are you going to handle each situation?"

He was asked how today's version differed than the one he forged at Bowling Green. "The same," he said. "We added very little."

The Meyer manual, of which the Plan is a part, was born out of his own experiences. Meyer was aware that new assistant coaches, like himself, often struggled to learn the ways and philosophies of their new boss. That's why he put it all together into one manual.

"I never got a book like that from a coach," he said. "I just kind of put that together myself. I wanted to have a resource when the situation called for it—I didn't want to have to grab from air."

It works like this: When new assistants are hired, they are immediately given a copy of the Plan and the manual. Meyer even follows it when choosing on which side of the ball to hire the most experienced and best coaches.

"They give you a pot of money to go hire coaches. How do I decide where to put that money? Well, let's go to the Plan to Win," says Meyer.

"'Play great defense.' So put most of your resources in defensive coaches."

When it comes to personnel, the same rule applies, as it did when the talented and versatile Joe Haden signed on. The coaches knew he would be an outstanding receiver. But the commitment to defense is to be emphasized, so he became a corner.

Does anybody complain? "I don't want to hear about it," said Meyer. "And Dan Mullen [offensive coordinator] didn't say a word to me. Billy Gonzales [wide receivers coach] recruited him. Joe Haden would be a great receiver, but Billy knows the "Plan To Win.""

The second principle is the turnovers. Each assistant is told to teach the same ball security—handoffs, hanging on to the ball after a catch, etc. Meyer had been on staffs in the past where the receiver coach, running backs coach, and quarterbacks coach all taught players how to hold the football differently. On the Florida staff, it's all taught the same way. Coaches "clinic" each other over the summer on it. "We all teach it the same way. We all clinic each other every summer. We all spend five minutes each day on ball security," Meyer said.

It is only a paper document, not a hardback book, however, and Urban's Way is far more personal, direct, and persuasive.

3

The Book of Urban

Through application of the Plan To Win, Meyer has found a way to compete and excel in America's nastiest college football league. He feels strongly that these principles have elevated his program to the top. Now only history will tell us whether this set of tenets will keep Florida up there in the land of Big Boy Football.

The SEC was going to get even tougher, if for no other reason than the caliber of coaches was improving—Meyer at Florida, Steve Spurrier at South Carolina, Les Miles at LSU, Nick Saban at Alabama, Houston Nutt at Mississippi, Bobby Petrino at Arkansas, etc. That, along with the high quality of players being recruited, led some to believe SEC dominance was about to unfold. (The prediction came true as an SEC team won three straight BCS titles—Florida, LSU, and Florida.)

The rising tide of SEC play raised all ships in the league. The result of this parity, says Spurrier, is that "teams will have to win close games if they're going to win the SEC." Spurrier's 2006 Gamecocks lost four games by a touchdown or less, but wound up 8-5. The following year it would fall apart for them as they came out of the box 6-1 then lost five straight, finished 6-6, and failed to be invited to a bowl. In 2006, Florida's national championship was a by-product of winning close games, until the team matured in the postseason and flourished. There was always the potential for those South Carolina–like collapses, however, and that worried Meyer. Without veteran leadership on defense in 2007, he feared a potential downward spiral when times got tough.

The 2007 Florida football team would be a little too green to compete for another national title. And in the heart of the schedule, when the biggest of Big Boy football was played against Tennessee, Auburn, LSU, Georgia, and the like, solid coaching and preparation would make the difference.

Nothing in the Plan, however, would teach Meyer how to save him from himself. The real question about Urban Meyer was not if he could continue to succeed, but whether he would overextend himself, implode, and drop like a shooting star.

Those closest to Urban would all tell you he will continue to be successful—but with a caveat. His father, his sisters, his mentor Bruce, his closest friends, his assistant coaches, and his players all worry about his burning out.

Some coaches *say* they're "all in," but Meyer makes it the linchpin of his coaching philosophy. Like Amarillo Slim playing four of a kind, Meyer leaves nothing on the table. The concern for Urban by friends and family is how far he is going to push himself and for how long. Urban says he's working on trying to delegate more to his staff.

"The last two years I've delegated more than I've ever delegated in my life," Meyer said. "At Bowling Green I delegated nothing, I did everything myself. Everything."

That flashback to the Bowling Green version of Urban Meyer is not necessarily pretty to him. He didn't like what he had become—"a thirty-six-year-old coach out of control."

He was not only a control freak who was driving himself crazy, but everyone around him as well.

"I was in defensive meeting—you weren't allowed to start until I was in there," Meyer admitted. "Offense, I was there. I would drive people insane. But I would also drive myself insane. I don't think I was as good of a coach in many ways because I was spread so thin. I've gotten really good at that in the last two years. Plus I've got a great staff, so I really trust those people. It's the release of it . . . and that I'm still working on."

As demanding as Meyer is of his players and assistant coaches, he is maybe more demanding of himself. Driven by his desire to excel in an organized manner and on his own timetable, he races the clock constantly, with every segment of practice timed out by digital clocks.

"Let's go, let's go, let's go, let's go!" Meyer admonishes his players on the Florida practice field, always exhorting them to go faster. As players roll out from class and enter the practice complex, they are taught to be running when their first foot hits grass on the playing field. There can never be any wasted time or lost motion. "Hurry, hurry, hurry, hurry!"

There is always an implied message to go top speed, because speed wins in football. One of the mantras is "Four to six seconds of relentless effort." You often see that slogan in the locker room. In everything Urban Meyer does, he wants to get there in a hurry—just as he has done on the ladder of success.

So what's the hurry and where is Urban going next? And what's his motivation?

His oldest sister figures that it's only about the football, not all the fame, glory, or riches that come with the job.

"Urban's not into being recognized; he doesn't like it," said Gigi Escoe, an economist at the University of Cincinnati where she is the school's first vice provost for assessment and student learning. "He's not shy. If you meet him at a party and you have something to talk about, you can talk all night in an animated way if you've got the time for it and you connect. So he's not a wallflower. He was always very popular with girls and boys and had lots of friends. He just doesn't get impressed by impressing people.

"He's only in it for the football. He's not in it for the money. He's not in it for the prestige. He's in it because he loves football and cares deeply about football players. Because if he's going to start shaping them up on one side, he's got to shape them on the other because it's his obligation and he's taking up too much of their time and their life."

His father is pleased by his son's football intellect and creative approach to the game.

"He's innovative. He's a scholar of the game. He works hard at it. And he works smart," said his father, Bud. "He allows his intellect to be free. He isn't fettered by things that he's afraid won't work. He wants to do things that he understands will work."

One of Urban's former mentors, Sonny Lubick, agrees with Bud and sees Urban's openness to ideas and ability to learn by osmosis from those around him as a huge asset. "Urban is a sharp guy, and the thing I saw in him is that he is free to let himself learn from everybody," said Lubick. "And he surrounds himself with good coaches."

Dean Hood, one of his best friends from his growing-up years in Ashtabula, Ohio, sees Urban's success stemming from street smarts and a strong work ethic. Hood, former defensive coordinator at Wake Forest who was named head coach at Eastern Kentucky in early 2008, sees an unlimited future for Meyer.

"He's a very hard worker. Urban is a very, very intelligent person," said Hood. "It seems to me you get somebody who's either highly intelligent or street smart. Urban's got both. He's very, very streetwise, but he's a very intelligent person. You combine those two things with somebody who's a hard worker—man! The sky's the limit."

That "sky" apparently won't include pro football.

Urban claims to have "zero interest" in the NFL. One reason is that it would take too much time away from his priorities in life.

Simply put, when it's not about football, it's about his wife, two daughters, and son. Then there is the matter of planning and coaching the lives of 105 football players, which he and his staff do meticulously. Everybody's life is laid out in the Plan to Win.

"I'm just not going to do anything that doesn't involve my family," Meyer said. In the summer of 2008, he and his family planned to go on a church mission. Though he is not openly religious, he is a semiregular church attendee and, according to friends and family, very spiritual.

"The Lord is working on his heart and he is trying to get a better perspective on it," said Hood. "That's a struggle in this business, to keep a proper perspective. And I think Urban truly, one hundred percent believes that it's more important to use football as a platform to teach young kids how to become men."

In essence, Meyer's job as coach has become his ministry. This fiercely driven, tough, and dedicated football man is obsessed with winning, but equally committed to setting young men on the straight and narrow, and retrieving the lambs that have lost their way.

Urban Meyer is equal parts life coach and football coach who takes a "wholistic" approach. Each player is nurtured physically, nutritionally, academically, socially and, sometimes when they want it, even spiritually. Building trust is the goal.

Meyer also coaches everything that moves around his players. He coaches the alumni, the fans, his family, and his football assistants. If he had time, he would coach the cheerleaders and the band. He coaches his players in football, academics, health, decision-making, discipline, physical fitness, accountability.

When he is in his own personal classroom—the football field or the film room—the aura of the man and the coach begins to sparkle. The authoritative walk, the laser-beam eye contact, the commanding posture, and the direct vocal commands seem to elicit the players' attention.

Intensity, focus, concentration—all of that goes into Urban's Way. It carries over from the meeting room to the field, as well as to other members of his coaching staff.

In the special teams meeting room—they used to be called "film rooms" before the days of videotape—a bevy of coaches swarms among the players, who are watching video in the spring. One coach points out the proper technique to a player; another is in the ear of one about his timing; and yet another reminds the player of containment. You can feel the intensity. They are coaching in concert, like worker bees.

A few players are incoming freshman, who have just left high school a few weeks ago to enroll early for spring practice. There are baby steps to be coaxed. At one point, a coach realizes a player is lost. "That's our fault," says the coach. "You didn't know that. We didn't tell you that. So that is my fault." One of the cornerstones of Meyer's coaching philosophy is owning up. If you are a teacher, you teach, and if you don't teach your players properly, then it's on you. At Florida, the special teams are more than an afterthought. The special teams coach is also the head coach.

Across the way in a smaller room, defensive backs were getting tutored later that day. Some magic was involved here, because David Copperfield wears a coach's cap and goes under the assumed name of Chuck Heater at the University of Florida. When the cupboard is empty of defensive backs, he creates the illusion that it is full.

For three straight seasons, Heater, the thirty-two-year coaching veteran, has pulled bodies out of that cupboard and turned some of them into All–Southeastern Conference-caliber cornerbacks.

Dee Webb came out of nowhere to make the 2005 All-SEC first team. Heater made a starter out of senior Vernell Brown, who had been moved to cornerback the prior season, but had no experience. Reggie Lewis was brand-new on defense and, after several mediocre seasons as a wide receiver at Florida, blossomed into a starting corner.

The following season Heater and the staff would welcome Ryan Smith, a skinny, 155-pound, early graduate of Utah who, under an NCAA loophole, had remaining eligibility. Smith made first-team All SEC and second team All America after the 2006 season. More than halfway through the 2005 season, Heater had moved junior-college transfer Reggie Nelson from nickelback to free safety and turned him into a first-team All American in 2006. Nelson and Smith, Florida's version of Butch and Sundance, led the nation in interceptions. In his fifth season, the seldom-used Tremaine McCollum became the first-team nickelback.

In 2007, Heater's challenge was even greater, and sometimes he met it with smoke and mirrors. He would start true freshman Joe Haden at one corner and sophomore Wondy Pierre-Louis at the other. After an injury to Haden, he would be going to redshirt freshman Jacques Rickerson.

Heater was charged with filling everybody's cupboard, since he served as both cornerbacks coach and recruiting coordinator, leading one to wonder why he couldn't save something for himself.

"Chuck Heater is the best secondary coach in America," Meyer said.

Like Meyer, Heater is animated and will do anything within reason to get the player's attention. During one spring drill when he suspected a player wasn't going full speed, Heater screamed at him, "I want you to give me your best out here! I'm giving you my best that I have today, and I expect you to give me your best! You understand me?"

"Chuck is a lot like me," said Meyer, who noted that his trust level has been raised with veterans such as Heater on his "all-star staff," many of whom he had coached with at Notre Dame. Therein would lie the hope for Meyer's sanity one day: that he could delegate more to aides such as codefensive coordinators Greg Mattison and Charlie Strong (both former Irish coaches); strength and conditioning coach Mickey Marotti; Heater and safeties coach Doc Holliday; offensive coordinator Dan Mullen; receivers coach Billy Gonzales; offensive line coach Steve Addazio; and tight ends coach John Hevesy.

The aides had a high visibility after winning the national championship, and attrition on the staff, as expected, began to take hold.

Watching them work up close, however, was a treat to an outsider.

One day in the spring of 2007, Heater and Holliday were in their "office," the secondary coaching/video room. Numerous printed signs on the walls suggested some type of call to action. Those that stuck out were GET ON TOP and AMNESIA, the latter obviously suggesting that a badly beaten defensive back get over the trauma quickly.

The lights were down, and from the back of the room, the silhouettes against the video screen of these extremely young and inexperienced athletes reflected the body language of a focused and intent but slightly nervous group. The conversation with Heater was low-key and professorial in an atmosphere of reverence and respect from the players.

Suddenly, a shadowy figure stood up and seemed to move toward the dark side of the room. In a few moments, safety Tony Joiner returned, still buckling up his practice pants from what appeared to be a trip from the bathroom, his upper body well-defined against the screen. "You're looking pretty good there, Tony. You ever think about doing some modeling?" Heater asked, not meant at all in a disrespectful or pejorative way. Nothing about why a player had left in the middle of the meeting. No criticism for leaving without permission. No disrespect meant and none given. Just playful banter.

Joiner was the only returning starter in the secondary—one of two overall for codefensive coordinators Mattison and Strong. (End Derrick

Harvey was the other.) Joiner, at the top of the pecking order, had cachet. Rank has privilege. It's OK to go to the bathroom without asking. He has earned that. In Urban Meyer's program, everybody earns his way, or loses it, by performance.

"You have to have a little bit in the bank," Heater would later say, explaining how the pecking order impacts how he treats players. "You have to have made some contributions around here. Certainly that was the case with Tony, who had proved his worth. You have to know your guys and you deal with them all differently. A player gets a little different treatment if he's a 'program guy' and is somebody you can trust."

Earn some of that trust and you make your way into the Champions Club, where the players get better athletic clothing, better food, and the ultimate respect of coaches and peers. It is a circle of trust based on adherence to team rules and putting forth a higher degree of effort in the classroom and on the field.

Once in the Champions Club, you are treated to special gourmet meals and the best gear Nike has to offer. The rest chomp on hot dogs and wear hand-me-downs. If they do good things in class, on the field, and in the community, players get virtual Champions Club brownie points. Once inducted, they never want to go back to rubber hot dogs, crappy practice shorts and shirts, etc.

To emphasize the life of luxury in the Champions Club and what gravitas it warrants, Meyer will stage his theatrical-bit performance at some of the early inductions, almost taunting nonmembers. As he is badgering them, he will turn away from the uninitiated and toward one of the Champions and say, "Hold on just a minute! How is your steak cooked? A little too rare? OK, let me get that back on the grill." Turning back, he then says to the non-Champions, "Excuse me just a minute. I've got to go over and cook his steak a little for him, it's too rare." He then takes the steak back over to the grill, cooks it some more, and returns it to the Champion's plate.

Urban Meyer knows how to cook up a scheme.

"He loves football," said his former Ohio State and Colorado State coach Earle Bruce, "and he loves coaching. And he's a great communicator. He gets very explicit with his players."

Urban and Shelley annually invite the new recruits to their house for a cookout, and after the fete, the breaking down of the "over-recruiting" is unleashed as Urban tells each of them about every weakness or flaw in his character, game, or academic regimen.

Straight talk has worked so far for Meyer, who puts his rules of governance in writing and believes a football scholarship is a contract with the family, the player, the university, and the coaches. He backs up what he says. As proof, once when players kept showing up late to class, he went to the next session after receiving a call from the professor about the players' tardiness. Next time, the Gator head coach was there waiting when three players walked in late. "You do that again, you're out of here," Meyer announced upon their arrival.

That kind of talk and action also resonated with parents on the recruiting trail, where nearly all of his Florida classes have been ranked top five or better. To Meyer, it's all about the future players' investment in core values. In a letter to parents, Meyer tells them:

> *I continue to believe that the University of Florida and your son have a mutuality of responsibility and accountability. When we are aligned and are working to accomplish the same goals, success is attainable. Players, coaches and staff that live life the right way, attend classes and tutorial sessions and put forth great effort cannot be stopped short of success because they are too invested in making sure they cannot fail.*
>
> *All of us will work diligently to teach the student-athletes how to make this investment. They will be introduced to the core values by which they must live and abide on a daily basis. Honesty, Respect of Women, No Stealing, No Drugs, and No Weapons are the core values of our team. I believe you will agree with me that these core values can be values that can guide your son throughout his entire life and enrich and reward his family life.*

In the manual Meyer hands out to players, they are reminded, among other things:

- You have responsibilities/obligations; not entitlements.

- Do your job, nothing else.

- You've done nothing; thank those who gave us what
  we have at Florida.

- Selfish people fail.

All of these principles came straight out of the Book of Urban.

Getting his players to apply those principles—that is the greatest challenge. It is called coaching.

Meyer claims that what makes a good coach "is what makes a good father."

Some coaches would call that babysitting.

"You're damn right it is," Meyer admits. "If you are a position coach, you need to know everything there is to know about your player, where he is, what he's doing, who he's hanging out with, how he's doing in class, and what girl he's dating. If you are a coach at Florida, yes, you will become a babysitter. And so will your wife."

Keeping up with every player's personal life is, of course, impossible, as was seen in the death of Avery Atkins, but Meyer says coaches have got to try. Atkins was a gifted defensive back with NFL first-round potential who got sideways with the law over a domestic violence charge and was kicked off the Florida team. After a struggle with drugs, Atkins played a few games for Bethune-Cookman in 2006 and was hopeful of getting back with the Gators in 2007. They found his body in a car parked in Port Orange, Florida, July 5. The Daytona Beach Mainland High School product was the prize recruit of Meyer's first class in 2005.

Shelley Meyer e-mailed Franz Beard of GatorCountry.com, who had written a warm, sympathetic piece entitled "The Avery Atkins That I Knew." Shelley's e-mail said: "Avery was wonderful and [your story was] heart-felt and reflects what we all feel about him. The smile for sure was a trademark I'll never forget about him. However, my last encounter with him while trying to convince him to stay with us (because *here* is where he belonged), and having him tell me 'that's your opinion,' is, unfortunately, what I'll always think about. It's just real tough to save them all."

The line "tough to save them all" was first uttered to Shelley by a doctor in her psychiatric ward after the loss of an addicted patient to suicide.

Urban's "family" includes his players and coaches. He also brings his wife and children into the mix. Past, present, and future players are familiar sights at the Meyer household, where Shelley treats them as extended family as they snack and watch TV in the family room.

When an Avery Atkins dies or one of the players is suspended, it gets very personal with the Meyer family, the players, and the coaches. They all know they must not give up.

"We worked hard and failed to reach him [Atkins], but we must keep working. We know we cannot save them all, but that is what we must try to do. In the end, that is a coach's responsibility, and not what people think," said Hiram de Fries, Meyer's friend and staff member.

Meyer usually imposes stiff penalties when players violate core values, team rules, or bring embarrassment to the University of Florida and the Gator football program. Football programs differ across the country in penalties for disciplinary purposes; Meyer seemingly seeks to hit the offenders in the pocketbook. The disciplinary possibilities are endless, from suspensions, community service, return of bowl gifts, to academic and behavioral requirements.

Although sometimes sensitive and forgiving, Meyer has also been known to be harsh after the repeating of stupid mistakes and the loss of games because of poor effort. At times he's borderline brutal with his demands, but would no doubt argue that he's pushing the players to their maximum. He hurts when his players hurt.

Yet he seemingly has this uncanny calm and cool in a crisis and often knows just the right touches at the right time. Eric Jacobsen, an All–Mountain West player at Utah who still lives there, recalls the day of the 2006 Auburn game when Meyer delivered that touch. At one point, Meyer reached offensive coordinator Dan Mullen on his cell before the team bus pulled out and told him, "Make sure you sit up front somewhere with Chris Leak. You get in his ear and you make him feel like he's on the way to being a national championship quarterback. He still has to lead us to a national championship game."

Which is what Leak did, despite the loss to Auburn. This set the tone for the remainder of the season and the championship run. When Leak was needed, he stepped up. The whole team seemed to stay composed in a crisis.

Keeping composure was a learned response and at key points along the way, Urban would reach into his pocket to grasp a medal on a silver chain.

When Buckeye speed-burner Ted Ginn took the opening kickoff back for a touchdown in the BCS National Championship game, there was a temptation to explode. Meyer's players watched him closely for any crack or change of emotion, but saw no panic in his face. One reason was, as he was about to unload on somebody, linebacker Brandon Siler grabbed him by the arm and said, "We got it coach, we're OK." After that, Meyer didn't even blink when he called the offense in a huddle.

Chris Leak took the field and promptly led the Gators to a game-tying touchdown drive, and Florida scored three straight times to take a 21–7 lead. Leak had the game of his life and was voted Most Valuable Offensive Player in the BCS Championship game. Thanks to Siler, and Meyer's willingness to listen, he didn't panic, though as a young coach he might have.

What we now know is that Urban, though seething inside, calmed himself after the talk with Siler. He then returned to the sideline where he reached inside his pocket and grasped a medal on a silver chain that has become almost like his rosary beads in times like these. This very private moment has been shared with only a few people, although much has been speculated about it.

Some people guessed that Meyer, an Ohioan who grew up on Ohio State football, was rubbing two lucky buckeyes together. They couldn't have been more wrong. Instead, he was grasping a religious medal in his pocket. This was a common way of reminding himself of his late mother, Gisela, and something he did often during stressful times on the sideline of games.

From Gisela, Urban had learned about nurturing and reaching out to others. As much as he admired his father, Bud, and was brought up under his strict discipline, he learned from his mother about bringing people together around food for social interaction.

4

"Winning Prevents Anarchy"

One of Urban Meyer's biggest attributes has been inclusion and the bringing together of all factions. That has included former players—those of all nationalities, races, and religions. He has involved the fans, the bands, the support staff, and the faculty.

Perhaps Meyer's success is the by-product of what he calls "a culture of winning." It is a shared culture. And that meant there could be no divisive lines.

The task was not always easy and the road was sometimes full of potholes.

At Utah, he had the challenge of blending Caucasians, Polynesians, Hispanics, and African-Americans in a Mormon-dominated community.

He has not only been a champion of diversity, but has become sort of the godfather of the Gator Nation, with a mission to heal all wounds and mend all fences. Various misunderstandings, tiffs, and disses have caused estrangement of some former Florida players over the years. Meyer has brought many defectors back to the Gator Family by inviting them to functions, such as the annual Captain's Dinner, during which current players get a live lesson in the team's heritage.

Working with Director of Athletics Jeremy Foley, Meyer welcomed former players back for special ceremonies, including the centennial in 2006 and the Florida Football Ring of Honor.

Two of the first four Ring of Honor inductees were Emmitt Smith and Steve Spurrier. Smith had remained somewhat distant from the Gators ever since declining to come back for his senior year and join Spurrier in 1990, instead opting for the NFL.

Meyer not only invited Emmitt back, but trusted him to speak to his team,

"Something I am very, very cautious about doing."

The legacy of winning was slowly making its way back into the culture of Florida football. Sometimes that winning legacy can work against you, because new players and young fans tend to feel they should inherit those rights as champions. As Patriots coach Bill Belichick warned when he spoke to the Gator team in the spring of 2007, talking directly to the newcomers, "Some of you woke up on third base and don't even know how you got there because you did not hit the triple."

Meyer has successfully recruited top players, but tempers the allure of their potential with common sense. That's why he says he can't really judge a recruiting class until four seasons later.

Each year when Meyer invites the new recruits to his house, he hands each of them a card with pictures of four rings on it, signifying the high-water mark set by the 1993 class, which won four SEC rings and a national championship. One of the players from that era—such as linebacker James Bates or running back Terry Jackson—will speak to the newcomers and offer the challenge. The message is clear: This is going to be your heritage, so aim high and shoot for the best.

Four and five-star recruits are the lifeblood for the "culture of winning."

Yet history shows that everywhere he has been head coach, Meyer has also relied on the heavily "unrecruited" walk-on and has been a champion of those who earn their scholarships with battlefield promotion. He knows it takes them all to win. And he never loses sight that winning is the ultimate goal—otherwise, there will be no platform from which to help young people. Just in case he does, he's always got Hiram de Fries around to remind him that it is about the W's.

When Hiram isn't dealing with at-risk players or checking on player academics or enforcing and interpreting policy or assisting with community "leader/mentor programs," he is on the field watching out for the welfare of those around him as the team's "safety officer." You can tell how much Meyer values de Fries by the 2006 BCS championship ring he was awarded and proudly wears.

The big man with the shiny ring was negotiating a healthy lunch of broiled scallops when he paused to reflect on the elixir for all coaches. Although a professional life-skills expert, de Fries is also a football guy. He wouldn't be around to coach life if the football team didn't win games.

On this day he was lunching with a writer friend in Cross Creek in the backwoods of north-central Florida, halfway between Gainesville and Ocala—up the road from the old homestead of Pulitzer Prize winning author (*The Yearling*) Marjorie Kinnan Rawlings. The topic was the necessity for winning, which the big man with the shiny ring said was not just the lifeblood but also the petrol that drives programs and propels coaches.

Hiram de Fries knows about petrol. He is an attorney and retired Shell Oil executive who advises Meyer on numerous issues and is an administrator of policy. "Hiram is like my uncle," Urban says of the former Colorado State lineman, who grew up in Hawaii and began helping a twenty-five-year-old assistant coach named Meyer recruit players to Fort Collins, Colorado, while coaching at Mission Viejo and Mater Dei high schools in Orange County, California.

"During the gas crisis of the 1970s we learned firsthand about the law of supply and demand. It was a major inconvenience and some people even died," de Fries said with careful deliberation. "But that's not the real danger. The real danger is that if we run out of oil and gas, we have anarchy."

There was a long pause in his conversation with the writer, who was practicing his own version of supply and demand on his fried catfish, cheese grits, and hush puppies right from the kitchen of the Yearling Restaurant.

"It's like that in college football," said de Fries, continuing with the metaphor for his closing argument. "Winning prevents anarchy."

There is no danger of anarchy around the University of Florida anytime soon. But just as the price of gas continues to rise, so do the expectations of people about Meyer.

A constant vigil is needed, however, to keep focused on the ultimate prize: winning. What coach would dare say that was not the No. 1 priority?

Therein lies the challenge for Meyer, who is caught between missions both a top priority and yet essential to each other. As de Fries says, winning is the panacea, and without it a coach has no pulpit. Yet, as Tim Tebow says, the shaping of young men's lives is more important to the Gator coach. Literally, that is almost a daily struggle for Florida's coach. His good friend from Ashtabula, Ohio, admires Urban's commitment and the price he pays for it.

"When he loses, my man will not be eating, will not be sleeping. That's gut-wrenching to him," said Dean Hood. "But you can take all that stuff and wad it up and throw it in the trash can . . . compared to the importance of being a good dad and a good husband. The importance of using football as a platform to teach kids how to be a good husband and a good dad. That's the true Urban Meyer and that's what's important to him.

"That's one of the things I love about Urban. Yeah, that stuff—he can't eat, he can't sleep, whatever. And he still does it . . . he still runs that fake punt against Iowa [in the 2006 Outback Bowl win]. If that doesn't work, you want to talk about the abuse he's gonna take for that? That's what I love about Urban Meyer."

As Hood points out about his childhood friend, trying to find the right balance between mentoring players and winning football is the dilemma of every coach with a strong faith.

"How do you keep that balance of that and winning?" said Hood. "It's like Satan still dangles that carrot of winning in front of your face. And it's all well and good, but you still gotta win. That's the struggle in this profession—to do that in perspective. Just to trust that God is sovereign. Just be obedient and faithful and [know] he's going to take care of you. Rather than thinking that either you're going to have to win or you've got to sell your house."

One key ingredient to winning is the so-called chemistry, which Meyer wants de Fries to monitor. "Hiram is my 'chemistry coach,'" Urban said. "When I was a young coach, I always said I wanted to have an older guy as the chemistry coach on my staff to help us all get on the same page."

Heeding Billy Donovan's warning about his team being infected by "poison," Meyer said he detected some of that in his 2007 team and was counting on good chemistry among players to offset it.

A coach also just can't get enough Tim Tebows, which is what every culture of winning needs to support its ideals.

So a culture of winning also carries over to the fans, sometimes producing unrealistic expectations.

Some of the younger fans who tend to think all sports began with the arrival of ESPN in 1989 also assume it's their inherent right to cheer for a champion. They, too, are spoiled. Seven SEC titles and two national championships were achieved over eighteen years from 1990 to 2007, during which the Florida Gators had a .782 winning percentage and an average of 9.7 wins a season. No wonder the fans enjoy chanting "It's great to be a Florida Gator" after each win.

However, Meyer believes victory comes at a price and like everything else in his program, it should be earned. That is how he was taught when he was raised by Bud and Gisela Meyer in Ashtabula, Ohio.

5

The Good Life in Ashtabula

Ashtabula, Ohio, on the southeast bank of Lake Erie, just a few miles west of the Pennsylvania border, is usually character- ized as a "blue-collar town" with a rough-and-tumble lifestyle. Hardly the Garden Spot of America, Ashtabula has a harsh climate and a high rate of unemployment.

Urban's sister Gigi believes Ashtabula gets a bum rap.

"That stuff always shows up in interviews, that it [Ashtabula] was a 'hard town' and very 'blue-collar.' Our life was not very blue collar," said Gigi. "We went to Europe, our mother was the chef at the coun- try club, and we ate all kinds of things. My grandparents were fairly wealthy. We weren't really affluent but we weren't *not* either.

"I feel sorry for Ashtabula, because every time I read an Urban Meyer story, it makes it sound like he grew up in this horrible place, but it was kind of bustling. The lake was doing well. The chemical industry was doing well. Union Carbide was up and going. Ashtabula was just fine."

Urban thought Ashtabula was "awesome," but admits he lacked knowledge about climates and geography. "I didn't know there were warm places to live," he said. That kind of Midwestern naïveté and simple, uncluttered perspective made it an even better environment for youngsters to focus on sports and academics.

Urban's good friend Dean Hood didn't know much better, either, and found it the perfect setting for him.

"I ate my Wheaties, went to school, had great teachers and coaches, practiced after school—did things that kids do," said Hood. "I didn't notice any socio-economic deal. I was just living a normal life and I thought this is how everybody did it: get up in the morning and shovel six inches of snow so you can get your car out of the driveway."

Urban was raised at the stern hand of his father, but with the tender touch of his mother and was a self-proclaimed "mama's boy." He became an athlete, with a preference for football, baseball, and a little sailing. In the pursuit of his boyhood dreams, he discovered an almost magical quality of reinventing himself at just the right time as a new and improved model.

Meyer aspired to play baseball in the majors and football for Ohio State, but he also shared a dream with just about every Catholic boy who loved football: to become coach of Notre Dame. His mother affirmed that dream, telling him almost every day that those dreams could come true. They did in fact—or at least could have.

Hood, who attended a local public school, Harbor High, became friends with Urban through a passion for sports. Dean dated a girl who attended St. John, Terri Herpy, and the three of them often hung out together. Hood remembers the first time he went to Urban's house and met his father. "Urban said, 'Dad, this Dean Hood, he's the captain of the Harbor football team.' And Bud said, 'I don't give a crap. You want something to drink?'"

There were only a few hard-and-fast rules outside the mandate of giving your best efforts in studies and athletic competition. One cardinal Bud rule was "no motorcycles." But anytime Urban wanted a beer—which he rarely did because he was an athlete—Bud allowed his son to go to the refrigerator and take one. Drugs, of course, were out of the question, and if any of the kids ever used them, they knew they could be kicked out of the house.

Bud would later also use athletics as a form of punishment and a tool for learning self-discipline.

Sports were a part of the culture in the Meyer house, as well as the town. Despite his commitment to higher education, Bud told Urban at an early age to stay away from taking a college curriculum that would usurp his time that could otherwise be spent learning how to become a good coach.

Bud was strict and sometimes harsh, but he wasn't an overbearing, screaming Little League father. Sometimes Bud sat quietly in the stands and talked into his tape recorder, making notes for postmortems to be shared later. And he wasn't shy about sharing those opinions or dishing out discipline for mistakes made.

Running was Bud's weapon of punishment for failure. He was so strict that he once made Urban jog all the way back to the Meyer house from a baseball game played several miles away. Urban had made the last out when his high school team was behind and subsequently lost. Dean Hood remembers that day well.

"I went to watch him play a baseball game, and Urban played great, maybe going three for four, with some RBIs and played perfect in the field leading up to that," said Dean Hood. "But I think he made an out in the last inning and they ended up losing the game. Urban knew I was coming to the game and we were supposed to go out afterwards for a cheeseburger. I was with the girl from St. John that I was dating, and he was supposed to ride back from the game with us, so we were sitting in the car waiting and he comes over and throws his baseball cleats in the car.

"He said, 'I can't go.'

"I said, 'What do you mean?'

"He said, 'We lost the game and I'm running home.' And it was a long way from his home—and it was miles away."

So Urban learned at an early age that failure comes with a price. Perhaps that is part of the reason today for his self-flagellation following a defeat.

While Bud Meyer was strict and believed in strong discipline, he also took a keen interest in his three children and gave them leeway in making their own decisions.

The children were being prepped through higher education, and the odds were against their remaining behind in northern Ohio to work with their hands. They were expected to excel in school. "I got a C once in sophomore English," said Urban, "and I didn't think the sun was going to come up the next day."

Urban has nothing but fond memories of Ashtabula with his parents and two sisters, Gigi and Erika. That's because the two daughters and the son were the main focus of Bud and Gisela Meyer's life.

Urban was the middle child and began competition at an early age.

"If you weren't playing sports," said Hood, "you were working out to get ready for sports—at the weight room or the local YMCA. Sports was it."

The entire town shut down on Friday nights and most everybody went to high school games. On Saturday the locals watched Ohio State, and on Sunday they watched the Browns and Bengals. Athletics were everything. Woody Hayes was The Man. "You got beat up in school if you were not a Buckeye or a Woody Hayes guy," said Urban. "And I certainly loved him."

Playing sports was not an option in Bud's house.

"Everybody had to do sports," said Bud, a retired chemical engineer. "I don't know how you didn't do sports. We're one of those families, tragically, that have absolutely no artistic ability whatsoever. We can't even write a decent poem. None of us plays a musical instrument. I'm not proud of it. But everybody has to do something sports-wise just because that's how you're supposed to do it. I don't know things differently."

Gigi, who actually broke that stereotype by acting in a couple of plays, was also captain of her high school swim team. Erika was the first girl on a boy baseball team in Ashtabula, took up golf, and became an excellent baseball and softball player. Urban excelled in football and baseball.

"They all did that because that's what you do. Nobody made a conscious judgment about it—just get your butt out and play," said Bud. "Urban did well."

That commitment to sports and education got Bud and Gisela's full support, including their going to see their kids play or Urban coach, no matter how far away. And it carried over into Urban's adult life, as he was struggling to break into college coaching.

"They were both phenomenal about getting in the car and driving twelve hours to watch me," Urban said. "I'm coaching at Illinois State—I'll never forget this—making six thousand dollars a year. Illinois State played Indiana State. Maybe the two worst teams in college football, both about one and nine. They [Gisela and Bud] get in the car and drive twelve hours and watch the game when I only am the quarterback coach, then get in the car and drive home. What is that? That just tells you the kind of support I had growing up.

"And we're kind of the same way with our own kids. Shelley's everywhere. If I'm available, I go. So that's why I drive to Atlanta to go watch [his daughters play in] a volleyball tournament. That came from them."

Bud and Gisela also gave their children the gift of parenting.

"They were all around us kids, doing this, doing that," remembers Urban. "They had no life. And, really, that's what you're supposed to do. That's the way God made it. You are supposed to sink every ounce into your children. I always remember that about my own."

It was such a precious gift that Urban almost feels guilty. "I had a great family and a great childhood," Urban said. "I hear some of these stories about how these kids [on his team] without families were growing up. Why am I so fortunate?"

While Bud built discipline in his young son's life, the nurturing love of Gisela provided Urban with an underpinning of his dreams.

Bud was the hammer, Gisela the velvet.

There was plenty of sports competition for Bud to oversee and lots of gourmet cooking by Gisela. On "Popcorn Days" when snow fell and there was no school, the Meyer kids were allowed to stay home and hang out with Mom and Dad. They were entertained by the show out the front window: people walking, or riding in their cars, slipping and sliding down Lake Road, a main thoroughfare with big ditches on each side.

Sometimes those unfortunate people who couldn't negotiate their way past those ditches would come to the door to use the phone and call for help. Gisela would offer them hot chocolate. Nurturing was her thing, and she was generous to a fault, able to even connect with total strangers.

Perhaps this was part of the reason that Gisela, as a young girl, was able to negotiate her escape out of Nazi Germany, where she was a member of an affluent family.

A Prussian soldier she had befriended said he would be on duty that night, but would let her cross over because he would be leaving the next morning. Gisela's father had died in the war. She and her mother left everything behind as they fled on a river bed through Bavaria.

Gisela (Geez-a-la) was a gourmet cook trained in Switzerland and had worked at some well-known restaurants. She made her way to America as a young woman in her twenties and went to work as a server at a famous French restaurant in Cincinnati. The Maisonnette, until it closed in 2005, had the longest run in America with a five-star rating. Restaurant management asked Gisela to change her name to the more French-sounding Giselle (Je-Zelle). There she met Bud, a customer and a wine connoisseur of sorts.

Bud and Gisela married five months later. They had their first child, Gigi, in Cincinnati, but Bud was transferred to Toledo for six months, during which time Urban Frank Meyer III was born. Bud soon moved his family to Ashtabula, where he was employed in the chemical business and Erika was born. The close-knit family stayed busy with sports and school activities and enjoyed what Ashtabula had to offer.

"Winters were really cold," said Gigi, "with lots of snow."

Summer brought sailing, swimming, softball, baseball. Fall brought football. Everybody in the Meyer household participated in some kind of sports except Gisela, who had enough to do as nurturer and chef, either outside or inside the home. When she was cooking at the local country club, she got some help around the house from Gigi, Urban, and Erika—each was assigned a room to clean.

The Meyers were boat people. First was the smaller boat named *Puppe*, followed by a larger, twenty-four-footer called *The Gisele*—both named after Gisela Meyer. (*Puppe* means "doll" in German.)

"We hung out on the boat, slept on the boat . . . lived on the boat," said Gigi. "Urban and Erika and I all sailed on other people's boats as a part of crews that raced—especially Urban. He and Dad did the Bermuda Cup as sailors together. My dad was navigator and Urban was strong, so he could winch when he was told to."

They were members of Put-In-Bay and most Sundays they were on the lake—Urban usually in a Tartan Ten, a forty-foot keelboat that can sleep six.

Otherwise, they were a typical upper-middle class family growing up in the Midwest, with three kids who were taught to become achievers. And if you screwed up, Bud made you run laps or do push-ups. Urban did his fair share.

Bud and Urban watched a lot of football games on TV, and the younger Meyer, an excellent chess player, would question why the coaches made certain moves. "I remember that's how they connected," said Gigi. "Urban would say, 'Hey Dad, I wonder what would have happened if they had run these four plays instead of those four plays.'"

At an early age, Urban showed an interest in playing and coaching. Ken Sims, a basketball coach and friend of the Meyer family, now retired in Ocala, Florida, says he recalls Urban asking questions about coaching at around age eight. "He was very curious," said Sims. The only advice Sims remembers giving him—and he's not even sure Urban remembered it—was "don't start out in high school."

As a young boy, one day while heading to his seat to watch a college game in Cincinnati, Urban passed by the Wichita State football team. He saw what he believes now was the defensive coordinator scribbling on a chalkboard, barking out orders to his players. "He's just going after the players with intensity, and I just stopped and started watching him," said Meyer. "I'm a little guy with my dad, and I'm stopped, holding up people. I wouldn't leave and I was just mesmerized. To this day I can remember that coach with that chalkboard, coaching those guys up. I looked at my dad and said, 'I want to be a coach someday.'"

Meyer didn't know it at the time, but on that same Wichita State staff as offensive line coach and, later, linebacker coach was a rookie assistant named Phillip Fulmer, who would take over as head coach of the Vols in 1992.

Urban's first love back then was baseball.

In his prepuberty days, young Meyer lacked the body mass and strength for football. He had come from a long line of baseball players—two great-uncles who played in the minors and a dad who was an amateur. It was no surprise, then, when Urban began to do well in the sport. His knack for reinventing himself and improving in spurts seemed to mystify members of his family. And Urban would carry over that trait of metamorphosis from his days as an athlete to his being a coach.

Every time sister Gigi turned around, her little brother seemed to grow in size or stature as an athlete.

Like all siblings, the three Meyer kids fought on occasion.

"If you want to know what Urban was like," said Gigi, "then just look at Nate [his son, who was turning ten in 2008]. Except a little bit more mischievous."

The worst trouble Urban got into was over playing ball in the house and breaking a glass horse brought back from Europe by his grandparents. But because he was playing ball when it happened, he wasn't severely punished.

"There was anger, but not a lot of anger," said Gigi, "because playing ball was something that happened a lot in our house. I mean, we ran patterns out in our front yard a lot. Dad would say, 'This on two . . . you're blocking,' and off we'd go."

Urban did well early enough in high school sports that his parents began thinking maybe he could earn a college scholarship. Bud was famous for his declarations, having forecast a dim future after one of Urban's bad baseball performances as a sophomore. "He acted like he had never been on a ball field before," Bud said. "He made wild throws from the infield, struck out, made mistakes. I remember saying, 'We can just forget about scholarships.'"

Urban was a skinny kid who didn't reach one hundred pounds until he was midway through his freshman year. About that time he took one of his patented quantum leaps. He had a growth spurt accompanied by a sudden advance in athletic skills.

"Urban was a great baseball player," said Hood, who didn't play the game but sometimes shagged balls for his friend or attended his games as a spectator.

"I was good at baseball because you didn't have to have much strength and size," said Meyer. "And I could turn a double play and I would practice with my dad all the time. But I was really not a good player. Between my sophomore and junior year, I went from being a guy who didn't play much, a skinny little guy who was 115 pounds, and I went on a growth spurt."

One day Urban found that secret weapon that he hoped would be his equalizer. He wanted to buy a set of weights—"and this was before guys were lifting weights." It came to him while he was watching a TV program about Nebraska football. He somehow got his hands on some national strength magazines and pasted the torn-out pages on his bedroom walls. "That's my edge!" he proclaimed.

Bud Meyer had heard that weights were bad for some athletes, however, and initially declined to buy them for Urban. But after going to a doctor to learn how to use them properly, Bud purchased an inexpensive set—"plastic with cement in the middle," Urban recalled. They set them up in the dining room, where quite often Urban would bump the dining room table during his workout.

"I went from 115 pounds to 175 pounds, running, and hitting home runs, and started getting recruited. And that was astonishing. I would wake up sore. But I had a growth spurt that most kids don't go through."

Of the four high schools in Ashtabula, Urban chose St. John because it was noted for excellent football and baseball teams.

Gigi remembered Urban was not very big in his early teens and preferred baseball over football. Then one day she turned around and he was a star on the St. John High football team. She attended a nearby private girls' boarding school because she could compete in swimming there, but when she returned home, it was obvious to her. "I was gone, came back, and I went from—in my mind—being able to rest my head on my brother's shoulder to [not being able to do] that quick."

Then Gigi went to college, came home, and found out her brother was a high school football star.

"I was so amazed. It was like he had come from this little guy playing outside to [playing] both sides of the ball," said Gigi. "I actually came home to see about three games in a row because I was so blown away that it was Urban out there doing that. It was really cool. I was very proud of him."

Football was always in his mind, and as he grew, Urban was good enough at a smaller Catholic school to start at both free safety and tail-back. St. John was known as a school where football and baseball players could excel.

"In that environment, he was pretty good," said Bud.

St. John coach Paul Kopko was demonstrative and very physical in his coaching technique, often grabbing the face masks of players who failed to execute plays properly—and sometimes worse. At an early age, Urban learned to deal with criticism and responded to Kopko's hands-on approach by getting bigger, stronger, and becoming a leader.

While playing at St. John, Urban's coaches became an inspiration to him. Kopko and assistants Jim Mackey and Ken Petrochello taught him an understanding of the game and the importance of sound fundamentals.

"I had great coaches at St. John and great experiences," Meyer said. "Coach Kopko and his staff were the reason I got into coaching football."

Petrochello, Urban's defensive coach at St. John, saw a leader emerging at the middle safety position. He remembers seeing Urban for the first time as a "skinny, five-foot-five freshman who was very enthusiastic.

"He was very intense about getting stronger and bigger so he could make an impact on the football team," said Petrochello. "He started doing weights with a friend and you could see the results: He started getting stronger and taking a more dominant role on the football team."

As a senior, Urban called defensive signals and was known as a hard-hitting tackler who often separated the ball from the receiver. And when needed on offense—St. John ran the run-and-shoot—Urban filled in as backup tailback. He often played both ways.

"He was a fiery competitor," said Petrochello, "and he did not want to be out [of the game] at any time—did not want to be off the field. And if he had an injury, he would play through it."

One vivid scene Petrochello will never forget was when St. John was in the state play-offs against Mogadore Christian Academy from Akron. St. John's starting tailback was out with an injury. Meyer was also hurt with a leg injury, but would saddle up and play both ways. That night as Urban was getting his leg wrapped on the trainer's table, Petrochello looked up and saw a determined athlete who was willing to sacrifice his body for the team.

"He was getting taped from his hip almost down to his ankle," said Petrochello. "Standing on the top of the table, he looked almost ten feet tall. The idea was he was showing all the other kids: 'Hey, this guy is going to play whether he's hurt or not.'"

Meyer played hard, but St. John lost, 10–7.

Urban was named to the all-state football team. But it was baseball that took precedence.

Urban made faster progress as a shortstop. As a junior, he had begun to develop into a solid infielder who could go deep into the hole, then rocket his throws to first. At the end of the year, he made the all-star team and in the tournament had a strong at-bat.

Urban remembers one game where the scouts were watching and, almost like divine intervention, he hit a home run and made several big defensive plays. "It was like God put it there," he said. "I hit a home run and shortstops don't usually hit home runs." On a play between short and third, he backhanded the ball, planted his right foot, and rifled it to first to get the out. He surprised himself. "I just let it fly," he said, "and it was like *bap*! 'You're out!'"

Those kinds of plays began to get him followed by scouts.

Three years later in 1982 when Urban was drafted in the thirteenth round and signed a professional baseball contract with the Atlanta Braves, Bud had to eat his "there goes the scholarship" words. Gisela served Bud's critical comment on a platter in what must have been one of her favorite recipes for gourmet broiled crow.

The night before he was to leave, Urban's friends threw a party. When they were able to get alone together, Urban and his teenage friend Dean Hood, an aspiring college football player, dreamed the dreams of seventeen-year-olds. Maybe someday, said Hood, the two of them would wind up on the cover of *Sports Illustrated*—"me for football and you as a baseball player." Urban made it to the cover of *SI*, but in a different sport: as a college football coach. So far Hood hasn't.

After he was drafted by the Braves, Urban's mom, dad, and baseball coach all traveled to Atlanta. Urban was nonchalantly flipping a football—he wasn't sure why, but perhaps it portended things to come—as he and his family walked into a motel room and proceedings began. He turned the negotiations over to his dad, unconcerned about financial details and eager to start playing. He and his baseball coach began chatting.

"My dad is a chemical engineer and he's real smart," Urban said. "We are getting calls from agents who want to represent me. And dad said, 'I'm going to handle it.' I just wanted to go play ball. So they [the Braves people] come in and sit down. Not minutes later you hear, 'Congratulations!' And they're shaking hands. So I go over and sign it—I'm not paying attention . . . I want to say it was a thirteen-thousand-dollar signing bonus . . . And they're going to pay for my education. So I don't think twice about it."

Next, Urban traveled to Sarasota for the Rookie League in the summer of 1982 where his baseball education began. He was sitting around the table at the dining hall, talking with fellow players. "Eighteen- and nineteen-year-olds just babbling," he said. "One loudmouth is sitting right there, he's like the forty-second-round draft pick. He started talking about the amount of money they all signed for. And I'm listening to the amount of money this guy is talking about and I said, 'I didn't get that kind of money.' And this guy said, 'Can you believe they tried to get me to sign on the first offer and my agent wouldn't take it and so they doubled it?'

"So I called my dad and said, 'By the way, the forty-second rounder got double what I got."

Life as a professional baseball player wasn't all it was cracked up to be. Being away from home and baffled by his inability to hit professional pitching, he soon decided to give up baseball and return home to Ashtabula in pursuit of football. When he called Bud, however, that idea was quickly quashed. Urban made every excuse possible—"the coach didn't like me . . . didn't like the way I talked . . . didn't like the way I parted my hair," he told his father. To which Bud responded, "OK, you're seventeen and you're grown. So you're capable of making your own decision. But by the way, you're not welcome back here. I'm sure your mother would want to see you at Christmas, but other than that, you're not welcome. There are no quitters in the Meyer family."

It's a story Urban repeats every year to his class of new recruits.

Predominantly a glove man, Meyer found pitching at that level difficult to hit, but he was diligent about staying in shape. Since the physical conditioning had paid off before, Urban wanted to keep it going. His roommate, however, had a different workout routine. "I was doing pushups every day, running, lifting, and getting in bed early every night," Urban recalled. "My roommate stayed out drinking until 2:00 A.M. and I could smell it on him when he came in."

It just didn't seem to help. Perhaps the real sign for Urban was the day his roommate had a big day at the plate with a couple of home runs. After hitting his second one, the roommate returned to the bench, reeking of alcohol, and sat next to Urban, who had struck out three times that day. "He looked over at me and said, 'Maybe you should do less of what you're doing, and more of what I'm doing.' And you know, I began to think maybe he was right."

Urban finished that summer, and the following year he returned to the Braves organization, reporting to the Pulaski, Virginia, Class A team of the Appalachian League in 1983. Developing arm trouble and unable to connect with the curve ball, Urban began to realize baseball wasn't his thing. Bud was willing to accept that decision. So Urban returned to Ohio, enrolled at Cleveland State for a semester, and began to make plans to walk on at the University of Cincinnati—the place where he had seen that unknown Wichita State coach who had so inspired him ten years prior.

The best thing Urban ever did as a baseball player, as far as Gigi was concerned, was to present her with a birthday present of his only home run ball in a professional league—even if it was late. After she turned eighteen, she was asked by Urban what she wanted as a gift, and she said, "I want your first home run this season."

It finally came six months later.

"He called up one day and said he was sending me something in a box," said Gigi, who still treasures that baseball today. She displays the baseball on a shelf in her Cincinnati home. It is signed *Urban Meyer*, with the date of his homer.

By the time Urban arrived at Cincinnati the Bearcats were struggling, having gone through four coaches in five years. Dave Currey, Urban's coach, hung on for five seasons before losing his job following a 19-45 record and two years of NCAA probation.

In Urban's first season, 1984, the team went 2-9 against a schedule that included Auburn, Alabama, Miami, and the Florida Gators. That year marked Urban's first trip to Gainesville, but Florida Field wasn't even nicknamed the Swamp yet. Galen Hall's team, which wound up being named No. 1 by the *New York Times* before being derailed by NCAA sanctions, hammered Currey's Bearcats, 48–17.

As a junior, Meyer played free safety and special teams, but there were also disciplinary issues among the players that bothered him. This was the time to end his career as a player and begin as a coach. Urban had told his father as a sophomore in high school that he wanted to be a coach someday and was encouraged by Bud to pursue it. So when Urban received a call from St. Xavier, which needed an intern for defensive backs, he was recommended and took the job.

Exiting without fanfare, he quietly launched what would become a brilliant career, setting the stage for his first step toward college football, where he would serve for fifteen years as an assistant.

The dream he had shared with his mom was about to become real. One of the few regrets he would have was she would die before ever seeing him become a head coach in 2001.

When Gisela first got ill with cancer, Urban and his sisters had already left home. Although the Meyer family was scared, Gisela made it known she didn't plan on dying any time soon and said she wasn't taking it as a death sentence. She lasted fifteen more years. She didn't quite make it to five years cancer free, but did get to see all of her grandchildren. Her family rallied around her.

"Everybody loved my mother," said Gigi. "There are people in this world who leave this footprint, which she did. She was one of these women who was the kindest, sweetest, most sincere, most benevolent, nongossiping, nontypical woman that you've ever met.

"It's probably because she lived in bomb shelters growing up and saw things that most other people don't see. So she could not get excited or worried about the kinds of things that bother people in Ashtabula, Ohio. Or the kinds of things that set my dad off—'Oh Bud! Stop that!'—and so she kept him in perspective and kept life in perspective for us. And even her own cancer, she kept in perspective."

Gisela possessed that rock-solid quality of "perspective" that Urban came to treasure as mother's wisdom. She thrived on the good news about her son's career as a bright assistant coach on the way up and was happy that he was hired at Ohio State.

After Gisela died, Urban still thought of her every day and would carry a memento with him in his pocket all the way to the national championship game.

6

Bud and Earle

The genealogy of Meyer's coaching dates back to the Woody Hayes DNA that was injected into the veins of Earle Bruce. Meyer did not inherit that Woody affliction of the Three-Yards-and-a-Cloud-of-Dust offense that dominated the Ohio State legend's archaic thinking—albeit that the Buckeyes had the running back talent, blocking muscle, and technique to overwhelm.

At Ohio State as a graduate assistant under Bruce, Urban became hooked on the pageantry of college football, but he also learned about the importance of toughness and the necessity of speed. This was the beginning of the enlightenment stage for Meyer about how far he could push an athlete and the need for a coach to involve himself in the lives of his players.

Urban choked up the first time he ever touched an Ohio State jersey.

For a kid who grew up bleeding scarlet and gray and wore number 45 in high school because he idolized two-time Heisman winner Archie Griffin, simply walking into the Horseshoe—Ohio Stadium in Columbus—was the emotional equivalent of a baseball fan first setting foot's in Cooperstown, New York.

"I had tears in my eyes . . . I remember grabbing a scarlet and gray jersey and going, 'Wow!' I mean, 'Wow! I'm here.' Every kid growing up in Ohio wants to do that," Meyer said.

Urban's hiring by the Buckeyes seemed more than coincidence. While spending a year interning at St. Xavier High School in Cincinnati, Meyer met Ohio State's quarterback coach, Tom Lichtenberg, who was recruiting "St. X" quarterback Greg Frye (the Buckeyes signed him). Lichtenberg was also in charge of Bruce's graduate assistant program and offered Urban a job, which he took immediately.

In what would become one of the most meaningful life-changing experiences ever, Urban was introduced to Earle Bruce and got the opportunity to learn about the game from one of Woody's trusted disciples.

Bruce was head coach in Columbus from 1979 to 1988 and he would own the second best record in school history at that time (81-26-1). Under him, Ohio State went to eight bowl games and won four Big Ten titles. His Buckeyes beat archrival Michigan five times and his 5-4 record was the best any Ohio State coach ever had against Bo Schembechler, including that of Woody Hayes. His 1979 team went unbeaten and played for a national championship, barely losing to Southern Cal, 17–16, in the Rose Bowl. But it didn't spare him from the coaching guillotine.

The young graduate assistant from Ashtabula with the piercing whistle and the combustible coaching personality looked to be right out of the Woody Hayes Coaching Catalog. But Bruce himself was soon on the hot seat and would be winding down his final two seasons there.

Meyer was being trained at the knee of a coach who would be fired by Ohio State, but Urban would one day gain a measure of vindication for his old coach when his Florida Gators beat the Buckeyes out of a national championship twenty years later.

Aside from Urban's "two fathers," three other coaches became his mentors—Sonny Lubick, Lou Holtz, and Bob Davie. However, the little man in the fedora from Pittsburgh who became a legendary Ohio high school coach by going undefeated at Massillon two straight seasons had the biggest influence on Meyer's career.

Earle's direct, nose-to-nose approach and the Way of the Scarlet and Gray had rubbed off on Meyer, who is still such a huge fan of Woody Hayes, that a sketched portrait of him hangs in Meyer's Gainesville home. Meyer became an even bigger fan of Bruce, whose photograph appears there several times over.

However, coaching at Ohio State would prove to be the first half of double jeopardy for Meyer, who would lose his job twice because of hitching his wagon to Bruce's star.

If you asked him if he'd do it all over again, Meyer would respond with a resounding yes. Furthermore, going from high school to college and getting hired to coach at his beloved Ohio State as a graduate assistant was like jumping over the moon.

In Earle, Urban saw a mirror image of his father, who had guided him toward coaching and suggested it as a career. After meeting and working under the iron hand of Earle, Urban was convinced that he'd run into Bud Meyer's clone. "If you cut those two open, they'd be the same person inside," Urban said of Bruce and Bud.

Bud didn't disagree. "One person who is the second father to him is coach Earle Bruce," said Bud Meyer. "He's the only coach he's ever had in his life."

Urban was in awe of Bruce, whose gruff exterior and sometimes abrasive style with players impacted the Boy from Ashtabula as he was learning College Football Coaching 101. However, because he had grown up with Bud, Urban didn't wilt in the face of conflict or harsh criticism. Besides, he was way too far down the totem pole to feel the wrath of Bruce very much.

Bruce was focused on doing everything "the right way," but was far from perfect. "He lost his temper and sometimes his self-control," said Urban. "But [there was] never cheating. No chance of cheating on your wife. The loyalty, all the things that he taught, to this day is still the key."

Bruce was loyal to his boss Woody, his players, and his coaches, but his employers didn't reciprocate and they fired him. Perhaps he rubbed some people wrong with his frankness—a frankness that resonated like a true high C on a coaching piano to people like Urban.

"He's the best. He's a man's man," said Urban. "Nowadays you talk to some people and you're not sure what the guy's saying. Coach Bruce tells you what's going on. At the end of the day I hope people say that about me. There's no BS. Coach Bruce is the best."

All along the way, the voice of Bruce would always resonate in the ear of Urban Meyer, whether real or imagined.

Bud mentored his son well at a young age and pushed him toward excellence, influencing Urban's choices without making them for him, but with a demanding disposition almost identical to Earle's. Urban would benefit from Bud's suggestion that he pursue coaching. Meanwhile, Earle was pounding fundamentals in his brain, and later, Urban's wife, Shelley, kept insisting that her husband stick with it.

As Urban began coaching at Ohio State, some of that toughness displayed by Bruce was embraced and later modeled by Urban.

In Columbus Meyer also began realizing the fragile nature of the coaching business after his mentor was fired. Just before the final game of the season against Michigan, Bruce was told he was going to be dismissed. Bruce beat Bo Schembechler's Michigan team for the fifth time, causing Bo to say that if he had to lose to Ohio State, "I didn't mind so much today."

After getting fired at Ohio State, Bruce went to Northern Iowa. He was there for one season before heading to Colorado State, where his team got off to a mediocre 5-5-1 start. But he and Urban were going to team up again several years later.

When Urban left Cincinnati for Ohio State, his girlfriend and soon-to-be fiancée Shelley had stayed behind to get her degree. Almost every weekend she hit the road for Columbus and attended the football games before finally moving there with her girlfriend and taking a job as a nurse.

"He made nothing and he worked all the time," Shelley said, but she did enjoy attending Buckeye football games. She would take that newfound enthusiasm with her when she moved to Illinois and married Urban.

Shelley says her Ohio State experience opened her eyes in many ways. One of them was her husband's potential as a coach. Another was the amount of sacrifice that it was going to take.

At Ohio State, Meyer became vaguely acquainted with a young

strength and conditioning coach from Ambridge, Pennsylvania, who would become a close friend, strong ally, and key player in his football coaching future.

Mickey Marotti was also serving his graduate assistantship in 1987 when Meyer arrived at Ohio State. His first impression of Meyer was "that he was just a football GA who had no time for strength guys—just kind of a 'guy'—and there was no dialogue. Just 'How you doin'?' and that was it."

Marotti and Meyer would go their separate ways, Mick heading to West Virginia next to work for two years as an assistant to Don Nehlen. But they would later hook up at Notre Dame to begin their partnership in pursuit of football excellence.

Meyer received his masters in sports administration at Ohio State after two years, but when he went to look for work he didn't find much to choose from. After all, Earle had moved on to Northern Iowa.

Had it not been for the comforting words and strong encouragement of his wife, Urban Meyer the coach might have been Urban Meyer the banker or insurance man.

Twice, college football nearly lost a bright and shining star.

Having always wanted to be a lawyer, Urban figured now would be the time to pursue it since opportunities in coaching were so sparse.

"I always wanted to be a prosecutor. I grew up watching too many courtroom movies—like *Jagged Edge*," he said. So he came home from his job in that second year at Ohio State—Earle having been fired and his graduate assistant's job about to end—and announced, "I've had enough, Shelley. I'm going to take six months off, study real hard, and go to law school."

"I'll never forget this," she said. "I said to him, 'You're making a mistake. You are meant to be a coach.'"

At times, coaches' wives make a huge difference in the careers and lives of their husbands—as well as the football future of some schools. Without her diligence and willingness to sacrifice and survive on very little money, college football would have been deprived of a brilliant coach in the making.

What was it that Shelley saw?

"I saw that the passion for that job was incredible," she said. "When you start out at Ohio State, I don't know how you can't not have passion for the game."

Urban finally found employment at Illinois State, where he struggled for two years (1988–89)—first as outside linebacker coach and then as quarterback and receivers coach for fellow Ohioan Jim Heacock, who would eventually become the Ohio State defensive coordinator and face Meyer's Gators in the BCS title game.

Life, however, was anything but normal for Shelley and Urban in Normal, Illinois.

Illinois State is noted for winning the championship in the National Forensic Association tournament. Perhaps its most famous alumnus is former NBA basketball player, coach, and broadcaster Doug Collins. A football mecca it isn't. Football wasn't much of a priority in Normal, and it showed.

If Meyer learned anything in his first real coaching job at Illinois State it was that without good players, coaches would surely become candidates for roadkill, because the Redbirds would certainly get run over. They went 1-10 and 5-6 for the two seasons Meyer coached there under Heacock.

Urban also found his way as an offensive-minded assistant coach, but only after encouragement from his wife that dissuaded him from making a career change.

"We got our brains kicked in that first year, but I learned a lot of football," Meyer recalled. "I actually thought about getting out of coaching. I was worried about surviving. It was so competitive to get a job, so saturated."

Urban had a special feeling for young people and his communication skills with them were extraordinary, Shelley said. Besides, she felt this was her husband's calling. "I definitely didn't want one situation to ruin all that. I was encouraging him: 'Let's give it a try somewhere else and see.'"

It was more than just a job for Urban—it was beginning to feel like a calling. He and Shelley were about to embark on a partnership of mentoring players by providing them a family environment, encouragement in schoolwork, and counseling about personal problems.

The longer Urban coached, the more the two of them began to

discover how many players came from broken homes, or that one of the players' parents might be in prison or addicted to drugs or alcohol. Shelley began to pay closer attention to the conduct, attitude, and behavior of players. Her job as a nurse trained to work in a psychiatric ward would pay dividends to Urban in his career.

Another part of Urban Meyer was about to surface on the next move. In Colorado, according to Shelley, "His spirituality took a turn."

Just before Urban bailed for another profession, the good news came. Earle Bruce was becoming a new head coach again. Urban and Shelley were moving to Fort Collins, Colorado, a place they would grow to love, where their daughters would be born, where she would make a whole new circle of friends, and where Urban's newfound faith would begin to change his whole thought process.

From the Hayes/Bruce seed, however, grew the branch of Sonny Lubick. From Lubick, Urban learned the importance of treating people right. That meant compassion for players and respect for all members of the football organization—from secretaries to janitors to ball boys. While in Fort Collins, Meyer also began to develop his spiritual side while learning a little football, too, and the production of his receiver group drew the attention of the man from Notre Dame.

Actually, it all began with a not-so-impressive meeting with Johnny Square, the Colorado State team chaplain.

7

Loving Fort Collins

Earle Bruce's call to arms in Fort Collins was the 911 rescue that brought Meyer back to football civilization. Once Urban was reunited at Colorado State with the man who was like his second father, schooling him in hard-nosed ways, Urban became one of Earle's enforcers. He didn't understand all of Earle's strict policies or even totally agree with them, but as a young coach in his impressionistic stage, Meyer was laying the foundation of his career—sound fundamentals and a no-nonsense routine.

At CSU, Meyer became more intrigued with the passing game, although the Rams were running out of the I formation. There wouldn't be many passes, and as coach of the wide receivers, Urban expected his players to execute. Sometimes he would snatch them by their face masks when they dropped a ball or missed a downfield block.

When the call came from Bruce, rescuing Urban from Normal, Illinois, Urban was thrilled. He'd never been to Colorado before—"I didn't know a thing about it"—but the chance to be reunited with his father figure/friend/mentor seemed promising.

It didn't take long for Urban and Shelley to fall in love with the cool, clean, crisp air and brilliant sunshine that enhances life in the foothills of the Great Rocky Mountains.

Fort Collins, an ideal midsized college town, population 130,000, sits just fifty-seven miles north of Denver. It was named by *Money* magazine as America's Best Place to Live in 2006. The "fort" was established by the Ninth Kansas Volunteer Cavalry in 1862. Today it is more noted for its vast number of microbreweries and pubs.

"Everybody said it was cold out there, but it's a great town, still one of my favorites," said Urban. "Some of my best friends are still there."

Shelley loved Fort Collins so much that she never wanted to leave.

As a young coach in his midtwenties, Meyer set out to make his bones under Bruce. Known on the staff as a no-nonsense wide receiver coach who drove his players hard and demanded near perfection, Urban often made his point at their expense.

Meyer also learned about the stringent rules of Bruce. One rule was that players had to always wear socks when traveling in street clothes. This particular rule caused Urban a great deal of anxiety one day when he was about to get on the bus and leave for a game. One of his starting wide receivers wasn't wearing socks. "I got his room key and ran back up fourteen flights of stairs to get them, ran back down, and made him put them on before he got on the bus," Meyer recalled.

While there was much football coaching to be learned under Bruce, Meyer also had some rough edges that needed smoothing.

Meyer helped Bruce turn the Rams program around quickly with a 9-4 record. Urban was so tough on his players, however, that attrition became an issue. He would scream at them, grab them by the face mask, and generally humiliate them in front of their teammates.

"I was out of control," Meyer admitted years later. "I grew up on Coach Bruce and Coach Hayes. When I grew up it was not uncommon for my high school coach [Paul Kopko] to get physical with a player. I had not known it, but I was doing the same thing. I would grab a kid's face mask—but I was out of control."

The growth and maturity of a young coach would evolve through some painful lessons—among them, watching Earle Bruce stumble and fall prey to his detractors.

Back-to-back losing seasons (3-8, 5-7) spelled the demise of Bruce at Colorado State after the 1992 campaign, putting Meyer's future in jeopardy. Urban witnessed from the inside what he considered mutiny as staff people turned on his mentor and he made a mental note about the importance of loyalty. Once the new boss arrived, however, Urban would also learn the value of treating other members of the staff with respect.

Watching Earle get done in again was painful for Meyer.

"I was at home, but I remember seeing coach Bruce's press conference," said Shelley. "I was sitting there crying, in the house. Before that point, it really didn't make that much sense to me, and I hadn't really thought about all the consequences of that action. And then I saw Coach Bruce and saw [his wife] Jean go up and comfort him, that really brought home how serious it was."

Most of all, she felt badly for Urban. "That's one of his favorite people in the world getting hurt and it's the second time. It had happened at Ohio State as well."

Urban was also about to become exposed to some different thinking about the manner in which a head coach treated those around him.

The new coach, Sonny Lubick, at first said he had no place on his staff for Meyer. With no money in their savings, a two-year-old daughter named Nicki, and one on the way (Gigi), there was cause for concern. Shelley said she never panicked because she was confident something would work out for them, but she sensed that Urban was frantic.

They had a mortgage and few job prospects, except maybe at University of Texas at El Paso. Urban began thinking again about getting out of coaching. He had two good friends who were encouraging him to come and try finance. "One offered me a job at Coldwell Banker and one offered me a job in Equitable. I was going to go into insurance or banking," he said.

Then came the good news. Lubick, a former Miami defensive assistant, had a change of heart and decided to retain Meyer. He had gotten a call from a local booster whom he respected about Urban's potential and decided to revisit the idea of keeping him. Meyer was eternally grateful, and what he said next, Lubick claims, "I will never forget."

"You don't know who I am, but you will never be sorry for keeping me," Urban said.

The learning curve was about to get steeper for Urban, whose feisty attitude and combative coaching style would get him reprimanded by the boss. It started with the day a good player quit and Urban was called into Sonny's office.

"This kid quit. You know why he quit?" he asked Meyer.

"No."

"Because of you. He can't take you anymore."

In silence, Lubick stared at Meyer, then said, "I just want you to know that."

It stunned Urban, who said he had a hard time dealing with the reality of his own harshness. "From that day forward I changed," he said.

Urban studied Lubick's demeanor and watched how he motivated people. Urban became more of a teacher and less of a drill sergeant. He began to blend in with Lubick's methods. The team began to click.

"I had grown up in an era when the louder you are, the more you get done," Urban confessed. "Just to watch coach Lubick operate, the way he treated everybody—secretaries, everybody! And our success rate was off the charts. We went ten and one that year.

"Coach Lubick was more of the 'hug 'em up' type and get people to work with you. And he was phenomenal."

Lubick says he did appreciate Meyer's toughness, however. "He coached those guys hard and he coached those guys good," Lubick said. "But we were at Colorado State and we had to keep those guys around. But I think it helped him, because all of us have gone through that one time or another."

More lessons were to be learned, however, and the next one was not about football—it was about life and how to put the game in context. Urban was about to meet up with the Reverend Johnny Square from the nondenominational Iasis Church in Fort Collins, Colorado.

Johnny Square says their first meeting "wasn't all that promising" as he was introduced by Lubick, who said, "Hey, I'd like to introduce Johnny, a former player, and he's our chaplain. I need you to welcome him because he's going to be working with our kids behind the scenes."

Something didn't seem right between Urban and the reverend at first. Basically, Urban didn't seem all that impressed with the idea of a team chaplain.

"On my first look at him, as Sonny was communicating that information, it didn't look too promising," said Square. "Not because Urban gave me a bad look. It just seemed like maybe somewhere in his life, before he met me, that whole religion thing might not have been something that he had cared for in that setting, at that moment.

"So I just said to myself, 'Maybe one of these days I'll get a chance to meet that man at the right time—maybe we can sit down and be friends.'"

Exactly that happened. The ups and downs of his career, the revelation of his own mortality and, perhaps the illness and eventual death of his mother, had a profound impact on Urban, who had begun attending Square's Bible classes for Colorado State coaches.

Square's lessons caused Meyer to stop, take stock of his profession, and check the latitude and longitude of his personal life.

Urban had many questions.

"Urban would come to the coaches' Bible study by an act of his own will," said Square. "One day we were studying the book of Job and he began to ask more questions. And when I said to him, 'Urban, if you measured eternity from one wall to the other, we would be a spec of dust in the corner.' And that seemed to have caught him, because right then he got a perspective on life. Urban began to realize that, from my perspective, that God put eternity in the heart of man. He put it in all of us, and we, at some point in time, have to come to grips with the short time we are here on earth."

"That kind of humbles you," Urban said. "When you think it's really important beating Tennessee, keep in mind that it's a dust particle. But it's the foundation that gets you from here to there."

Meyer also had questions to himself about his own life and contributions to the world. Such as:

"Are you changing people's lives? Are you really involved? Are the forty-yard dash and the vertical jump more important than trying to save a player's life? And that's when I changed. When he first started talking, I said 'Wow!'

"And together we actually changed a couple of kids' lives. The high you get from that, as opposed to kicking the winning field goal—it's not even comparable."

Urban says he then began to see the need for a team chaplain, something he hadn't before, and would continue discussing faith with Square at the coaches' Bible study. Urban softened somewhat his hard-nosed approach to coaching, says Square, who remembers one particular game when a Colorado State receiver dropped a sure touchdown pass.

"Normally, Urban would have ridden that kid, just really beat him down with some colorful metaphors," said Square. "I happened to be standing right by Urban when he brought the kid to the side. And he looked at this kid and said to him, 'Don't worry about it, we'll come back to you.'" That player's name was Erik Olson. Not that long ago, Meyer would have been grabbing the face masks of Olson and his fellow receivers in practices, screaming at them.

Several weeks after the Olson incident, Square said he was approached by Meyer, who told him, "I want you to know something has changed in my life. Not because I don't confront them [players] anymore. It's different now. I still confront them with a purpose. Years ago I would have beat that kid down, but just because you were standing there, I knew something was different."

Meyer was never going to be the same, Square said. "And I said, 'Urban, it wasn't because of me. It was because of what's in your heart now.'"

"Urban wanted to be good at everything, whatever it took," said Lubick. "He wanted to learn that it was more than X's and O's and grabbing face masks."

Meanwhile, the CSU football program was rapidly improving.

The Rams began a string of successful seasons, including their Western Athletic Conference championship years of 1994 (10-2) and 1995 (8-4). One of Urban's biggest success stories had been in 1992 with the development of Greg Primus, who set a school record of 192 catches and 3,200 yards, the latter of which was, at the time, ranked tenth on the NCAA's all-time yardage list.

Shelley gave birth to their second daughter, Gigi. Urban began to blossom as a coach. Life for the Meyer family was enriched by close friendships and by the beauty of the Rocky Mountain setting. Johnny Square's powerful lessons had taken hold, Urban's faith was growing, and now he could share it with his wife, who had always been hoping for a more spiritual marriage.

"I could see Urban, in those Bible studies, begin to ask questions," said Square. "And he got ahold of Christ, of God. It became personal to him. And that's what Jesus was about. And when he got it, you could see that things began to align. It first touched him as a man, in the sense that the relationship with Christ was real. And it was what he was all about. And then it began to touch him as a father because he began to talk about his love for Shelley and what God had done between those two. And then it began to touch him as a coach."

Colorado State's success—the Rams won eighteen games, two WAC titles and went to two Holiday Bowls after a 5–6 start—began to draw attention to the program and Lubick's staff.

The offers began to come in for Urban—Syracuse and Pitt among the first. Pitt offered to double his salary. There could be no moving without Shelley's approval due to their prearranged deal, and she was getting firmly entrenched. "I just never thought coaches had to move around to be successful," she said. "Why couldn't Urban just stay there and just be a good wide receiver coach?"

Urban had told her *she* was always going to be instrumental in any career decision for the family, not just the career or the money.

"She was more levelheaded," said Urban, "Because I get very emotional—'Let's go, let's go do this!' And she's the smart one and she says, 'No, this is how this is going to affect our children.' So she vetoed a bunch of 'em."

There was this one caveat: If Ohio State, Notre Dame, or Michigan ever called, Urban was gone.

8

Lou Holtz Calls

Urban Meyer was coming to lunch, but Notre Dame coach Lou Holtz didn't know it. This face-to-face meeting would have a huge impact on Urban's future, although it didn't seem so at first blush.

Skip Holtz played sort of a trick on his father by inviting Urban to their luncheon, where Urban was hoping to inquire about an opening on the Notre Dame staff. Urban and Skip had a mutual friend who had coached at Colorado State, Mike Trgovac (who later became defensive coordinator of the Carolina Panthers). The lunch didn't achieve the desired result—at first.

At the coaches' convention in January of 1996, Lou had already decided he was going to hire somebody else for the position—but that was all about to change. Shelley kept rooting against the idea, anyway, telling herself that Urban wouldn't get the offer.

"We got married and I said, 'You're in charge of our career and can veto any decision if it's for the right reason,'" Urban said of the arrangement with his wife. "'Except if it's Notre Dame, Michigan, or Ohio State. If those ever call, then your majority now goes to a forty-nine percent veto.' And so coach Holtz called."

The phone rang one early morning in Fort Collins, and when Shelley answered, the voice on the other end said, "This is coach Holtz. May I speak to Urban?"

The glare of the Golden Dome was blinding. Shelley knew this was going to be a tough one, but somehow she just felt like Urban wasn't going to get the offer right up to the time she answered the call.

Later, she was shocked to learn Holtz had tendered the job over the phone. She knew full well what the answer would be. After all, Notre Dame was one of those Big Three.

Shelley immediately called a friend and began bawling about leaving her circle of good friends and a place she had grown to love.

"I did *not* want to leave there [Fort Collins] at all," said Shelley. "That was where I wanted to stay forever. I didn't care if he was a receiver coach the rest of his life. When we took that job, I didn't know that you could bounce around and move around. That wasn't in it for me and I didn't know that coaches did that. I just knew I loved it there and my best friends were there.

"We'd had two kids there. I was in Christian Women's Club. I was ingrained in that community. And I'm not even Catholic [she is a nondenominational Protestant], so [at first] going to Notre Dame didn't have that much appeal.

"Then I got to thinking, 'This is stupid. This was Notre Dame.'"

Shelley did have to admit to herself that this opportunity looked like another piece of Urban's destiny.

When he informed his boss at Colorado State, Sonny Lubick didn't hesitate to say, "You better get out the door!" Lubick felt the association with Notre Dame and Holtz would enhance Urban's career.

After all, this was the Great Notre Dame, with all the echoes of college football tradition and history.

The Great Knute Rockne and his "Win one for the Gipper" speech.

The Great Notre Dame with seven Heisman Trophy winners and thirteen national championships.

That Notre Dame, the place of Urban's dreams.

How could he possibly turn down Notre Dame?

He couldn't—and didn't.

In the spring of 1996, Urban and Shelley bought a house in South Bend. They couldn't afford any furnishings or curtains, and Urban warned Shelley about spending money, knowing his future was uncertain.

When Urban was hired at Notre Dame, Lou warned that it might be his last year there. That didn't deter Urban from going all out, using what he had learned under his previous mentors and having immediate impact. While less harsh, Urban was still no pussycat with his players.

It didn't take Meyer long to make an impression.

Wide receiver Malcolm Johnson recalled how shocked he was by Meyer in their first meeting. "Before we ever introduced ourselves, he said, 'Stand up and take your shirt off, I want to take a look at you,'" recalled Johnson, who at first thought his new coach was kidding. "After about thirty seconds I could tell he was serious. He closed the door. I'm standing there in the room with a guy in a coat and tie that I've never met before and I have nothing on from the waist up."

After which Meyer said, "You look like you're about half of what a scholarship athlete at the University of Notre Dame should be. This meeting is going to be pretty short, because you obviously need to get in the weight room."

The fiery wide receivers coach who was known for his explosive personality also set a school record for throwing remotes during film sessions.

"He was like Bobby Knight intense," said Johnson. "In your face. His way or the highway. But the man could coach."

In his first season there, Urban got so outraged at one player that he flung the remote through the projection screen. Johnson remembers the day Meyer was confronted at practice by Holtz, who wanted to know about "the problem" with the projection screen, which reportedly cost $5,000.

"Yeah, I had an accident," an embarrassed Meyer told his boss.

"Well," said Holtz, "what are we going to do about it?"

Johnson said he recalled Meyer turning red, being stuck for a response, and he feared that his position coach might be paying for the screen out of his first pay check, which he had yet to receive. After a tense moment on the practice field, everybody found out Holtz wasn't serious about Urban having to pay.

"Nah, we've got you covered on the [cost of the] remote," Holtz finally said, meaning Urban wouldn't have to pay for the projection screen, and laughter broke out among the players.

That's about the last time anybody at Notre Dame ever laughed at Urban Meyer.

Johnson said Meyer's abrupt style was quickly accepted, and that his players began to develop a deep affection for their position coach. "He treated people with respect who earned that respect," said Johnson, now a vice president at Bank of America in Los Angeles.

Sure enough, at the end of the '96 season, Holtz resigned and got out of coaching for three years. Urban was left dangling. It was felt that Bob Davie, already on staff, might get the job, but there was no guarantee Urban would be retained. Meyer hadn't been there long enough to establish a relationship with Davie. "We really didn't know each other that well," said Meyer.

Then Joanne Davie called Shelley and asked how she was doing.

"I said, 'I'm fine. I'm a little worried,'" Shelley said. "This was before Bob had retained anybody. And she said, 'Why are you worried?' And I said, 'Well, we don't have a job right now and I don't know what's going to happen. We have two little kids and we just moved here.' And she said, 'Don't worry, you don't need to worry.'

"So I called Urban right away. And he said, 'OK, tell me exactly what she said.' And I had to go over it word for word for word. Of course, that said to me that Bob was going to retain Urban. And then we knew."

Then the next day Davie walked into Urban's office and said, "I'd like to keep you." Urban called Shelley and said, "Go ahead and order the window treatments."

Things began to improve immediately for the Meyer family in South Bend. Shelley soon became comfortable in her new surroundings.

"I loved my neighborhood," Shelley said. "It was the best we lived in anywhere over our career. There were about thirty kids on our little cul-de-sac that just hung together all the time. All the people that lived on our street were our age. We had a great time together. We did block parties.

"I loved Notre Dame football. Saturdays in the fall there were amazing. But I'm not really getting attached to it because I don't like the winters at all."

As a psychiatric nurse, she often dealt with people who suffered depression in the winter.

"The whole time I lived there I'm doing season affective disorder [SAD] for different groups," Shelley said. "It's rampant out there because the sun goes away. But I loved the people, everything—except the weather."

Nate, their third child, was born on November 24, 1998, the Tuesday before the Southern Cal game. Shelley had induced labor five days early so Urban could be away at Los Angeles for the game.

In the Meyer house, everything revolves around the football schedule—even birth.

As the up-and-coming wide receiver coach for the Fighting Irish, Meyer would refine his coaching skills and begin to raise his football IQ. Though Holtz would only be there for one year after Meyer arrived, Urban felt Lou's influence as a leader and motivator. The relationship continued to grow over the years and Urban would tap into the vast experience of Holtz as he wrestled with issues during his rise as a head coach.

As much as anyone else, however, in his five years at Notre Dame, Urban would also learn from his peers, fellow assistants, and players.

This was Urban's chance to work under a Hall of Fame coach (Holtz was named to the College Football Hall of Fame in the spring of 2008). "It was a privilege and an honor to work under Coach Holtz, whose legacy will always be a part of Notre Dame and all college football," said Meyer.

At Notre Dame, Meyer would begin bonding with assistant coaches who would someday become members of his staff at Bowling Green, Utah, and Florida. Reuniting with strength and conditioning coach Mickey Marotti, Urban would consult with him in laying the groundwork for future head coaching jobs.

Marotti would become one of his closest allies and friends. In fact, it was through Urban's lobbying with Bob Davie that Marotti got the job at Notre Dame.

For Meyer and Marotti, this was the second leg of a long journey together. They had crossed paths the first time at Ohio State, and the second time when Mick was the head strength and conditioning coach at Cincinnati.

In their first meeting years prior, Meyer had been extremely impressed with the intensity of Marotti's workout with players at Cincinnati. Several times Mickey had looked over in the corner and seen a familiar face. For nearly three hours, Meyer had stood there and observed Marotti's routine, taking mental notes. At the time, Urban was working at Colorado State and visiting his sister, who was teaching at Cincinnati. Marotti, realizing that they had been on the same staff at Ohio State, walked over to greet him.

"My shirt's out and I'm all sweaty and I go, 'How you doin'? Mick Marotti.' And he goes, 'Urban Meyer, I met you at Ohio State.'"

The work ethic of Marotti had impressed Meyer so much that when Meyer got back to Fort Collins, he wrote Marotti a note saying, "Great seeing you—you guys were really working hard."

It was 1998, and when Marotti arrived in South Bend to work for Davie, Urban was already there and one of the first to welcome him to the staff.

Right there in the hallowed ground of South Bend, where the legendary Knute Rockne is buried not far from the Notre Dame campus, the seeds of a powerful new coaching tree may have been planted.

A core group of assistants would emerge and ultimately begin their journeys toward Gainesville: defensive line coach Greg Mattison; strength and conditioning coach Marotti; offensive line/tight ends/special teams coach Steve Addazio; linebacker coach Charlie Strong; and offensive graduate assistant Dan Mullen. (Secondary coach Chuck Heater, who first met Urban at Ohio State, later joining him at Utah and Florida, had also coached at Notre Dame, but had arrived several years prior.)

Because he sweated with the players in the weight room and knew their innermost thoughts, Marotti had learned about their psyches. He was convinced that to get the best out of athletes, it would take more than regimen, discipline, and veiled threats. He and Meyer would scheme up ways later at Florida to entice the players to work harder—a sort of a caste system of the locker room. Those who worked hardest on the field, in the classroom, and in the weight room—plus kept their personal lives in order—would be rewarded with better living. That meant better gear, better food, and more privileges.

"We spent a lot of time together," Marotti said of his relationship with Meyer. Shelley Meyer and Susie Marotti also connected. Said Mickey: "We just kind of hit it off. Our kids were about the same age. The friendship of just 'Hey, we're going to come over' or 'We're going to have some players over' or 'Come on over and let's have a cookout.' We'd come to her house and they'd go to our house. Gigi, his daughter, would come stay with my kids, who were a little bit younger and idolized Gigi."

The two coaches became pals and would hang out, playing Ping-Pong, drinking beer, and hosting players. One common interest was nutrition, which Meyer would supervise for Davie and concerned Marotti a great deal. "We were always bitching about our training table," said Marotti. "'Why can't we get another sandwich?'"

Strong, Mattison, and Meyer frequently visited his weight room to check on their players, which impressed Marotti.

Mattison had come from the University of Michigan, where one of his fellow assistants, Mike DeBord, had already told him, "There's a guy there you're really going to like: Urban Meyer." Greg was a little puzzled how DeBord knew him, because "I'd never heard of Urban Meyer."

The year when the Mattisons arrived in South Bend from Ann Arbor, Michigan, they bought the home across the pond from the Meyers, and the two families began to interact. Greg enjoyed working on the lawn, and sometimes when he was digging in the dirt, Urban would come out in the backyard with his pitching wedge and hit a ball over the pond; Mattison would go get his club and hit it back.

"Jim Colletto, our offensive coordinator, lived across the lake—and we'd put down golf balls and hit them to his house, which ticked him off," Meyer said in a fond memory.

DeBord was correct: Mattison was, indeed, impressed with Urban Meyer—especially his coaching intelligence. Meyer also began to appreciate the football IQ of his fellow assistants.

"That's when I really got it how good they were as coaches," said Meyer. "Not just X's and O's, but they were really good with players. Greg Mattison was unbelievable. Players were over at his house all summer long. It was almost like a battle: Who would have more players over at their house, me or him? He really believed in helping players. Steve Addazio also. And Mickey, he's the best strength coach in America."

Relationships with players became everything. Credit Mattison and Marotti for raising Urban's consciousness about the best way to reach his athletes. Mattison did it by being there as a father figure, with off-the-field mentoring and nurturing in the privacy of his home. Marotti coached Urban up on the modern player's hot buttons.

The high coaching IQ of Meyer began to surface and the pace of his intel gathering picked up as he moved closer toward becoming a head coach.

Marotti knew Urban was formulating a plan for when he would become a head coach because his boss-to-be was always scribbling on a notepad. At Notre Dame, the plan would escalate.

"Urban Meyer is tremendously intelligent," said Mattison. "He studies things. When things happen he has a great knack [for finding the right answer]. I think you have to be an intelligent person to handle things the way he does it. He doesn't do things too fast without thinking about it."

Weighing heavily on Urban's mind and heart was the health of his mother.

He kept a constant reminder of her in his pocket which the press had never known about: a sacred medal.

A friend of Urban's, Dan Sweet, had brought back water from Our Lady of Lourdes in the south of France. According to the Our Lady of Lourdes Web site, many pilgrims go there every year, "principally because of the apparent healing properties of the waters of the spring that appeared during the apparitions of the Blessed Virgin Mary to a poor, fourteen-year-old girl, Bernadette Soubirous."

"I believe in that," Meyer said of the story of the water.

Urban arranged to have a special service with his mother at the Log Chapel in South Bend, and Gisela was sprinkled with the water by Notre Dame Team Chaplain Father James Riehle, who became close friends with the Meyer family.

Soon after that, when Gisela's condition was worsening, Urban went to church—before every noon Notre Dame game the team attended a morning service at the basilica—and he was handed a medal depicting the girl seeing the Virgin Mary. He didn't always keep those kinds of things, but this one had a special meaning.

For two years, every day or night, Urban stopped by the grotto on campus to light a candle and pray for his mother.

She lived another year and a half.

"I coached every game with this," he said, pulling from his pocket a chain with several medals. This he would carry with him on his ascent toward the top of the coaching profession.

The Notre Dame receiving corps enjoyed a run of success under Meyer, who worked comfortably in tandem with Davie, whom he began to admire greatly. The two coaches became close friends and Davie enhanced Urban's growth. After posting an 8-3 mark under Holtz, the Irish followed with records of 7-6, 9-3, 5-7, and 9-3 under Davie.

At first, Meyer wasn't sure he wanted to take his head coach up on the offer of becoming special teams coordinator. During the special teams meetings, Urban would often find himself bored and doodling passing routes on paper just to kill time.

At Davie's insistence, Meyer accepted the assignment and coaching special teams would add an important dimension to his repertoire for future head jobs.

Learning about the importance of special teams would prove to be a blessing, because that would become a cornerstone of his coaching philosophy. Realizing special teams were one-third of the game and that some head coaches didn't emphasize them, Meyer knew he could gain an advantage.

Subsequently, Meyer would take charge of special teams at every place he became head coach and elevate those players to a stature above that of the offensive and defensive starters. Among the privileges for special teamers when Urban became a head coach: First in line to eat team meals and flying first class on the team plane.

With this newfound responsibility, Meyer began developing a strategy. Special teams, after all, were the soul of the team, a place where desire often won out over skill, where speed and athleticism were advantages, where sneak attacks and the element of surprise were almost like guerrilla warfare.

Combining speed with surprise, Meyer determined that by loading up the punt and kickoff teams with some of his fastest players and overloading the return man, he could often force the opposition into mistakes and misjudgments.

Special teams would truly become one of Meyer's favorite weapons. He often stopped practice to heap praise on a special teams player. This was where battlefield promotions were awarded— sometimes even full scholarships, right on the spot—and it dovetailed nicely as a payoff in the Pavlovian theory of conditioned responses.

"His big thing was that he loved to single out guys who had the big balls on special teams and would make the big hit," said former Irish receiver and special teams player Joey Getherall. "He called the special teams his 'Special Forces.' He took a lot of pride in those special teams."

Meyer soon learned another good thing about coaching special teams: His courage to resort to trick plays under pressure would exemplify courage to his players, because he had something at stake, too. Over the first seven years of his head coaching career, the fake punt would be used—and executed successfully—in quite a few big games.

Meanwhile, Urban's 1999 receiver group broke the Notre Dame season record for pass completions (192) and yards (2,858). The year before, Malcolm Johnson finished his career with the seventh most receptions (110) in school history. Johnson and Bobby Brown had become the most prolific pair of pass-catchers ever, both exceeding 40 catches, as the team caught a record 190.

This was accomplished despite a conservative offensive attack.

More significantly, at Notre Dame Meyer began to search for a way to get the ball in the hands of his best players.

It was no surprise to Getherall and Johnson that Meyer would become such an accomplished head coach so quickly. "I knew he'd be successful," said Getherall.

Finally, there was a bit of a breakthrough, even if it was a baby step. It took almost a virtual epiphany after the second game of 2000, when No. 5 ranked Notre Dame lost in overtime to No. 1 ranked Nebraska, 27–24. Meyer's star wide receiver, much to Meyer's amazement, had not touched the ball.

David Givens, later to become an NFL receiver with the New England Patriots and Tennessee Titans, was despondent.

"After the game he was uncontrollable and crying, I mean sobbing," Meyer recalled. "He was a competitor, a great football player. And I'm trying to console him."

"You don't understand," Givens said.

"I do understand," Meyer responded. "It's going to be OK; we'll come back next week."

Looking through tears, Givens said, "I just want to help the team win."

"I understand that."

"Coach, I didn't touch the ball today."

His words jolted Meyer. He realized that he had not put the ball in the hands of his best playmaker and he vowed never to do that again. "'You have to fire me immediately if I ever let that happen again.' I didn't do my job that day. My job is to get that kid the ball."

Out of David Givens's tears the idea for the Spread would be born—at least Urban Meyer's version of it. The previous spring, Meyer and graduate assistant Dan Mullen had visited Scott Linehan in Louisville, where the Cardinals offensive coordinator for John L. Smith was blowing off the doors of defenses. The former quarterback at Idaho under Dennis Erickson was a codesigner of this powerful attack and was generously willing to share his information. (Linehan later became coach of the St. Louis Rams.) So enthralled was Meyer that he stayed in Louisville several days longer.

Meyer and Mullen also visited Northwestern offensive coordinator Kevin Wilson of the late Randy Walker's staff (Walker died suddenly of a heart attack in 2006) where they learned how to make zone option reads. They also began to study Purdue's passing game.

"We came back with great resources and now we're educated with a different approach, and I could speak [about it]," said Meyer. "Otherwise it would be uneducated babble for me to talk about how to isolate, playmakers creating great matchup issues, and all that. After that, I was educated in something other than just a dream. Now here's how we do it."

Bits and pieces of the Spread began to surface in Notre Dame's offense for the duration of the 2000 season, but it was only embryonic because Meyer was just learning about it.

Johnson recalls that the tweaking of the offense did help after Holtz left and Davie took over. "We used to beat our heads against the wall because we wished we could have utilized more of our weapons. It was an effective offense my senior year—we finished nine and one my senior year—but it was nowhere near what he did later with Tim Tebow and those guys," said Johnson.

So much more could have been implanted at Notre Dame, except that Meyer hadn't totally invented the Spread just yet. By midseason 2000, the Irish were showing that look in their pre-snap formations,

"Most of the time we'd just do the Spread and it was the quarterback draw or the running back draw, or we'd run a seam route," said Getherall. "It wasn't too much of what Urban does now. The formation was there, but we never threw the ball out there and never really worked the passing game into it. It was more spreading the defense and see what they were playing . . . from that point on they'd run the ball a lot. But at least they gave it a shot."

The seeds of the Spread fell from the tree of the fertile mind of a Louisville offensive coordinator, and together with his young graduate assistant/quarterback coach Mullen, Meyer gathered them up, dusted them off in South Bend, and then was about to transport them to Bowling Green, where they would be planted and then harvested.

"When Urban got the job at Bowling Green," said Mullen, "we

went around to all these places and took the thoughts and beliefs back together with us. Instead of saying we were going to run 'this offense' or 'that offense,' we took all the different ideas and philosophies, put them together, and said, 'OK, which direction do we want to go in—we want to run our own offense.'"

Notre Dame was a rich experience for Meyer, who became attached to his players and good friends with his coaching colleagues.

Little did Meyer know how quickly his reputation was becoming enhanced. He began to get noticed and job offers started coming in.

First he turned down a chance to interview for the job at Kent State.

Bowling Green called Earle Bruce looking for a new coach in late 2000, and he recommended Meyer. When Urban balked, the salty-tongued Bruce cursed him out for his reluctance to take the job.

"I called Earle and he creases me for fifteen minutes," said Urban.

His three mentors—his father, Bruce, and Holtz—insisted he look at it.

"This is not a very good job," Meyer told Holtz.

To which Holtz responded, "Of course it's not. If it was, why would they call you?"

Shelley was skeptical and at first thought about invoking her veto right. She had become a huge Notre Dame fan. "I said no at first—'No way, I'm not going there.' I couldn't understand why he would want to leave Notre Dame to go to Bowling Green," she said. "It was such a small town. And I said to him, 'That's the wrong way! I want to go west or south!'"

Both Shelley and Urban were happy in South Bend, but they began to research Bowling Green. She was surprised to hear from a high school friend who had lived there seven years and told her, "I *love* Bowling Green!" Then the reality of the opportunity to be a head coach hit her. "That's what really finally said to me, 'He probably really does need to take this.'"

He did.

On the trip back to South Bend after accepting the job at Bowling Green, the pilot of the private airplane gave Urban one more chance to say good-bye to the place he so dearly loved.

"He took us down lower and circled the Golden Dome several times," said Urban. "It was really an emotional experience."

Notre Dame would give Urban the last two pieces of his repertoire as a head coach: the Spread offense and the Plan to Win. Both were formulated in his final days there.

Urban heeded the advice of his father about always having an orderly approach to decision-making and problem solving. He scribbled out one page on what would be the schematic for his head coaching debut.

Both Urban and Shelley would fall in love with their new home.

At age thirty-six, Urban Meyer became the head coach of the Bowling Green Falcons, who were about to be introduced to that day of infamy: "Black Wednesday."

About his only regret was that his mother wouldn't be alive to see her son become a head coach.

In 2001 at Bowling Green, the Spread would be unveiled as 100 percent of Urban's new offensive philosophy.

9

The Bowling Green Boys

Bowling Green was a quaint northern Ohio community located just south of the Michigan state line. In football geography, the school was about twenty miles south of Toledo on I-75 between The Ohio State University and the University of Michigan, but a million miles away from the football world of Buckeyes and Wolverines. That made it even more obscure and difficult to recruit football players.

Enrollment at Bowling Green State University during those days was about the same size as the town population—eighteen thousand. Bowling Green had a rich history in the Mid-American Conference with outstanding coaches like Doyt Perry, Don Nehlen, and Gary Blackney. The Falcons biggest rival was Toledo and thus the nickname of the rivalry: "The Battle of I-75."

As Meyer had correctly assessed it, however, it wasn't "a very good job" at the time. After success in the early nineties, the program had fallen on hard times. Falcon fans were ready for a fresh start—something new and different. Athletic Director Paul Krebs, who would become Urban's boss and good friend, was going to give it to them.

Thanks to the wisdom of Krebs, the Bowling Green job would

give Urban his own laboratory—a place where he could indoctrinate his assistant coaches into some of his own thinking, try out new offensive theories, and explore ways to get the student body and the faculty more involved. He was also going to be learning about the limit of how far he could push players.

In his final days at Notre Dame, Meyer had carved out his future, writing the Plan to Win in one week. He brought rough sketches of a new offense with him to Bowling Green in his notebook filled with thoughts from his conversations with Linehan in Louisville. As head coach, Meyer would build and install those as key components.

Meyer also framed an early version of what would eventually become the Champions Club. He was adopting a philosophy about player regimen and motivation. Having read John Wooden's book on coaching many times, he followed the UCLA legend's advice that players shouldn't be treated equally, but rather rewarded for how they contributed to the team.

This would become part of his programs in the next two head coaching jobs. He also planted the seeds of what would become, on a more grand scale, the pregame ceremonial Gator Walk.

While it may have seemed Meyer was making it up as he went along, in reality he was cherry-picking the best ideas and cobbling them together with his own fresh, imaginative perspective and growing his football IQ.

These were the fruits of all his note-taking over the years, which is what Marotti meant when he said Urban seemed "always to be writing down things that he wanted to do differently someday as a head coach."

As always, those innovations were tied to the core values of physical conditioning, teamwork, living right, and education.

Meyer realized there would be no extended honeymoon, because modern-day coaches were expected to produce right away. This was a different place than in the past, when Bowling Green coaches went there to die.

Well, not really die, but at least get fired.

Meyer knew the risk, but he also knew the opportunity. And he knew there were limited resources. Despite all that, some of Bowling

Green's former coaches had nothing but good things to say about the town and the school—to a fault.

"What happens is that guys go there and they never leave," Meyer said, noting that Bowling Green gets comfortable and it's hard to depart. "And eventually you're going to lose and get fired," Meyer said.

That's what happened to Blackney, as well as others who went on to success at other places. Don Nehlen coached Falcon football for nine years and would later guide West Virginia to national prominence. Denny Stolz, a former Michigan State head coach who was fired following an NCAA investigation but resurrected his coaching career at Bowling Green for nine years before leaving to become coach at San Diego State.

Perhaps the school's most famous coach prior to Urban was the legendary Doyt Perry, a member of the College Football Hall of Fame.

"The previous coach [Blackney] told me, 'Be careful—win and get out. If you win you'll die there. You'll fall in love with the town, you'll fall in love with the people'—and I did. But it's difficult to sustain," Meyer said.

That was certainly the case with his predecessor Blackney, who had begun his career with a bang at Bowling Green in 1991 by winning 11 games, posting 19 straight Mid-American Conference victories, and becoming the school's first coach ever to win a bowl game. When Blackney took an assistant's job at Maryland, he left behind an overall record of 60-50-2.

By 2001, six straight seasons of losing had taken a toll on Blackney's program, which hadn't seen a winning year since 1994. That added up to a 24-42 record, a .364 winning percentage, which included the 2-9 team that Urban would inherit from 2000.

Some of Meyer's new assistants already knew his coaching style because they'd worked with him in the past. Offensive coordinator Gregg Brandon, who came in from Colorado, was in on the origination of the Spread. Quarterback coach Dan Mullen was brought in from Notre Dame, where he'd been a graduate assistant. Wide receiver coach Billy Gonzales, who played for Urban at Colorado State, was brought in from Kent State. Meyer also hired John Hevesy from Brown to coach offensive tackles and tight ends. (Mullen, Gonzales, and Hevesy would wind up on his Florida staff; Brandon would become head coach at Bowling Green.)

Also on that staff was Greg Studrawa, who coaches guards and centers, and who would go on to coach at LSU as member of the national championship 2007 staff. That means that on his Bowling Green staff, Meyer would have five coaches who helped win a crystal football: himself, Mullen, Gonzales, Hevesy, and Studrawa.

Just as he had reinvented himself as an athlete, Meyer would do so as a head coach, jettisoning bad habits as he moved from St. John High School to Cincinnati to Ohio State to Illinois State to Colorado State to Notre Dame.

Keeping up with his cohorts from his past, Meyer tinkered with his new toys and began recruiting new staff—such as a strength and conditioning coach. "He called me three times a day every day when he got the job for three months," said Marotti, who was still at Notre Dame. "Every day! And if he didn't call, he'd have Hevesy, or somebody, call from Bowling Green."

The coaches emphasized academics, following another Bud Meyer tenet: Thou shalt not make poor grades. And thou shalt go to study table. Urban had warned the players in his first meeting that if they missed classes, they could expect repercussions. Meyer's strong conviction that players should get an education and a degree was the motivation for calling out the "Bowling Green Boys."

Armed with all this coaching newthink, Meyer set about to change the losing culture. The toxic waste of failure was so deeply ingrained in the football program that Meyer would have to go deep to remove it, and in doing so, he would go over the line with his disciplining.

Given the lack of recent success, optimism in 2001 about Bowling Green football wasn't exactly soaring. Sometimes Falcon football players were ridiculed and disrespected, if recognized at all.

Defensive end Ryan Wingrove remembers how painful it was. "We were to the point where we were pretty tired of losing and being laughed at when you walked around on campus and heard people say, 'Do you play for the football team? Are you an intramural team or a flag football team?'"

"It really gets to the athletes who want to win. We'd pretty much had enough."

There was no way the Bowling Green Boys could be prepared for what was about to unfold. In test-pilot lingo, Meyer was pushing the envelope almost beyond acceptable boundaries with something called "Black Wednesday." On Tuesday before that infamous Wednesday, rumors were afoot that a team meeting would be held the following morning at five thirty in the Perry fieldhouse. The message was: Bring shoes and shorts.

If there was any doubt that life was going to be different for Falcon players, that quickly changed when Wingrove, Josh Harris, and their teammates reported the next day in January 2001 at 5:00 A.M.

Wingrove recalled of that fateful day: "It was cold, it was dark—and we were all nervous."

How far could Meyer push players to achieve their maximum effort? The players would be introduced to the pedal-to-the-metal style that characterized a young Urban Meyer, who would put them through a rigorous test right off. Given the number of behavioral problems and the losing tailspin, Urban knew the situation called for a quick and stern action.

Upon meeting the new coach for the first time, Harris was pretty sure Meyer meant business, and as he recalls, the coach had reminded everybody about not missing study table. A few players apparently didn't listen well.

"One thing that I noticed was there were no smiles, there was a sternness in his voice, and he was definitely setting a tone that things were going to be different, and it was going to be his way or the highway," said Harris, the quarterback from Westerville, Ohio.

Harris began hearing rumors about trash cans being open in the field house. "We were going to get run into the ground," recalled Harris. "When my roommate and I get there in the morning, the trash cans are not open—and I hate running with a passion—and so I was excited to see that the trash-can lids were closed and there were no coaches in sight yet."

That was the good news.

"Every trash-can lid got opened and my stomach dropped into the bottom of my feet," said Harris. "Because I knew it was not going to be over. They were going to kill us."

Inside the field house, a large plastic trash can was strategically stationed at each corner of the field, and more at midfield—and the players knew they weren't put there for picnic trash.

Meyer told the players in advance what to expect: The doors to the field house would be locked and "We're going to figure out whether we're going to be coming together or we're going to be going apart. If at any point and time you want to leave, you're more than welcome to quit. But I'm not going to quit on you."

Meyer was going to teach them a lesson about not showing up for study table. He told them, "People are going to go to study table. You are going to get your grades." Then he called out a group of people who had been skipping and he said as they were standing before their teammates, "Why do you guys think it's not important to go to study table? Why don't you care about this team?

"Now we're going to run."

He probably didn't realize it, but Urban was applying that old Bud Meyer rule: If you screw up, you run.

More than two hours of running and exercising commenced, along with the puking. Even when they stopped to vomit, they were pushed to move on and not hold up the line.

Wingrove remembers feeling as if his legs were moving fast, only to realize he was barely running.

"I have never run more or harder in my life," Wingrove recalled. "I remember looking at other guys and thinking, 'Man, why are they walking? I know I'm running as hard as I can.' I looked down—and I'm a guy who has a high motor and I just don't quit—but I was almost walking and telling myself I was running. It was an amazing thing. You just pushed yourself to that point because you just knew you had to . . . there's nothing else you had to look forward to except coming together."

Harris remembers that they ran several hours, but it wasn't a distance run. They ran sprints, starting with 300-yard shuttles, full gassers, and 30-yard suicides, touching every yard line every five yards and returning to the goal line.

That morning was the turning point, said Wingrove, a senior. "We were either going to die together or keep going together."

That wasn't the worst part.

(Warning: The following paragraphs are graphic and may not be suitable for reading at your dinner table).

The worst part, said several of the players, was having to wait in line to get to one of the trash cans and barf.

Meyer had warned them in advance, "Don't you throw up on the turf! Don't you throw up on *my* turf!"

"We're like hugging the trash can," said Harris. "Guys were waiting in line to throw up in a trash can that's full of other people's throwup. It's probably the most disgusting thing that I've ever [seen] . . . it was like a *Fear Factor* moment. You couldn't even think about the fact that somebody else had thrown up in this trash can and it wasn't clean. All you wanted to do was hurry up and throw up so you could get a little bit of relief before you had to run again."

Several players did quit that day, and eventually the number grew to more than twenty, leaving only about fifty on scholarship. But the team began to shape up, at least what was left of it. To fill out the roster, Meyer began recruiting walk-ons for the kickoff team by advertising in the school paper. But there was immediate progress. Those who did stay began to go to class and come to realize that Meyer was going to whip them into shape—physically and academically.

So disgusted with losing were the players that they welcomed coaches who offered a personal touch, who invited them over to their houses and encouraged them to stay committed to their education.

Meyer, himself, tutored the players. He used the old tried-and-true method of teaching through baseball statistics. Since his family had not yet arrived from South Bend, he would often stay up until 11:00 P.M., working on the math board in the math lab with players. Other assistants did the same.

"And that's when our players fell in love with them [assistant coaches]," he said. "Every player just wants to be helped. We were physically helping players. We owned them after that."

Meyer said the upperclassmen responded immediately—"We had a great group of seniors"—and that was why he was able to get his program across in a short time. Because Meyer paid tribute to his seniors and said he wanted to send them off on a good note, they felt a sense of purpose and responded positively.

Almost to a man, the players who remained felt Meyer's stringent measures were necessary to get the program righted. Administrative Assistant Jon Clark, who was a Bowling Green student and manager when Urban arrived, said he, too, learned about how much of a commitment it took to succeed and the "hard work" required.

"We had guys on our team that weren't good athletes, but played amazing football our senior year, guys that the year before barely even stepped on the field. Some of our seniors were playing above themselves," Wingrove said. "It was just amazing. There were three seniors on that defensive line, and all three of us played in the NFL. And one linebacker, Khary Campbell, is still in the NFL with the Washington Redskins."

Wingrove felt sure Meyer had X-ray vision. "The first time I saw him, I saw this intense guy who I thought there was no way he was going to let anything get past him," Wingrove remembered. "He's got this look when he looks at you—almost like he's looking through you . . . like he can see whether you're a good person or a bad person.

"He walked into the team meeting room and just starts looking at us—basically staring us all down and telling us things are going to change. It's not going to be the same anymore. He's not putting up with mediocrity. Basically, calling us a One Double-A football team—that we were nowhere near where a Division One football team should be or is. That we were either going to get better or get worse. And he was going to make sure we got better."

The result at Bowling Green would be in athletes attending class regularly and setting a course to obtain their degrees, as well as learning valuable life lessons. At the same time, the football team would be regaining respect and creating a little bit of a national reputation. As a result of that, Meyer matured and became a hot commodity as a young coach.

Camp Meyer for the Bowling Green Boys wasn't as hard-core as Bear Bryant's famed Junction Boys, who survived the Lone Star State heat and rigors of the Texas A&M coach in that small, dusty town, going on to win a national championship for the Aggies. But it may have been a cousin.

Urban won't ever do Camp Meyer the same way again, however.

"It was dangerous," Meyer said of Black Wednesday.

"What I know now is you can't do that. What happened that day at five o'clock that Wednesday—you can't do that now."

If his Black Wednesday was over the top, then the Spread was ingenious. Meyer brought a pretty smart offense with him, one that would continue to evolve after conversations with some of his peers such as Rich Rodriguez of West Virginia, now at Michigan. As much mystique as there was about the Spread, it was really just going to be a personnel-driven option out of a spread formation designed to get the ball thrown, handed off, or pitched, or snapped to speedy athletes in space.

The Spread was about matchups: an offensive versus defensive numbers game—not unlike basketball's fast break, with the added twist of the option read. But there was no set way to run the Spread, because it differed with the personnel. At Bowling Green, the success of the Spread, as always, would depend on who was executing it.

With Harris as the triggerman of the Spread, the Falcons and Meyer's formation would make an impressive debut with an opening win against Missouri, but not until after some anxious moments from the head coach about being short-handed. Urban began to brood about losing so many players. He told Shelley before the first game, "What if we lose every game? How long will they keep me? Two years? Three years?"

It all started with a bang—literally.

The 20–13 upset of Missouri, the first of three straight victories, became a signature win for his program. It also spoiled a Labor Day weekend fireworks display planned for Tiger fans, which gave Falcon players a chuckle and reason to say glibly, "Wasn't it nice of coach Pinkel to have fireworks for us?" Knocking off Gary Pinkel, who was making his debut at Missouri after ten years at their rival school Toledo, was extra sweet. Toledo had trounced Blackney's team in the last 2001 regular-season game, 51–17, before leaving for Columbia.

The good start was almost jinxed, however, when Meyer became frantic because he'd lost his good-luck charm—the medal which he carried in his pocket in remembrance of his late mother. He sent staff member Jon Clark back out on the field before the kickoff to search for it. Clark had four managers with him, combing the grass, up until they were chased off by the Missouri band in pregame entertainment.

This was to be Meyer's night, however, and finally the medal was discovered, having been stuck down inside his valuables bag.

Soon the Falcons were enthusiastically singing that familiar old Bowling Green postgame refrain, "Ay Ziggy Zoomba," in the locker room and on the campus of Bowling Green again.

Meyer's presence immediately brought recognition to the school and the players. In Meyer's first season, quarterback Josh Harris was responsible for 6 touchdowns and 498 yards of total offense as the Falcons beat Northwestern, 43–42, becoming the first MAC team to beat three opponents from the BCS in one season.

Thus began the two-year run of success for Bowling Green, starting with the biggest turnaround in the country, from a 2-9 season to an 8-3. The Falcons were not only heard from around the Mid-American Conference, but around the college football world. It wasn't easy being Bowling Green, because the media didn't know how to find it. That's why Urban was so happy when an *ESPN Game Day* reporter came to town—but was in for a surprise at the spin by Curry Kirkpatrick, who used the sport of bowling as a metaphor for his story line.

"It was awful," Meyer said. "He does something on bowling because of 'Bowling' Green. I thinking it's going to be about our quarterback [Harris], a Heisman candidate, leading the nation in scoring. I'm ready to do a great story. I remember jumping on J.D. Campbell, our SID, and saying, 'What is this s—?' But it was still Bowling Green getting on *ESPN Game Day*."

Meyer was named MAC Coach of the Year by the MAC News Media Association in 2001. Junior receiver Robert Redd, who would set the school record for catches in one game (14) before graduating, was named first-team all-conference, along with defensive lineman Brandon Hicks.

Starting out 8-0 in 2002 with a team that averaged scoring 40 points a game (third in the nation), the Falcons stumbled to a 1-3 finish after a 26–17 loss to Northern Illinois, which denied them that championship they had worked so hard to attain and from playing in a bowl game. But Meyer had taken the Falcons to great heights—all the way to No. 16 in the ESPN/USA Today poll and No. 20 in the Associated Press. They stayed ranked for five weeks. The 9-3 record and overall 17-6 mark in two seasons had proved that the Boy From Ashtabula knew how to coach.

Urban's Way began to have an impact with players, who were not only driven on the football field, but nurtured in the homes of their position coaches and given hands-on help with their studies.

There would always be a place in Meyer's heart for the Bowling Green Boys, especially those who gutted out Black Wednesday with him.

His players feel that way about him. "If he walked into a room today, I would literally run through the wall for that man," said Wingrove, who represents an orthopedic company that produces knee braces for football players.

"I think he's a great life coach," said Wingrove. "Everything I learned my senior year at Bowling Green has made me a better person. Made me better understand how to have a work ethic. How to keep motivated. How to be personal with people. How to trust people. How to earn respect from people. The things he helped teach you as a college athlete and through education is just as important as what he teaches people [about] how to be winning football players."

Cole Magner remembers Meyer for a different reason. As a freshman, Magner arrived in the fall, thereby avoiding Black Wednesday—but still recalls a long string of back-to-back, two-a-day practices in the late summer of 2001.

"The first day I thought I was going to die," said Magner. "The second day I was sure I was going to die. And by the end of the week I was hard as a rock."

What he remembers most about his relationship with his coach, he can cite, verbatim.

"One of his sayings that stuck with me forever was 'If done correctly, the player-coach relationship is the most meaningful relationship, second only to the parent-child relationship,'" Magner said. Being from Alaska, he "had no family anywhere close to there. I needed to feel like I had a family I was part of. He and the coaches adopted that motto, and it really made me feel at home."

Meyer kept telling them, "If you guys can make it through, you'll be playing for a championship one day."

That's when the Bowling Green Boys were trained to the whistle of Urban Meyer.

"I could probably pick out a coach Meyer–blown whistle out of a hundred whistles blown by coaches all over the country," Harris said of the early workouts under Meyer. "Two quick bursts—at least that's how he was blowing the whistle when he was getting ready to kill the Bowling Green Boys." He didn't kill them—he raised them up.

They never won the championship, but a core group of fourteen players on that team did make it through and will always have a special place in Meyer's heart—and in his home. "If you walk in my house, there's a big picture of them in my rec room. There's the national championship [from Florida] and then there's those fourteen kids."

The feeling was mutual for many of his players, including Magner, who said of Meyer, "If he was a politician today, he'd be running for president."

For a short time they all had seen a glimpse of a little football Camelot in Bowling Green.

"Bowling Green is a great place and still some of my best friends live there," Meyer said. "I could have stayed there forever. But they don't have the budget. The weather's difficult, but it's a great place. Great place to raise a family. Not a good place, a *great* place. To the point where it's almost like a magnet."

Earlier in that second year, however, when Bowling Green was breaking through, Meyer had gotten a signal that it was over for him there, remembering that the former coaches had warned him to "win and get out." The prophecy would come true, and the advice was a telling wisdom, because as much as Urban and Shelley Meyer began to like their life in Bowling Green, it wasn't going to last.

Urban met with a group of seven boosters at the local country club and asked them for help for new facilities—for which he got promises that night to the tune of $200,000 in pledges—but was called on the carpet the next day by the school administration.

"They told me that [fund-raising] was somebody else's job," he said. "I didn't argue, because I'm respectful." Although he didn't tell anyone but Shelley, Urban knew in his heart it was nearing the time for him to move on.

Those former coaches were right: Bowling Green *was* a place Urban would grow to love and could have become too comfortable. Except that people came calling on Meyer, who started getting feelers from schools: East Carolina, Baylor, Michigan State. The latter one got his hackles up.

"Michigan State was the big rumor out then," Meyer said. "I got a phone call from a headhunter who said, 'You're doing a great job and I understand there's a lot of innuendo and speculation, but you're not a first-tier coach. You're second-tier.' I'm like, 'What does that mean?'

"He said, 'We've got our guys and it looks like one of them is going to take it. If they don't take it, then we'll get to you.' I didn't take that one too well." (The Spartans took John L. Smith, who, ironically, was a relative of quarterback Alex Smith, who would play for Urban at Utah.)

It wasn't long, though, until Urban's name surfaced in the Utah mix.

When Utah first called, even though Shelley kept telling him she wanted to move to a warmer climate, Urban said at first he had no interest in it.

Meyer had a change of heart and would take a stealthly route on his way to Denver for an interview with Utah athletic director Chris Hill, with whom he would become very close. Urban had Clark go online to purchase his airline ticket to Salt Lake and informed him to tell no one.

"Only about three of us knew," said Clark. "Several people asked me, 'Where's coach?' And I would say, 'Gee, I don't know.'"

Utah seemed an odd fit for a guy from the Midwest. Besides, Meyer knew nothing about the lifestyle of Mormons and such. It was not a football powerhouse, and the Utes played in the Mountain West Conference, not the Big 10 or Big 12 or Pac 10 or SEC.

"Then I go out to interview with them and I meet Bernie Machen [now the president at the University of Florida] and they were the most professional to that date I've ever met."

So Urban flew back out for a second interview and, once on campus in Salt Lake City, fell in love with Utah. He loved the beautiful facilities. He loved the athletic director—"to this day we're still great friends."

When he walked into the $6 million academic center, overlooking the Rocky Mountains, he was overwhelmed. "They kind of give me a tour. I walk in the back of the room and I call Shelley and I say, 'I'm going to take this job.' And she said, 'Why?' And I said because at Colorado State Sonny Lubick is the kingpin and we have so much more than they have: academic facility, unlimited resources, beautiful city—a million people right there.

"I couldn't get over that. There are a million people to draw from! At Colorado State, there's a hundred thousand. At Bowling Green there's eighteen thousand and you've got to fill a thirty-five thousand seat stadium."

The Latter Day Saints (LDS) community offered many resources. Urban knew about those resources and was about to learn their culture.

The next day he was offered the job; he accepted and began trying to find a way to tell his players. He had a topflight quarterback coming back in Harris and was certain Bowling Green was going to be in the preseason top 20 in 2003.

He was leaving with regret, however, because he had not only begun to like the town, but he had grown close to his players, liked his staff, and felt the program was still going to be advancing. This was going to be a tough announcement for him, as well as his players.

Harris was devastated, as were others. It took Harris a long time to come to grips with the fact that this man who had come into his life, who had such a powerful influence on him, would be walking out on him and his teammates. Not until years later when Meyer returned to Bowling Green did they have a chance to talk.

"I hugged him and told him that I loved him," Harris said. Meyer then explained why he had had to leave and Harris said he understood.

"I'm extremely happy for him," said Harris, who was drafted in the sixth round by the Baltimore Ravens. "I have no hard feelings. I think he's one of the greatest coaches and greatest mentors—one of the *hardest* mentors—that I've ever met. And that I will probably ever meet. He has also had the largest impact on my life, beside my mom, my wife, and my kids."

Harris has stayed connected to Meyer as a fan of every team where he has coached. As they watch his games, Magner and Harris like that it's like watching the Bowling Green Boys all over again—"except with different players."

The night after accepting the Utah job, Urban walked downstairs to awaken his sleeping daughter, Nicki, who was ten.

"I said, 'Hey, babe, I think we're going to have to move, I'm going to take this Utah job.' She jumps up and starts crying and says, 'Daddy, you promised me you wouldn't do this. You promised me, you promised me!' She's crying, hysterical. I calmed her down. I walked upstairs, called the AD and said, 'I'm not taking it.' Shelley and I sat there and talked for six hours, right through the night. At 6:00 A.M. she convinced me. I picked up the phone and took the job."

Shelley, of course, knew that Nicki, like any other young girl of ten, was overly emotional. "He hadn't seen that very much," Shelley said, "and I knew that in twelve hours Nicki would be over it and be fine." And, of course, she was. So the Meyer family began to pack up—again—for the adventure out West.

As Urban looked over his shoulder at Bowling Green, he was shocked at the angry response of some people. Although many did appreciate Meyer's efforts, others seemed to feel he was a traitor. That he wouldn't give the media the answer it wanted as the negotiations with Utah got under way seemed to offend some.

"I thought they'd be saying, 'Congratulations and thanks, see you later; boy, you really helped us.' Because we won seventeen games in two years and the last two years before that they won like six," said Urban.

If he left them sad and angry in Bowling Green, he would find people happy and thrilled in Salt Lake City, where Urban Meyer was about to make another of his famous leaps.

10

Utah: The Land of Diversity

U tes" is the name of a proud Native American tribe, as well as the nickname of the Utah football team. It was also one of eighteen politically incorrect names on an NCAA hit list back in 2005, but the issue was settled when the Ute Tribal Business Committee agreed that having their ancestors honored in such a manner was a good thing.

Utah is far more about Mormons than Utes. The two groups were once enemies, having engaged in armed conflicts back in the 1860s. Today, members of the Latter-day Saints Church far outnumber the Ute tribe in Utah, which has just over three thousand members, and they appear to be getting along just fine.

Urban discovered that Ute football was also about a lot more than just Utes and Mormons. His team was a virtual melting pot of Mormons, Polynesians, Hispanics, Protestants, and Catholics that needed to be forged into a team.

Meyer realized that by encouraging players to embrace their diversity, racial and religious barriers would come down and the result would be better team chemistry. That's what it would take for Utah football to achieve national stature, and Urban Meyer was just the right man for the job.

All Urban Meyer had known about Utah was that it was one of those square states out there in the great Rocky Mountain West with lots of Mormons. It turned out to be a great place for Urban's personal revelation and growth.

By the time Meyer arrived in Salt Lake City, the Utah program had begun to slip. A six-game losing streak in 2002 had resulted in a 5-6 record—and the Utes had to win their last three just to do that well. Their lackluster season spelled the demise of Ron McBride. McBride's 88-63 mark represented the second most wins in Utah history. His 1994 team's ten wins were the most in school history and he had taken the Utes to six bowl games. None of that was enough to save his job.

Meyer would tell his players their team should be among the country's elite, but few believed that possible at first. Meanwhile, Urban went about assessing his talent—wherever it could be found.

As with all of Meyer's teams, the talent came from everywhere, including the downtrodden, the forgotten, and the volunteer corps. Meyer retrieved several players from the football scrap heap. They came from all walks of life—sometimes even gangs. Some had drug and alcohol issues, just as there were on other campuses. He would come face-to-face with how to deal with troubled players.

That's where he was introduced to the near tragic story of Marty Johnson.

It took two medical redshirts, a trip to jail, and a mulligan from his Ute teammates and his coaches before Marty Johnson could get there. Equally amazing was that, after seven years of college, Johnson would also get his degree.

The long and winding road that got Johnson to Utah in the first place—Boise State to Butte Junior College to Salt Lake—was almost longer when he arrived, mostly uphill. Between injuries, Johnson proved to be a formidable runner. The problem was that while he was injured, he tended to self-medicate with alcohol. Trouble for him began the night when he rammed into the back of a car, left the scene of the accident, and was arrested on a DUI.

When Meyer first met him, Johnson was already beleaguered with that DUI. He also had a football injury. Disappointed because Meyer didn't have him listed at the No. 1 tailback spot in the spring of 2003, Marty admitted "I had a chip on my shoulder." Then he hurt his foot— the third year in a row he'd gotten injured—and was on the shelf again.

Johnson went out one night "and shared some drinks with some friends." On his way home, Johnson was stopped, arrested, and charged with his second DUI. He made bail, but told no one for a while. When Meyer found out, he immediately suspended Marty and was ready to boot him off the squad for good. Urban was furious.

It was virtually a foregone conclusion that Johnson was done at Utah, but suddenly Meyer had a change of heart when Shelley stepped in to plead Johnson's case.

Between Shelley's advice and a story that Meyer saw on the front page of a newspaper about an innocent victim getting killed by a drunk driver that day, Urban rethought Johnson's dismissal. Shelley convinced her husband that if football were taken from Johnson, he might return to drinking and wind up killing somebody while behind the wheel. Meyer also knew that he had no real family, as his mother had been murdered.

Shelley followed up to let Johnson know somebody cared. With personal communication, she began to fill the void left by the absence of Marty's family. Johnson immediately responded positively, later revealing he had been lonely and missed his parents.

Shelley and daughter Gigi, then only nine, struck up a friendship with Marty. Gigi was like his little sister. "I loved the way she played sports with boys," he said.

Johnson, however, still had to face a jury of his peers in more ways than one.

Marty's teammate Bo Nagahi remembers how upset Meyer was, but that he finally decided to let the matter be decided by the Leadership Committee. Several of them spoke frankly, including defensive back and captain Morgan Scalley, who said, "We told him we didn't really need him because we were winning without him."

That was Urban's Way: Your teammates decide your fate.

"He always kind of put all the decisions in our hands—whether it was ranch dressing or Italian dressing, or what jerseys and what shoe color or what kind of socks we were going to wear," said Nagahi. "When that issue came up with Marty, it was a tough one. It took some time because Coach Meyer was really, really upset at Marty. He said, 'Driving drunk, you could kill a member of my family, not only hurt yourself, but hurt other people.' So he gave us a day or two to think about it."

The courts were even harsher, as Marty was sentenced to jail at the end of 2003 and would serve twenty-nine days.

The Leadership Committee decided to give Marty another chance, but only if he could meet what he remembers was "a list of about fifteen" conditions. He would be suspended from the team for 2003 and told to complete the list of demands.

Johnson said he felt maybe they doubted his strong desire to play again, but was glad to get the reprieve. Eventually he would meet every one of the conditions, including sobriety.

When he went to jail, Shelley and Gigi stayed in touch. The Meyer family even visited him in jail and the sight of Marty in an orange jumpsuit was shocking to Urban. That day Urban told Marty he was wanted back on the team. The healing had begun, and the whole Meyer family took part.

Marty wrote Gigi a letter from prison in which he admonished her to "listen to your parents because they know what they're talking about." He also told her she was "the coolest little girl around."

Shelley has that letter framed, along with a photo of Marty and Gigi at an amusement park in Salt Lake City.

Once out of jail, Johnson began to rebuild his life with the help of Urban and his family. Marty spent lots of time around Gigi and Shelley, flourishing in a family environment. He'd never really had that and often wondered what it would be like to have the support of his mother. Shelley became his surrogate.

"I just always tried to imagine that she was what my mother would be like and it made me feel good," Johnson said.

The junior college transfer from California received a second medical redshirt and, once out of prison, would return to the team in the

spring of 2004. That fall he was the starting running back on the unbeaten Utah team, rushing for 848 yards and scoring 15 touchdowns.

"Football is a great thing because not only does it sometimes keep
you out of trouble, but it's your second family," said Nagahi. "A lot of
players don't have what some of the other fortunate players do—two
parents, a father and a mother. Or even any parents, for that matter. He
[Meyer] brought that to our attention, too—that not everybody comes
from the same setting. You kind of had to keep an open mind, we kind
of wrote it all down, and we said, 'OK, we're going to give Marty another chance.'

"Because obviously, if he didn't get any help from us, who would
he get help from?"

Marty says he was extremely grateful for the support of his
teammates, his coaches, and the Meyer family. In 2008 he was
working in Sacramento, California, with no wife and no girlfriend—
but still in love with the game of football. He signed as a free agent
to play in the NFL, but was released by the Philadelphia Eagles in
August 2006. In the spring of 2008 he was hoping to catch on with
Team Florida in the All-American Football League, which had a
team in Gainesville, but the league never got off the ground.

Urban Meyer vowed that he would never kick a football player off
his team unless it was the absolute last resort.

From that day forward, Urban had a new unpaid assistant coach in
charge of counseling: Shelley.

Utah had a rich football heritage, but was never a football powerhouse
and had achieved only above-average success in midlevel competition.
The school was not without colorful history: The shovel pass, or "Utah
pass," a forward pitch by the quarterback to a receiver or running
back—was invented there. Quarterback Lee Grosscup was a magazine
cover boy in the mid-1950s, played sparingly for the New York Giants,
and later become a broadcaster.

Some of the former Ute players of note included NFL head coach
(San Francisco 49ers/Carolina Panthers) and Super Bowl–winning
coach George Seifert; Miami Dolphins defensive lineman Manny

Fernandez; Cincinnati Bengals player and TV announcer Bob Trumpy; Pittsburgh Steelers-Baltimore Colts-Washington Redskins receiver Roy Jefferson; and Carolina Panthers receiver Steve Smith.

The Utes won twenty-three conference championships and ten bowl games through their first 115 seasons. The program had gotten an uptick during Ron McBride's era of the early 1990s, so the cupboard wasn't bare.

Starting off with good players to coach was not just luck, because Urban Meyer says he would never take over a losing program without inheriting some talent. Urban was very aware of McBride's recruiting prowess and that Utah had beaten Southern Cal in the Las Vegas Bowl two years prior. (Just as he had known about Blackney and about Zook, whose players he would inherit at Florida.) While McBride was an excellent recruiter and left behind good players, the players needed shaping into a solid team.

Meyer also knew he needed immediate success, as there are no longer honeymoon periods for highly compensated coaches to build programs. The key to his success at Utah would be the blending of the cultures.

The strong presence of older Mormon players would have a big impact on the makeup of the football team. Meyer would have to accommodate the more mature athletes who had returned from their Mormon missions, most of whom were married with children. One of them was Morgan Scalley.

Scalley got a telephone call from his sister, a Utah football fanatic, who said she had heard something about a guy named Urban Meyer being Utah's next coach. "I had never heard of his name before," said Scalley, "so that was kind of a weird deal for me."

Scalley, a twenty-three-year-old sophomore safety who had just gotten back from his mission in Germany two years prior, was a punt returner and defensive back whose father, Bud, had played at Utah. Like some of the other regulars, Morgan began to feel the disappointment of a losing season the year before. He was also somewhat skeptical about this new guy whose name he had just heard. At first, there was a feeling-out by both parties—coach and players. Most of the players had already heard of Meyer's reputation as a taskmaster. Soon Scalley and his teammates would become impressed.

"He had a vision, he had a purpose, and he knew where he was going," said Scalley, reflecting on the first team meeting with the new coach. "The first time he met with us he said, 'You know there are really only about eight teams in the nation that ever do things the right way. And we're going to be one of those football teams.'

"He was speaking to a bunch of guys who had gone five and six the year before. So he was speaking to a bunch of doubters in that room."

When winter workouts began, Scalley found out how committed this new guy was to the concept. "The more we did, the more he asked us to do, the more we started to believe in what he was telling us. He had a vision . . . but I don't know if he expected it to come within a year."

Sophomore quarterback Alex Smith and a few others began to hear the stories about Bowling Green's Black Wednesday which preceded their new coach. Sure enough, when Meyer arrived in Salt Lake, out came the trash cans, on the doors went the chains, and the windows were covered with black paper—and the running commenced. This time it wasn't as harsh and there wasn't as big an exodus, but there was some negative reaction—and some attrition. Smith himself was coming off a frustrating freshman year and considered transferring before Meyer arrived.

As in the case of Marty Johnson, at this point in his life and coaching career, Meyer would have to decide about how far he was willing to go to demand and achieve maximum performances from his athletes.

If a player had a checkered background without a solid family upbringing, even if he had taken a wayward path somewhere along the way, playing for Meyer was going to provide him with at least one mulligan in life.

One such player was senior tight end Ben Moa, whose troubled past kept chasing him down from behind. By the time the new coach reached Utah, Moa was on the road back from being a gang member, but had previously been kicked off the team and out of school at least once for stealing. The big tight end/running back was, however, about to learn Urban's Way. Meyer, in turn, would learn to trust Moa on one of the biggest play calls of his career.

"Ben Moa was a gang member who was shot, and he shot at people," recalled Meyer. "When I got there, he was late to practice and had some major issues. He had a great wife and I became very close to them. And he changed his life around.

"We had him over to our house all the time, and I found out the guy was a good kid. He was just a mess. We kept working with him, working with him. He became like a son to me."

That bond of trust would pay dividends in more ways than one. Such as the day that Moa stepped up in Meyer's face to demand that he be given the ball on a crucial play in a triple overtime.

Utah was without starting tailback Brandon Warfield, or anybody to play behind him. So it fell to Moa, a 260-pound senior with no running back experience, to fill that void.

In the third overtime, nationally ranked Air Force scored to go up, 43–37, but failed at a 2-point conversion. Utah took the ball at the 25 and drove it to the 1, where on fourth down Meyer called a timeout. Standing on the sidelines, Meyer called "twenty-four jump pass," a play that years later Florida quarterback Tim Tebow would execute as a freshman to help defeat LSU.

Moa had another thought and challenged the decision by his coach.

"Coach, give me the ball," said Moa, who had rushed 8 times for 25 yards to that point in the game. "I'll score."

Meyer was staring into Moa's eyes, which were now full of tears, as the emotion rippled through the entire offensive unit.

"I swear, I'll score!" Moa kept insisting.

Meyer grabbed him by the face mask and said, "OK, you'd better score!"

"I swear to you on my family's life, I'll score!" Moa kept screaming.

Meyer waved off the original pass play, putting the ball—and the game—into the hands of his part-time tailback.

Moa kept his promise, diving into the end zone to tie the game at 43.

But there was more to come.

Under college overtime rules, Utah was forced to go for 2 points.

Now Meyer could use the jump pass on the conversion, a play Utah had practiced many times.

Moa received the snap, moved forward as if to run, then stopped and delivered the only scoring pass of his college career perfectly into the hands of tight end Matt Hansen for the 2 points.

"We tricked them a little," Moa told the Associated Press after the game. "I knew they were going to bite. We had run the ball every time I was the quarterback—six times, maybe more. They didn't cover any receivers. They blitzed everybody in, and I knew Matt would be wide-open. So I threw it over the top, soft."

Final score: Utah 45, Air Force 43, in what Meyer would later call "probably my favorite game I ever coached."

The Ben Moa and Marty Johnson stories, Meyer feels, reflect what his program is all about.

At first sight, walk-on freshman Casey Evans was pretty much viewed as a reject. In an interview with Meyer before workouts started, the coach told Evans to "go back and talk to coach [Kyle] Whittingham again" to make sure he'd be a worthy candidate. The Utah defensive coordinator gave Evans the thumbs-up, despite his skinny frame.

"He totally didn't think I looked like a football player," Evans said.

As drills got more difficult and players started quitting, Evans was still there. He would become one of the team's leading tacklers and an All Mountain West defensive back as a senior. First he had to endure twelve straight workouts in the weight room, the difficulty of rope climbing, and the grueling tugs-of-war. Their motto became "Don't let go of the rope" that year.

Evans survived the drills, but was stuck on the scout team until one day he made a few good plays and got a battlefield promotion. "Put this guy on the kickoff return—you've got a spot on special teams!" Meyer said, pointing out the exceptional effort of Evans.

When the Champions Club started that year, Evans was a reject. He couldn't make the cut because his bench press wasn't good enough. Angry at this rejection, Evans began to work even harder. "It made me so mad that I didn't make it that I spent every way imaginable trying to improve my bench," said Evans. Then Evans made it.

"The majority of the team makes it," Evans said. "You don't want to be that kid over there eating hot dogs when everybody's eating steaks."

Looking back, Bo Nagahi said, Urban's Way was really the only method that could have worked. At times in the beginning, during those rigid workouts, Nagahi would ask himself, " 'Who *is* this guy and *what* are we doing?' "

Nagahi was an established special teams player and defensive back when Meyer arrived, so he naturally liked the new emphasis on special teams and the way players were singled out with great enthusiasm and intensity. Respect came right away.

"Anything he asked me to do, I would do it," said Nagahi. "I don't care if he said be a long snapper. Even if I had never done it before, if he asked me to do it, I would have done it. I would have tried my best, knowing that if he had the confidence in me, I would be able to do it."

Meyer spent an inordinate amount of time teaching techniques to individual special teams players. Nagahi said the players were all well prepared and knew they could never use an excuse of "I didn't know" if they screwed up. "Because he made sure that you knew."

Meyer also made sure they knew about the correct techniques for a balanced life. He wanted them to learn how to run the proper routes for success in education, have a meaningful family experience, and he assisted them in whatever spiritual journey they might be taking.

First, however, Urban had to win them all over. And that was going to take a few months, because not everybody shared Nagahi's immediate acceptance.

Meyer soon found resistance from a number of older players on the team to some of the hard-nosed drills imported from Bowling Green. In March 2003 of the first off-season, those players decided to push back.

Scalley's recollection was that "the first two months he beat the crap out of us," to a point where Scalley and some of the veterans spoke out against it. Scalley, junior defensive lineman Sione Pouha, aged twenty-four, and several older players were among those who went to Meyer's office and told him they'd had enough.

"This is not Bowling Green," one of them said. "You're not dealing with eighteen-year-olds anymore. You're dealing with returned missionaries, guys who are twenty-five who are married with kids."

In this dissidence, they were risking a Meyer meltdown and a Mount Saint Helen's–like volcanic eruption, but they didn't get it.

Scalley knew the risk involved. "There were a lot of coaches who would have said, 'You know what, guys—forget you! You shut up and listen.' But Urban is a guy who will listen to his leaders if they have proven he can trust them," said Scalley.

"He was great. He told us 'You know, you're right. This is as new to me as I am to you guys, and I'm learning just as much as you are. And we're going to have to work through this together.'"

Meyer followed that up by embracing the culture of the school, the program, and the state—all of which impressed his players, who also knew their coach was on a mission of his own.

Urban would use that lesson of diversity. First, however, he had to learn about the Mormon culture.

"I didn't know a thing about Mormons," Meyer admitted. So he and Shelley read a book about the LDS and found out that they embraced many of the same family values as did the Catholic Church.

Like most other non-Utahans, Shelley and Urban were not all that familiar with that religion. Shelley's friends had been teasing her about Urban perhaps adopting the Mormon lifestyle and marrying more than one wife. (Plural marriages are, in fact, fairly rare among Mormons today and practiced mostly by a small number of fundamentalists.)

Urban also befriended a church elder, Elder Joseph B. Wirthlin, a former Utah tailback of the 1940s who had become one of twelve LDS apostles, "one of the greatest guys I've ever known." Urban also became friends with a former all-conference Ute player, Eric Jacobsen, who is a Mormon.

While in his eighties, Wirthlin would become a guest of Urban's at a Gator game in Gainesville. Likewise, Urban would later be invited to speak at one of those Mormon firesides with one of his players, at which, according to that player, "He talked about how important it was that his kids knew he believed in God . . . and he kind of got choked up when he was speaking." (Wirthin died December 1, 2008, at the age of 91.)

The more Urban learned about Mormonism—particularly about the principles of family, education, discipline, missions, etc.—the more comfortable he felt. His defensive coordinator, Kyle Whittingham, was a practicing Mormon and also helped explain his religion to Urban. "He helped me with this and I fell in love with Utah," said Meyer. "Fell in love with Utah and learned a lot about the religion."

Then there were the Polynesians. Urban just had never seen them in their formal attire. Thankfully, Meyer already had a friend and cohort, Hiram de Fries, who was born in Hawaii of Dutch and Polynesian descendants and helped educate him about the Polynesian culture in his days at Colorado State.

At Utah, Hiram helped explain some of their customs, such as the day that the "Poly" players showed up to ride the bus wearing a shirt and tie for what the team calls Dress A when traveling to airports or to stadiums.

The Polynesians were resplendently dressed in their finest Sunday church clothes, with ties and white shirts tucked into the traditional black-cloth lavalava, the Samoan name for the kiltlike sarong or skirt worn for centuries by the warriors of Polynesia.

It was a cultural shock for Meyer, seeing his football players in "skirts" for the first time.

"They can't wear that," Meyer said to de Fries.

"Why not? They wear them to church," said de Fries.

The Polys were, indeed, allowed to wear their lavalavas.

Meyer came to appreciate his association with this new ethnic group. "Of all my experiences, the Polynesian culture I have the most respect for," Urban said, "because they don't just *say* 'family,' they *are* family. Everybody knows everybody's cousin. They all care about each other. There's no disrespect. There are things you have to get in order, but all you have to say is 'I'm going to call your mom.' And it's done, just like that."

Meyer, however, drew the line at the "magic mud" out in back of the hotel where the Utah team stayed the night before games at Rice-Eccles

Stadium—a product from the previous regime. Utah had been gifted with the magic mud by a group that alleged the substance had belonged to a Polynesian chieftain and should be used as a ceremonial walk-through for good luck.

The magic mud didn't make the cut and was covered. Nobody seemed to mind, and that certainly didn't stop the magic from happening.

At the first "Champions Banquet" held at the Meyer household, Urban and Shelley noticed something unorthodox—even if maybe it *seemed* orthodox to the players. As they dined, they were grouped by ethnicity, race, or religion.

"The married LDS kids were sitting over here, the black kids sitting over here, the Polynesians over there, the Hispanics over here," said Meyer. "Nobody's talking. They couldn't stand each other. I looked at Shelley and we said, 'What is *this*!?"

Some of the LDS players, white Protestants, and white Catholics seemed to intermingle. One Persian, or Iranian, player even crossed over and says he simply sat with his position group.

"This has got to stop," Meyer announced to them, and he quickly broke up the divisiveness. Most of the players didn't realize they were doing it.

There would be no more cliques on Urban Meyer's football team.

At the insistence of their coach, the Ute players began to find out the family backgrounds of their teammates, their hometowns, their high schools, their likes and their dislikes. If they didn't have the correct answer, they had to run.

Little by little, the group of individuals started to become a team. In the off-season, after scrimmages, the Polys taught others about their festive picnics, featuring pig roasts.

Once they had gotten past the rough spots in the first two months and the weeding out had taken place, Meyer and his football team began to bond. After year one, that bond was stronger than Krazy Glue.

One spring day the following year when Urban was leaving his office, walking to his car, he happened upon one of his captains, Morgan

Scalley. "I gotta run," Scalley said to Meyer, who inquired where he was going in such a hurry. Scalley said he was headed to the park for a "Poly party" pig roast with the defensive lineman Steve Fifita and several other Polynesian teammates.

That's when Urban knew it was working.

Once inside his car, Meyer called Shelley and said, "Unless I screw this up, we will win every game we play next year."

Shelley remembers that he also said, "And win them by a bunch."

"They finally got it," Meyer said. "They cared for each other. All that hard work was paying off."

That prophecy would come to pass.

Meyer remembered what Earle Bruce always said about the huddle, "The huddle is the greatest in football, because it doesn't matter whether you or black or white or Hispanic or Polynesian or Chinese, Catholic or Jewish. On fourth down and one, everybody grabs a hand and squeezes tight and says, 'Let's go.' Churches aren't like that. Businesses are not like that. Some families are not like that. But the huddle breaks every barrier—religious, racial, rich or poor."

As the stories of Ben Moa and Marty Johnson would attest.

"We went twenty-two and two," Meyer said with fondness of his two seasons at Utah. "A skinny kid named Alex Smith takes over in the third game of our first year, and it was like a freak show from there."

Inside that huddle of diversity that Bruce had talked about was a sophomore from San Diego, six-foot-four Alex Smith, a superstar in the making with a good football pedigree—his father coached and played in college, and his uncle was head coach at Louisville. Wanting to play Division I football, Smith was signed by McBride, but the coach allowed Smith's redshirt year to be burned by just seven plays. Smith was so discouraged that he was thinking of transferring to an Ivy League school.

Then he heard the name Urban Meyer for the first time, but didn't recognize it. He had never heard of Bowling Green, but the more Alex investigated it, the more he heard "crazy things" about Meyer's style of coaching at Bowling Green—crazy workouts and a crazy offense that featured a running quarterback. "I'd never run the ball and I was kind of a slow kid," he said.

Meyer, hearing Smith was upset, phoned Alex and made immediate arrangements to meet with him and his parents. The new Utah coach made a favorable impression. "He was up-front," said Smith, who felt right off that Meyer "was a person that demanded respect."

Even so, Alex had some uncomfortable times at first because of the stories of Urban's aggressive style, his screaming and hollering as he pushed athletes to the edge and beyond—and they were all true.

Still a gangly teenager, Smith began to get "rubbed the wrong way" by the motivational tactics. "At the time," said Smith, "it was blunt to have your head coach screaming and yelling that 'you're too weak, you're too slow, you're too little, and you're never going to be able to play like that!'

"Looking back, it was something that really pushed me and I really wanted to be that type of player for him. But as you played for him, you came to appreciate it so much."

Smith found out in a hurry that he, as the starting quarterback, would be no more important than the 115th player on the team, or the walk-on who gave his best in the classroom, on the field, and off the field.

Everybody, however, had to endure those brutal weight room workouts and go through the mat drills in which you often were a mismatch for wrestling a teammate.

"I've never been ridden so hard in my entire life," Smith said of the weight room workouts. "I'm eighteen years old and I'm doing a bench press workout with a couple of quarterbacks."

Smith had just finished with one set and was warming up, helping set his teammate when he began hearing some of the strength and conditioning coaches talking about him.

"They're talking about how I can't bench press three hundred pounds and I need to get down and do pushups. So they got me doing pushups in between workouts, then they bring over a ball, and I've got my feet on the ball doing pushups between bench presses." All of a sudden somebody sat on his back, "Pushing down as I'm trying to push up. It was such an intense environment!"

Later, once the workouts became more regimented, Smith said the coaches quit coming to the weight room and let the players police the workouts.

"There were times when you asked yourself if you were capable of doing everything they were asking of you," said Smith.

Such as the time in the mat drills when the quarterbacks were asked to wrestle the linebackers who were sixty to seventy pounds heavier.

"I am just getting killed out there," said Smith. "My nose is bleeding, my shirt is ripped, I've got rug-burn all over me, and they're telling me to do up-downs because I just got beat and to get back in line because I just got beat.

"At times you say, 'Man this is insane, this is crazy.' But everybody's doing it. He treated everyone the same—everyone is getting pushed. I learned to appreciate it because everyone is so tight because we've been through so much together. Those mental barriers are broken down. You found yourself really engaging that stuff and really wanting it, knowing it was going to make you better and pay off. It was something I'm so thankful I got to go through and to play for coach Meyer. It's something that's going to change my life forever."

It was a different kind of quarterbacking, too. You were no longer just handing off or passing the ball—you were the focal point of the offense. As Smith found out, you had to "totally buy in." If you did, things would start to make sense—such as the game when Alex had a lightbulb go off over his head. In the 2003 Cal game on national TV, Smith came off the bench to start for the injured Brett Elliott. Early in the game, Cal brought a blitz with no safeties to defend, and the automatic read for Alex was to go deep. Somehow he recognized the coverage, as did his receiver, and Alex hit the pass for 14 yards and a first down.

"It wasn't a great pass, it wasn't a great play by me, and the receiver made a nice catch, but it was easy and it was just doing your job," said Smith. "After that it seemed to really click. All eleven players were just doing their job."

Smith drove the Utes down the field late in the game and executed an option for the winning touchdown. That 31–24 win was the first of twenty-two victories Smith would engineer as the starting quarterback over the two seasons and jump-started him into fame.

In his mind, Alex Smith said to himself: "This could really turn into something special."

It did.

From that point on, Smith's huddle was full of eleven guys, many of them different from the guy next to him, who pulled together with defense and special teams to achieve a dream that almost nobody but they and their coaches thought possible.

Though the Meyer family was, once again, getting firmly entrenched, it was much different in Utah from Bowling Green, where Meyer had won no championships nor gone to a bowl. Another quantum leap unfolded in the second year at Utah.

Undefeated and untied teams are rare in college football anymore, but Utah was about to show the world what one looked like in 2004.

Coming from behind to beat Air Force, 49–35, in their Mountain West Conference opener and go 4-0 was a big stepping-stone. Just a few days after Meyer had called Marty Johnson "an average back," his senior tailback set a school record by scoring four touchdowns against the Falcons.

Johnson, Morgan Scalley, and their senior teammates such as Sione Pouha, Chris Kemoeatu, Paris Warren, and Travis LaTendresse were leading the way.

After Utah beat North Carolina, 46–14, some of the players who had been grousing about Meyer's tactics began to get the vision. Meyer called them "the most 'invested team' in the country."

A lot of good karma and vibes were coming from everywhere. According to a story in the *Salt Lake Tribune*, defensive lineman Steve Fifita's play had been inspired by a book entitled *The Game of Life and How to Play It,* by Florence Scovel Shinn, a metaphysician, given to him by teammate Reza Williams, who would wind up enrolling in law school. The book contained material about positive thinking that was more than eighty years old. Williams had been given it by a seventy-five-year-old janitor at his apartment building. Fifita gave several copies to teammates.

Apparently these Utes had their own version of the magic mud.

So far ahead were they against Colorado State—and no doubt because of his respect for Sonny Lubick—Meyer took quarterback Alex Smith out with nine minutes to play in the third quarter in a 63–31 rout of the Rams for win No. 9.

About here, Meyer's name began being mentioned for openings at Washington and several other places.

"It was almost like people were expecting us to go," Meyer said. "Everybody was saying, about nine or ten games into the season, 'This is going to be coach's last year and he's going to go somewhere else.'"

To his credit, Meyer never let it get him off his message. If ever he really needed to keep his concentration, it was in Laramie, Wyoming, when the lights went out due to a power failure.

It was 17 degrees with a windchill factor of minus 10. The game was supposed to be on regional network TV, but when the lights were turned on, it blew a main circuit breaker, and the entire stadium went dark fifteen minutes before the kickoff.

Utah returned to the locker room, and, to prevent a slowing of metabolism, members of the support staff were sent to town to buy energy food (fruit). The players were fed and kept relaxed.

After seventy-five minutes, partial lights were restored, and Utah beat Wyoming, 45–28, and headed for the airport. However, no one had bothered to call the airline charter service. The airplane was already on the tarmac with its engines having run for an extended period of time since the Laramie airport was not fully equipped to restart them.

That also meant the plane would have to land in Denver to refuel for the trip over the Rocky Mountains to Salt Lake. The team could have taken buses and gotten home sooner. Such was life in the Mountain West Conference.

The Utes had clinched their second straight Mountain West title even before the game with big rival BYU. Urban had no idea how big the game was against the Cougars until his athletic director, Chris Hill, reminded him that a $14-million payday was on the line should Utah win and make it to the Fiesta Bowl. Also, for the first time ever, *ESPN GameDay* would be at Rice-Eccles Stadium.

That $14 million was a huge windfall for any school, but for a football program that rarely even broke even, it was a lottery win.

The Utes clobbered BYU, 52–21. Fans celebrated the Fiesta Bowl by mobbing the field, tossing sombreros, taking down the goal posts, and tossing tortillas on the field.

As Utah began practicing for the Fiesta Bowl, there were more rumors about Meyer leaving.

Urban made his first call to a friend and former associate to feel him out about joining his staff—without being able to say what the name of the school would be. Some of them guessed Florida, and before long, UF director of athletics Jeremy Foley called to meet him for an interview.

Meyer was almost set to say yes to Foley, but Notre Dame called, suddenly putting his dream job within grasp and Florida in jeopardy.

When it became evident Urban was leaving, he asked if the team wanted him to stay on for the Fiesta Bowl.

Foley and Gator fans would have been a lot more nervous if they'd known how close Urban came to changing his mind. Once again, Shelley was there to help him through the night and to reach a decision that he wasn't going to regret anytime soon.

PART TWO

Becoming a Gator

11

Shelley, the Go-To Girl

Counselor, friend, mother, sweetheart, homemaker, cheerleader—Shelley Meyer can do it all, and sometimes does. Shelley rocks! But she is also the Rock when it comes to a family crisis—the sound thinker under pressure and the logical one.

Shelley's counsel provides stability for the Meyer household in those key life-transforming moments. She has become the ultimate coach's wife, according to Urban's good friend Dean Hood. Perhaps her background as a psychiatric nurse is the perfect credential.

"He's got a great wife," Hood said. "In this business, if you don't have the right wife, it can hinder you. She's wonderful—a perfect coach's wife. And he's been blessed."

Shelley Meyer is the Go-To Girl. In football lingo, she would be the Playmaker in Crunch Time. And she has made plenty of big plays. Maybe none bigger than the day Jeremy Foley came to Salt Lake City and offered the Florida job to her husband.

Shelley's Energizer Bunny enthusiasm abounds in everything she does. She feeds off the energy of her family, her friends, and her community activities, but she's also the No. 1 fan of Gator football. In fact, she once agreed to do a stunt with the Gator cheerleaders whereby she was hoisted to the top of a human pyramid—much to the horror of her husband watching on TV. "Don't do that again," Urban said in his text message to her.

She even cuts the grass with great enthusiasm.

The farm girl from Chillicothe, Ohio, just can't help herself. When it's time to mow the lawn, she straps on the iPod headphones, fires up her thirty-two-inch, walk-behind Toro (it was a Mother's Day gift from Urban while they were living in Bowling Green), and sets out to mow the two-acre tract behind what Billy Donovan has dubbed Shelley's "double-wide." When Donovan drives past, he offers up what she describes as "the ol' fist-pump high five."

Her reward? She trades off the lawn mowing for having someone clean her house every other week.

To some, this might sound like a role reversal, but she calls this three-hour task her "personal time" for a busy wife and mother. Shelley's schedule includes everything from carpooling to teaching spinning (cycling) classes to volunteering to help wipe tables in the lunchroom at Nate's St. Patrick school.

It was while playing football at Cincinnati that Urban found his future fiancée and wife—someone to enhance and enrich life and to help him get through the valleys after a loss. He met Shelley Mather (May-thur) in May of 1984 at a party.

"The first time I saw him I didn't realize who he was or what he was or anything," she recalled.

Shelley remembers asking one of her guy friends, "Who's that?"

He said, "Oh, that's UB."

"UB? What kind of name is that?"

"That's his nickname, his real name is Urban."

"Urban? What kind of name is that?" She said she had never heard that name before.

Shelley thought the Boy From Ashtabula was handsome and interesting, but she had a boyfriend back home.

"That was it. I didn't think anything else about it. A day or two later they ran into each other again. And he told his friend, 'I want to talk to that girl.' And his friend said, 'This guy wants to talk to you.'"

Urban came over and talked, asking her to go out on a date. The first time she said no. A few days later she saw him again. When he asked her for a date this time, she said yes. That was three weeks before school was out for the summer. They would spend most of every day together until school was out.

"And we completely and immediately fell in love," Shelley said.

They split up for the summer—she was in southern Ohio and he was in Ashtabula, in northeastern Ohio. It wasn't convenient for visiting, so they just wrote letters over the summer. When classes resumed at UC, they reunited and the romance bloomed. Soon they were married and on the coaching trail.

A coaching trail that would one day be leading to Gainesville, Florida.

From the early days on, once Ron Zook had been fired, Urban had been targeted by Florida as its No. 1 candidate. At first it seemed like an easy answer to a question that was raised all the way back to October 23, 2004, when Zook was let go a few days after losing to Mississippi State: Who would be Florida's next coach? Smart money was on Bernie Machen's bringing his man from Utah, but contrary to rumor, it was hardly a cut-and-dried deal.

Shelley says—and Jeremy Foley backs it up—that nothing was offered to Urban until the regular 2004 season was over, despite rumors to the contrary. Foley had an intermediary contact Urban to measure his interest. All parties contend that when Chuck Neinas of Boulder first talked to Meyer, only generalities were discussed.

Neinas became a familiar voice on the other end of the line to Shelley. "Every time he called I'd say, 'Oh no, Chuck, what now?' I loved Chuck, but I was so glad to see him and be able say, 'I'm glad you don't have to keep calling us anymore!'"

Foley found Neinas, a sort of college football headhunter, trustworthy and confidential in his business dealings. "He helps you find out information on the front end that helps," Foley told the Associated Press. "You find out who's interested, who's not interested. He's responsive. If you call him, he calls you back. If you ask him to find something out, he finds it out."

Neinas had given Foley the thumbs-up that Meyer was interested, but no terms were discussed, and Urban said he wasn't sure about which school wanted an interview with him. Though Foley would make no official contact yet, Meyer had a good enough idea of what jobs were available and knew that if it was Florida that the state was loaded with talent.

Lou Holtz, then at South Carolina, told Urban about linebacker Brandon Siler and wide receivers Bubba Caldwell and Chad Jackson. Holtz also said the state's talent level was good enough to make the Gators "one of the two or three best teams in the SEC."

As soon as Utah finished off the regular season unbeaten with a victory over BYU, the Urban Meyer watch was on. Washington had already contacted Urban.

Foley called Meyer the day after the BYU game and made arrangements to FedEx a package of information to him before flying on the down-low out to Salt Lake right away. Now Meyer was beginning to get excited, flashing back to that day in 2000 when he had stopped to visit the Swamp while recruiting for Notre Dame. Meyer loves telling the story—how he once got ticketed for illegally parking just outside Ben Hill Griffin Stadium after going down to stand on the 50-yard line of the empty arena just to drink in the atmosphere. He immediately phoned Shelley to tell her, "Now I know why I have such a tough time getting these kids out of Florida to come to Notre Dame."

"Tell me about it!" Shelley said.

"It's an awesome environment for football!" he said.

It wasn't so much just the atmosphere that day in Ben Hill Griffin Stadium—Meyer had visited Florida Field while playing for Cincinnati—but the aura it had attained during the Steve Spurrier era. As a football coach, Meyer admired the style and panache of Spurrier's teams. "When I saw them come across the TV," Meyer would later say, "I sat down and watched because of their swagger."

The Florida job was very appealing. Meanwhile, Washington made a pitch, and Utah began its counterstrike to possibly retrieve the best coach in its history—a thirteen-year contract that was tantamount to a lifetime deal. Shelley and Urban knew right away that Washington wasn't it, but they felt they owed it to Utah to listen to any counteroffer.

At the same time, Foley began to zero in on his prey.

Given that reporters had chased Foley across the country the last time he conducted a search for Spurrier's replacement, the Florida director of athletics was going to take a different route, literally and figuratively. Instead of flying from Gainesville, he would come in from another airport. After spending Thanksgiving at his second home in Vermont, Foley flew from the Northeast to Utah "because nobody up there would know who I was."

Right away Urban was impressed with Foley, and Foley was impressed with Meyer, who, he said, "was organized, straightforward, and asked a lot of questions." Foley needed to get this one right, since he'd gone through a tumultuous search for a replacement coach last time before settling on Zook, so the Florida AD brought his A game to Salt Lake. Though he made no offer yet, Foley knew Meyer was the right guy. The feeling was mutual with Urban. So they said good-bye and Foley told Meyer he'd make a return trip soon.

"Jeremy Foley is like Chris Hill, my AD at Utah—the ultimate professional," said Urban. "He [Foley] had put together a book which he handed me that contained a testimony from the coaches—including Billy Donovan. He had Billy call me. More importantly, he had Christine call my wife to talk about the church, about the schools, about places to live. He had it all covered. He did his homework on me and knew all I cared about was my family and recruiting. And whether I can get it done there. He had all that, A to Z. Phenomenal. That's what makes Jeremy the best there is."

Basically, Urban was sold on Florida without visiting Gainesville, but held his cards close to his vest at the moment. Shelley was long ago sold, and so was her family. Daughter Nicki had told them, when she first heard by the grapevine that Gainesville was on the family radar, "I'll go to Florida!" And Nicki's and Gigi's sentiments would be a factor in the final decision. Nate was still too young to care.

During the process of all these job negotiations, there was something called a BCS game, the Fiesta Bowl against Pittsburgh, and a $14 million payoff. Urban was now in what he called "the tenth or eleventh hour of our discussions with Florida," but he didn't want to tell Foley yes until he had given Utah's offer fair consideration.

During a Utah practice for the bowl game, Meyer turned and saw what looked like a caravan of TV trucks pulling up to park nearby. When he inquired what was going on, he was told, "Notre Dame has just fired Tyrone." That was Tyrone, as in Coach Ty Willingham. That set things on fire, Urban said, "And that whole next week was unbelievable."

As much as Urban loved the idea of going to Florida and was impressed with his boss-to-be, one school could knock Foley out of the box. The one that his mom, Gisela, always talked to her son about—the dream job of Urban Frank Meyer III. Now that job was going to be his for the taking.

Everybody, including Foley, knew Notre Dame would come after the former Irish assistant coach.

Meanwhile, learning of Notre Dame's trip to Salt Lake, Foley had scrapped the idea of going through a "process" to hire Meyer and had flown to Salt Lake, contract in hand. He met with Meyer the day of the scheduled discussion with Notre Dame and tried to sway him with an attractive offer, but to no avail.

Foley and Associate Athletic Director Greg McGarrity went back to the hotel room that Jon Clark had reserved in his own name to throw off the press, but there was no rest to be had for either. "We're both kind of nervous Nellies anyway," said Foley.

Once Utah practice ended, Urban drove home and was greeted at the door by Shelley, who told him the meeting had been moved to the Grand American Hotel in downtown Salt Lake. Notre Dame athletic director Kevin White had said they had encountered a group of Notre Dame media trailing them. Urban was told to take the hotel's back entrance and meet White and Notre Dame president Father John Jenkins in room 328.

Urban considered White his friend and "I loved Notre Dame, because that's my dream," so naturally he was going to give serious consideration to the offer from the Irish.

Jenkins and White came with their A game, too.

Urban discussed matters of the schedule, admissions, and facilities with them. "That's what we talked about—how to make Notre Dame more competitive for national championships," Meyer said.

"All things were addressed and all things we were going to have some leeway in—which was big for Notre Dame."

That night during a family discussion, as Foley awaited word, Urban told his wife and children he was rethinking his decision about accepting the Florida deal.

"We go home and there's no sleeping," recalled Shelley. "Urban was in turmoil over this, pacing, trying to lie down and getting up. Talking about every factor. Many phone calls to coaches—Bob Stoops, Coach Bruce, Bob Davie, Coach Holtz—and to his father."

Earlier that day Foley had gone for a walk to find a church.

"I found an Episcopal church—I'm an Episcopalian—and I knocked on the door," said Foley. "It was closed because it was Thursday afternoon, but the minister came up and opened it. And I said, 'Can I spend a few minutes here just by myself?' and he said, 'Sure.' And so I went in just to settle my nerves, obviously looking for a little assistance."

Certainly not wanting Notre Dame to have an advantage of any kind, Foley wasn't going to rule out the possibility of divine intervention.

After all, because Foley had kept his eye on Meyer for several months, he had missed a chance to bring back Steve Spurrier earlier that year—which didn't make some Gator fans very happy when the Ol' Ball Coach wound up signing on with South Carolina just two weeks prior. (Had Meyer not taken the job, Foley's backup plan was Bobby Petrino, then at Louisville.)

Later that night to kill time, McGarrity and Foley went to a movie, waiting for Urban's call. "I told Urban, at the very least, don't make me go all night wondering," said Foley. When Urban did call, he told Jeremy that he and Shelley still had some talking to do, that the interview had gone well, but he didn't sound as if he was wavering. Although he was.

Foley's—and Florida's—biggest advantage would turn out to be Urban's and Shelley's desire for a strong family life, because he could recruit closer to home.

At one point during the night Urban told his family he would be taking the Notre Dame job.

"I wanted to go to Notre Dame," Meyer admitted, "but my family wanted to talk about going to Florida."

Shelley knew how tough it was for her husband because "he left his heart at Notre Dame when we left there last time—he really, really, really loved Notre Dame."

Shelley did not want Urban to regret the decision of turning down Notre Dame, so she gave him time to work it out.

Urban loved the talent pool in the state of Florida and figured his best chances of winning a national championship would be in Gainesville.

One key factor in Florida's favor: Notre Dame was a national school, meaning Urban would be flying coast to coast in the search for recruits. That would preclude Urban being home to see his son and daughters compete in sports. In talent-laden Florida and adjacent states, only short hops would be necessary to recruit some of the best players in America.

Remember now, Shelley still had "veto rights" on all but three schools—and Notre Dame was one, where she only had 49 percent of the vote.

At the end of the night, way into the wee hours of the morning, Urban and Shelley sorted it all out. They were going to Florida. The next morning they called Foley, who rushed over to their house.

Shelley remembers Foley coming to the Meyer house the next morning and shaking hands with Urban, who said, "I'm coming to Florida." She was so happy that she screamed. Later, after Foley left, he would get a phone call from somebody saying that the word was out: Urban Meyer was the new Florida coach. It had been leaked out inadvertently by a family member in another city.

Florida's—and Foley's—prayers were answered. Nevertheless, some Utahans felt jilted and questioned the sincerity of Urban's and Shelley's affection for Utah.

This is the dilemma for coaches, whose job offers often come suddenly. They are asked to address issues prematurely. There are delicate negotiations which, if played out in the media, could be harmful to either or both parties. Therefore, when either party isn't forthcoming with direct answers, fans usually get angry and frustrated. Perhaps this was the case when Urban and Shelley found themselves considering one of the best job offers any coach could want, but at the same time, feeling sad to be leaving a place that they liked so much in Utah.

Urban had a career coaching ladder to consider, and that included being coach of a major college and winning a national championship. He felt he could do that in Gainesville. The Go-To Girl had gotten him back on track for that challenge.

We pulled up two cushy chairs in the front room of their home. Shelley provided the lemonade and cookies as we chatted for two hours about the life of the Meyer family and, more specifically, how they work as a duo in this unique role as life coaches and mentors for Gator football players. She worries about Urban because of his self-inflicted negativity when things are going badly for his team or one of his players.

It has sometimes been a long, dark, and lonely road for Urban, whose off-season between the 2006 and 2007 season was the worst he'd ever experienced.

In his eighth year as a head coach, Urban became convinced that Shelley was right and that winning back the lives of players was more important than winning football games.

She may have been a little naive at first about the gypsy life of a football coach, but once she adjusted and got it after signing on with Urban, she committed with a vengeance, and her inner toughness taught even her husband a lesson.

"When I was making six thousand dollars as year, I watched her," Urban said. "We couldn't even go out to dinner. She never said a word—other than when I was trying to get out of coaching. She said, 'No, you want to be a coach.' Zero point zero dollars in the bank, living paycheck to paycheck. Couldn't go eat on Friday night, because we couldn't afford it. She never said a word, other than, 'Let's go, let's go . . . let's keep it going.'"

There is nothing in the Meyer household that she doesn't get involved with—nothing!—and if need be, she could probably help Urban with his game plans and play calling. For certain she knows the mood swings of a football coach and how to deal with them—a least most of the time.

Meyer's style of all-in coaching, his proactive approach to player issues, and intense personality made it even tougher.

"Urban is a Type A personality who's always going," said Shelley. "He worries a lot. A hundred and five players. So-and-so is homesick. So-and-so's girlfriend broke up with him. So-and-so is having academic issues. And this stuff weighs on him. And so he worries. And sometimes he needs some help in getting past all the worry and all the issues in order to get refocused. He needs somebody to talk to.

"When we lose a game, it's bad. I try to remind him of why we're here."

She can also be the toughest member of the Meyer family, as Urban points out. Part of his resolve comes from Shelley's Spartan personality and willingness to sacrifice early in their marriage when even a night on the town for cheeseburgers wasn't affordable.

Urban needs that balance because he doesn't want to go back to those dark days on the coaching sideline when his emotions overwhelmed his body and the physical stress overpowered his nervous system. Urban promised himself to keep emotions in check following an episode at Notre Dame when he fell to the ground on his knees from excruciating pain in his head.

That "why we're here" message has come across loud and clear to Urban, who now says his priorities have been changing and that he feels he and Shelley have their own mission.

"That has been a process developing," said Shelley. "Winning used to be the main goal. It has come about as we've matured and have dealt with more and more troubled players—and Urban getting more spiritual."

There is a sense of purpose about the Meyer family being at Florida—and not just about football. Urban admits that part of his attraction to Gainesville was his fascination with watching Spurrier's team play, but knows now that's not the real reason.

"There's a certain spiritual element that's taken over me, too, in the last several years," he said. "And I really believe—and my wife's this way, big time, and she's always saying, 'There's a reason we're at Florida—and it wasn't because of the orange stadium.'

"I'm thinking it was because I loved watching them play in the nineties. And, 'Man, that would be kind of neat.' I believe now, and it's her opinion, that has nothing to do with it. We've been put at

Florida for a reason. We took over a team with some serious issues and we still have issues we're dealing with—more so than I ever dreamed of, more than I ever wanted to."

Trying to get young men to live right can be perplexing and exhausting. A failure in the game of life is even harder for Meyer to take than losing a football game.

"You're not going to win every battle, but the ones you win, what's going to place a price tag on saving a life?" he said. "And maybe failing if the guy doesn't change. Go ask the [Louis] Murphy family. Let's get a price tag on that one. Or a Steven Harris. Or a Marty Johnson. Or a Dallas Baker. And you go on and on. And the ones who didn't change."

Urban learned not only to lean on Shelley, but at times on his Florida staff as well—a staff he pulled together in January of 2005 which would help coach the Gators to a national championship twenty months later.

As Meyer put that staff together, he placed a high priority on wisdom and experience. The only person Urban called, even before he had the job, was Greg Mattison, who was still in South Bend awaiting the outcome of Notre Dame's search for a new head coach. Urban told him, "I'm onto something big," but said he couldn't tell him what.

Mattison knew that both Florida and Notre Dame were looking for a new head coach and figured it was one or the other.

"Just tell me this," Mattison said from his South Bend home to Meyer. "Am I going to have to move?"

Meyer said he couldn't tell him yet, but when he put down the phone, Mattison knew in his gut it was going to be Florida.

Urban had two more pieces of business before he could bring his staff together and get on with life in Gainesville: First, winning the Fiesta Bowl game and, second, seeing his assistant Kyle Whittingham inherit the head coaching job at Utah.

"I wanted Kyle to get that job, because if he leaves, everything we worked for goes up in smoke," said Meyer. "So half my heart is back there because I love those players."

Nagahi remembers Meyer saying, "I would love to coach you in the bowl game, but if you don't want me to do it, then I won't." The team met and, according to Nagahi, said, "We got here together and we're going to leave together."

Utah won everything it could win, including the 35–7 thrashing of Pittsburgh in the Fiesta Bowl, and Alex Smith was off to the NFL, where he was made rich as the No. 1 pick.

"We went twelve and oh and beat teams where the game was over in the third quarter," said Meyer.

Many contributed to that dream season, not the least of whom were All–Mountain West Conference players such as defensive linemen Sione Pouha and Steve Fifita, offensive lineman Chris Kemoeatu, wide receiver Steve Savoy, Smith, and Scalley. Scalley was named the Mountain West scholar-athlete of the year.

"Utah was the ultimate team," Meyer said proudly. "The twelve-and-oh team, just to give you an example of how tough they were, I couldn't break them. We were so hard on them the first year. And that next year we had a bunch of good, veteran players who just took control of the team."

They took it over to the point that Meyer at times could leave to deal with issues about his new job at Florida. Those veteran players helped keep the Utes focused and on target for Fiesta Bowl opponent Pittsburgh.

As Urban had predicted, Utah would become an elite team. The Utes finished No. 5 in the USA Today Coaches poll and No. 4 in the Associated Press poll. All that hard work, after all, had paid off for everyone.

Off that Utah coaching staff from the 2005 Fiesta Bowl, he would bring Dan Mullen, Billy Gonzales, John Hevesy, and Chuck Heater as assistants; also strength and conditioning assistant Matt Balis, administrative assistant Jon Clark, Hiram de Fries and video coordinator Brian Voltolini, and his assistant Wayne Cederholm.

Offensive coordinator Mike Sanford became head coach at University of Nevada-Las Vegas, taking with him Utah assistants tight end coach Keith Uperesa and linebacker coach Kurt Barber. Defensive line coach Gary Anderson stayed behind to work for Whittingham.

———

After Whittingham got the job at Utah, he called Urban at 2:00 A.M. to tell him.

"Now I'm relieved," Meyer said.

That done, Meyer got on with the business at hand: filling out his lineup card of "all-star" coaches for his Florida staff.

12

Getting the Band Back Together

Much in the way many young women dream of their wedding day, young assistant coaches dream of becoming head coaches. Brides-to-be may make mental notes at other weddings about their future bridesmaids and maid or matron of honor; coaches scout the football landscape for future associates.

Urban Meyer was no different.

Meyer always wanted to hire his dream team of coaches one day. When he was named Florida's new coach, he already had that list ready. Previous relationships would play a big part in the selections. It didn't take long to get the band back together, sort of like a reunion of Urban's rock'n' rollers.

The group of coaches that Meyer put together to help win the 2006 national championship were excellent teachers, strong motivators, dogged recruiters, good in-game decision-makers, and dedicated staff members. They had good chemistry and shared a common vision.

Because of their success, their coaching profiles were elevated, which would ultimately lead to staff changes.

Urban had planned for the day when he could round up his stars.

"The last four or five years when I thought this might happen, I made a list of names," Meyer confessed. "I wanted to pick the best coaches I'd been around and have them on my staff. And then you need a bunch of recruiting fools that don't mind spending six nights in a row in a hotel."

The last thing he wanted was a staff of yes-men.

"You have to have somebody who's got enough balls [to disagree]," he said.

"Disagreeing" doesn't mean openly arguing the call on fourth-and-one over the headsets or locking horns with each other and making a spectacle on the practice field. What it did mean was that behind closed doors—and especially in the annual staff retreat when they openly challenged each other's theories and philosophies—they would be encouraged to give their opinions and challenge fellow staffers, even when their opinions were different from those of the boss. Those differences of opinion were not to be turned into personality conflicts—or disrespect.

Disloyalty, however, would get you fired.

"If you don't believe in something . . . that's why we have these retreats," Meyer said. "There are no egos and you're not going to lose your job. You lose your job by being disloyal."

"Disloyal" meant something different from disagreement.

"The last page of the coaching manual says 'Disloyalty of any form will not be tolerated,'" Meyer said. "It says there right there in the book: disloyalty to the point of where I ask you to do something and you don't do it. Or you are negative about the program in a public place. Or cheating on your wife. It's over. You are finished."

Otherwise you were free to loosen your seat belt and enjoy the flight with your peers. Surprisingly, Meyer gives his assistants a wide range of flexibility, especially for a guy who has such hyper focus about everything else. Assistants know the parameters of their jobs and they are left pretty much to their own styles of coaching. This is a different Meyer from the one who once intruded on meetings and openly challenged his assistants.

"I think what they learn from me is that I'm not rigid," Meyer said. "I've been on staffs where it's 'This is the way, shut your mouth, and go to work.' I always want to hear a better way of doing things. We've altered things when somebody feels really strong about it."

The "Do your job" mantra goes for assistant coaches as well as players. If there is an issue with a player that is a problem for the position coach. Assistants are expected to take on the responsibilities for their players—whether babysitting them, tutoring them, counseling them about their girlfriends, or simply teaching them better fundamentals on the field.

"I don't want to deal with 'issues,'" Meyer said. "I want to coach football. And a lot of times the head coach becomes the 'issue coach.' If I spent eight hours working on guys who miss class . . . that's not my job. It's the position coach's job. And some are better than others."

The best at that, Urban said, was Kyle Whittingham, who replaced him at Utah.

"Kyle is one of my great friends and one of my top assistants I ever had. There are no issues. He just took care of everything. He was the best."

As Urban recruited his all-stars for the Florida staff, however, Whittingham was staying behind to succeed him at Utah.

Putting together that all-star staff wasn't going to be difficult at a school such as Florida. Meyer got more than his share of phone calls and e-mails from applicants, but already knew pretty much whom he would hire and/or retain.

Greg Mattison and Charlie Strong would be a lock as his codefensive coordinators, Urban having worked with both at Notre Dame. Strong was gone from South Bend and already at Florida when Meyer was hired.

Mattison, a graduate of Wisconsin-La Crosse and former coach at Navy, Texas, and Michigan, was in South Bend, awaiting word about who would take Ty Willingham's place at Notre Dame—thinking it might perhaps even be Meyer.

Strong and Mattison were no-brainers because Meyer was already familiar with both and they possessed three important characteristics he wanted: They were excellent coaches who knew how to take care of their players; they were strong recruiters; and they were committed to being good fathers and husbands.

Mattison's hiring would prove to be a vital piece of the puzzle, as he would bring an element of toughness to the defensive line which would fortify the Gators' national championship run.

Like Meyer, Mattison is a big proponent of inviting players to his home and treating them like family. Meyer knew that Mattison would set the curve in building relationships with his defensive lineman. With players such as Ray McDonald, Marcus Thomas, Jarvis Moss, Derrick Harvey, Steve Harris, Jeremy Mincey, Joe Cohen, Javier Estopinan, and Clint McMillan, a world of talent was awaiting Mattison. In subsequent years he would stash away superb young talent such as Jermaine Cunningham, Justin Trattou, Mike Pouncey, and Carlos Dunlap.

Among other things, Mattison and Strong shared a conviction about the importance of discipline and hard work. They also both came from small-college backgrounds—Charlie received his bachelor's from Central Arkansas State, but also holds masters from Henderson State and Florida.

"From the first day I met him," Mattison said of Urban during their Notre Dame days, "I always respected Urban for the way he recruited and the way he worked. He always had his guys doing the right thing. When you take pride as a coach in being a disciplinarian like I did, you kind of look around at other guys to see who else does it. And Urban was really good at it. He was always right on it."

While at Notre Dame, Meyer and Mattison also traveled together on recruiting trips and encouraged each other in their efforts to land prospects. Because they were neighbors, their families interacted. More than ten years Meyer's senior, Mattison brought gray-haired wisdom to the job.

"Greg is a friend, but I just admire the way he handles players," said Meyer. "He and his wife, Ann, just love players. He can recruit. He can motivate."

Mattison and Charlie Strong, who coached linebackers, would be an excellent tandem of codefensive coordinators.

"In South Bend we became great friends," Meyer said of Strong.

"We lived about five houses apart. The thing that impressed me was that he was one of the best fathers and best husbands I'd ever been around. The correlation of that to coaching I think, especially nowadays with the stakes and the changes . . . I don't know how you do it now. If you are a bad husband and a bad father, you are a bad coach, man. I sincerely believe that."

Another trait Meyer admired about Strong was his pleasant attitude and perpetual smile. Charlie would be a calming force in a cauldron of intensity and an encourager when times got tough. Strong never seems to have a bad day.

"I could be six feet under and he's 'OK, we'll be all right, we'll be all right,'" said Meyer. "And he's even a better coordinator than I thought. He calls a great game."

As a longtime Florida man who worked under four previous regimes, Charlie also knew where all the bodies were buried and how to get in and out of places such as Oxford, Mississippi, alive. He was hired by Charley Pell and served under him, Galen Hall, Steve Spurrier, Ron Zook, and now Meyer (as well as Lou Holtz at Notre Dame and South Carolina).

"Coach Meyer is a combination of those. He has so many of those same great qualities," Strong said. "Coach Pell was very organized. Urban is very organized. You think about Coach Spurrier and the way he changed the game. You think about the offense that Urban is running right now and it's changed the game. His relationship with players—I think he developed that from Coach Holtz, having those strong family ties.

"He's an outstanding football coach, a great organizer, a great disciplinarian, and really concerned about the welfare of the players. He will tell you in a minute: Coaches take care of the players. Your whole life is around these players."

With team leader Brandon Siler as his middle linebacker, veteran Earl Everett on one side, and Todd McCullough or Brian Crum on the other—plus a promising set of young linebackers in Brandon Spikes, Dustin Doe, A. J. Jones, and Ryan Stamper coming up behind them—Strong's presence would be felt on the defense. (Especially after the loss of Mattison, which would take place after the 2007 season.

Urban would say many times how valuable his defensive coordinator was to him and would express astonishment that Strong, an African-American, was not already a head coach someplace.)

The choice of a secondary coach was a slam dunk: Meyer always knew Chuck Heater would work on his staff again, ever since they were fired at Colorado State—one of four places they would work together.

"He's one of the best teachers," Meyer said of the Michigan grad. "He adapts his coaching style. He's nonstop teaching, nonstop coaching. There's no other coach I trust more than Chuck Heater because he's been through it all."

Heater, the old-school secondary coach, brought experience and savvy to the mix.

They briefly crossed paths in the mid-1980s when Chuck was secondary coach at Ohio State and Meyer was a graduate assistant. Heater remembers Urban as "a serious guy who took care of his business and worked really hard, but never drew a lot of attention to himself. He was just a grinder—which is kind of what he is today."

Heater and Meyer bonded at Colorado State, where they both lost their jobs under Earle Bruce. (Meyer was rehired by Sonny Lubick, but Heater wasn't.) "I'd never been fired before," Meyer said. "I come home, and this is after Sonny told me he couldn't keep me. My wife and I are sitting there and I'm distraught, like bankrupt distraught, like 'What am I going to do?' He [Heater] came walking through that door. He didn't call. He just showed up at my house. I'll never forget that for the rest of my life. He said, 'How you doin'? Just hang in there. I've been through it a few times.' He was the guy who guided me through that difficult time."

They hooked up again at Utah. Heater's call to Meyer in Salt Lake came as a surprise.

"He said, 'I understand you got a secondary spot open, defensive backfield,'" recalled Meyer. "I said, 'Who you got?' And he said, 'How about me?' He was at Washington. I said, 'Chuck, I can't pay you.' He said, 'Try it.' I go, 'You're kidding me.' Because I was already going to hire another guy. He called me and I said, 'Here's what I can pay you, if you want to come.'

"I went to the AD and got another fifteen grand so at least he wasn't in poverty. He changed our program. That year we went twelve and oh, he had a major impact on that team—major! We had no cornerbacks starting that season who had ever played and we ended up twelve and oh."

Heater was such a committed assistant that he slept in his office in Salt Lake for most of the first season until he could move his family. "I tried to keep it from Urban, because I knew he would feel badly about it," said Heater. "He kept asking me where I was living and I'd try to avoid telling him."

Heater was impressed to see how Meyer had advanced. Meyer was diligent in his chores, but not particularly upwardly mobile. Urban was more about getting the work in front of him done rather than campaigning to become a head coach. "And that kind of impressed me," said Heater. "He never worked at being a head coach. He worked at being a good coach."

Right before Heater's eyes, Meyer was maturing as a head coach.

"He was a duck to water—he knew it," said Heater. "He'd been taking really good notes, and he jumped in the seat behind that F-16 and he knew how to fly it. I've been around a lot of guys, so I see how comfortable they are in that leadership role. He was comfortable, had a tremendous vision, and knew what he wanted to get accomplished."

At Utah, Heater began his remarkable work of coaching up Ryan Smith and Bo Nagahi—"kids who had never played before," Meyer noted—to become starters. "Just like he did at Florida in our first year when he got Reggie Lewis to play and Vernell Brown to play," Meyer said.

That night in Glendale, Arizona, when Meyer looked over and saw Tremaine McCollum lined up to cover All–Big Ten Ohio State wide receiver Anthony Gonzales in the BCS championship game, he was reminded of Heater's teaching genius. McCollum had previously been buried on the depth charter at the start of the season as a third-string corner before becoming the No. 1 nickelback.

"And he does it," Meyer says of McCollum. "That's not supposed to happen."

Once again, together with safeties coach Doc Holliday, Chuck Heater made his magic, although he plays down that quality. Holliday was especially effective in the maturity of safety Reggie Nelson, the All American and winner of the 2006 Jack Tatum Award as the country's top defensive back. Nelson would be taken by the Jacksonville Jaguars as the overall twenty-first pick. (At the end of the 2007 season, Holliday returned to West Virginia, his alma mater, as associate head coach, coach of tight ends and fullbacks, and recruiting coordinator.)

Holliday was one of the few people Meyer hadn't known before, but took him upon the recommendation of former West Virginia coach Don Nehlen, for whom he has "a great deal of respect." Meyer wanted a recruiting machine: He got it in the guy whose real first name was John. (Holliday picked up the nickname from the legendary Old West figure and running mate of Wyatt Earp.)

"He's an 'octopus' when he recruits, because he wraps his tentacles around everybody," said Meyer. "He not only recruits the player, but also the thirteen to fourteen people around him. When I go out recruiting with him, he beats me senseless."

As an example, Meyer talks about the day he and Holliday buzzed through the small town of Belle Glade, Florida, just to meet the brother of a prized prospect. Deonte Thompson's brother "Speedy" worked for the water department.

"So here's the head football coach, national championship coach at Florida—didn't eat all day—and he's got me driving through Belle Glade sixty miles an hour to get to a crack in the sidewalk where the water main broke so I can say hello to his brother, Speedy. And we ended up getting Deonte."

Doc always knew how to recruit them, but he learned how to better guide and nurture players under Meyer.

"I think the thing I learned from Urban is how important that relationship is with the kids, how to get involved in their lives and how to develop their trust," Holliday said before departing for Morgantown. "We've always done that wherever I've been, but not to the extent that he does it. He's got a good scheme on both offense and defense, but just his managerial skills and the way he attacks things is really special."

Another key figure would be the strength and conditioning coach, whose role would be more important than normal in Meyer's strategy.

From a long, long time ago when he first watched Mickey Marotti work at the University of Cincinnati, Meyer had his eye on him. They became close friends at Notre Dame. "We kind of grew up in the coaching profession together and we think alike," Meyer said.

It was a given that Mickey, who holds a bachelor's from West Liberty State and masters from West Virginia and Ohio State, would be Meyer's first choice for that job.

Mattison had already been hired and left for Gainesville, but his wife Ann remained behind to oversee the packing. It took what Marotti called "a sign" at the Mattison residence for Marotti to see the light and finalize his decision. Mickey's wife, Susie, still wanted some assurances that Urban wouldn't be leaving Florida anytime soon because she was uprooting her family from her relatives in nearby Pittsburgh.

"Deep down we wanted to go, because we knew everybody and it's time to go," recalled Marotti. "We're all close and they are like my best friends. I'm talking to Urban, walking around the Mattisons' house as they're packing boxes. I look down . . . there's this stuff on the floor. And there's this picture." Mickey saw the sign he needed.

"There on the floor is an eight-by-ten photo of Greg Mattison and Urban Meyer, arm in arm, with their Notre Dame coaching gear on. And I said [on the phone to Meyer], 'All right, we're coming. I got the sign. That was it.'"

Urban felt Marotti was a key piece. "I have to have him. I *have* to have him!" said Urban.

By hiring Marotti and pairing him with Matt Balis, the strength and conditioning coach at Utah, Urban knew he had the strongest possible combination. Matt and his wife, Lanette, became part of the Gator family and, following the national championship season in 2006, he went on to become the strength and conditioning coach at Virginia.

"Matt was an integral part of our team and player development. He was tremendous," said Meyer.

Strength and conditioning is a vital part of Meyer's program.

"That whole position has created a value of its own for the last ten years," Meyer said. "He's [Marotti] the most valuable guy on your staff. He's a motivator. He disciplines. He's in the middle of every kid's life.

He has them over at his house constantly. His wife, Susie, is involved. He's the best there is in college football."

Probably nobody works closer with Meyer than offensive coordinator Dan Mullen, who was there from the beginning when Urban began crafting the Spread. Mullen also is entrusted with the crown jewels: He gets to call plays, but with the oversight and veto power of Meyer.

Starting at Notre Dame as a graduate assistant from Syracuse, Mullen was brash, outspoken, and sometimes annoying.

"I was ready to fight him when I first met him. He was asking, pushing, 'Why are you doing it this way? Wouldn't it be better to do it this way?'" Meyer said. "I had been a receiver coach for sixteen years at the highest level, and here comes some GA guy who's going to challenge me? I wanted to say, 'You want to just shut your mouth and go set the cones up for me as my GA?' But then you start listening to him talk, and he's got a great mind for football. And when you cut through all the six or seven layers, he's a great person. Now those layers aren't there anymore."

That same confidence, that honesty, from the New Hampshire native soon endeared him to Meyer enough to become his offensive chess master.

"He's grown as much as any coach I've been around," Meyer said. "To think that he's the offensive coordinator. I always knew mentally he could do it, but [his] maturity and people skills needed improvement. But he's always had a great mind for football. We challenge each other, talk about it, think about it. Have very similar beliefs on how to move the football. But now his people skills and his ability to lead have really improved and he's using each to become a better coach. He was nowhere near that—on a different planet for a while."

Tebow calls it an "ongoing relationship" with his quarterback coach, which began when he was still playing at Nease High School near Jacksonville. He wasn't terribly fond of Mullen and almost didn't come to Florida.

Tebow had become friends with then head coach Mike Shula of Alabama and hadn't yet befriended Mullen. Also, frankly, Mullen had another quarterback prospect he liked as much as Tebow.

The uncertainty of their relationship caused them to get off to a slow start, but it would soon evolve into a close friendship. If it hadn't, Tebow might have been wearing a Crimson uniform with a big "A" on the helmet. Despite his love for the Gators—because Gainesville was only sixty-five miles away and because of his fondness for Meyer—he was giving Tuscaloosa strong consideration. Tebow said he prayed about it and decided to sign with Florida.

"Tim almost didn't come to Florida because of him [Mullen]. We had to overcome our quarterback coach to get Tim Tebow to come here," Meyer said, laughing at the irony. Tebow's father and his high school coach warned Meyer of that. And Meyer points out that Mullen has had the same kind of beginning relationship with every quarterback he's ever coached.

"Chris Leak had that problem and wound up loving Dan. Josh Harris [Bowling Green] didn't like Dan at first," said Meyer. "Now he and Josh talk all the time. When he first got Alex Smith [Utah] they didn't hit it off right away. He and Alex are best friends now. Alex invited him to go to the NFL draft."

In fact, Mullen and his Utah quarterback became so close that Dan asked him to be in his wedding when he married Megan. "That's when he started calling me Dan," said Mullen. "I told him, 'if you're going to be in my wedding, you don't have to call me 'Coach' anymore.'"

Mullen, who holds a bachelor's from tiny Ursinus and a master's from Wagner College, admits that he was "tough to get to know, and right at the beginning I was a little rough around the edges," but said that during the recruiting process he and Tebow became friends and he felt they had "a good personality mix."

Like Tebow, Mullen has a strong drive to win. "I love football and I want to win and I want my quarterbacks to be the best in the country," Mullen said.

By nature a perfectionist, Mullen demands excellence from all his quarterbacks and that means paying attention to the tiniest details of execution. And, as he has proven in his short tenure as an offensive assistant, the final product speaks for itself.

Tebow's sense of humor and pleasant personality, plus a platinum work ethic, made Mullen's job much easier. Nevertheless, it took a while.

"It's hard getting used to," Tebow would say of Mullen's style with players, "and some of his tactics you don't always agree with. But it is meant to make you the best player you can be. Once you align with that and learn that, your relationship can grow and develop. He wants to win. He wants to do everything he can. As a player, hopefully that's what you want, and you're going to buy in and try to become the best that you can."

Over the first two years together, as they got to know each other, Tebow's passing mechanics, grasp of the offense, and leadership improved under Mullen. Tebow sometimes hung out at the Mullens' house in the off-season, chatting, watching movies, and sometimes winding up asleep on the sofa. (In December of 2008, before the national championship game, Mullen was named head coach at Mississippi State, but stayed to coach the game against Oklahoma.)

"He knows I have his best interest at heart," said Mullen. "Because I want to win and the best thing I can do to make that happen is to make him the best quarterback I can make him."

In those first two years, with one Heisman already to Tebow's credit, it would appear that Tebow and Mullen are doing just fine.

Mullen wasn't the only coach who almost lost a prized pupil. Meyer very nearly let his former player at CSU and current receivers coach get away. After one year at Florida, Billy Gonzales got so discouraged that he was about to take another job at a rival school for quite a bit more money.

"I got too hard on him," said Meyer, himself a former receivers coach. "That would have taken the wind out of my sails." Urban didn't say what changed the mind of Gonzales, but he was thankful that Billy stayed because he is such an integral part of making the Spread offense click. (Gonzales had to be retrieved again in 2009 when he received offers from rival Tennessee and the Cleveland Browns.)

Nobody plays a bigger part than the receiving coach, one of the toughest jobs on the staff—if for no other reason than he has to convince the receivers that they must become good blockers.

"To get a receiver to block is one of the most difficult things a coach has to do," said Meyer. Urban thinks Florida's receivers went from being "pathetic" blockers in 2005 to "the best in the country in 2006."

Gonzales, shuffling ten players in and out of the game to line up in various sets, often looks like a New York City traffic cop. His performance has impressed the boss.

"I think he does a great job," Meyer said. "He's a great father. Great husband. He's like a son to me."

While Gonzales was playing for Urban as a Ram, he saw qualities that would someday make him a solid head coach. "As a player, you knew he was going to be successful as a head coach because of the hard work, his desire, the passion for the game, and at the same time the influence that he had on us as players. He was always there for us," Gonzales said.

Gonzales was also building his coaching résumé after CSU, starting with small college jobs that led to Kent State. Meyer brought him to Bowling Green, then to coach at Utah, where he developed all-conference receivers Paris Warren and Steve Savoy, two Utes who helped lead their team to an unbeaten season and Fiesta Bowl win. At Florida, Gonzales inherited senior Chad Jackson, then developed Andre (Bubba) Caldwell, Percy Harvin, Cornelius Ingram, and Louis Murphy into topflight receivers.

For offensive line coaches, Meyer chose two familiar faces and then interchanged them. Steve Addazio coached tight ends in 2005, then switched over to the offensive line. Following Notre Dame, Addazio spent two years at Indiana before he was summoned by Meyer.

"Steve, if you take football away, we'd be real close friends," Meyer said. "But it's hard to be close friends when you're the head coach and he's the assistant. I love him, I love his family, his approach, his outlook. Steve and his wife [Kathy] love players. He's the same kind of guy as me. You say, 'OK, Steve, let's go around the world six times and then go play golf.' And he'd say, 'Why? I'd rather go play with my son Louie.'"

It says something that Meyer and Addazio, who consider themselves recruiting road warriors, met up on the recruiting trail when they were recruiting a lineman from Central Bucks High in eastern Pennsylvania.

"I was kind of checking him out, so that I could see how Notre Dame recruited—Notre Dame was larger-than-life to me, because I grew up Italian/Catholic," recalled Addazio, who holds double degrees from Central Connecticut State.

The next time they hooked up, Meyer was in South Bend and Addazio had been hired by his friend Kevin Rogers, who was then offensive coordinator for the Irish and became the quarterback coach for the Minnesota Vikings.

"I loved the way he [Meyer] coached the wide receivers," said Addazio. "He was like a line coach. He was up in their jug, on 'em—he was a wild man and I just loved that about him. I always felt he was a real guy. Hardworking. Wears emotions on his sleeve. Got a lot of juice. Kind of how I am, and was."

Because they were friends, they stayed in touch as Meyer began his ascendance. When Willingham came in at Notre Dame, Addazio was let go. So he went to work for Gerry DiNardo at Indiana, who was fired after Addazio's second year there. Then came the phone call. Around 11:00 A.M. in mid-December 2004, Addazio was offered a job at Florida. In three hours he was packed and on a flight to Gainesville—the first staff member to arrive.

"I'm really grateful," Addazio said. "When you get a head job like this at Florida, people come out of the woodwork. You've got a lot of friends, but you've got to hire the best people for the job. It was real meaningful that he had enough faith in me to hire me. We were friends and that's all well and good, but everybody knows you can't always hire friends. I'm forever grateful to come down here and be a part of this whole deal . . . And I didn't want to let him down. I just love the hell out of him, to tell you the truth."

Besides, if Meyer was Captain Emergency, he needed the other superhero with him—"Captain Panic," as the emotional Addazio was nicknamed.

"There was always a crisis," Addazio said, laughing at his reputation as a Mr. Get-It-Done-Now-or-Else guy. (With the departure of Mullen, Addazio was named offensive coordinator. Meyer hired quarterback coach Scot Loeffler from the Detroit Lions via Michigan. Both Tebow and backup Johnny Brantley said in the spring of 2009 that Loeffler had helped their throwing mechanics already.)

John Hevesy, a Maine grad who began as offensive line coach and moved to tight ends/line, was coaching at Brown when he was hired at Bowling Green by Meyer.

"We've been together for the duration," Meyer said. "I first met him when I was at Notre Dame. He did a brilliant job at Utah. Kind of took over that offensive line."

Hevesy thinks listening and learning from others has been one reason for Meyer's ability to stay ahead of the curve.

"His mentors are Earle Bruce, Lou Holtz, Bob Davie, Sonny Lubick. And each of them has his own little niche," said Hevesy. "He takes something from each of them. You hear them all talk and you know where he got it from. It's not all coach Holtz, or all coach Bruce, or coach Lubick . . . it's some from each. Or, I don't know, maybe it's his dad. They give him ten things and he takes four of them. And that's staying ahead of the curve."

Meyer's No. 1 asset as a coach, Hevesy says, is the ability to motivate. "I don't think I can ever say that in seven years that I can recall kids coming out and not playing hard," Hevesy said. "They're always ready to play. Maybe if we weren't ready to play or somebody was better than us, but never because the kids were not motivated to play."

As a team, Hevesy and Addazio coached and developed such players as tackles Phil Trautwein, Lance Butler, Carlton Medder, Jason Watkins, and Randy Hand; centers Steve Rissler, Mike Degory, and Drew Miller; guards Jim Tartt and Tavares Washington.

The replacement hire for Hevesy, who went to Mississippi State, was tight ends coach Brian White, former assistant at Harvard, Washington, and Syracuse who had spent eleven seasons as the offensive coordinator and running backs coach at Wisconsin.

Urban first met Stan Drayton when he was hired, briefly, at Bowling Green. "He stayed about three months," said Meyer.

Even though they parted by mutual consent and Stan went to the camp of an archrival (Tennessee), Meyer still says, "He's got a great family, and he's a great father, great husband."

Although popular with his peers and regarded as a good recruiter, Drayton wasn't getting the production out of his running backs. Also ball security, which is one of the four mantras of Urban Meyer's Plan to Win, became a serious issue. So did the inability of some backs to learn pass blocking.

Kenny Carter was eventually brought in from Vanderbilt to replace Drayton. Carter's presentation on ball security impressed the boss. That staff replacement was followed by the hiring of a new cornerbacks coach, Vance Bedford of Michigan, who was a member of Bruce's staff at Colorado State when Meyer coached there. Bedford's Wolverine secondary had played effectively against the Gators in their bowl loss to Michigan.

That meant Heater would move over to coach the safeties.

If they didn't already know it, all of the coaches would learn Urban's Way, including immersion in the lives of their players, putting a high priority on their comportment and education. The word "discipline" would take on a different definition from what most coaches consider it to be:

"Discipline," says Meyer, "is ninety percent anticipation, not reaction. Everybody thinks discipline is making him do one hundred wind sprints. No, discipline is, if the kid's an alcoholic, get him to a counselor before it becomes an issue. Discipline is also if you hear there's a big party going on and there's going to be a problem, not wake up in the morning and hope something's not wrong—or, if there is, then punish them. That's not's discipline.

"Discipline is making sure you talk to them before that party and then have someone there if it happens. So that's in our book. It comes straight from Coach Bruce." Which, of course, means that it also came from Woody Hayes. Now this third generation of Woody-isms, handed down by Earle, would make their way into the fabric of Florida football.

With his all-star staff intact, Meyer was off and running toward the ultimate prize.

13

The Spread for Arizona

The first day Urban Meyer set foot on Gainesville soil as the official coach of the Florida Gators and announced that he would run the Spread offense, he drew mostly blank stares and some obligatory nodding of heads.

Some of us football snobs pretended we knew all about this potent, exotic Utah Spread, which in 2004 averaged more than 46 points and 520 yards per game. We even knew his unbeaten Utes hadn't trailed at halftime all season, but were still not convinced it was right for this level of play.

This wasn't the Mountain West Conference, and a wide-open offense wasn't new to the Gator Nation.

After all, hadn't Steve Spurrier spread the field with his receivers and "pitched it around" effectively against SEC competition?

It wasn't going to be an easy sell. But Meyer soft-pedaled his offensive theories and wrapped them inside his message about education, discipline, and support of the Gator program as he took it on the road.

In the spring of 2005, Meyer played to packed houses on a statewide tour of twenty-two Gator Clubs in such places as Jacksonville, Tampa,

Orlando, Lakeland, Ocala, Leesburg, Melbourne, Fort Myers, Palm Beach, Fort Lauderdale, Miami—all of them showing substantial increases in attendance over the last year. People sometimes asked him about the Spread, but really, nobody understood it. His messages about the new program resonated with crowds, which were clearly buzzed about the man who would be asked to restore the glory to Gator football. The tough talk, however, would need to translate into wins.

Those of us who had been around Gator football for many decades were anxious to see what Urban Meyer was all about. The first taste was in the Orange and Blue spring game, which drew a record fifty-eight thousand fans to the Swamp for a glimpse of the future.

We thought the Spread was just a formation and questioned whether it could work against SEC football defenses.

Turns out we were fairly ignorant about that which we spoke.

"What do you call your offense?" I had asked Meyer on December 7, 2004, the day of his first press conference.

'The Spread," he answered.

"No, I mean, do you have a name for it? Like 'the Mountain West Offense?' Or maybe you could call it the 'Southeast Coast Offense,' " I said jokingly.

"That's for you guys to decide," he said politely.

We still didn't realize the Spread merely represented a concept in which to showcase the best players. There was talent at Florida, but because of injuries and the lack of depth at wide receiver, the offensive results in 2005 wouldn't prove to be a fair representation. Among the missing pieces was a running quarterback. Meyer could live with Chris Leak as the starter by making some adjustments. Trouble was, he waited a little late in the season to make them.

Although the Spread didn't blow anybody away in Meyer's first season, he would eventually make believers out of skeptics, as well as most of the SEC opponents—many of whom would copy his offense. But what was the Spread offense and where did it come from?

I had begun to trace the roots of the Spread. Having been taught by veteran football coaches over the years that there was nothing really new in the game—that it all just goes around in cycles—there had to be something in the archives. I found out that Dutch Meyer had run the Spread formation at Texas Christian University in a scheme much like Urban's direct snap, four or five wide receiver formation.

Feeling pretty smug about my discovery, I sprang it on Meyer.

"Did you know that the Spread was first run in this country many years ago?"

"No."

I explained that the version of the Spread run by TCU's Meyer—and Coach Matty Bell before him—had been the perfect offense for Slingin' Sammy Baugh, who led the Horned Frogs to consecutive postseason victories in the 1936 Sugar Bowl and 1937 Cotton Bowl. "And I might add," noted author and TCU expert Dan Jenkins had told me, "that with Baugh and O'Brien, Dutch mixed in the double wing and triple wing with the Spread."

I could tell from Meyer's expression that he was not all that impressed.

Meyer had frequently tolerated people like me asking questions and making uninformed comments about the Spread without losing his patience.

Finally, he'd had enough. It was time to set the record straight all these years later.

"First of all," he said, "there is no 'offense.' We don't have an offense. People say the Spread, because we like to spread the field. It's all personnel dictated. If I get some really fast receivers here, I'm convinced we can win with the Wishbone—if you have good players, you can win. So that's why I always take offense at that."

OK, I get a half point for saying the Spread was a formation, right? Well, not really.

"When you start saying the Spread offense can't work . . . no, not if you have bad players. Can you run the I formation? Yeah, Eddie George did it real well. Can you run the Spread offense? Well, yes, if you have Tim Tebow and Percy Harvin, Louis Murphy and those kinds of guys. But if you don't have those receivers, you can't win the SEC."

So it turns out that the secret of the Spread is the same secret of the Wishbone, the West Coast offense, the I formation, and the Single Wing: If you've got superb material, you can win with any of those.

It's more about recruiting—getting the right people on the bus—than it is about calling ball plays and formations.

Nothing infuriates Meyer more than for a coach to say he can't run a certain offense because he doesn't have the right players. When he hears somebody say he wasn't successful because he ran a West Coast offense and he "didn't have a West Coast quarterback," Meyer goes bonkers. So he couldn't blame Chris Leak for a lack of success in the 2005 season. It wasn't so much about Leak's deficiencies as a runner as it was about his not having enough deep threats that first year.

Anyway, Meyer would never use that as a crutch, because he thinks that is a flimsy excuse for a coach.

"If I'm the athletic director, I walk down the hall and fire him immediately," said Meyer. "Because your job as a coach is to utilize your personnel, not to design some scheme. There's no magic scheme. You better get your tail out and recruit, because the result is that it changes and you need to match your personnel."

It took Urban half the season in 2005 to adjust, but he finally did it. We didn't know it yet, but we had only seen a mere shadow of the Spread.

But what, exactly, was the Spread?

"When you say 'the Spread,' do mean just like 'spread the field'? Meyer asked. "Because there are a lot of people who use that word 'spread.'

"Here's what that word means: 'Spread' is a style of offense. Like, Steve Spurrier doesn't run the Spread—or, at least our Spread. He might spread the field and try to throw it. With a 'spread formation'—that means the Rich Rodriguez (Michigan), Gary Crowton (LSU), Urban Meyer version—we're trying to equate numbers. That means we'll never hand the ball to an offensive player if every player is not blocked."

Now I'm really getting confused—so the "Spread" is a formation, but the Meyer "Spread" is also an offensive philosophy, right?

Meyer was out of his chair, animated and laying it all out there like a football professor.

For the next twenty minutes I got schooled at Urban's personal, one-on-one "Instant Spread" clinic. He emphasized the importance of gaining advantages in numbers and matchups. As he had explained earlier, it was similar to basketball teams hoping to get three-on-two or two-on-one fast breaks.

I learned about quarterbacks reading defenses and leaving one player unblocked on the option play; about them looking for clues such as the "one high" and "two high" defenses, meaning one or two safeties—or maybe none.

Scribbling in my notebook, Meyer drew up a standard defense with four down linemen, three linebackers, and four defensive backs— one safety, or "one high."

He talked about "plus" and "minus." The idea is for the offense to have one more blocker than they have defenders—or "plus one."

You've got six defenders over here, make sure you have no worse than an equal number of blockers.

"If we were just to turn around and hand the ball off," Meyer explained, counting off the blockers versus the defenders, "they have one-two-three-four-five-*six* on defense and we have one-two-three-four-*five* blockers—we are minus one. But because we are in the shotgun, we read one defender, we don't block him."

That's what Meyer calls "hats for hats on everybody." The quarterback reads the off-side end or linebacker, who goes unblocked, and at the point of attack he simply runs the option play.

The trouble with that defensive approach against the Spread is that it's predicated on single coverage and it frees up athletes such as Percy Harvin, who cannot be covered by one defender.

So the next move for the defense is "two high," or two deep safeties.

In his first meeting with quarterbacks every year, Meyer re-teaches the Spread. He will draw up a two-high defense, which features double coverage of receivers, and ask his quarterbacks what to do to "plus one" the defense. The answer: run the football.

"Now watch this," Meyer said, scribbling another set. "This is where recruiting comes in. This is why matchup football is important. This is what David Givens said to me that night [at Notre Dame]."

The third way to defend Meyer's offense, he said, is the "no deep" look. What some defensive coordinators will do, said Meyer, is to drop the second safety into "the box," and that leaves nobody deep in coverage.

"If they play no deep," said Meyer, "that gives them a one-man advantage. Except for one thing: This guy is Percy Harvin, that's Bubba Caldwell, that's C.I. [Cornelius Ingram], and that's Louis Murphy.

"Do you really have four players who can cover our four best receivers?"

The answer to that today is no.

So when quarterbacks see the no deep, they are trained to think about hitting the long pass and "we expect them to score."

Meyer put down the pen. "What I just told you," he said, "is the Spread offense."

Like every good teacher and coach, however, he wanted to review:

1. **One high: Equal numbers, you can run the ball and be OK. You're equal.**
2. **Two high: You're plus one. Run the ball, because they outnumber you in the passing game. They can double your receivers.**
3. **No deep. Can you run the ball (meaning just a hand-off)? No, they took the extra defender and put him in the box. Now there are two answers: You run option, or you throw it. And if you throw it, you better have a better checker (receiver) out there than their checker (defensive back).**

So in the end, what I learned is that this newfangled offense is really about recruiting the fastest and best players, putting them in favorable matchups on the field, and finding a way to getting them in space with the football. And, yes, it is kind of like basketball.

It was a good primer for a sportswriter of average intelligence, but there were still many questions, such as: Isn't this really another version of the single wing, especially when the offense is in the red zone? And weren't all those veteran coaches correct about trends being recycled every fifty years?

Indeed, there's a little bit of old school/new school in Meyer's offense, which is now being emulated by many of his SEC opponents. He noted that Tennessee, Kentucky, Vanderbilt, and Auburn had recently switched to some form of it. LSU ran components of it in 2007, mixed in with the I formation, in winning the national championship. Texas ran it in 2005 in winning the national championship. Meyer noted that the majority of the BCS teams winning bowls were having success with the Spread.

"Yes, it's the single wing to a T," said Meyer, not realizing the pun he had inadvertently just made. "The single wing is right back. And that's exactly what it is."

Meyer said Spurrier was ahead of his time and ran some facet of the Spread, but mostly in terms of formation. He is a huge admirer of Spurrier's individualism.

"He didn't care. If he wanted to throw it fifty times, he was going to throw it fifty times," Meyer said. "He did it when everyone else wasn't doing it. And he was different. I liked his aggressiveness and his breaking of the mold. He was the Spread offensive coach of the nineties, but it wasn't 'Spread Option.'"

Spurrier had long ago left town, however, and Gator fans were going to need education on the Spread.

At the first sign of struggle in the 2005 season, there would be some grousing about this Mountain West offensive mentality. Even some Gator players had doubts in the early indoctrination period of the offense and the physically demanding drills. Those same doubters would turn out to be the biggest Meyer advocates and future leaders, but at the beginning they balked at Urban's offensive philosophies and questioned the necessity for the harsh training tactics.

One such player was Jemalle Cornelius, who would become one of the captains of the national championship team.

"We definitely thought he was crazy," said Cornelius. "The first thing he did was when he came in and talked about there were going to be a lot of changes. He talked about the mat drills and the different things he had done at Bowling Green and Utah. I just remember me and a lot of guys were kinda like, 'Who does he think he is? This ain't Utah or Bowling Green. That stuff ain't going to work.'"

Early on, the thought of transferring occurred to some players, including Cornelius.

"It was January and we had this thing called Full Metal Jacket on Friday, and they had us in there doing all this crazy manual resistance stuff," said Cornelius, then a junior. "They're talking all this trash. The workout was so hard that it was to the point of 'Well, this is a new coach, do I need to transfer?' I didn't know if I could put up with this every Friday, with all them in your face and challenging you."

The days of the laid-back Florida athlete were soon over. As it got more competitive in the weight room and on the mats, however, the players began to respond. "They were trying to see who would break and who wouldn't," said Cornelius. "I think that right there was the turning point."

Another day in spring practice Meyer called all his receivers together after an unimpressive practice and showed them tape of his receivers at Utah running their routes—which didn't sit well with top flight players such as Cornelius, Chad Jackson, Bubba Caldwell, and Dallas Baker.

At the same time, Meyer was plugging holes in other places and had to find every able-bodied man. One of them turned out to be seldom used Vernell Brown, a mere 5' 8", 165-pound redshirt senior from right there in Gainesville who had already planned on getting his degree and leaving. He had been moved to defensive back the year before and didn't see much of a future. After his meeting with Meyer, Brown changed his mind because he was promised, "If you deserve to play, you'll be on the field."

Being in that first wave in the first season, Brown didn't know quite what to expect from Meyer. Along with others, he often wondered about some of the drills and how exactly they related to playing in a football game. "If you weren't strong-minded and didn't have any heart, man, you definitely wouldn't survive on his team," said Brown. "Because he put you through some stuff when at lot of times you looked at each other and said, 'What the hell are we doing this for?' and 'how does this pertain to football?'

"Later on down the road in a speech during practice or after practice or before a game, he refers to that kind of stuff. And that's when it comes around to you: 'So this is why we did that!' Regardless of how out of the ordinary the exercise or drill seemed to us, it always came back around and tied in somewhere in the game of football."

As a physically fit athlete who considered himself a "workout warrior," even Vernell found out in early 2005 how tough such events as the "Valentine's Day Massacre" in the weight room could be.

Over the summer, the players met at nearby Lake Wauburg at 8:00 A.M. Once he got into the drills, Brown said, "I thought I was training to be a navy SEAL."

Out of all this came a starting cornerback retrieved from the scrap heap who, under the tutelage of Chuck Heater, became a solid player. Brown was such an important part of Meyer's program that he became Urban's first "Face of Florida Football," as a player who earned his job the hard way with his platinum work ethic and inspired his teammates.

Brown also later became instrumental in helping Meyer counsel teammate Cornelius Ingram, the promising tight end/receiver from Hawthorne who had decided to quit the Florida team. Through that friendship and the willingness to listen to Brown, "C.I." eventually stayed, became a starter, and developed into a key player for the team's future.

When Meyer came along for the 2005 season, most players didn't really know what to expect.

Others lost their way, such as Reggie Lewis of Jacksonville, a promising wide receiver recruit who was originally going to LSU when Ron Zook talked him out of it. Lewis says he "got off to a rough start and I wasn't playing like I should be" in his early years under Zook. He was getting discouraged and was about to transfer when Meyer came aboard and found a way to appeal to Reggie's competitive nature as a defensive back. Later, Lewis became a starter in Urban's first season, and Meyer began to look for ways to motivate his cornerback.

The road ahead for the 2005 squad was full of surprises. Right off they were introduced to Meyer's philosophy of earning your way. The new coach stripped down some of the old ways and even threatened to dismantle some traditions such as the Gator head—or so they thought.

At the same time, players could also be making progress toward their membership in the Champions Club, which would reward them at another level for their "investment."

Meyer would wind up keeping the Gator head, which suddenly reappeared one day, along with some other remnants of past glory. After all, it had worked fairly well.

Most of us in the media didn't really know what to expect.

Could Urban Meyer make us forget Steve Spurrier? Well, no, but could he at least put the Gators back into contention for the SEC title?

Entering into my fifth decade of observing and writing about the Gators, I was both curious and a little skeptical, not having seen Bowling Green or Utah play but a couple of times.

Nobody said it wasn't going to be fun, however—especially for those of us who consider watching Florida football a privilege.

Although you can never escape your passion, I once put mine on hold, leaving the sports writing profession, moving to New York and Colorado—even getting out of the newspaper business. Your passions always find you, however.

I heard my first University of Florida football game on the radio, circa 1950, and it became my theater of sports. As a preteen, I acted out my fantasies in the living room of my Ocala home, listening to "the Voice of the Gators," Otis Boggs, while dodging imaginary tacklers, stiff-arming chairs.

This was a connection for life. I still remember Kynes, Montsdeoca, Griffin, Hunsinger, D'Agostino, French, Jumper, Oosterhoudt, Poucher, Oswald, and the like. I saw my first game at age thirteen.

To grow up and get paid for covering Gator football games was the equivalent of Willie Sutton being hired as a bank teller.

The spectacularly colorful drive on autumn Saturdays from Ocala to Gainesville on old U.S. Highway 441 was worth the trip alone—a journey I have taken hundreds of times and yet never get tired of making.

Over the years, I had seen Florida Field more than double in size and witnessed the growth of the program from consistent mediocrity to consistent excellence. When you start out watching Bob Woodruff's teams, everything else looks like a July Fourth fireworks display.

I'd personally interviewed the last ten Gator coaches. Meyer struck me differently from the rest, yet nobody measured up to Steve Spurrier in my eyes.

Spurrier, coach No. 19 at Florida, was the gold standard.

Without Ray Graves, No. 14, there would have been no Spurrier, discovered by Graves's brother at Science Hill High School in Johnson City, Tennessee. Graves had taken over for Bob Woodruff, No. 13, fired because he thought offense was from the evil empire.

Graves was moved upstairs prematurely to accommodate the transition to Doug Dickey, No. 15, a move that was bungled by back-room politics.

Charley Pell, No. 16, brought Gator fans pride in their school colors and rebuilt the infrastructure, but got caught cheating and was fired.

Galen Hall, No. 17, was a good football coach, but not media savvy or pretty enough, so he was fired, and Gary Darnell, No. 18, held the reins for fives games until Spurrier arrived.

Ron Zook, Florida's twentieth head coach, was a decent, hard-working, honest man with the near impossible task of trying to follow the Gators' greatest coach. He was relieved by Charlie Strong, No. 21, as an interim until Urban arrived.

Spurrier had been such a favorite of mine that some of my friends and newspaper readers got tired of reading about him—even my own doctor. I was undergoing a physical examination from my Alabama-educated physician, Dr. Jerry Cohen, when he said, "All you media guys love Spurrier because he gives you good interviews."

It was true, but I lied.

"No, because he wins. Don't you still miss Bear Bryant?"

"Yes," the doctor admitted sheepishly. "And my life is pretty much over."

Help would eventually be on the way in Tuscaloosa; Alabama hired Nick Saban.

Help had already arrived at the Swamp.

I covered the debut of Florida's twenty-second head coach on opening night, 2005. He would come away with his fifth straight opening-day win as Florida beat Wyoming, 32–14.

Truth be known, he'd heard all about the Swamp and its loud, impassioned fans, but Urban wasn't terribly impressed at the noise when he took the field for the first game—but said he played along as if he were bowled over.

"Running through the tunnel—it was everything [former Gator] Lito Sheppard said it would be," Meyer said, indulging the fans and the media. "That's as big time as it gets for a home game."

OK, it was a little bit of an exaggeration, but he had expected so much more (eventually he would get it).

The following week against Louisiana Tech, Florida won, 41–3, and the crowd didn't get all that amped up either. The excitement was about to unfold the next week, however, with the Tennessee Vols coming to town, because Florida had lost to them the last two times at home and three of the last four times overall. And Urban was about to get baptized in the SEC Holy Wars.

For Tennessee, 90,716 were in Ben Hill Griffin Stadium, the most people ever to see a football game in the state of Florida—college or pro or even the Super Bowl—and bodies were flying all over the turf. "That was like seeing two sledgehammers going at each other," Meyer said after his Gators beat the Vols, 16–7, to win their third in a row.

About that crowd? This time Urban got an earful.

"When Dee Webb blocked that field goal," he said of the play by his starting corner and special teams player, "I was kind of waving and my headset slipped back and I heard that crowd. And I thought a jet had landed in the stadium. That's the loudest I've ever heard it anywhere."

This time he really meant it.

While the Gator Nation was getting educated on the Spread, Urban was getting educated on the road woes of playing in the SEC.

With Andre Caldwell injured in the Tennessee game and without a depth of talent at wide receiver, the Gator offense ran up against defenses that put the extra safety in the box and made life tough for Chris Leak. One of those teams was LSU, and the result in Baton Rouge that day was not pretty, as Leak and his unit struggled in a 21–17 loss. But even that had been an improvement over what had happened in Tuscaloosa two weeks earlier when the Tide clobbered the Gators 31–3.

Fears and doubts about the Spread were rearing their ugly heads. After the tough loss in Baton Rouge, a columnist wrote:

> There is the matter of the paltry 99 yards rushing and 107 yards passing with four sacks Saturday. With only half an offense and without the talent to run Meyer's "spread option," it's not likely to get better. You can't rely on the other team gift-wrapping five turnovers every Saturday as LSU did.
>
> I'm not seeing a lot of conviction in this offense, nor am I seeing improvement. In fact, it's becoming more predictable by the week. Meyer admits his players are still far behind the learning curve and that all he has been able to install so far is the base offense.
>
> There are no game-breakers in the lineup. With Andre Caldwell gone for the season, the Gator offense lacks that breakaway speed that can turn a game around. Yes, Dallas Baker and Chad Jackson are solid receivers, but they can't seem to get open much in clutch situations.
>
> There isn't even a good trick play in the bag.
>
> Chris Leak is Chris Leak—and he's never going to be an option quarterback. And though DeShawn Wynn has improved—Meyer said he believes after Saturday that he's become "a real Florida Gator tailback"—you can't build an offense around him.
>
> Say this for the defense: They've played hard and keep their team in the game, but getting the ball back for the offense doesn't seem to end in a good result most of the time.
>
> The game against LSU was there for the taking. The Gators had three cracks in the final eight minutes, but couldn't generate any points.
>
> With an off week to get healthier before the showdown in Jackson-

*ville with SEC East leader Georgia, Urban Meyer has a lot to work
on these next two weeks. He's going to need it.*

The guy who wrote that was me.

The lesson learned in 2005 was that to win on the road in the
SEC, Meyer was going to need a more consistent offensive attack, and
that without all the components to run the Spread as it should be run,
he would have to adapt. He hadn't been minding the store. Because
Meyer was out and about most of the year on his exhaustive public
relations tour, Florida's offense hadn't received the kind of attention it
needed from the head coach.

Meyer gives himself a poor grade for not adjusting his personnel
quickly enough during the 2005 season, partly because he was so busy
trying to change the attitude of the student body and the football culture. Almost every night during the week, Meyer was out speaking to
a fraternity or a student group about bringing the factions together. He
pushed himself to the point of exhaustion.

There was a dichotomy between the students and the football
team, largely because of a brawl Zook's team got into with a fraternity,
and Meyer wanted that to heal. But it would come with a price.

"He'd [Meyer] practice for three and a half hours," said Assistant
Athletics Director for Sports Information Steve McClain, "and then
he'd get in the car and go speak to three fraternities every night." This
was a routine he'd learned from Earle Bruce. Except at Colorado State,
Bruce didn't also have the twenty-two Gator Clubs at which to speak
as Urban did in his first year.

"If I'd kept doing that," Meyer said, "I'd be ten toes up."

By the time Florida reached the Georgia game, having lost two of
its last three games, some thought his team might be going ten toes up.
With a 5-2 record and facing the unbeaten Bulldogs, some changes
had to be made—especially in the sagging offense.

That's exactly what Meyer did for the Georgia game. After meeting with his offensive coaches on the Sunday after the LSU loss, he
brought back Billy Latsko from the defensive side to play fullback and
used a tight end to pass protect. Options on offense were limited once
Dallas Baker was injured and Chad Jackson's hamstring slowed him.

During bad times, Urban turns to the more veteran coaches on his staff in late-night meetings and sometimes seeks phone counsel from Earle Bruce and Lou Holtz.

"That night at my house, after LSU, I had Dan Mullen and Steve Addazio come over until the early morning hours," said Meyer. "Instead of complaining about how bad we were at certain positions, we changed our whole offense that night."

Against the unbeaten Bulldogs, Leak took the Gators 80 yards on the opening drive. Meyer pulled out all stops, including a fake punt, which didn't produce any points but took valuable time off the clock as Florida hung on to win, 14–10. After pulling off the successful fake punt, Meyer noted that punter Eric Wilbur "was better than any playmaker" at his disposal. His defense also held.

Out of that stellar defensive performance, the names of Reggie Nelson and Reggie Lewis began to crop up. Nelson had seven tackles and would duplicate those numbers the next week against Vanderbilt and again against FSU.

The Commodores gave the Gators a scare, as Jay Cutler took them to overtime before Lewis's game-clinching interception salvaged a 49–42 victory. Meyer had called for somebody to "make a play" on a sideline huddle, but few had expected it would be Lewis, who was starting because of a season-ending broken fibula to Brown.

Then came the one that really stung Urban: A 30–22 loss to Steve Spurrier in his first head-to-head matchup, just three weeks after the LSU loss. Urban was so upset after the trip to Columbia that he had the captain park the airplane and called a team meeting at the gate, challenging any potential quitters to leave the team.

Vernell Brown said the flight home from Columbia and the subsequent brouhaha on the plane may have been the turning point for the program.

The flight attendant made an announcement over the intercom, catching everyone by surprise, "Coach Meyer would like to see everybody, so please remain in your seats."

Brown was figuring there would be a short announcement and they'd be on their way home.

"This turned into—and I kid you not!—an hour-and-a-half or

two-hour speech," said Brown. "He's got everybody on the back of the plane coming up front and standing up. And it was basically a man-to-man, heart-to-heart speech. I think that was a turning point. Instead of guys going off in left field, they went to right field, the way they were told to go.

"I think we were at a turning point then, coming off a loss to South Carolina . . . especially with the things that we could have lost had we not lost that game . . . and that was one of the tactics he used, having that man-to-man conversation in front of each and every one. Not letting anybody get off the plane and not talking to this person and that person, but talking to everybody!

"He let you know that if you didn't want a part of this, now was the time to leave. 'If you want to get off, get off now. But when it's all said and done, we're going to get the train back on the track with you or without you.'"

Meyer's concern was that his team was losing and it lacked quality depth. "What ate me up was not only the loss, but who's gonna make plays for us?" he said. "Was it that somebody just didn't play good, or somebody's got a sprained ankle and will be back? Or, 'We're not very good.' And that was my concern against Georgia, 'we're not very good.' Especially on offense."

He knew that he was lacking offensive talent, so he did what had to be done: "We went out and recruited for it."

There would be no trip to Atlanta for the SEC title game, but some of the pain of the South Carolina loss was eased by a 34–7 thumping of Florida State, which got Meyer and his Gators to the postseason.

Florida beat Iowa in the Outback Bowl, 31–24—thanks in part to a fake-punt call—and finished a respectable 9-3.

The first season of what may become the most exciting era in the history of University of Florida sports was under way. This would be the setting of the table for what would happen in Arizona a year later. But there needed to be a different kind of "butter" on that table, which was the symbolism Meyer used for reevaluation of the Gators' road routine.

14

The SEC Stairway to Heaven

Nobody could really blame Chris Leak for being a little skeptical on how the 2006 season was going to go down. The highly recruited senior from North Carolina must have felt like a quarterback without a country who had been asked to call signals in three different languages, given all the offensive coordinators he'd been coached by in three seasons.

No wonder Leak had taken a while to find his bearings. Starting as a freshman under Ron Zook's quarterback coach, Ed Zaunbrecher, Leak was then handed off as a sophomore to Larry Fedora. As a junior he was introduced to Dan Mullen and a new system, an even more radical departure. After a rocky start between the two in 2005—Mullen admits, "I take some getting used to"—there would be an eventual meeting of the minds and development of a trusting relationship.

The 2006 season wasn't starting out all that well, either. Leak's own coaches and teammates accused him of poor leadership. Down the stretch, his teammates would challenge his manhood. And the critics began to wonder if Leak was the right driver of an offensive machine that was built for a more physical quarterback.

Now in his final season, Leak would also be asked to share duties with true freshman sensation Tim Tebow. Would this ever end? Was this superstud-rock-star-campus-hero-freshman-kid Tebow trying to steal his cheese, too? His coach assured him that wouldn't happen.

"The day we signed Tim Tebow," said Meyer, "I called Chris and said, 'We've signed Tim Tebow, but you're our quarterback.' And he said, 'Thanks, I needed to hear that.'"

The experts all said the two-headed, Leak-Bow quarterbacking monster just couldn't work. There was simply too much difference between them: The righty and the lefty, senior and freshman, the African-American and the Caucasian, the show pony and the pack mule.

Leak was the starter. Tebow would come off the bench in short yardage situations and, like a smashmouth fullback, polish off the final few yards of the drive for the touchdown—after Leak had done all the heavy lifting. That's how it must have felt in the innermost ego of Chris Leak. But if so, you'd never have known it.

Meyer and Dan Mullen kept a tight lid on things and refused to allow petty jealousies between Leak and Tebow to arise and creep into the huddle.

Tebow was clearly the crowd favorite, bounding with the joy of a frisky puppy dog suddenly detached from its leash. Each time No. 15 jogged onto the field, electricity rippled through the Florida section of the stands. Nothing, however, could alter Leak's focus or deprive him of his anointment as the wiser, more mature, more experienced quarterback.

Besides, Leak had the backing of the boss. Meyer made sure to reinforce the fact that Leak, not Tebow, was the starting quarterback— and that simply wasn't going to change.

As a result, not only was the two-headed quarterback monster tamed, but the talents of Leak and Tebow were blended so perfectly that the desired result was exceeded. So efficient was the Leak-Bow model that admiring coaches around the country would eventually emulate it.

The success of the two-quarterback system at Florida didn't come about by chance, but out of Meyer's conviction that he needed to get the best players on the field. Urban knew after seeing Tebow in the spring game before his freshman season in 2006 that he was coaching a "once-in-a-lifetime" player.

"Chris was an excellent quarterback, but you have this weapon. And you have to use it. How do you do that?" Meyer said.

Meyer had noodled over that dilemma all summer. "Not many people have had success running a two-quarterback system," said Meyer. "And especially when they are very different. If you have two of the same type players, like I know coach Spurrier did, then you rotate them and there's no issue. But these are two very different personalities—very different strengths and weaknesses. How do we make that work?"

Therein lies the true originality of Meyer, who won't hesitate to go against the grain of the coachthink. Especially when he knows the gamble is worth it.

"You have to play him [Tebow]," Meyer said. "It's not fair not to. But then how do you handle the ego of another great player, Chris Leak, and do right by both of them? And ultimately, win games? That occupied about ten hours of my day."

It was ten hours well spent. After a slow start, Leak would find his grooves. Leak was the passer and the field general of the long drives. Tebow would immediately find his new niche, becoming the short yardage back who compensated for the lack of an inside power game. This ideal one-two changeup kept opposing defenses off balance. Even when opponents knew Tebow was coming, the 235-pound hammer was virtually unstoppable.

Meanwhile, for the first time in his career, Leak had the same coordinator for two successive seasons and that would eventually produce a comfort level, consistency in his game, and solidarity among his teammates.

While the Spread offense still didn't always hit on all cylinders, Leak was also backed up by a defense with seven NFL draft choices on it—including two first-rounders.

Thus the championship journey of Chris Leak was under way. But he would still encounter a few more rough patches. Even the offense would have to undergo change. More changes came, too, beginning in January before the title run. Leaders were being called out. Dallas Baker was one.

It had taken a while for Baker to grow up, although after a short stint in a Massachusetts prep school, he was playing football where he had wanted to play: Florida.

Baker's uncle, Wes Chandler, had become a star wide receiver at UF in the 1970s and gone on to a successful NFL career. Dallas had been a fan of Steve Spurrier's Fun 'n' Gun and arrived in Gainesville with a sense of history and a desire to excel for the team he had always loved. Dallas could even remember the names of the wide receivers who had played for the Ol' Ball Coach.

"I can name some of them back as far as Ernie Mills, Jack Jackson," Baker said proudly.

Yet Baker seemed to be taking things for granted early on. In 2004, away from the comforts of small-town New Smynra Beach, Florida, and on his own in Gainesville to play for Ron Zook, Dallas struggled with the temptations of his newfound freedoms. Studies were not a priority. He was sort of a team clown and seemed to put more effort into being funny than being a student. On the field, Baker's ample talents weren't enough to erase some of his bonehead plays in 2004. There needed to be some changes, but they would come slowly.

The first adjustment began in 2004 before Meyer's arrival—the night of Baker's sophomore season in Knoxville against the Vols when a stupid penalty may have cost his team the game. Baker engaged Vols defensive back Jonathan Wade in hand fighting, countering with a head slap, and as usual the officials only saw the retaliator. The subsequent personal-foul penalty, with 55 seconds left in the game, gave Tennessee the field position to drive down and win the game, 30–28, on a James Wilhoit field goal.

Baker kept making those types of blunders that season. He didn't run an all-out route on a key pass against LSU, and Florida lost the game, 24–21. He dropped a pass in a 38–31 loss to Mississippi State, a defeat that many people feel was the final straw in the firing of Zook.

Even with all his screwups, Baker ranked second on the team in touchdown catches that season, thus beginning to earn his nickname Dallas Baker, the Touchdown Maker, proffered by Gator Radio Network play-by-play man Mick Hubert. Without a midcareer switch in direction, however, he might have become known as Dallas Baker, the Trouble Maker.

Once Meyer arrived on campus in December of 2004 and held his team meeting, Baker could sense things were going to be different. He just didn't realize that meant for him, too.

"He said, 'I understand some of you guys may not want to be here,'" Baker said. "He told us some of us needed to grow up. Some guys were upset . . . they thought maybe he was going to be too strict."

That's when Meyer introduced them to Captain Pain, Mickey Marotti.

"He [Marotti] was telling us how to work out," recalled Baker. "We used gloves so that we wouldn't scratch our hands [in lifting]. The first thing he told us was we weren't going to be able to wear gloves. We felt like, 'Well, this is going to be a completely new school.' A couple of guys were kind of butting heads with him, saying it behind his back: 'Who does he think he is?' I was from New Smyrna, where you were taught to say 'yessir' and 'no sir.' I wasn't too hardheaded."

Yet another wakeup call coming for the gangly 6'3" Baker, who figured he was ready to buy in for a new start with the arrival of Meyer. But he wasn't really prepared for the chewing out he was about to get from his new coach. Among other things, Meyer informed Dallas that his teammates thought he was funny "but they don't think you're very smart."

Here came the Meyer missive about poor academic habits and the importance of Baker getting his degree.

"In the summer I was doing OK, but I was still messing up," said Baker. "In May, me and Coach Meyer had a one-on-one meeting where he spoke to me like a man, telling me he was going to send me home, that he met both my parents and they were great people and he didn't want to disappoint them like that, but he can't have me 'messing up' his program. And that I could be a great player and I just don't know how much talent I have and I'm wasting it. I guess that just hit home, because I've never had anybody talk to me, telling me how great I could be . . . but my goofing up was going to mess it up.

"So I just thought, 'Well, how about I try it his way and see how everything works?'"

Dallas stopped the "goofing off" and became a productive performer on the 2005 squad, which went 8-3, with a trip to Tampa for the Outback Bowl.

Following the 31–24 Outback victory over Iowa in January 2006, Meyer brought Baker into the media room as the game's MVP and pointed him out to the press as "the Face of Florida Football."

Deep down, Meyer was calling on Baker for leadership on the offensive side, where there was a deficit. But the Gator coach wasn't concerned about leadership on the defense, because Brandon Siler was there to go forth with his coach's message that mental toughness would be a requirement for all.

"We saw we were losing close games," said Siler, who was approaching his junior year, what would be his final season. "Whatever we were doing in the past wasn't working, and that's what coach preached to us. Even in our off-season workouts a lot more of the stuff was team-oriented instead of individual stuff.

"If a teammate fell down, you had to have his back. You don't want to be that weak link. I think that was the difference. Mostly it was our mind-set, the way we did things. We weren't going to lose. Something was going to happen, somebody was going to make a play, but we weren't going to lose those games."

So Siler would help "change the butter," which Meyer used as the metaphor for altering the Gators' regular road routine. In reality, it was a reevaluation of "everything from A to Z," according to Urban.

Seeking advice from his mentors on how to do that, Meyer was burning up his cell minutes with calls to Lou Holtz and Earle Bruce.

Starting in 2006, road trips were to become pleasurable. The mornings of the games would be more about waking players up with a purpose and interacting with assistant coaches the moment their feet hit the floor. And making it fun.

"We didn't change a whole lot," Meyer said. "This came from Coach Holtz: It's an unusual environment for them, so the coaches go in with a glass of orange juice and a newspaper—rip the door open, throw the sheets back, turn on the TV, throw the drapes open, get real loud, have fun with them. They're in an uncomfortable environment—it's not their bed they're sleeping in. I noticed the players started getting a kick out of it.

"'The other thing we did was place more emphasis on toughness. I thought we were a very untough team our first year. You can't win on the road unless you are tough. And I think that was a testimony to the kind of team we were our first year—a very soft team."

Along with Tebow, among the other new faces who would play significant roles in those changes and the run for the championship: Percy Harvin, Louis Murphy, Brandon James, and Ryan Smith.

Everybody was going to be needed for the impending brutal six-game stretch of consecutive SEC opponents: Tennessee, Kentucky, Alabama, LSU, Auburn, and Georgia. The last four, in particular, seemed insurmountable. Even the media experts were discounting Florida's chances at national prominence because of that "Murderer's Row" lineup.

Ever so slowly, however, the pieces began to fit together, with the fabric tightly woven. The toughness that Meyer spoke about would begin to surface. Urban, looking for every conceivable way to motivate his team, turned to his good friend and confidant Bill Belichick of the New England Patriots, who makes an annual spring visit to Gainesville. In particular, Meyer wanted to raise the level of play in his secondary and of players such as cornerback Reggie Lewis, who had become one of Meyer's favorites.

Meyer learned about a routine used by the Patriots coach with one of his defensive backs, Frank Minnifield, who was so competitive he didn't even want passes completed on him in practice. Not even in a walk-through. That became a battle cry.

"Not even in a walk-through," Belichick would say to Minnifield in warm-ups before a game. Minnifield would echo, "Not even in a walk-through."

Meyer borrowed that slogan to use on Reggie Lewis. As secondary coach Chuck Heater would be working with his corners, Meyer would come by and mutter, "Not even in a walk-through," and Lewis would acknowledge same.

They would exchange those words before, during, and after games.

When the team took its customary Saturday walks around the hotel in street clothes—Meyer would always lead the way—they spoke in their own private code.

"I would say, 'C'mon Reggie, get up here and let's go,'" said Meyer. "I would always have 'Not even in a walk-through' written on a yellow sticker. As we started walking, I would slip it over to Reggie. He would take it and put it inside the top of his helmet or his shoulder pads before a game."

This player-coach relationship grew out of trust. "He was a man of his word and he gave me the opportunity," Lewis recalled. "And I made the best of it."

As for the "Not even in the walk-through" mantra, Lewis said, "That's what gave me the personality that I had. I lived by that quote every day I touched the football field. It just meant I didn't want anybody to complete a pass on me." And Lewis defended well most all season.

Looking back on it now, Lewis says he wishes he could have played his entire career under Meyer. Even with some of the physical demands of the early workouts, Lewis bought in because he was tired of not winning.

"It was time for a change," said Lewis. 'We said, 'Why not give it a shot?' We had a fantastic coach and conditioning coach. He brought in the right people. And we were going back on top where we had been when I first got there. We had to take a look at his offense, because he had been successful at every school he'd been at. So we decided we were going to do what he said to do, and it worked out."

There was something special about this one hundredth year of Florida football and "the Boys From Old Florida" who were playing in it. Not that you could tell from the first two games—romps over Southern Mississippi and Central Florida in the Swamp by the combined score of 76–7. But you could tell that night in Knoxville, Tennessee, on Urban Meyer's first visit to the cauldron that is Neyland Stadium, when the Associated Press's seventh-ranked Gators mounted a late comeback to nip the AP's thirteenth-rated Vols, 21–20.

Winning the first SEC game of the year for Florida or Tennessee has always been as vital as, say, winning Pennsylvania was to Hillary Clinton or Barack Obama. Now Meyer had done it on his first two tries.

With key blocks by Steve Rissler, Drew Miller, and Jim Tartt, Tebow, a freshman quarterback running like a fullback, picked up a crucial fourth-and-two first down to keep a 72-yard drive alive. Then Baker caught Leak's touchdown 21-yard pass as Florida rallied after trailing 17–7. It was the second Leak-to-Baker touchdown of the night.

Leak was brilliant. The defense held Tennessee to minus-11 yards rushing, led by the seven tackles of Brandon Siler—one of them a sack on the Vols' last drive. Tebow came through in the clutch. And Dallas Baker was finally serving notice that he was going to be a leader.

Knoxville 2006 wiped away some of Baker's bad marks from 2004, and he was on his way. He had become a member of Meyer's Leadership Committee. Wanting to step up in his new role, Baker had an understanding with Siler, the leader of the defense, that he'd do his part by helping inspire the offense.

Right away, Baker began to encourage young Percy Harvin, a star in the making, who had gotten a celebration penalty. "I told him, 'Don't make the same mistakes that I've made. Don't go down the same path'" Baker said. "I said, 'I've done some stupid stuff since I've been here. Next time, just hand the ball to the official.'"

During the game, Harvin suffered a high ankle sprain that would limit his play for the next few weeks.

With Baker's help, the leadership was starting to show up on both sides of the ball.

After rolling past Kentucky 26–7 to go 4-0, these 2006 Gators proved they knew how to come from behind against SEC competition. They would prove it again the next week against Alabama. Trailing the Tide 10–7 at halftime at the Swamp, Leak found Bubba Caldwell for a 16-yard score and a 14–10 lead. Nursing a one-point margin in the fourth period, Leak then hit Baker with a 12-yard scoring pass. The win was sealed with a splendid 70-yard touchdown return of an interception by an emerging star, newcomer Reggie Nelson, who was about to crash on the scene as an All-American free safety.

Nelson and cornerback Ryan Smith had larceny in their hearts and would wind up as the two biggest thieves in the SEC. They worked so well as a tandem that when Smith picked off his second pass of the day and fumbled it, Nelson was right there to recover it in what Meyer would call "the biggest play of the game."

Meyer nicknamed Nelson "the Eraser" because he covered up so many mistakes—just like that one by Smith. In addition to quick bursts of speed, which enhanced his ball-hawking skills, Nelson had brilliant instincts and tackled with the thunder of a linebacker.

"Playing cornerback with that guy behind you was so easy," Smith said of Reggie Nelson. "A lot of my interceptions [he made eight] I can credit to him, and I think we helped each other throughout the year. Being able to play with somebody that talented who puts the fear in the receivers makes it easier to play my position."

Smith marveled at the skills of Nelson. "The way he runs, the way he moves, the way he covers ground is almost inhuman," said Smith. "He's just trotting out there and it looks so effortless. But at the same time he covers so much ground. He's an amazing athlete."

Nelson was a bit reclusive with the media, possibly because he carried the burden of a mother ill with cancer. He rarely talked to the press, but did share his innermost thoughts with some teammates, such as Louis Murphy, whose mother also suffered from the same disease.

Secondary coach Chuck Heater could see Nelson developing into the premier free safety in Gator football history. "He loved to play football and he had a play-making component," said Heater. "Some guys have more propensity than others—some guys seem like they never make a play on the ball, and others always end up with the football."

What Nelson brought to the safety position were those cornerback-like skills. "He got there in a hurry, he liked to run downhill and swat people pretty aggressively," said Heater. "He set the standard for that position for here, probably forever. Every guy who comes along will be compared to that standard."

The Alabama win also produced another new wrinkle: Leak, who would never be mistaken for the next Herschel Walker, actually broke off a 45-yard run against the Tide. Ironically, it fell to Tebow to finish the job and score from the Alabama 2-yard line. Beating Alabama, 28–13, settled one score, but that was just the first leg of Murderers' Row.

Next Saturday would bring LSU to town, and that was another issue of redemption for the spanking in Baton Rouge the year before. However, Siler had a little something for the Tigers. He and defensive lineman Ray McDonald would team up to make the biggest defensive play of the game, but it was somewhat overshadowed by Tim Tebow's now famous "double-pump jump pass."

Siler's crucial recovery of LSU quarterback JaMarcus Russell's fumble at the Gators' 1-yard line ended the Tigers' bid to take the lead. That was even a bigger game-changing play than Tebow's pass— if not season-changing. With the score tied at 7 apiece in the second period, Siler told defensive tackle Ray McDonald to line up on the center's nose but to shoot the left gap.

"Ray went left and shot off the ball and it shocked the center," Siler said of McDonald, "and I came in on the right side and the center leaned that way. And I just fell straight down and went down there fighting for it [the ball] and came up with it." While Siler couldn't have picked a more timely spot to make that play, he certainly picked the wrong occasion to get any publicity for it (not that Siler really cared), because this was the breakout game for the left-handed quarterback from Jacksonville via Nease High School.

Against LSU, Tebow accounted for three Florida touchdowns, including one of the grandest moments in the one-hundred-year history of Gator football—both for its beauty and its ugliness. Ironically, it was the first career touchdown pass of the future Heisman Trophy winner, all one yard of it.

Tebow had always run the ball in short-yardage plays on the goal line and never thrown a TD pass of any kind. This time he took two steps forward, looked to the end zone, jumped in the air and did a half pump, then did another as he released a wounded-duck pass to a falling-down-backward tight end Tate Casey, who held on for the touchdown. Imagine the surprise for a stunned LSU—just as Tebow's own teammates had been surprised in practice the first time they saw the play.

Siler couldn't help but chuckle, and he loved the boldness of the call. The day in practice drills when the Gator offense had sprung it on his defense, Siler had cried foul. "Ah, that's cheatin'! You can't do that kind of thing!" he complained to the coaches. "And now they were doing it in the game!" said Siler, who was loving it.

That kind of aggressiveness by the offense got Siler's heart beating and would send a message to rest of the defense.

"Sometimes when a coach calls plays kind of on his heels, scared to be too aggressive, it makes you play the same way," said Siler. "You know he's backing off, so you back off a little bit, too. But when you call an aggressive play, you're sending 'em the message, 'Aw, man, we're going to get 'em!'"

Utah's Ben Moa had run the same play for the 2-point conversion to win the triple-overtime game against Air Force. Tebow's pass to Casey was much uglier.

While the Tebow play was memorable, perhaps forgotten was the interception by another newcomer, Smith, which gave the ball over to Florida to start a 72-yard Florida drive. Smith's ball-hawking was going to be a huge asset in weeks to come.

Also almost unnoticed was the debut of a young wide receiver named Louis Murphy, a speedy freshman from St. Petersburg who had been buried in Meyer's doghouse. Murphy had been booted off the team as a freshman for missing curfew, but given a second chance. He rewarded his coach by catching a 35-yard touchdown pass from Tebow against LSU, Tim's second career touchdown pass and second of the day—and Murphy's first ever. Murphy was so excited that when he came down inside the goal line he didn't know at first he had even scored.

Nobody was prouder of Murphy than Meyer, who was seeing the beginning of what he would call "the biggest turnaround of any player I've coached." Much in the manner of Dallas Baker, Louis Murphy had one foot out the door in 2005 when the light turned on.

Originally recruited by Zook, Murphy was signed by Meyer, but quickly got on his wrong side for missing curfew during two-a-day drills. Meyer said Murphy was also hanging out with the "wrong crowd" and headed for trouble. To earn a spot back on the team, Murphy would be put through a brutal routine. "I told him [Meyer] that he could try, but he was never going to break me," Murphy vowed after receiving the details of the punishment.

Murphy knew in his heart that he had needed a fresh start.

"I was hanging with people who weren't going anywhere, just trying to fit in with the 'in' crowd," Murphy confessed. "I needed to start showing myself around the Dallas Bakers, Jemalle Corneliuses, the Bubba Caldwells. I don't know, I guess that was just a teenage thing . . . not knowing what you want for yourself . . . going with the wind . . . following the crowd.

"I seemed to get in trouble. It wasn't working."

This was in contrast to the good family life Murphy had growing up. His father, Louis Sr., was pastor at Mt. Zion Progressive Missionary Baptist Church in St. Petersburg. His mother was a teacher. Louis was a star in football and track, as a sophomore having been the anchor on Lakewood's state champion 4×400 relay team.

"I came from a good upbringing," said Murphy. "I don't know what it was—trying to rebel and do the wrong thing. You live and you learn. I learned a lot from a lot of my mistakes. But look at me now! I'm trying to live my life right and the way my mom would want me to live it. Help the team win."

Murphy says one of his inspirations had been his mother, who loved seeing her son play football, but became ill with cancer. She was especially pleased that Louis was back on the field at Florida.

Another of Murphy's inspirations was Tebow, with whom he grew close during off-season workouts in 2008. "Our chemistry is becoming second nature," said Murphy. The future was beginning to look bright, especially after another signature win by Meyer over SEC rival LSU.

Eighteen games in, Urban Meyer had elevated the Florida football program to dizzying heights heretofore not seen since the Spurrier days. The 6-0 start to the 2006 campaign had vaulted the Gators up to No. 2 in the polls as they departed for Auburn, Alabama, and the place once known as "the Loveliest Village on the Plains." Except this time, it was also going to be "the Loudest Village on the Plains," because a souped-up public address system was blaring music so loud that Auburn would be fined $5,000 for piping in "artificial" sounds.

Frankly, the Auburn crowd was so loud that Tommy Tuberville didn't really need the extra juice. Especially on the two plays that changed the game's momentum in favor of his Tigers. After an impressive 17–11 halftime lead, Florida imploded on a blocked punt and a controversial forward pass/fumble.

Auburn had taken the lead, 18–17, when Eric Wilbur's punt was blocked and Floridian Tre Smith from Venice scampered with it into the end zone. However, it looked as if things were under control as Leak hit a 32-yard pass to Baker and pitched out to Bubba Caldwell for a 27-yard gain. Trailing 21–17 at the Auburn 6-yard line and about to take the lead, Leak dropped back to pass, tried to hold up, and watched in horror as the ball slipped from his hand and fell to the ground, where it was scooped up by Tray Blackmon.

Leak, his teammates, and his coaches wanted an incomplete pass called, but after a replay the fumble recovery was allowed to stand. Among those who questioned that call was CBS analyst Gary Danielson, broadcasting the game with Verne Lundquist.

As the game wound down, a desperate, last-play lateral attempt by Jarred Fayson was fumbled and picked up by Patrick Lee, who raced in for a score to end the game. Auburn won, 27–17. The loss was devastating to Florida coaches, players, and fans and a big blow to any championship hopes.

"Even with all the stuff that happened that was negative we still had a chance to come out and claw our way to win a big SEC game on the road," said Jemalle Cornelius. "That was kind of like our first real game when people started taking us seriously on that [national] stage.

"For some reason, we could not get going on offense. We had played so well in the previous games, then to come in there and have a letdown like that was very, very frustrating."

There was about to be a meltdown in the Gator locker room.

Siler still could not fathom that his team had lost to Auburn, however, and still thought "five or six minutes after the game . . . we were going to come back somehow. And the game was already over. It didn't hit me until I got back into the locker room."

Shock set in when the reality finally did hit the Gator players. They began to boil over with emotion, and a spontaneous ten-minute player meeting ensued, with feelings made known. Players called each other out, or, as Siler put it, "We came together and had meetings amongst each other that 'it can't happen again.'"

Vocal encounters became more heated and players screamed at each other. Leak was the focal point of criticism by his teammates, several of them calling the offense "a bunch of BS." Helmets were thrown.

One of his assistant coaches warned Meyer that he'd better break things up. Meyer declined, remembering a similar incident at Colorado State and how Sonny Lubick had handled it.

"Let it go," Meyer told him.

"I wanted to hear what they were saying," Meyer said. "If they think Chris Leak's not very tough, I want to hear it. If they think the offense sucks, I want to hear it. Go ahead and get it out. Catharsis. I'm a big believer in that. You've got to release a little bit. So I let them release. Once it started to calm down and I got control of it, we knelt down and said a prayer."

This was pure Lubick, who had done the same thing after his Colorado State team went unbeaten for seven games and the streak was halted by Utah, 45–31. That day, Lubick walked into the locker room after the loss and declared to his Rams, "We *are* going to win the Mountain West Conference!"

"Everybody quit crying," Meyer recalled of that incident at Colorado State, which had happened almost twelve years ago. "I kind of looked up and in my mind I'm going, 'No we're not!' But I'm not eighteen years old, either."

Meyer was relating now to how Lubick had handled that situation.

"When they [the Florida players] left that locker room I wanted to make sure they knew they still had a chance. I told them they were still going to win the SEC Championship and maybe more," Meyer said.

Urban let his team brood over the rest of the weekend. On Monday he reached into the archive and dusted off a ten-year-old proverb from Danny Wuerffel's postgame interview following the devastating 24–21 loss to Florida State. It was, after all, possible to gain enlightenment after a loss, as this story from the 1996 Heisman Trophy winner would prove. Wuerffel's words would be the inspiration for "one of the greatest team meetings we ever had," said Meyer. With an assist from Lubick, of course.

"He came in and played us an audiotape of Danny Wuerffel, talking to the media when they lost in 1996 to ruin their ten and oh season," Cornelius said. "It looked like, at the time, it ruined their chance to play in the national championship.

"He [Wuerffel] was just saying how much they had poured everything into it and how all that evaporated . . . how their feelings were all let down. He talked about how important it was for senior leadership—and I'll never forget that he said, 'James Bates, Lawrence Wright, and Jeff Mitchell . . .' rallying them up and getting them ready for the SEC championship game.

"And then he said, 'There's one thing about being knocked down and getting back up: It's easier to win and win them all, but there's something about a team getting knocked off course and end up finding a way to come back and do something special.' Coach Meyer gave us a card of that, with the whole quote of Danny's, and that little thing we kept to ourselves—a card with the SEC championship rings on it. It was something we kept with us the rest of the year."

Cornerback Reggie Lewis, who a year or two later couldn't remember exactly what Wuerffel's quote was, said he felt it was effective at the time.

"Whatever it was Danny Wuerffel said to the team, we lived by it the rest of the year," said Lewis. "Coach Meyer said for us to keep it on us, so I kept it in my wallet. I would look at it and say, 'I want to win a ring.' It was our goal from that point forward, having lost to Auburn, to get to the national championship game. And not only to get there, but to bring back the title to Gainesville."

Those 2006 Gators already knew how Wuerffel's story had turned out: With outside help—other contenders getting knocked off—Wuerffel's team wound up playing No. 1 ranked FSU in the Nokia Sugar Bowl and winning the national championship by pummeling the cross-state rival, 52–20.

Now Meyer's Gators had to write their own ending. They would heed the advice of Wuerffel. Over the open date, they would "get back up" just in time to play their oldest rival, the Georgia Bulldogs, whom they had only lost to twice since 1990, but still trailed in the series at 46-37-2.

This was also the beginning of a disturbing trend by the offense, which never really got off the Gator bus in Jacksonville. The defense carried the day, luckily for Meyer, but he admitted "in six years I've never felt this way about an offense." What offense? The leading rusher was a wide receiver, Percy Harvin, with just 37 yards. Except for Bubba Caldwell's eight catches—one for a touchdown—and his 12-yard run for another score, there wasn't any offense. Florida made four turnovers—three interceptions thrown by Leak and a fumble. Luckily for the Gators, Georgia committed five.

"Thank God for great defense," said Meyer, and in a way he was thanking Him for the gift of Ray McDonald. If ever a player stole Meyer's heart for pure courage, it was the 6'3", 280-pound senior from Belle Glade, Florida.

McDonald stepped up against Georgia in Florida's seventh win, scooping up a fumble by Bulldog Kregg Lumpkin on the first play of the second half and taking it 9 yards for the final Florida score. The trouble was, the Gator offense shut down after that 21–0 lead and allowed Georgia to creep back in at the end before finally winning, 21–14, in a victory that was uglier than Georgia's bulldog mascot, Uga.

Meyer was almost gloomy, despite his team's going to 7-1. His press conference was such a downer that he had to catch himself before he got into trouble with Shelley for being so negative. Despite his offensive woes, Meyer didn't know there would be more trouble on the horizon.

(McDonald would move to tackle to take up the slack against Vanderbilt. Interchangeable parts such as McDonald would prove invaluable. Mattison called McDonald "as good a defensive lineman as I ever coached.")

Though it hadn't been made public yet, Florida would be losing its best defensive player and the anchor in the middle of the line. Having rejoined the team against LSU after a two-game drug-related suspension, Marcus Thomas was kicked off for good after the Georgia game for violating the terms of his reinstatement. This was yet another serious blow to the Gators' championship hopes.

Right here is where the nurturing and care of players was about to pay off for Meyer. Each game after that, another player came out of mothballs or redeemed himself in some fashion for the coach who had stood with him in stormy times.

If there was going to be any good news about the loss of Thomas, it was from the response of players such as Ray McDonald, who with the help of head trainer Anthony Pass and physical therapist Susan Tillman, was now healthy. He was also durable, reliable, and played with heart. McDonald's career stretched over two football administrations, forty-five games and thirty-six starts. He was the only freshman in school history to start twelve games under Zook, but played in only five games during Meyer's first year because of his bad knees.

McDonald loved the no-nonsense approach of his new coach and was glad all the conflict on campus with other students was no longer a factor. He wasn't a part of the incident, but some of Ray's teammates had gotten into a scrape with several members of a fraternity. The incident was exacerbated when Zook, at the suggestion of his boss Jeremy Foley, showed up at the fraternity house, but became angry and combative with the students.

That incident also caused a rift between the football team and the student body and led to Zook's doom as coach.

Looking back on how things had gone wrong for Zook, but without wanting to be critical of his former coach, McDonald said, "It felt like a whole bunch of chaos. You wanted to focus on football, but you really couldn't because you had fighting on campus with other students at a fraternity house—stuff like that going on—and you don't want to be involved in that stuff or hear about it. You just want to play ball."

McDonald had a vivid recollection of how rapidly things fell apart in late October of 2004, "Then we lost to Mississippi State and it was like a domino effect. Everything just started going down, man."

That wasn't all that was going down that season, according to Ray's mother, LaBrina. She and her husband, Ray Sr., were worried about their son.

"Before Coach Meyer came, we were in the valley," said LaBrina. "So when Coach Meyer came in and we met with them and I realized Ray is going to be fine, we felt better. coach Meyer and coach [Greg] Mattison, they are going to take care of our son. We felt like we had turned our son over to some other parents.

"God didn't make enough coach Meyers. He's a genuine caring person, not just a football person. He treated Ray like his own son. You can feel the love and the passion from him and his family."

Ray Jr. had known about Meyer's reputation before he arrived and readily welcomed the new coach. "Our [senior] class pretty much accepted him because we got tired of losing. If you love football and you've got somebody coming in to help you, then why not accept them?

"When he talks, he knows what he's talking about. When you're playing for somebody like that, you really believe in what they are saying and you want to make them happy."

Ray Jr. found Meyer's routine refreshing—even "the Midnight Lift."

Players came into the weight room at midnight in the off-season for a hard two-hour workout, but more important, they began to talk to each other. "We just sat down in the middle of the floor and talked about life situations and what was going on—where we came from and the kind of stuff we went through," said McDonald. "Doing stuff like that gives you a bigger bond with your teammates."

Ray grew up around football in a family where the game was revered and his roots ran deep. His father, Ray Sr., was a former Gator player who was featured on the cover of the November 11, 1985, *Sports Illustrated* issue after making two touchdown catches in a 14–10 win over LSU. Ray Jr. was one year old at the time.

Ray Sr. and LaBrina were delighted with their son's progress and deeply appreciated the efforts of Meyer in getting their son healthy, back on the field, and on cue for his degree.

A rough road lay ahead for Ray Jr., who would be operated on by Dr. Pete Indelicato for torn anterior cruciate ligaments in each knee. The operations were done five weeks apart following the 2005 season, thereby allowing him to rehabilitate both knees at the same time and get ready for the 2006 season during which he would play a key role.

"One of them was bad," said Indelicato. "He had both significant cartilage and ligament damage. My biggest concern was that he had to rehab both knees in the spring and summer. But he was a great kid and he had great support from his family. We made sure his mom and dad was there when we told him he had to have the surgery."

All his teammates and coaches were impressed with the way McDonald worked his way back from surgery. When the 2006 season rolled around and his teammates needed him most, McDonald would be ready. During a dry spell for the Spread, the defense of co-coordinators Mattison and Charlie Strong would be leaned upon heavily.

As the team prepared to play Vanderbilt, ever so quietly some players were filling in the cracks like putty. One big crack was the one left behind by the suspended Thomas, but that news wouldn't come until halftime against Vandy and would be viewed as one more obstacle in Florida's run for the national title, which didn't really appear to be on track at this point.

The Gators were ranked fourth behind Ohio State, Michigan, and USC. Truthfully, though, Florida really wasn't in the national title conversation. There were other offensive struggles and player conduct issues to be resolved. National analysts were spurning the Gators for lack of so-called "style points." They weren't scoring all that many football points, either, but they were riding the wave of good special teams and defensive play.

As well as good will between a coach and his players.

In the 25–19 victory over the Commodores, Smith and Nelson both blocked punts—something that Meyer works on almost every day in special teams practice. The two of them were becoming forces in the Florida secondary, as Smith had ten unassisted tackles against Vandy. Defensive end Derrick Harvey notched his eighth sack to lead the SEC.

Baker, all grown up as a big-time receiver, made seven receptions for 135 yards and eclipsed the 2,000-yard career mark.

With a 9-1 record, the Gators were preparing to host the Ol' Ball Coach on his first return to the House That Spurrier Built and nicknamed the Swamp. Still with a bitter taste from their experience the year before in Columbia, Meyer and his players would feel intensity like they had never known in a football game.

By virtue of Tennessee's loss to Auburn, Florida had clinched a spot in the SEC title game for the first time in six years. If there was such a thing as good karma, it was beginning to peek around the corner.

Former Gator star defensive back Lawrence Wright had once coined the phrase "You're either a Gator or you're Gator bait." In the case of Steve Spurrier, it was wrong—because he was both. Though Steve Spurrier claimed he would always be a Gator, tonight he was wearing the colors of an SEC East opponent,

The sight of Spurrier on the opposite sideline, wearing colors of the enemy, was almost too much for some Gator fans to fathom.

They may have respected him or even loved him—some said they hated him for going to South Carolina—but in the final seconds of the game with the Gamecocks, they were getting the bejabbers scared out of them by the Ol' Ball Coach. Spurrier was on edge, too. Meyer was nearly a basket case.

A wave of emotion rolled over the Swamp like evening fog.

The man once called Darth Vader Under a Visor, Steve Superior, and Evil Genius by Florida opponents was steeling himself against an emotional outburst in the final ticks of a game in which his South Carolina team trailed, 17–16, with the winning field goal up for grabs.

For older Gator fans, this picture looked out of context. Spurrier had only coached from that east sideline once before—in a scrimmage for the 2001 spring game—and had gotten beat. In our phone conversation earlier that week, Spurrier remembered that occasion.

"We didn't usually keep score, but this time I told Jon Hoke [defensive coordinator] to take the defense on the home side and we'd go over on the visitors' side. We always had a rule that the losers had to run. Well, we got beat that day and the offense had to run."

Being back on Florida Field turf wasn't new to Spurrier that season, so it wasn't exactly like a homecoming. Twice earlier that year Spurrier had visited the stadium where he starred as a player and a coach—once during ceremonies for the opening game honoring his 1996 national champions and again when he came back to be inducted into the Ring of Honor prior to the Alabama game.

South Carolina's coach wasn't the only one feeling the heat. Urban Meyer didn't want to lose two straight years to the Ol' Ball Coach and be reminded of it by his critics. Meyer was tied in emotional knots, trying to figure out how to win.

Across Florida Field on the west sideline, Florida had called another time out, attempting to freeze Gamecock field goal kicker Ryan Succop, whose kicks had already been blocked twice in the game. Urban was considering calling yet another.

In the coaching booth, Meyer's assistants thought they had spotted a weak link in the South Carolina offensive line—a guard who was vulnerable to the rush. They were afraid if Florida called a second timeout, Spurrier's special teams coach would realize it and have a chance to replace that guard. (Turns out that guard wasn't in the game anyway.)

Every player knew how vital this game was to Meyer, to the program, and possibly to national championship hopes. Siler's knee was banged up and he played in great pain at less than 100 percent. In this case, Siler's heart was more important than his knee and his spirit kept his teammates pushing their limits.

An exhausted Jarvis Moss had not taken a play off all night and came to the sideline needing every tick of the second timeout just to stay upright. This was the first season in a while Moss had been able to go full speed. Only in the past year had doctors and trainers been able to correctly diagnose the staph infection on his pelvis bone that had kept him from gaining sufficient weight, causing him to be weak of body and flagging in confidence.

Some days over nearly two years when he couldn't eat—a bag of chips and a soda might be all he could get down—Moss was so discouraged that he considered quitting on several occasions. But he had remembered something his grandfather the late Bill Moss had told him while growing up in Denton, Texas, "Just when it's the darkest, there's always light."

After playing in only a few games in two years, Moss had found his way back as a defensive end who, at times, was a dominant force. Moss says he will forever be grateful to the medical assistance of the doctors and trainers who helped him recover and salvage his football career, especially head trainer Anthony Pass.

Perhaps because Moss had missed so much for so long, he didn't want to miss a single moment now. When they told him somebody else was going to take his place on the attempted field goal block on the game's final play, he fought against that idea.

Defensive tackle Steve Harris says he and McDonald talked about knocking South Carolina's guard backward and lobbied with the coaches for the "middle block" by Moss. After all, Moss had blocked Succop's field goal attempt earlier in the fourth quarter and McDonald had blocked one in the third quarter.

In the defensive huddle, co-defensive coordinator Charlie Strong informed Moss of the change in plans.

"Moss," said Strong, "let's let Harvey jump."

"Nooo way," said Moss. "No, I'm not coming out of the game, coach!"

A few seconds later, Strong asked, 'Moss, are you good?"

" 'Yeah, coach.' "

"Well then how come you look so tired?"

Moss says he thinks Strong was trying to motivate him.

"I had played the whole game and there was no reason I should come out on this last play," said Moss. "I hate to think what would happen if I had come out, because I felt like it was my fate and Florida's fate at the same time."

So there was no way Moss would be standing on the sideline watching the field goal attempt. "I just felt like I had to be out there with guys like Ray McDonald and Steve Harris, just to back them up," he said. Once on the field, the three of them began plotting strategy.

Moss said a prayer as he walked back on the field and lined up, waiting on the officials to whistle the ball in play, studying the body language and kicking motion of Succop, who was timing out his practice kick while drawing a bead on the north goal post.

Eight seconds were left on the clock when Succop stepped off the yardage, the ball was snapped, and he stuck his foot into it at the Gators 38-yard line, an attempt of 48 yards. At the snap, McDonald and Harris took out the "weak guard," giving Moss room to step forward and leap with all his might.

"And he blocked the kick," said Meyer. "We were that close to taking him out. But we didn't take him out because he convinced us he could do it."

The 6'6" lineman from Denton (Texas) Ryan High School used all thirty-six inches of his vertical leap and caught the ball flush with his hand, tipping it off course—and preserving the 17–16 Gator win and hopes of a national championship.

Moss, now a member of the Denver Bronco defensive line along with Marcus Thomas and Harris, remembers vividly how history could have been altered by one tiny push of his blocker.

"When I jumped up in the air, the South Carolina lineman had his hand on my chest," Moss said. "He just placed it there. If he would have shoved me just a tad, I honestly think there's no way I would have blocked that kick. In one of the pictures, you can see it."

Harris didn't see the block, but he heard it and knew what happened.

"That was like the most exciting play ever," said Harris. "I just remember hearing the ball get hit, because I had my head down, trying to knock the dude back as hard as I could. So I wasn't looking at anything else. Then I heard the whole crowd screaming, so I figured he had blocked it. I looked up, and it was blocked. It was crazy. Some teammates were crying. Fans screaming. It was just crazy. The field goal was right on track. It hit right in the middle of his hand. If he [Moss] would have missed any part of it, the ball was would have gone through."

Blocking that kick also helped Moss fulfill a guarantee to his teammates that these Gators would have a shot to win it all. Moss remembered what it felt like in Denton when Ryan won the state high school 4A football championship and it was starting to be eerily similar. In the locker room, when Meyer asked him to speak, Moss said, "I'm starting to get a special feeling about this team."

Jarvis Moss had jumped over the moon to deliver on his promise.

"If anybody thought we were going to win the national championship it was Jarvis Moss," said Jemalle Cornelius. "He had so much confidence we were going to win it. Even though we lost to Auburn and
came back and won the rest of the games and won the SEC, we still had
a lot of things that needed to happen for us. And Jarvis, the whole year,
said, 'I guarantee you we're going to play in the national championship.'
That's one guy I remember having supreme confidence."

While some people might call that fate or luck, Meyer says defi-
antly that the blocked field goal was the result of players training hard
in practice and executing in games. The blocked kick was fate, perhaps, in a spiritual sense, but Moss also agrees with his former coach
that design and rehearsal played a big part.

"We practiced that play numerous times and in every practice,"
Moss said. "But I never blocked it one time in practice. But we still
practiced me jumping every practice, and it paid off, because when it
came time, it was in my mind what to do."

The play and the game would make a lasting impression on all Gators, but especially Cornelius.

"That was one game I will never forget the rest of my life," Jemalle
said. "The electricity in that stadium. Some of the guys were so emotional after that game. That was just a great win for us. Our winning
streak at home was on the line—we had a lot of things going on in that
game . . . it being coach Spurrier's first time back in the Swamp in a
while. All the stuff that was riding on that game made it such a big deal."

The commitment and effort by Moss were inspirational to Cornelius and his teammates, who were starting to believe maybe there was,
indeed, something special going on.

"For a guy like Jarvis to come in the way he did, battling the
whole game and sucking it up and making that play was great," said
Cornelius. "I definitely knew after that game that we had a shot at doing something special with that team."

After the game, resigned that his team couldn't get in the way of
destiny, Spurrier said to me as he left his press conference, "I think it
might be the 'Year of the Gator.'"

For longtime Gator fans, that "Year of the Gator" phrase was a well-worn bumper sticker that had been spun both ways over the past fifty years. It could be a derisive commentary about the empty promises of the sixties and seventies, once spoken mostly in sarcasm. Or, when the prophecy was finally fulfilled under Spurrier in the nineties, it took on a new meaning. I knew Spurrier meant it as the latter and wasn't just being frivolous with a wisecrack. He was, after all, still half-Gator.

The victory was gift-wrapped for twenty-one Gator seniors on their last night in Ben Hill Griffin Stadium, a night when Meyer's ninth win of the season pulled him to within one of Spurrier's mark after his first twenty-three games at Florida: Nineteen wins, four losses.

Quietly, the team was starting to jell. The impact of Meyer's coaching personality could begin to be seen and felt.

Just as the Plan to Win worked at Bowling Green and Utah for Meyer, it was working at the University of Florida. Ryan Smith had experienced it in his second season with for the Utes—this convergence of hard work, intelligent decisions, teammates trusting each other and making a commitment to a common goal.

There was little difference, Smith said, in the Urban Meyer of Salt Lake City and the Urban Meyer of Gainesville. (While Smith graduated from Utah and enrolled in UF graduate school without missing a season, special teams player Butch Rowley transferred to Florida and redshirted in 2005, becoming the regular holder.)

"A lot of people ask me this question, but he's the exact same person," said Smith. "There may be some things he had to change because of the demographics of the people he was coaching. But as far as coaching style and the way he communicated with the players and the way he ran his program, everything was the exact same. It was his blueprint for success, obviously."

The only different wrinkle, said Smith, was that Meyer backed off a little on some of the grueling workouts because the athletes at Florida were the elite recruits that he didn't have at Utah. "At the same time he kept his sternness about him, but the players at Florida weren't used to it at all," said Smith. "It was big-time football and people could never tell them anything because they were big-time recruits."

Smith, a toothpicklike corner—so skinny that even Meyer was floored to see him with his shirt off—had arrived at Florida through sort of a fluke loophole.

"It was crazy how we found out," Ryan said.

One day his father, Lance Smith, was looking through the NCAA manual when he discovered the rule: A player who graduates early with eligibility remaining could transfer without sitting out a year, provided he enrolled in graduate school. Ryan got his degree from Utah in July of 2006 and still had two years of football left.

At first Ryan considered transferring to an all-black college such as Howard to play the game for fun. Having played for both Meyer and Heater at Utah, however, he had always dreamed of experiencing big-time football.

"My dad called me, I called Coach Heater, and Coach Heater called the academic advisor at Florida," said Ryan. "And it just went from there."

Smith wound up right in the thick of it and would play a big part in helping his team win a championship again, even as a featherweight defensive back. If he was anywhere close to the 165 pounds he was listed at on the roster, Smith didn't look it. But he was smart, gifted with great ball instincts, and extremely quick.

And he knew the system—though you wouldn't know from his debut on Florida Field.

What Ryan found out right off, playing in front of ninety-thousand people, was that it was best "not to think, just to react." Obviously, he wasn't thinking when he lined up against Southern Mississippi in his first game, because he was on the wrong side.

"They yelled at me, 'Get back on the other side, it's not man coverage—it's zone," he said. "So my first play in the Swamp was an MA [Missed Assignment]."

It quickly got better, as he went on to lead the SEC in interceptions and make All-Conference.

"It was like déjà vu," Smith said of watching Meyer operate at Florida. "I've already seen it happen to players at Utah and I've seen what it did for us and how we ended up twelve and oh and a top five team. I've seen it work. To see the process—it was a good experience for me . . . and basically the same thing happened again."

Most of all, Smith could see tangible results of Meyer turning boys into men and his off-the-field priorities had a major impact on the young Californian.

"I think his whole aim is to change lives," Smith said of Meyer. "A lot of coaches go into the job saying, 'I'm not your babysitter, I'm your coach.' He says, 'I am your football coach but at the same time, I'm going to hold you accountable and I want to make you a better man.' And that's what I really loved about being under him."

Meyer and his staff made Smith's dreams come true. "To be able to play in that arena was a treat, and I really appreciated being able to do that," said Smith. "I thank Coach Meyer and his whole staff, because if there was anything I ever wanted in this world, it was to be able to play on a big stage in big-time college football. And they made that happen for me."

The big-time football and the big stage had not been enough to impress many of the voters that these Gators were championship material, however, because they were not mentioned in those conversations much as they went after their tenth win of the season.

Clubbing Western Carolina, 62–0, for win No. 10 wasn't going to do much for their polls standing, but some of the younger players got their chance to shine. Freshman Brandon James returned a punt 77 yards for a touchdown and set a school record with 155 yards in punt returns. Freshman wide receiver Riley Cooper caught three touchdown passes. And freshman Tim Tebow scored twice rushing and also threw for a pair of touchdowns.

There was still no love from the critics, who brought up that "style points" deficit thing again. Urban declined to campaign at this juncture, saying later "I didn't really know" how good his team was because he hadn't had the time to compare the competition. "I'd much rather worry about beating that school out West [Florida State]," he said. "You have to make an educated statement, don't just babble. I don't ever want to be accused of that. If I make a statement, it's because I'm pretty firm on what I'm saying—it's not just 'Hey, this is kind of neat.'"

If he wasn't going to overvalue his own team, he certainly wasn't going to undervalue his next opponent, because as usual Florida State was loaded with talent despite its 6-5 record. The 10-1 Gators had a chance to hold serve on their No. 4 ranking going into the postseason by beating Bobby Bowden's Seminoles for the third straight season.

This changing-of-the-butter thing was working nicely for Meyer. It would be field-tested for the final time in 2006 on the trip to Tallahassee, but it wasn't going to be easy.

Remember the Plan to Win admonition to "Play great defense"? Down the championship run in 2006, none other than Moss, McDonald, Siler, Smith, Harris, Nelson, Lewis, and Harvey would help turn games around along with the usual defensive reliables such as Earl Everett, Joe Cohen, Clint McMillan, Tony Joiner, Brian Crum, and Kyle Jackson.

Moss and McDonald came out of a M*A*S*H unit. Smith worked his way through a legal loophole just to have a chance to play for Meyer again. Lewis found new life as a starting corner. Nelson was a junior college transfer. Dallas Baker had done a 180-degree turnaround in his life and career. Cornelius Ingram changed his mind about quitting and came back to provide some big catches. Harris had fathered three children out of wedlock and wouldn't be allowed back until he took responsibility for them. Harvin snapped back from his ankle sprain.

On offense, growing leaders was difficult. Seniors such as captain/ wide receiver Jemalle Cornelius, tackle Steve Rissler, and wide receiver Dallas Baker were doing their best to lead. Where the coach needed it most, however, was at quarterback.

Finally, at the very time when Florida needed Chris Leak, the senior quarterback would come through against the nation's No. 12 ranked defense and display the leadership Meyer believed he always had. All those disappointing seasons and the reluctance of the Gator Nation to accept him were going to be chewed up and spit out on Bobby Bowden Field in the next 74 yards in the chance to break the 14–14 tie and cap off the victory.

Florida's running game was on the bench, with DeShawn Wynn and Percy Harvin injured, so Leak wanted the ball and wanted to do it his way. "Let's open it up and let me pick 'em apart," he said boldly to his coach. His coach said OK, delighted that, for the first time he could ever remember, Leak wanted to take charge of a game like this.

Chris Leak knew how to drive this big Orange and Blue machine after all, 74 yards right up Bobby Bowden Field. Seven completions later, on third down, Leak found Dallas Baker for 25 yards and the winning score. Florida's 21–14 victory was the third consecutive over Bobby Bowden and second straight in Doak Campbell Stadium—only the Gators third win in Tallahassee since 1986, the place where Danny Wuerffel's 1996 team nearly lost its national championship dream.

Meyer had stuck by Leak, who had been slow to fulfill that leadership role until his wake-up call during the fourth quarter against FSU. In the final regular season game of his senior year, Leak was learning a valuable lesson in life: If you want something, you have to ask for it.

The football had been there for the taking during the past twenty-five games. Until now, Leak hadn't grasped that when you want what's inside the piñata, you must reach up and poke it with a stick to break it open. Finally, Leak's instinctive reach to take a risk/reward responsibility not only produced the winning drive against the Seminoles, but provided an adhesive his football team had so badly craved.

Leak's leadership role turned out to be more than just a one-game duct-tape fix. Maybe he wasn't the Rock that Brandon Siler was, but at least the senior quarterback was now willing to assume command. Leak grew up as leader that night in Tallahassee. Meyer was impressed with how Leak asked for the ball.

"Part of playing quarterback is improving the level of play of the other ten guys around you," Meyer said later. "It's also having communication with your coaching staff, giving recommendations, and that was nonexistent a year ago. When he would come over to the sideline, everybody would sit there and look at each other. There was no discussion. Chris has done a great job, and that was his best job as far as discussion, recommendations, and then more importantly than all that, execution."

The Florida Gators were on track toward championships and the two-quarterback system had been validated.

Leak's newfound leadership skills were boding well for Florida. "He needs to go to Atlanta and get himself a ring," Meyer said of his quarterback.

Meanwhile, the players were starting to understand their roles and appreciate Meyer's theory about the SEC title game being the Stairway to Heaven.

"When I came to Florida and heard Coach Meyer talking about winning the SEC, I told him, 'Coach, that's not going to be good enough—I came to Florida to win the national championship,'" said Siler. "And he told me, 'You win the SEC and you've got a chance to play for a national championship.'"

The Gators were starting to muster up their defensive forces for the two big championships ahead with maturity of players such as Nelson, who logged another six tackles and an interception. Smith made his seventh pick, best in the SEC. The emergence of Harris in the middle of the line was going to play a big part in things to come in the Desert. Harris had four tackles and a sack.

The big question was whether the pollsters and football pundits were going to make Meyer out to be a liar. The Gators were going to Atlanta to find out.

15

Two Battles to Win in Atlanta

After winning five SEC titles in six seasons and six in nine seasons, Florida was pretty much the face of the championship game. But that face hadn't been seen around the Georgia Dome in a while—since 2000, to be exact.

The game against Arkansas marked the Gators' eighth appearance out of the fifteen championships. They were not so much thinking about a national title at this point because any scenario that would have them leapfrogging Southern Cal—or maybe even Michigan—seemed unlikely. Of course, they only had to make it to No. 2 for a chance to play No. 1 Ohio State.

The challenge ahead for the Gators was to win the game as well as the propaganda war that was being waged against them for a lack of style points. Florida's national worthiness was being discounted by almost all of ESPN's so-called experts to the point where on my radio shows in Colorado (KKFN) and Florida (WMOP/WGGG) I began a counterpunch against "the ABC/ESPN cartel."

Kirk Herbstreit was the poster boy for the cartel as far as Gator fans were concerned, because he had openly campaigned for a Michigan-Ohio State rematch.

More and more, Florida looked like a candidate for a good hosing: A 12-1 team that had lost once on a controversial call at Auburn could very well end up not getting a shot to play for the national title.

Honestly, the Gators were just hoping to win the SEC and get a bid to the Sugar Bowl. Even that looked in jeopardy as reports out of New Orleans began to surface that LSU might be the Sugar Bowl's team of choice, unless the Tigers wound up playing in the Rose Bowl. Then some funny quirks of fate began to happen—the kind not even Urban Meyer would be able to deny: help from the football gods.

The matchup between the Gators' league-leading rush defense (Florida, No. 5 nationally) and the SEC's most potent rushing offense, featuring the spectacular Darren McFadden and the fleet-of-foot Felix Jones, figured to be a test of skills and wills. McFadden had rushed for 1,485 yards and 14 touchdowns, averaging 6.1 yards per carry. In Fayetteville, they called him Run DMC.

McFadden rolled up 182 yards against LSU, which hadn't allowed 100 to a back all season. Jones rushed for 137 against the Tigers, not including a 40-yarder that was called back. McFadden was extremely effective lining up in what Coach Houston Nutt called the Wildcat formation and later the Wild Hog formation, featuring a direct snap to McFadden in the tailback/quarterback position, similar to the old-fashioned single wing.

Meyer would spend extra time on tackling drills, knowing that the Gators would have to wrap up McFadden and Jones to bring them down. The Razorbacks were not purely a power team, because they used lots of misdirection.

The Gator defensive front seven boasted agility, mobility, and quickness, with linemen such as Moss, McDonald, Harris, Cohen, and Harvey. Linebackers Brandon Siler and Earl Everett led the team in tackles during the regular season, but would need to react quickly against McFadden and Jones to plug holes. Beyond that, the secondary would be chasing hard after the Razorback runners, and that meant safeties Tony Joiner and Reggie Nelson would be asked to hog-tie those wild Hogs.

Florida's running game had been anemic, with the oft-injured De-Shawn Wynn accruing only 648 yards for the year, and a quarterback, Tebow, second with 407. Of foremost importance, the Gators would have to get the ball in the hands of their playmakers, chiefly freshman sensation Percy Harvin, who had sped 41 yards for a touchdown against FSU in the same kind of direct-snap formation that Arkansas deployed. Harvin had recovered from the neck strain received against the Seminoles. Wynn, who'd also left the FSU game with an injury, was back up to speed. And so was wide receiver Dallas Baker, who had been dinged.

Leak was aiming to build on his success against FSU, adding to his résumé, which included back-to-back years with wins over archrivals Tennessee, Georgia, and FSU. Leak's 21 touchdowns and 2,540 yards passing might not have been Heisman-like, but his performance on the road had certainly been. He needed only 65 yards to break Wuerffel's school career passing record. As for the Heisman, it was going to belong to Ohio State's Troy Smith.

While critics were ignoring Florida's talent or dissing the Gators' opponents, Meyer was focused on the road ahead. As for style points, another SEC championship trophy in their case would be plenty of style for the Florida Gators.

In playing for the SEC, Meyer was sticking to his Plan to Win, but adding a few accoutrements. He remained true to his "Play great defense" commitment. He would also continue to rely on his special teams delivering. He also kept his promise about doing everything within his power to give his players a chance to win, including the calling of surprise plays deep in his own territory with Florida trailing Arkansas.

Following the pregame meal at the Atlanta hotel, Urban went back to his room to finish out his game plan call sheet and try to unwind, but he couldn't relax. The weekly body punches were adding up, and Urban was reeling a bit from the pregame pressure, what with so much riding on the outcome. All of a sudden on game day he was balled up in a knot of anxiety.

The men in the room with Meyer could feel the tension. Bud Meyer knew what was riding on this game for his son, as did Earle Bruce, who decided to intervene.

The wise seventy-five-year-old coach suddenly stood up and got into the grill of Florida's head coach. Bruce began screaming and poking his index finger into Urban's chest as if the Florida coach were about to suit up and take the field.

"I'm sitting there, and I'm so uptight about this game—for some reason, I'm blocked up," Meyer said. "Coach Bruce is sitting there and I don't even know he's sitting there with me, and he grabs me. Here's a seventy-five-year-old man doing this and screaming at me, 'Are you OK?'

"And I go, 'No, coach, I'm not all right.'

"And he looks right at me and says, 'Now listen'—he starts screaming and cussing me—'you let that go, you hear me! You let it go, you take your chances, you shoot everything you've possibly got at it.' He starts lecturing me.

"It was the best lecture I've ever had.

"So on my game plan sheet, right at the bottom, I wrote down, 'Let it go.'"

He didn't yet know what that meant, but Meyer's quarterback came out smoking, taking over where he had left off in the fourth quarter against FSU. Leak scored on a 9-yard run, then hit Harvin with a 37-yard strike for a touchdown. On that play Florida took a 17–0 lead and Leak broke Danny Wuerffel's career yardage record of 10,875.

At the half, Arkansas trailed 17–7, but came storming back with a touchdown pass from McFadden to Jones. Suddenly Leak had a lapse in judgment on the option play, as his pitchout was intercepted by Hog defensive lineman Antwain Robinson, who ran 40 yards for the score and a 21–17 Arkansas lead.

Meanwhile, something was also going on with the national rankings.

The buzz had started somewhere in the first half of the UCLA-Southern Cal game. Writers covering the SEC championship game in Atlanta congregated in front of TVs in the rear of the press box.

Word got out in the Georgia Dome that TV sets were in the men's bathrooms and hundreds of spectators gathered there in the final minutes to watch UCLA and USC. The pervading feeling was that USC would rally to overcome the Bruins' 13–9 lead.

Tim Tebow's "bad moment"—he got a penalty in the 2009 National Championship win over Oklahoma for "taunting" Sooner defensive Nick Harris (No. 5)
(Tim Casey of Gator Country)

Urban Meyer and Percy Harvin pondering a plan in the 2009 National Championship game.
(Tim Casey of Gator Country)

Although he's not as intense as he once was on the sideline, Urban does show his emotions.
(Tim Casey of Gator Country)

Louis Murphy celebrates a touchdown with Tim Tebow.
(Tim Casey of Gator Country)

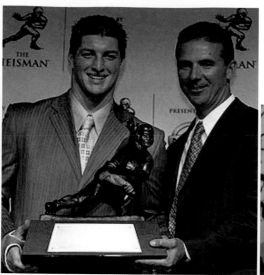

Tim Tebow and Urban with the hardware at the Heisman ceremonies in New York.
(Tim Casey of Gator Country)

That's Urban and his son, Nate, on the lake for their morning cruise.
(Tim Casey of Gator Country)

Urban looks at his special mementos, which he keeps in his pocket at all times.
(Tim Casey of Gator Country)

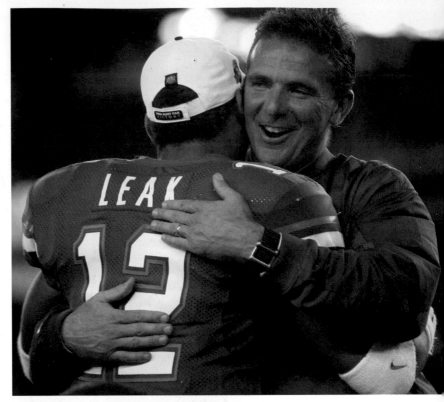

Urban says good-bye to his national championship quarterback Chris Leak.
(Tim Casey of Gator Country)

It's a bird, it's a plane, it's Super—no, it's Tim Tebow!

(Tim Casey of Gator Country)

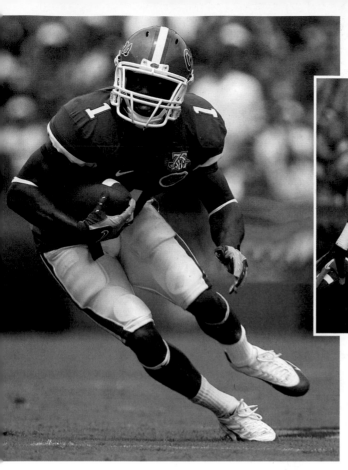

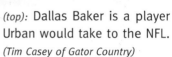

(top): Dallas Baker is a player Urban would take to the NFL.
(Tim Casey of Gator Country)

(left): Percy Harvin motors like a sports car.
(Tim Casey of Gator Country)

A moment with Bubba Caldwell, star receiver.
(Tim Casey of Gator Country)

Gigi shares a moment with dad after a win at "the Swamp."
(Tim Casey of Gator Country)

(top): The Meyer Boys, Urban and Nate, take a moment to relax in practice.
(Tim Casey of Gator Country)

(left): Urban and daughter Nicki at football practice.
(Tim Casey of Gator Country)

Michael "Sunshine" Guilford, seen here with his friend and teammate Tim Tebow, was killed in a tragic accident.
(The Guilford Family)

The Gatorade Shower after national
championship victory.
(Tim Casey of Gator Country)

Sometimes Urban gets a little intense
in the heat of a game.
(Tim Casey of Gator Country)

Urban going to work at the Swamp.
(Tim Casey of Gator Country)

Urban speaking to the media in
Arizona at the BCS title game.
(Tim Casey of Gator Country)

Shelley and Urban listen to the press
conference at the Times Square Hard
Rock Cafe after the Heisman Trophy
Award Presentation on Saturday,
December 8, 2007 in New York City.
(Tim Casey of Gator Country)

Urban hoists the crystal ball
as Chris Leak looks on.
(Tim Casey of Gator Country)

Meyer pretty much knew what was going on out in California, but wanted his team to stay focused on Atlanta, where at the moment he had all he could handle.

Things had taken a turn for the worst and this was beginning to look like a replay of the second-half meltdown at Auburn. Emotions were churning in Meyer's gut as the game was slipping away.

This was the time for Urban to screw up that courage that his good friend Dean Hood had been talking about when he said, "It's the old thing about 'What is courage?' Is that the lack of fear? No, courage is being afraid, but doing it anyway. That's what I love about Urban. It rips his heart out. But he still makes those tough decisions. And he'll throw his balls out there."

In the world of Urban Meyer logic, there would indeed be the time to "let it go," and this was it: fourth down and ten at his own 15-yard line and his team trailing 21–17 in the biggest game of his coaching career to date. It was a call, he admitted later, that "could have cost me my job."

Looking down at his game plan sheet, Meyer saw the notation of Earle's advice to "let it go." And so he did: One of the gutsiest calls I'd seen in four decades of covering football was about to be pulled off by the special teams coach, who was also the head coach.

Frankly, when Florida came out of the huddle and Eric Wilbur took the snap of James Smith, and ran to his right as if to make a rugby-like kick, some of us in the press box thought Meyer had taken leave of his senses. We did not know this play had been rehearsed for weeks, honed over and over in practice by two reliable seniors, Wilbur and wide receiver Jemalle "Cap" Cornelius.

"The play is called Blitz at Nine and we ran it almost every single day," said Cornelius. "We used to kid about when we were going to put it out there. He [Meyer] looked over at me and said, 'Cap, you ready?' And I said, 'Yeah, I'm ready, coach.' And he said, 'Get the first down.'"

As he jogged on the field, Cap got a bit nervous. He hoped the Arkansas defense didn't detect his presence, because he hadn't played on the punt team all year. He was also a little fidgety because he hadn't touched the ball all night.

As Wilbur moved to his right with the ball, all of a sudden he flipped it back to Cornelius going in the other direction. The captain from Fort Meade, with the aid of fullback Billy Latsko's block, skirted up the left side for what looked like an eternity—but was, in fact, just 17 yards.

"I saw nothing but green," said Cornelius, "and I was just running, running, running. I saw the back of Kyle Jackson, because he was sealing a guy off, but otherwise all I could see was green, and I was thinking, 'get the first down, get the first down, get the first down!'"

One of the greatest calls in the hundred-year history of Florida football didn't even go for a touchdown, but it accomplished the momentum shift, got a first down, and sent a message that Urban Meyer was willing to do anything to try to win this game—just as Brandon Siler had said.

"I think that completely changed the momentum of the game," said Jarvis Moss, watching from the sideline.

"That just shows the heart your coach has to run that kind of play," Siler would later say. "It's one kind of play when you make it, it's great. But when you miss it, everybody goes, 'What were you thinking on that?!' But he had no problem, because he believed in it."

How was that for style points, Mr. Herbstreit?

Since that had worked so well, Meyer was tempted a few minutes later when Florida was faced with a fourth-and-one at its own 41-yard line—hey, what's a measly one yard when you've made ten? But he got talked out of it on the headset by co-defensive coordinator Greg Mattison, who could tell Urban was contemplating another gamble. "Let's kick it away and go play some defense," Mattison said, perhaps reminding his boss of his own tenet. Meyer did, and he was rewarded.

Razorback punt returner Reggie Fish, obviously looking to make a big play, tried to field the ball at the Arkansas 2-yard line. Fish looked up and saw three Gator gunners coming after him, fumbled the ball in the end zone, and Florida's Wondy Pierre-Louis was there to cover it for a touchdown. The 24–21 lead didn't lock the game up, because there was still some work to be done, but that sequence of plays probably best defined what Meyer's football coaching philosophy was all about.

The commitment to Urban's Way means sending extra gunners on kicks and punts. It means practicing special plays over and over and over in the hot Florida sun and putting the ball into the hands of invested veterans who have the skill set for success—all of them coached thoroughly about ball security.

"I believe in well-trained guys who work hard in practice and hang on to the ball," Meyer said. "It's called competitive excellence. If you believe in fate, why do guys work hard? Why not just hope fate takes over?

"We don't believe in luck. If we did, why don't you put a rabbit's foot in your hat, rub a bald head, and win the game? We believe in hard work and being trained for that moment when your number's called. Some people don't believe that.

"Some people believe that kid from Arkansas dropped a punt because of lights or something going on. I think he dropped a punt because he knows our punt coverage is so good. If you've ever watched our punt coverage, you know how many guys were around him. Six! How many of these other people have punt coverage like that? He dropped the ball because he knew he was going to get whacked. That's how we teach our players: There's no such thing as luck. It's competitive excellence. So when your number is called, you make that play."

The good news was rolling in: There on the video wall was the evidence in big, bright white lights, a final score, UCLA 13, USC 9. The Gators had a clear shot to the title game—providing they could put Arkansas away.

Could this be déjà vu ten years later? Were the football gods lining up in Florida's favor for a second time in a decade?

With a little under eight minutes to play, Gary Danielson of CBS weighed in on the style points controversy as the network flashed up a graphic comparing the Gators' schedule to Michigan's.

"OK, here's another way of looking at it: Michigan or Florida?" Danielson asked the viewer. "Everybody, you can TiVo it, stop it—here's your ballot. I've ranked, I think, from most impressive win to the least impressive win.

"You can see Florida has the tougher schedule," said Danielson. "That's style points!"

Basically, Danielson went through each team's opponent, side by side, and concluded that Florida deserved to play Ohio State for the title because the Gators had won the championship in America's toughest conference. And the graphic placed on the screen gave the statistics why. Later, this "tale of the tape" would cause a spat between Herbstreit and the CBS college crew, Verne Lundquist and Danielson.

Though that graphic was originally Danielson's idea, he pointed out that it was a collaboration of the CBS team, including producer Craig Silver and broadcast partner Lundquist. They got a third opinion of it from Gary's friend and CBS spotter David Moulton, Fort Myers, Florida, talk show host.

Herbstreit took offense at the graphic and told a Michigan radio station:

"When I was watching [the SEC championship], when they put that graphic up, the only thing I could think of was that the coordinating producer would force them to do something like that to kind of destroy any credibility they'd all built over the years, just obviously by standing up and talking about an SEC school."

Herbstreit later told me he had made a mistake in reacting to Danielson's comment and criticizing CBS for losing its credibility. Now he wishes he hadn't reacted that way to what he calls "an ambush."

Though he did not like Herbstreit taking a swipe at the credibility of his network and broadcast team, Danielson didn't want to pick another fight. He completely understood that in the role of analyst you can get trapped by your opinions. He points out that if his graphic had said that Michigan deserved to play for the title, he could have become the poster boy of Gator Haters instead.

"I'm not saying I was right or that I knew who deserved to play for the championship, because nobody knew that—not me, not Kirk Herbstreit, not Bob Davie . . . nobody," Danielson said later. "What I said needed to be said, but I only said it because Florida won the championship of the toughest conference in America, and Michigan had already had their chance. But I have to remind Gator fans that if USC had won, it would have been a different story and they would have been mad at me."

The disagreement about Herbstreit's official position concerning the Gators' chances of being in the BCS Championship Game against Ohio State stems from what he considers a bit of misunderstanding and maybe a misinterpretation. Angry Gator fans don't agree, as they think he was a total Michigan advocate at Florida's expense.

"The only regret I have is that people completely misconstrued my opinion in early December about who deserved to be in The Game when I said 'Ohio State and Michigan,'" said Herbstreit. "Once that discussion was over, it was time to talk about the next forty days—that argument's over, Florida's in The Game. Now, what do you think of The Game?"

Then there is the matter of the polls, how close they were down to the end and whether it was a conflict for either Danielson or Herbstreit to be taking an advocacy position for any team. Danielson's chart seemed to speak for itself. Herbstreit, said his critics, spoke on behalf of the Wolverines because of a Big Ten prejudice.

"It's a lousy system when guys like me can sway the outcome of the polls and the same for the coaches," admitted Danielson, who played collegiately at Purdue of the Big Ten. "I don't like it one bit. But I get paid to give my opinions. I didn't create this system that let's people like me vote in it. But it's not my job to change it."

Indeed, it is far from a perfect way to pick a champion, and the argument begs for a playoff. But for now and the foreseeable future, it must be settled by public—and media—opinion. That means announcers who see the same conference play each week are likely to have a bias. Danielson admits that is true and understands why. As far as his own regional bias, Herbstreit wants it known that his opinions are not influenced one whit by his personal allegiance to Ohio State, or the Big Ten.

Florida would win the game, 38–28, and the SEC title with the final touchdown coming on another razzle-dazzle—a Tim Tebow-to-Andre Caldwell-to-Tate Casey double pass for an 80-yard score, perhaps putting in a little "style" punctuation.

Siler had one of his biggest nights, leading the defense with twelve tackles as his teammates intercepted three passes for the fourth time that season. As for McFadden, the Gators held the SEC's leading rusher to just 73 yards and allowed Jones only 57.

As the final seconds ticked off on the Georgia Dome clock and the swarm of Gators gathered on the field, the blessings of the moment grew exponentially: an SEC championship—and maybe a whole lot more.

The next day, after arriving back in Gainesville, the Florida players were summoned by Meyer for some sort of announcement. Urban wasn't fooling anybody. These Gators knew they were going to get their championship shot.

When he reflected on it, Meyer couldn't help but marvel at the turn of events. Some days he'd thought playing for a national championship that season was purely a pipe dream. Between the rash of injuries early in the season and the national media's disregard for his team's "style" of winning, Meyer just couldn't find the silver lining anywhere.

On Saturdays during the season, after Florida had played in an early day game, Meyer would go home and watch football on TV, becoming subjected to the disrespect of the Bristol Boys.

Sometimes when the ESPN cartel commentators talked about what teams should play Ohio State for the national title, the Gators never got a whiff. In one late-season poll on ESPN of which team should play against Ohio State for the national championship, Florida wasn't even a candidate.

"I love college football and it's just part of the business," Meyer said on the Sunday after the SEC title win on his teleconference. "But it's amazing, the overanalyzing, how a team wins. I've never really studied that before. So, yeah, I thought there would be an issue with the respect Florida would get."

Finally, the Gators got that respect. Through an amazing turn of events, the stars became properly aligned, the computers and the humans reached the same conclusion, and after a roller coaster of an SEC championship win over Arkansas, the Gators moved to No. 2.

Meyer had been right. Winning the SEC would get his team its shot.

16

The Joy of Winning It All

Ohio State was a portrait of consistency, with the swagger of a nineteen-game win streak. And why not? The Buckeyes had the Heisman Trophy winner, the undefeated record, the No. 1 ranking. Las Vegas odds makers made them a little more than a touchdown favorite. Perhaps they also carried a bit of overconfidence and almost smugness into the holidays. But they were about to run into a well-coached team with a sense of purpose and supercharged emotions.

This was the football game fans in the South and Midwest had always wanted to see, but it had been precluded by conference tie-ins with bowls. And playing during the regular season probably wouldn't have been an option prior to 1970 because of segregation (Florida's team wasn't integrated until then).

An age-old argument about regional bragging rights in college football was about to be settled. At long last, there would be some kind of real measuring stick between the Big Ten and Southeastern Conference champions in the first-ever postseason meeting: the 2007 Bowl Championship Series National Championship Game. It was also the first time Ohio State and Florida would play in football.

If longtime Florida fans were honest, they were still a little

queasy about returning to the Valley of the Sun eleven years after
one of their worst butt-whippings in history. Steve Spurrier's unbeaten 1995 team was undressed by Nebraska, 62–24, in Tempe,
Arizona, and that didn't exactly inspire fond memories—even if the
2007 game had moved to Glendale.

Some people think that 1995 Florida club might have been Spurrier's best, but just happened to come up against one of the greatest
college football teams in history on a night when Tom Osborne's 1995
Cornhuskers played mistake-free football and caught an ordinary Gator defense napping.

Yet Meyer felt good about coming back to the place where two
years prior his unbeaten Utah Utes had pummeled Pittsburgh, 35–7, in
the Tostitos Fiesta Bowl—the school's greatest football moment. Just as
his Utah team was going to rock the college football world, so would
his 2006 Gators, who were still an unknown quantity.

The Buckeyes had to worry about cobwebs, their last game having
been against Michigan on November 15. They had been in dry dock
for over fifty days, and that would turn out to their disadvantage. They
may also have failed to note the evolving trend of triumphant under-
dogs. On the same University of Phoenix Stadium field one week ago,
Boise State had pulled off one of the biggest upsets in recent post season history: a 43–42 overtime victory over Oklahoma in the Tostitos
Fiesta Bowl. First-year Boise Coach Chris Peterson elected to go for
two and the win, which he got when quarterback Jared Zabransky
executed a beautiful variation of the old Statute of Liberty play.

Meyer would have some surprises for fellow Ohioan Jim Tressel,
too, but not of the Boise State genre. Instead of trick plays, Meyer
would stay true to his Plan to Win commitment about defense and
beat the Buckeyes at their own game of helmet-to-helmet football.

During preparation Urban would, of course, consult regularly
with his mentors. He called Lou Holtz, who advised him to keep his
team's emotions in check and evenly paced until the night before the
game, and then give his motivational speech.

Holtz, who had national-championship-game experience, warned
Urban against getting the team fired up too soon, telling him, "Don't
play that game night until January eighth. You don't need to play it

December thirteenth, you don't need to play it December sixth. You need to play it January eighth."

Out of the conversation with Holtz came the idea of breaking the forty-one days ahead into increments and keeping players on task for each segment of the plan. At the same time, Urban wanted his team to keep that chip on its shoulder. So he went a little old-school with his psychological warfare.

Meyer used the slight by the national media, circling the wagons in his finest Earle Bruce/Woody Hayes fashion. Preying on the angle that nobody was showing his Gators any love, he pulled out the oldest trick in the book: the dreaded Bulletin Board.

Most coaches don't believe players can be motivated by bulletin-board material anymore, but again Meyer went against that trend. After all, the body of work for his propaganda war wasn't inspired by just a single clipping from the local sports page, but an entire season of being neglected as a potential national championship contender—what he viewed as a clear-cut bias against Florida.

Some of the lack of respect by the media was perhaps justified because of the way Florida's offense struggled midseason, but Urban wasn't going to admit that. Besides, he had forty-one days to brainwash his players. The campaign would be so successful that he wouldn't even need to give his team a pregame pep talk.

This was not just any old bulletin board, but a ten-foot monstrosity strategically placed near the food table the week before the game, which Meyer called "ten feet of nonsense."

On it were clippings about Ohio State's superiority and Florida's fallibility, taken from newspaper or magazine stories, the Internet, and, in some cases, right out of a fiction book.

"Half of it was real and half of it was made up. And the half that was made up I signed 'Kirk Herbstreit of ESPN,'" Urban confessed.

Meyer told Mick Marotti, his partner in crime on the bulletin board, he wanted the material to be picked up by the end of the week, "but I wanted it where they were so disgusted with the team they were playing . . . I told them to make it up. They'd put it on the computer and make it look official."

Earlier in the week, as Meyer and Marotti sat back observing, they could see the message was getting through. They noticed players getting their food, reading something on the board, and remarking to one of their teammates, "Hey, look at this!"

Meanwhile, Meyer also showed his players a copy of Lindy's Fiesta Bowl preview, "A Championship Season," which someone had sent him. The slick magazine featured Ohio State Buckeyes plastered on every page but two. Stuffing the magazine in the back pocket of his coaching shorts, Meyer took it to practice daily. During warm-ups he would flip through the magazine—pages and pages of scarlet and grey, but no orange and blue—until reaching the tiny Gator segment. Then he'd skip over to a page with a photo of Buckeye quarterback Troy Smith and say, "Who's that? Chris Leak is a pretty good quarterback, too."

Next, Meyer would turn to a photo of the Ohio State coaching staff and say, "We've got pretty good coaches, don't we?"

He showed it to the players over and over and over. They got the point.

As they wound down for the holidays and prepared to leave for the desert, practice had been stellar and issues were almost nonexistent. However, Reggie Nelson had bad news about his mother a few days before Christmas. Mary Lakes had been battling breast cancer for more than three years and had tried, unsuccessfully, to keep her son from worrying about it. Sometimes she would wear a wig so Reggie wouldn't find out she had lost her hair due to chemotherapy treatments.

Realizing the gravity of the situation, and knowing the pain of losing one's mother, Meyer and assistant coach Charlie Strong had paid a visit to Reggie's mom in Melbourne, Florida.

A few days later, Meyer received a card from his All-American safety, which read, "Words can't express how much your thoughtfulness is appreciated. THANK YOU." Nelson's personal comment was printed neatly on the opposite page: "I truly feel that this card says it all, but I really want you to know that I appreciate you taking the time out of your busy schedule to visit my mother and me this week." It was signed, "Reggie Nelson, #1."

His mother died a few days later on December 21. Reggie understandably declined interviews in Arizona.

Urban knew how it felt. "I went through the same thing seven years ago," said Meyer. "If anybody's gone through that, the last thing you want to do is deal with other people asking how you're doing. He's doing much better."

Then there were the cold, hard facts: Ohio State's offensive line could not match up with the quicker Florida defensive linemen. Bryan Mattison was there to bear witness. The son of Gator codefensive coordinator Greg Mattison, the 6'3", 272-pound defensive end and captain of the Iowa Hawkeye defense, knew from playing against the Buckeyes that their guards and tackles were slower. Since Bryan was home with his father during bowl preparations and attended Gator practice, he gladly shared that information.

"He [Bryan] would tell me every day that there's no way they [Ohio State] could block me," Jarvis Moss said.

Bryan, his father, and the Gator linemen also studied Ohio State's offensive slide technique and knew their scheme so thoroughly that they could guess where the ball carrier or passer was going to be. It was as if they had a copy of the Ohio State game plan.

"Coach Mattison broke the film down and the way he explained things, 'If you get this or that, this is what you can expect,'" said All-SEC defensive lineman Ray McDonald. It also didn't hurt that in three-plus weeks of preparation, the Gator D-lineman watched three games of tape on Ohio State—one of them the Iowa game. Florida and Iowa played similar defensive fronts, so as regulars McDonald, Steve Harris, Derrick Harvey, Joe Cohen, and Moss watched the Hawkeyes versus the Buckeyes, they were interested to see how No. 99 of Iowa was doing, since they all knew Bryan personally. They never let on to coach Mattison that they knew his son was the guy on tape causing the Ohio State offensive line such a problem.

"I never said much," said Greg. "and they were sitting there watching one day and Bryan is playing really good against Ohio State. And Ray McDonald said, 'Coach, see that ninety-nine—is that how you want us to play that 'six technique'? He had knocked the tight end back and made a good play, and I said, 'Yeah, that's exactly right—step with that foot and knock him back.'"

A few plays later when Bryan ran downfield and caught the ball carrier, his father said, "You know what? If you guys will run to the ball like that number ninety-nine there, we'll have a heck of a chance." And they all had a good laugh.

Mattison's son knew from hearing his father talk about the talented Florida group he coached that Ohio State was going to have all it could handle. What really convinced Bryan that it was going to be a mismatch in Florida's favor was how easily the Gator linemen began to recognize Ohio State's formations and plays. When Bryan saw them work on pass defense drills, he was blown away at the speed of Moss and Harvey.

Later that night when the Mattisons went home for dinner, Bryan was asked by his mother, Ann, "How do you think they [the Gators] will do?"

To which the Iowa defensive captain replied: "Mom, I've never seen anything like those ends. They won't block them!" That "they" he spoke of would include two All–Big Ten first-team offensive linemen, tackle T. J. Downing and center Doug Datish. "Them," of course, were Harvey and Moss.

"We were watching film all month," said McDonald, "and everybody on defense was saying, 'Man, we're going to beat these guys.' Watching Ohio State on film, they were moving so slow. And it was like, 'Man, how can teams not stop this team? They do the same thing over and over!'"

The defense had such an air of assurance that they almost had to guard against over-confidence. All the Florida players were encouraged not to lip off or respond to anything said by the Ohio State players—even the stuff on Urban's bulletin board.

"Man, they said a lot of stuff about us," said McDonald. "When we got out there on the field, it was like caged animals let loose."

In his lengthy final press conference, Meyer was asked to reflect on his not-so-famous days.

Q. *Urban, when you are on the stage like this, do you think much about the days when nobody talked to you, nobody knew who you were?*

A: *Yeah. I look back and loved every minute of it. (Smiling) I remember my first press conference at Bowling Green up in Detroit. I came walking in as new head football coach. I sat in Media Day and, after a half hour, looked and said, "Am I done?" I grabbed my stuff and left. I cherish those days.*

Meyer also harkened back to his first game as head coach when his Bowling Green team was opening up in Columbia, Missouri, and he had begun to freak out: "Six years ago sitting in that hotel room before the game, I remember looking at my wife and saying, 'What happens if we get our brains beat in and lose every game, how long will they keep us?' She said, I bet you win them all.' And I said, 'No.' I thought there was no chance.

"We wake up and do a walk-through like yesterday, and I saw a look about them—that maybe you might find a way to do this. Our first series, first down, nothing; second down, nothing; and then we end up winning the game. I remember the time well." He would remember this time well, too, because nothing would ever compare to the memory his Florida team was about to make.

By now it had become tough to contain his optimism. Meyer was telling his staff members, closest friends, and relatives that he loved everything he'd seen on tape about the matchups. The night before the game, Urban pulled off his masterpiece. He had made up his own "Tale of the Tape," pitting position versus position and stat versus stat.

In his "How We Are Going to Win" speech, Meyer drove home the point that his Gators had played the toughest schedule in the country. "We can beat Ohio State," Meyer told them. "They have no idea what they are talking about. We're a better football team."

The irony of this is that Meyer was taking the very argument that ESPN's analyst had used against the Gators' chance of winning a national championship—because of the Murderers' Row schedule—and parlaying it into the rationale as to why they were going to win it.

Whereas he had played the hype game with the bulletin board, now Urban was giving it to his team straight. As he ticked off Ohio State's opponents, the Florida coach drew rapt attention.

He talked about Ohio State playing Illinois. Then Purdue. Then Minnesota. Then Indiana.

Then he ticked off Florida's schedule.

"My whole discussion that night was, 'You played Tennessee, Auburn, Alabama, LSU, Georgia, South Carolina . . . our 'easy' games were South Carolina and FSU—and those are no easy games."

Then he projected his masterpiece on an overhead screen, typed on two pages of plain white paper, emphasizing the difference in caliber of competition, under the heading:

No Confusion = How to Beat Ohio State
Get your Position Group to Play Better than Ohio State's

It contained eleven comparisons, position by position, and seven statistical categories. On the position comparison sheet, Ohio State was given a slight edge in the running game, fewest sacks allowed, most sacks by defensive linemen, and field goal kicking. One of the most telling comparisons was the first:

OFFENSE

QUARTERBACKS	COMPLETION %	TOP 25 DEF FACED
UF Leak/Tebow	63%	5
OSU Smith	66%	1

Ohio State was proud of its completion percentage, but Urban wanted to emphasize his quarterbacks faced better defenses.

Urban put a big orange "F" next to "Quarterbacks" for "advantage, Florida." And so on.

If there had been any doubt by any of the Florida players about whether they were the better team, it was pretty much erased.

"So those kids went to bed that night knowing that we had the advantage," Meyer said.

Certainly Ryan Smith did. The All-SEC corner totally bought in. "He told us the record of every team they had played and named the last seven teams and the records of the teams they had beaten," said Smith. "This was no bulletin board stuff."

Statistics could, of course, be made to prove anything, but by now Meyer had his team so convinced they were going to win that the players felt they couldn't be stopped.

Yet there was always this truism: You can draw it up, believe it, coach it—but sometimes it doesn't work out that way. How would it fly this time?

Not being privy to all that information right away, or being smart enough to figure it out, I had my doubts about Florida's chances and on several national radio shows had predicted an Ohio State victory, 31–28.

Meanwhile, the very idea that the Florida Gators would be playing for a national championship in Meyer's second season was remarkable, if not staggering. That the University of Florida could become the only school ever to win the national title in football and basketball in the same year was downright incredible.

The night before the game as I was about to retire, I thought about some of the great Gator fans, friends, and family members who were not there to share the moment. My late sister, Shirley Lovell Ritch, often my traveling companion for road games, had died eighteen months prior. I had made a note in my column for the next day to remember Shirley and some of the others, including three former coaches*:

"Good morning to Bob Whitfield, Shirley Lovell Ritch, Ed Kensler, Jim Niblack*, Dutton Long, Armand Lovell, Fred Montsdeoca, Red Mitchum, Charlie LaPradd, Ben Ayres and Charley Pell*—and all those other devoted Gator fans we have lost in the last couple of years. Your friends will be thinking of you Monday night."*

In the middle of the night, somewhere in the vicinity of 4:00 A.M.,

I awakened to the beeping sound of a cell phone belonging to my son Brenden, and, not wanting to awaken him, attempted to find my way in the dark room to turn it off. Having banged my shin on the furniture and fully awakened, I felt the urge to sit down at my computer and write about the revelation that had just come to me over the transom of my hotel room from the Great Unknown. Perhaps it had also banged some sense into my head.

I could see it now. Florida was going to beat Ohio State. It was clear, because certainly if Michigan could score 39 points on the Buckeyes, then the Gators could. I sat down and wrote in my blog:

> *A man has a right to change his mind, too. I like the Gators tonight.*
>
> *I'm dealing with my gut instinct, which has over the years been fairly accurate when it comes to handicapping Florida Gator football games. That's why today, when I make my final radio prediction on KKFN Denver, the* Irv & Joe Show, *I will be throwing them a curve. Both Irv and Joe are expecting me to pick Ohio State, 31–28. Instead, I will reverse that outcome, with Florida winning, 39–31.*

Boy, was I way off. It was going to be a lot worse than that.

Chris Leak was about to be both celebrated and exonerated, but it had taken every one of those previous forty-six games he had started over four years, beginning with the Kentucky game of his freshman year in 2003.

Yet, if there was any real continuity between the Spurrier and Meyer years, it was Leak, who kept the fires burning, propping up hopes of the Gator Nation with a 35-12 record as a starter.

Even when his own teammates questioned his toughness, Leak held it together. Sometimes it got wearisome—the losing and the negativity and the booing—and finally, the misguided-but-well-intentioned Tebow fans who wanted Leak to move aside for No. 15. If he never had many close friends on the team, he did have the support of his brother and parents.

"He has a great family," Meyer said. "His brother C.J. [who worked for Meyer that season in the football office] was right there for him and was a powerful influence for Chris."

The dialogue probably went something like this between brothers:

"It's OK, Chris, stay patient. Don't worry about those fans booing, Chris, just block them out of your head. Chris, just stay focused. This is your team, this is your time."

The cornerstone of Meyer's football philosophy was that lean-on-me trust among teammates and coaches, not easily achieved. Invested veterans didn't always trust incoming freshmen. Coaches didn't always trust players, and vice versa.

Until late in his senior season, Leak's teammates didn't always trust him. Their quarterback was aloof because he rarely hung out with them socially. He wasn't vocal. Some players were quiet—Leak was a church mouse. He wasn't forthcoming in interviews and usually only spoke to the media when he was asked to do so.

Many doubted Leak's heart, and his willingness to put his body on the line to win the game, the way Tebow would. If they didn't totally trust Tebow's experience, they at least trusted Tim's heart. At first Leak seemed interested in mentoring Tebow, but in the shank of the season, it became a distraction.

"When we're winning, Chris loves everybody," wide receiver Bubba Caldwell said.

With 74,628 fans looking on at the University of Phoenix stadium and tickets outside being scalped for more than $1,000 each right up to kickoff, quarterback Chris Leak was razor sharp as he was about to make a statement in the game of his life.

Only sixteen ticks into the game, Ohio State's quick strike sent shivers down the collective spine of the Gator Nation. The Florida Gators and their fans were given pause to wonder if this media buildup of Ohio State was, indeed, justified. Ted Ginn Jr. streaked 93 yards for a touchdown and a 7–0 lead. One of the fastest Gators, safety Reggie Nelson, was clearly held by a Buckeye as he was closing within two yards of catching Ginn, but it went unnoticed by the Pacific Ten Conference officials.

Ohio State had presented the challenge. Did Florida have the answer? Gator players were stunned, but began to gather themselves. Meyer was angry at first. Just when he was about to go after one of his special teams players, Urban felt Brandon Siler grab his arm. "Don't worry," Siler told his coach. "We've got you."

Over on the defensive side of the bench, once the initial shock subsided, Jarvis Moss turned to inadvertently make eye contact with one single, anonymous Gator fan sitting in the stands among Buckeyes. "He looked right at me and I looked right at him," said Moss, "and then he looked down in the stands and looked right back up. We made this connection. We were telling each other that things were going to be okay."

Ginn's touchdown made Dallas Baker "kind of nervous," but then he thought back to the regular season when his coach had reminded the team on how they react to a shot across the bow like this from an opponent.

"The whole year, Coach Meyer was saying something like, 'Something big is going to happen in the game, but don't let it get to you,'" Baker said, "because we had a couple of close games. And when I looked around, most guys were complaining that Reggie Nelson had been held on the return. Some guys were just amped up and ready to play. But mostly I was ready to get back on the field."

In times like this, Meyer would reach in his pocket for his chain of medals and grasp his favorite—the one that reminded him of his mother—between his thumb and index finger.

Since his days when he blacked out and nearly fell while on the sidelines as an assistant at Notre Dame, Meyer had tried to learn how to better control his emotions. It turned out he had an arachnoid cyst on his brain, benign, but it also caused severe migraines when aggravated by emotional stress. The doctors told Meyer to "cool it with the screaming and yelling," which he did until he became a head coach at Utah. During a game against Oregon, in a tense moment of the fourth quarter, he almost passed out. Doctors helped him pinpoint those emotional outbursts—usually, in the fourth quarter—and he began to alter his behavior pattern.

Before he had any more outbursts, he had to stop and think about that.

So this time, on the Florida sideline, with just sixteen seconds gone in the biggest football game of his life, Meyer turned and walked away calmly, almost dispassionate and expressionless. At least outwardly. Deep inside he was fairly seething, because he knew his team had to make an immediate answer.

Ryan Smith, as did other players, looked into the face of his head coach and didn't see any emotion.

Wide receiver coach Billy Gonzales walked over and tapped Baker on the shoulder pad, saying, "Okay, Dallas, your turn."

That set up what would be the first of "Urban Meyer's Seven Key Plays" to winning the national championship.

High above Florida Field where Meyer was utilizing a luxury suite for an office as the football staff's were being refurbished in the spring of 2008, he punched up a video clip on his computer and pointed a red laser at the giant Sony screen sitting near his desk. This was more than fifteen months after Florida's national championship win. Meyer had chosen "Seven Key Plays" for our national championship skull-session review and was about to roll the tape on the first.

URBAN MEYER KEY PLAY No. 1:
Brandon James kick return

Brandon Siler wasn't concerned about Ginn taking the opening kickoff in for a score, but Siler was mad because he and his defensive teammates had been talking all week about shutting out Ohio State, and now that wasn't possible. But he kept calm and kept his head coach calm.

Meyer said if his team, down by a touchdown, didn't answer, the game was in jeopardy of being lost. According to the Plan to Win, field position after the kickoff would be crucial.

Video tape rolls:

"This is double eighty-nine, right after the touchdown, and that means we want to double-team their eight and nine defender," Meyer said, counting left to right across the Ohio State kickoff lineup.

Ohio State squib-kicks to keep the ball away from Florida's ace return man, Brandon James, and the football takes a hop. "And we catch it on the dead run at the five-yard line, so we're in great shape here," Meyer says, pointing with his laser. "I think their intent was not to kick it to him, because he's obviously a very good kick returner, and by this time of year we had a pretty good kick return team."

From the end zone view, now we can see James coming clear with the assistance of two of Florida's blockers, Cade Holliday and Nick Brooks, as they execute their double-team.

"This is called the Ambush Technique, and that's Darryon Robinson," Meyer said, *pointing out a block by a special teams player whom most people had never heard of. Kestahn Moore is the lead blocker. Tony Joiner also makes a block.*

Meanwhile, the back-side is sealed off by Gators. One Ohio State defender dives at the legs of James and misses. The Buckeyes are about to make the first of several critical mistakes.

"Brandon James does a great job," Meyer says, *as the Buckeye defender drags No. 25 down by the face mask after his 33-yard return. Fifteen-yard penalty against Ohio State. Florida gets the ball at the Ohio State 46—favorable field position achieved.*

The face mask penalty was against Ohio State kicker Aaron Pettrey and James's return had set up the offense for its first of three unanswered scores.

That was part of the answer, and here came the rest.

URBAN MEYER KEY PLAY No. 2:
Leak's pass to Baker for a score

It's 7–0 Ohio State, and just as he had done in the 74-yard drive against Florida State, Chris Leak began slicing and dicing the defense with short pass completions. Knowing that cornerback Malcolm Jenkins loved to jump slant routes, on the eighth play of the 46-yard drive, with a second down and three at the Buckeyes' 14-yard line, Meyer signaled in Sluggo, for the slant-and-go route.

"When coach Meyer called that play, I kind of knew I was going to score," said Baker.

Videotape rolls:

"We went four by one, which we call quad formation, and we're trying to isolate Dallas Baker against one of their corners in a one-on-one situation," said Meyer. "And it's easier to do when you motion Percy Harvin out of the backfield."

Baker (No. 81) is wide left and draws single coverage, as hoped, as Harvin (No. 8) goes in motion right.

"When we started the game off, we had a feeling they were going to play us in zone coverage, because we didn't feel they could match up man-to-man," said Meyer. "So in zone coverage we want to be very patient, block the perimeter.

"You'll notice on the first play we run the bubble screen for eight yards to Percy—we just wanted to see how they were going to play. When we motioned out, we felt like the Will [weakside] linebacker was moving over, but you have to be sound in numbers. We have four receivers, they only have four defenders—if everybody gets their block, it's over. If they cheat the Will linebacker to our quad, that's going to isolate Dallas on this corner, with just safety help over the top. He does cheat over, the corner jumps inside."

When Baker sells his inside-slant fake, sure enough Jenkins bites, Leak lobs the ball over his head, and Dallas adjusts, catching the ball for the easy score.

"Dallas does a great job, sticks it like he's going in," said Meyer. "Chris holds it long enough and we score. Very good execution by Chris and Dallas."

Now there was an immediate mood change on the Florida sideline.

"When our offense came out on the first series of the game and scored, our defense got pumped up," said Reggie Lewis. "That's one of the best drives I've ever seen."

Chris Hetland's extra point kick makes it 7–7 with just over ten minutes gone. Florida has answered. "If you don't score here, it's a whole different game," Meyer said.

Now there will be a couple of exclamation points, lifted right from the text of the Plan to Win.

First there is a key defensive stand—Tremaine McCollum breaking up Troy Smith's pass, Brandon Siler tackling the Ohio State quarterback after a 4-yard run, and then the first of three sacks by defensive end Derrick Harvey. Smith is running for his life, and, indeed, the Gators are flying their "great defense" flag. Special teams are about to strike again.

URBAN MEYER KEY PLAY NO. 3:
Another James return

This is another special teams play and another Ohio State penalty, which will put the ball in play in Buckeye territory with two minutes to play in the first period.

Videotape rolls:

"They're punting the ball from their own twenty-two. We have on the return team and Brandon James returns it twelve yards, and watch what happens here: This guy hits our guy [Jemalle Cornelius] late and we get fifteen more yards. So this punt return with the personal foul penalty now gives us the ball on the plus thirty-five-yard line, going in again."

This sets up the first of two more first-quarter touchdowns, and it's beginning to look almost easy.

URBAN MEYER KEY PLAY No. 4:
Option to Harvin for a touchdown

Florida has the ball at the Ohio State 5. Now that he's no longer in-jured, Harvin is about to become an offensive force. He takes the op-tion pitch from Leak and executes Urban's next key play for the go-ahead score, 14–7.

Videotape rolls:

"This is Nine Speed," Meyer says. "We send Percy Harvin in motion, over the top, expecting pressure, and run speed-option to the left. Chris pitches the ball to Percy, and it's very well blocked on the perimeter and Percy gets in for the touchdown." Key blocks are thrown by Bubba Caldwell and Cornelius Ingram. "Chris did a good job by calling an audible on this play," Meyer says. Florida goes up 14–7.

It appeared in slow motion that Harvin's knee was down at the 1, but the review said otherwise and the touchdown stood.

Florida's defense was about to take over the game and keep pour-ing it on.

Reggie "Not Even in a Walk-Through" Lewis, he with the yellow sticker, had been studying the moves of Heisman Trophy winner Troy Smith on tape. Late in the first quarter, the Florida cornerback caught Smith just right, and made a diving interception at the Florida 39, where Leak set up again. DeShawn Wynn stuck it in for a touchdown. Florida 21, Ohio State 7.

Sloopy was barely hanging on. The Gators had the nation's No. 1 team down, rubbing its nose in the dirt, with a 14-point lead that was about to grow into abject humiliation. What Nebraska did to Spurri-er's Gators ten years ago in the Desert, the 2006 Gators were doing to Tressel's Buckeyes.

Ohio State finally found a pulse when Antonio Pittman ran in from 18 yards in the second quarter to make it 21–14.

URBAN MEYER KEY PLAY No. 5:
THE fourth-and-one stop.

Now came *the* moment for *The* Ohio State, a fourth-down gamble that would live in Buckeye infamy. It was also *the* play for Florida, one that would take Ohio State completely off life support.

After failing to make third and one at his own 29, Tressel paused to consider the big gamble—going for it on fourth with just under four minutes left in the first half and his team only behind 24–14.

Florida's defensive players, in semidisbelief, began chiding Ohio State's coach, warning Tressel not to do it.

Lewis remembers Joiner making the international sign for punting, telling Tressel, "Y'all are not going to make the first down—that was a bad decision." At the same time, Moss was admonishing him, "Don't do it! You'd better not do it!"

He did it anyway.

Videotape rolls:

"*There's a little over three minutes left in the quarter and the score is only twenty-four to fourteen,*" *says Meyer.* "*They decide to go for it on fourth down, and this is the big play of the day, as far as confidence and as far as their team showing they're in a little bit of a panic situation.*"

Smith handed off to Pittman on the right side, and No. 95 in a blue jersey shot from the off-side tackle position, chasing Pittman down the line.

"*They run an off-tackle power play and Ray McDonald comes from the back side with great effort—the same kid that had two ACLs a year earlier.*"

Nose tackle Steve Harris bull-rushes Ohio State All–Big Ten center Doug Datish, pushing him backward almost two yards. Seven Florida defenders— including freshman linebacker Brandon Spikes, senior linebacker Earl Everett, and senior safety Tony Joiner—are there to contain on their left side, plugging all the holes. There is no place for Pittman to run, and Ray McDonald, with his two surgically repaired knees still not at 100 percent, catches Pittman and stops him short.

It wasn't just the biggest play of the national championship game, or even just the best of McDonald's career, according to Meyer, who called it "one of the great plays in Florida football history."

The nation's No. 1 team was about to come unraveled, so discombobulated just seconds before halftime that the game was already out of hand—and about to get more so.

The defense of Greg Mattison and Charlie Strong is, just as McDonald had predicted, playing as if they had been "caged animals."

Now kicker Chris Hetland, who had made only four field goals in the regular season, was back in form. Out of the hold of Butch Rowley, with a snap from James Smith, he kicked his second straight of 40 or more yards and put the Gators ahead, 27–14. Meyer had refused to give up on his senior from Leesburg, Georgia, despite a cold streak, and Hetland would repay him by going three for three in the post-season.

URBAN MEYER KEY PLAY No. 6:
Moss sack, Harvey recovery

As Bryan Mattison had said, there was no way Ohio State's offensive line could handle the speed of Florida's defensive linemen. That would be obvious with the five sacks by Florida—three by the game's Defensive Most Valuable Player Harvey and two by fellow defensive end Moss.

Not so obvious to the average fan was the manner in which Harris was man-handling Ohio State's Datish, who was getting shoved into his own backfield. Such was the disruption of Heisman winner Smith that he gained only 55 yards total offense, completing just 4 of 14 pass attempts.

Almost as if he were looking for a place to hide, Smith would be contained at every turn, like a mouse in a maze frantically trying to escape. This time it cost him a turnover that led to a Florida touchdown.

On first down at his own 20, Smith dropped back to pass, and Moss fought through a double-team to sack the quarterback and strip the ball at the Buckeye 6-yard line.

Videotape rolls:

"Jarvis Moss does a great job. Harvey picks it up at the five-yard line. And it's over. The game's over, because this one sets up the Tim Tebow pass to Bubba Caldwell."

Mattison's two defensive ends are living up to Meyer's vow that his team will play "great defense"—and then some.

URBAN MEYER KEY PLAY No. 7:
Tebow pass to Bubba Caldwell

Videotape rolls:
Florida leads Ohio State, 27–14, and is about to ice the game with 1:28 still left in the first half. Tebow is the quarterback, and no doubt the Buckeyes are expecting him to run, as he had done almost every time in short yardage situations like this during the season. Tebow takes one step toward the line, then takes off running to his left, pulls up, and hits Bubba Caldwell on a short pass. The senior receiver takes it in for the Gators' sixth score in seven possessions. Florida 34, Ohio State 14.

Meyer, a chess player, calls this the "checkmate of the game."

Bobby Fischer couldn't have played it better.

As many brilliant defensive plays as there had been by Florida, none was more symbolic than Everett's "helmetless tackle." Ohio State had the ball at the Florida 49 with a third and twelve, desperately needing a big play to have even a flicker of hope. Smith was being pursued and scrambled out of the pocket for what looked like decent yardage when Everett came charging through and was inadvertently de-helmeted by

Pittman. Even without his headgear, the senior from tiny Webster, Florida, stayed in pursuit, somewhat uncertain what had happened, and made the tackle from behind. "I just knew all of a sudden I saw a lot of light," Everett said later.

This was a group of Gators not to be denied, even without full pads and gear.

Deep in the heart of Urban Meyer, a vein or two might have still bled scarlet and gray. Meyer would always be a little bit of Buckeye, the way Spurrier would always be a Gator. Although he only went to school in Columbus as a graduate assistant, the Buckeyes had always been Urban's favorite team to watch. Maybe that was why he showed a little mercy on them in the second half, calling off the shock-and-awe troops.

From there, it was a pure punt-a-thon. Of their final twenty plays, the Gators ran sixteen times.

The last time Chris Leak would touch the football as a Florida Gator—at least, a *leather* one—was when he took a knee to end the game and flung the ball to the domed ceiling in a celebratory act of sheer ecstasy. Meyer then received the crystal football emblematic of the national championship and hoisted it overhead, then passed it off to Leak, watched him plant a big kiss on it, and then relished the look of joy and relief on the face of his much maligned quarterback.

Leak was brilliant in his decision-making and execution, as reflected in his stats: 25 completions out of 36 attempts for 213 yards, 1 touchdown and no interceptions. The real stat, however, could not be quantified by a number: his leadership skills and the manner in which he rallied the offense following Ginn's 93-yard opening salvo. All that made him an easy choice as the BCS National Championship Game Most Valuable Offensive Player.

What a way for the University of Florida to end its centennial year of football! Florida 41, Ohio State 14.

"We're national champions—that's what you play for ever since you are a kid," said Leak. He said he was humbled, but felt rewarded for his patience and praised those teammates who kept the faith and did the work.

"When you work hard, when you keep doing the right things and you are a good person, you know, you get your schoolwork done, you graduate, when you are doing all the right things, eventually your time is going to come," said Leak. "This team has worked so hard, done all the right things. I am so proud of these guys, the way they have handled themselves."

In the end, because the Florida team knew it had played better competition, there was the assurance that it could not only compete, but win the game.

"During my career, we have played in some huge games," said Leak. "Coming into a game like this, you really just have to go back to all those big games you played in and all those great teams that you were able to play against. And that really helped me get a comfort level of going into this game, knowing what the atmosphere was going to be like and what was going—what I was going to have to do for us to be successful. My experience through my four years in college football really helped me out throughout the game."

It was quite an exit for Leak, who wasn't even invited to New York as one of the Heisman Trophy finalists. Somehow it didn't seem to matter on that night in the Arizona desert. The trophy Leak held in his hands was all he could have ever wanted out of his four years at the University of Florida. Both he and his Gator team definitely belonged.

"He's officially one of the top two quarterbacks to play at the University of Florida," said Meyer. "There have only been two quarterbacks in one hundred years of football to win a national championship and Chris Leak is one of them."

Meyer had imagined this moment for several years, but had begun thinking about it when he saw Texas quarterback Vince Young hoisting that crystal football a year ago, confetti raining, joy resplendent on the faces around him.

As precious as this moment was, Meyer knew it didn't define him or his team or even begin to tell the story of how the Gators got here, how they dug themselves out of the morass at Auburn, how they sorted things out in a family squabble as helmets flew across the room and made a pact that they would not come this away again.

After Auburn, Meyer had challenged his team to get off the canvas after taking a near knockout punch and respond with courage and fire.

"As far as a defining moment, you're not evaluated when you pick up a crystal ball," Meyer would say months later, looking in the rearview mirror at that night in Glendale. "Any nut can do that. You're evaluated when you get hit right in the mouth, as hard as you can, because you spit blood out and you go after the guy. Or do you put your tail between your legs? I've seen it handled both ways."

In football and in family, that measure of mental toughness is how Meyer judges himself and those around him.

He learned that from his father, from Woody and Earle, and even from his wife, Shelley, whose tenacity and fierce competitiveness kept Urban going at times when he wanted to quit coaching . . . when they were making poverty wages and there was no confetti—or anything else—falling from the sky.

That toughness is what had gotten Meyer and his Gators to that moment he had dreamed about ever since seeing Young with the crystal football.

Barely voted into the finals over Michigan in the season's last BCS poll and questioned about their validity as a contending team, the Gators proved once and for all that they not only belonged, but perhaps deserved an apology from some of the pollsters, analysts, and commentators.

The national championship was textbook Plan to Win, and it had worked to perfection. Great defense and special teams play produced favorable field position, which led to the desired short field. And in all those trips to the red zone, they scored almost every time down.

Many other moments during the regular season might not have been so visible to others, but were clearly evident to Meyer. Most of all, the Gator coach was proud of the comeback stories of players like such as Leak, Ray McDonald, Dallas Baker, Steve Harris, Reggie Lewis, Louis Murphy, and the likes.

On the night of the national championship game victory, the now graduated Vernell Brown received this text message from his two old coaches, Meyer and Heater: "You were just as much a part of this as the guys who played in this game."

"That really made me feel good," Vernell said. "Really good."

When they returned to the Swamp in street clothes a few weeks later for the national championship celebration, seventy thousand fans were there to salute the Gators.

"For over thirty days they said the Florida Gators did not belong," Meyer said. "Little did they know we had a group of seniors who were the most motivated group I've ever been around."

One of those twenty-one was Leak, who never realized his dream of a Heisman Trophy, but said he had always set his sights on something bigger: a national championship ring and an MVP trophy in the BCS championship game. Now he had both.

In a special ceremony, Leak received the mythical torch from Danny Wuerffel, who returned to Gainesville for the celebration just to pass it on. Wuerffel surprised everyone by showing up to present Leak with his award. Wuerffel's appearance was kept a secret from Leak and the team. "When I heard about Danny coming last night, I kind of got choked up," Meyer said.

The 1996 Heisman winner was also there as a Gator fan.

"It's great to be a Florida Gator. It was great one hundred years ago," Wuerffel said. "It was great ten years ago. And it's great today."

So this was more than just a celebration—it was also the handing off of a legacy. Wuerffel spoke of Leak becoming one of only two quarterbacks with a national championship ring, but then advised rising sophomore Tim Tebow, "There's room for one more, Timmy Tebow!"

The symmetry was not lost on the coach.

"It was neat to see Danny 'hand off' the baton to Chris," Meyer said. "Chris never had an opportunity to be handed off a baton. When he came here, they handed him the football and said, 'Go play.' A quarterback shouldn't have to do that."

The second Florida team to win a national title and the second to achieve a national championship in ten years watched highlights of their accomplishments on the big screen at the newly decorated stadium. Orange patches were removed on the facade of the south end zone, revealing a 2006 that had been added on the other side of NATIONAL CHAMPIONS 1996. At the end of the six Southeastern Conference championship seasons, the number '06 was affixed.

It took something like this for seniors such as Baker, Harris, McDonald, Cornelius, Rissler, Everett, Cohen, Leak, Billy Lastko, Eric Wilbur, Chris Hetland, DeShawn Wynn, Brian Crum, and Tremaine McCollum to realize just what they and their teammates had accomplished: a huge crowd of adoring fans at Ben Hill Griffin Stadium showing their love and appreciation.

Leak choked up a little when he was handed the mike, later lamenting that this would be his last appearance with his teammates. But he said he probably wouldn't feel the full impact until "I can come back later and see that '2006 National Champions' on the wall."

Meyer was hoping to add to that collection in the near future, but knew that probably wasn't going to happen in 2007.

The twenty-one seniors were off to the Yellow Brick Road, seven of them headed to the NFL.

Many tears were shed at the football banquet that spring, especially by the Ray McDonald family and by Dallas Baker, who sobbed as he was crediting Urban Meyer with turning his life around and Coach Billy Gonzales for being like a father to him. Urban Meyer said he cried for nearly a minute, and the tears had nothing to do with how much he was going to miss the leadership of those twenty-one in the upcoming 2007 season.

PART THREE

The Season Inside Gator
Football 2007

17

Making History—Maybe

The temporary nature of championships is good reason to cherish and celebrate them, but there is also a downside. Those championships have a dangerous allure and can turn a team into a pillar of salt, according to Urban Meyer.

"The national championship is a powerful, but potentially evil, thing, I found out," Meyer said. "Obviously it's great, but it also throws high expectations on people."

Unfortunately, those rings didn't mean a thing once the 2007 season kicked off. Gator fans were about to draw their last few breaths of that "Titletown" aroma from the stifling August heat in Florida. They were hoping their football team could pull off back-to-back national championships as Billy Donovan's basketballers had done a little over four months prior. Meyer knew better, but a coach can always pretend to dream along for a bit before reality sets in.

The biggest question mark for the Gators in 2007 was about experience on defense, with just two starters off the national championship team. He had a team of babies, some of whom were still acting like it. Almost ninety freshmen and sophomores were on the roster. Forty-nine of the seventy-man traveling squad were either first- or second-year players.

They were young and they were fast, but they were also foolish, which is why one soap-opera nickname for this team was "The Young, the Fast, and the Foolish." Soap-opera themes played throughout the season, beginning with two-a-day practices when Meyer had to deal with issues "that I've never had to deal with before."

To counteract the afterglow-turned-arrogance and false expectation, Meyer turned to his friend Bill Belichick of the New England Patriots again in hopes of working his team through the process. Belichick bluntly told the squad, "You woke up on third base, but you never hit the triple."

Meyer said to them, "You're not that good. First of all, most of you guys were wearing ball caps on the sideline, watching other guys do it—you certainly didn't pay the price."

Meyer was having his own doubts about his team. "What went through my mind going into the year—there was a little bit of fear. I was very concerned about this team, and a lot of those fears became real."

Then it happened. About six of those eighty-eight underclassmen still in their teens got into trouble by either breaking the law or breaking the team rules. Later in the season, several veterans did likewise.

At the SEC Media Days, when asked about discipline problems and the fact that his team had "more than we'd like," Meyer explained his theory about dealing with troubled players: "Discipline is not dismissal in our opinion. Discipline is education and correction, then doing what you've got to do. We're in the process of doing a lot of educating, a lot of correcting, and putting a product on the field."

The youth of the team, as Meyer expected, was about to surface.

Sometimes there was no choice, however. Sophomore guard Ronnie Wilson had been removed from the team earlier in the spring after being hit with felony charges for firing a gun, but those charges were later reduced. Sophomore kick return specialist Brandon James faced the loss of his scholarship for the fall semester for twice breaking team rules—including the purchasing of a small amount of marijuana from undercover cops.

There were also these challenges to address:

1. **How to best utilize the blazing speed of the team's playmakers, while also driving home the point to the defensive front to give "four to six seconds of relentless effort."**

2. **Finding leadership on the defense to go with returning starters Tony Joiner and Derrick Harvey.**

3. **Maintaining execution excellence against tough SEC teams such as Tennessee, LSU, Auburn, Georgia, South Carolina, etc., as well as Florida State.**

4. **Dealing with an unusually large number of underclassmen who had never experienced the heat of close games.**

5. **Finding the answer to "Can Tim Tebow pass?" and teaching him how to engineer fourth-quarter drives the way Chris Leak did.**

Summer practice was tough, hard, and hot. Meyer was going to make it even hotter for Joey Ijjas, who had just about nailed down the kicker position. A walk-on, Joey was on the short list of three that were close to earning a "scholly," Meyer's term for a full scholarship. He would be painted in a corner with a series of pressure kicks that would decide his fate.

Urban yelled to Ijjas, "Make this one from fifty-two yards and you have a full scholarship. Right here, right now."

The players began hooting and hollering. Urban stood right next to the holder and was screaming at Ijjas, who nailed it, long, high, and true, right down the middle. Meyer high-fived his new scholarship kicker. It was a good way to end a really tough practice.

As Meyer spoke to his team at a Gainesville motel the night before the opening game against Western Kentucky, he had an inkling that some big piece might be missing.

Urban remembers worrying about "egos, selfish approach to the game—all things that are conducive to not being a very good team."

Before the team meal, Meyer stood in front of the serving table, which was groaning with everything from chicken to roast beef and all the fixings, and gave his young team a paint-by-the-numbers scenario.

"Listen up now. Everybody turn your chairs toward me," Meyer said.

Then he instructed them in baby steps on how to take the field tomorrow. There was appropriate pregame and in-game decorum in defending the Swamp. This was more about ceremony and ritual than execution, because fifty-nine roster members were either redshirt or true freshmen, and thirty-four of them had never run on Florida Field at Ben Hill Griffin Stadium. And twenty-four of that fifty-nine were scheduled to play against Western Kentucky.

"You are going to a special place tomorrow," Meyer tells them. "I've been to all of them—Ohio State, Michigan . . . all of them. And there is nothing—*nothing*—like the Swamp. It's a place we need to respect and make others respect as well.

"There's another team getting ready right now to go on the field tomorrow. This is a place where we only go for regular season games and one other time a year for the Orange and Blue spring game. We're not like other schools, because we don't practice at Florida Field. We only go there a few times a year. We need to own it. We let it slip away a little from us a few years ago, but now we're taking it back. So we need to respect it and make sure others respect it. And the way to do that is not talk a bunch of crap to the other team.

"You go as hard as you can, as fast as you can, you hit them in the mouth and you get up and pat each other on the back. You don't talk trash to the other team. This is sacred ground. When you play, remember those who played your position before you at Florida Field. You owe them nothing less than your best effort, to treat that position with dignity and respect."

Following Meyer's address, Cornelius Ingram said the blessing, and the big receiver from Hawthorne, Florida, asked God to guide and protect them.

Since the culture of Meyer's football team was built on sweat equity, with players receiving status through their conduct on the football field, in the classroom, and in their social activities, there was an order to everything. Even who got to eat first.

The young men sat quietly as Meyer said, "Okay, we keep hearing a lot about this great group of receivers. Everybody says we got excellent receivers." Pause. "So the group that's going through the chow line first is . . . the punt team."

It is not by accident that Meyer, himself the special teams coach, elevates the special teams players to the level of offensive and defensive starters or even above. Another group is called next, then another. Soon, the players began to converse over dinner in a relaxed atmosphere.

Two large TV screens pipe in ESPN. Syracuse is playing Washington, and the Orange's throwback uniforms are almost as ugly as the final score (42–12, Huskies).

By now, some of the groups have split off, a few watching football. Some members of the defensive team, led by Tony Joiner, are playing cards. Offensive coordinator Dan Mullen is about to take his three quarterbacks up to a room for a tape-watching session. Co–defensive coordinator Greg Mattison has now occupied one of the tables in the corner, where he is going over his call sheet—what defenses he would like to call on certain downs and distances—as an administrative assistant types it in a computer.

A few linemen take advantage of neck massages from Hiram de Fries, himself a former lineman at Colorado State and longtime friend of the head coach's.

A smile breaks out on the face of Tim Tebow as he passes by. He will start his first game tomorrow, as he and Mullen perform a half leap-and-hip-bump for unknown reasons. Tomorrow the quarterback will have to answer the question posed by critics: Can Tim Tebow pass?

Tebow had developed a huge following and was becoming one of the most popular players in school history. He already was the subject of many "Tebowisms" on the Internet. The favorite was "Superman wears Tim Tebow pajamas."

On occasion there is laughter, but not loud or raucous. By now the ice cream sundae bar is open and a movie is playing next door—tonight's selection by Director of Football Administration Jon Clark is *300*.

Food, food, everywhere. The Gators eat well. Friday night at the hotel there is a team dinner of carbs galore. If you're looking for salad you've come to the wrong place. Pasta, beef, chicken, potatoes—topped off by sumptuous make-your-own ice cream sundaes. Then, after meetings, the groaning board reopens—hot dogs, hamburgers, fries, milk shakes and—oh yes, smoothies. Mickey Marotti's smoothie machine constantly whirs, and Tebow is a regular partaker.

There is also a little football homework on what Meyer likes to call "the best Friday night in football."

Idle chatter among support staff occasionally branches off into storytelling.

Chris Patrick, the assistant athletics director for sports health, has been at Florida since 1970 and has experienced a third of all Gator football history. When he arrived in Gainesville, Gatorade had just been invented and was about to become the drink of choice for athletes.

Dr. Robert Cade, the inventor of Gatorade, would mix his concoction back near the training room in a bathtub.

For a time in the midseventies Florida teams no longer drank Gatorade, Patrick said, "because I think Dr. Cade was upset with the university and how it was being marketed." But the matter was resolved a few years later and Gatorade went on to become standard fare for most every elite athlete. University of Florida coaches, players, and sports writers covering the teams have frequently been featured in national TV commercials for Gatorade.

Looking back at it now, Patrick wishes he'd had a better sense of history and valued the Gatorade remnants more.

"I thought many times that when they tore down that training room and took all that stuff out of there, I should have gotten my hands on that bathtub where Dr. Cade used to mix the stuff," said Patrick.

You just never know when you're going to become a part of history.

America's fastest and youngest—but hopefully not the most foolish—college football team got off to a rollicking start, brought to you by the numbers 4 and 6. Those numbers were printed in big block letters and posted on the locker room door leading to the South end zone with the admonition: 4 TO 6 SECONDS OF RELENTLESS EFFORT.

That "4 to 6 seconds" slogan wasn't just some inspirational bumper sticker on the wall, because it was a mandate drilled into the heads of Gator football players as if they were Manchurian candidates.

Meyer picked those increments because that was approximately how long it took to run a play and wanted that "4 to 6 seconds" to become instinctive effort, from snap to whistle. That was a trait of the defensive linemen on the national championship team, who were coached to play assignment football while giving maximum effort in running to the ball. Because the linemen on the 2006 team were mostly veteran players, they were allowed to take themselves out anytime.

At Florida, everybody's on the clock all the time, one way or another. For Tim Tebow, it was for the reverse—to slow him down. Meyer and Mullen wanted his game more under control in is first career start.

The new, mild-mannered Tim Tebow—more like Clark Kent than the other guy—began his career as a starter twenty-three minutes before 1:00 P.M. Tebow was throttled down by his coaches, given no predesigned running plays, and told to keep his raw emotions under wraps. If he came to the sideline facing would-be tacklers, he was to step out. He was learning how to manage a game.

His offensive unit and coaches huddled around him just inside the boundary, as the strapping young man with the square jaw and the eternal smile let his chinstrap hang loosely. Meyer went over the last-minute instructions. First he slapped his quarterback's shoulder as a show of encouragement, then slapped his open palm before Tebow jogged on the field and took his first snap as a starter in what was likely going to become a long and illustrious career.

A short gain by running back Kestahn Moore officially got the Tebow Era under way. Three plays later, Tebow finished off a 90-yard drive, sneaking over for the game's first touchdown. Fifty-six of those yards he got himself, running or passing. He was on his way to a four-touchdown day.

Most coaches would have been giddy. The Florida offensive staff was already focusing on the next series.

From inside the Florida coaching booth, it looked and sounded a little like the floor of the New York Stock Exchange about an hour before the closing bell. Not unlike other coaching booths, it was "organized chaos"—a roller coaster of emotion, with a little shouting and a few curse words tossed about.

If you didn't know the Gators were trouncing Western Kentucky, you might not have been able to tell it from the temperament in the compact glass booth as the second half began.

Three different coaches in the booth all have their roles. Secondary coach Chuck Heater, who calls the secondary coverage, is wired into co–defensive coordinators Greg Mattison and Charlie Strong and safeties coach Doc Holliday.

Offensive coordinator Dan Mullen, joined in the booth by tight ends coach John Hevesy to his left, is plugged directly into the headset of Meyer, offensive line coach Steve Addazio, and receivers coach Billy Gonzales—all down on the sideline. Mullen calls out the personnel groups and communicates with the backup quarterbacks, who signal in the plays. Addazio watches the side closest to the sideline, and Hevesy has the far side. Hiram de Fries handles administrative matters such as down and distance, the 25-second clock and time-outs. Mullen watches the corners, and graduate assistant Nick Schiralli watches the safeties and charts the coverages.

"Let's go Pony, Wristband 85," Mullen calls out. Then he repeats it. Running back Kestahn Moore carries to the left side for 8 yards.

The offensive pecking order in the coaches' box centers on Mullen, who often communicates with Meyer. The others only respond, but do not volunteer unless they feel really strongly there is something that will make a difference.

Next to Schiralli is Zach Smith, a recruiting intern who charts all offensive plays so the Gators can "self-scout." Graduate assistant Sean Cronin sits to the left of Heater and identifies the opponent's offensive sets and tracks the backs while Heater tracks tight ends, which is the key to identifying the personnel groups.

It's the opening game and there are bound to be blown assignments on offense. As Florida breaks out of the huddle, Meyer mutters,

"We're all screwed up. You'd better get the tailback in and get it straightened out!"

Mullen is not happy that the offensive players don't seem to have a sense of urgency. "Snap it up to the line of scrimmage," he yells to Tebow. Then he mumbles to no one in particular, "They look like they're out of shape!"

Most of the time Mullen works off his play sheet and establishes rhythm with the calls, but on occasion he'll ask, "Is that OK with you Urban?" Meyer rarely says no on this day. Once, when Florida was backed up on its own 2-yard line, Mullen was itching to go deep.

"Wanna take a shot here?" Mullen asks Meyer, meaning to have Tebow throw a bomb.

"No, I'd like to make a first down and then take a shot," Meyer tells him.

On third and one, Moore makes the first. A play later, Tebow hits back-to-back strikes of 43 yards to Andre Caldwell, down to the Western Kentucky 42, and then 42 yards to Riley Cooper for the touchdown, Tebow's third of four for the day in Florida's weather-shortened 49–3 win opening day over Western Kentucky.

If Don Meredith had been in the booth, he'd have sung that famous line "Turn Out the Lights, the Party's Over." Liberal substitution began. "Let' s get some of those other guys in there," said Meyer.

The long-asked question was answered. Not only could Tim Tebow pass, but he threw a deep ball with a deft touch. Instead of trying to run over would-be tacklers, he stepped out of bounds like an NFL quarterback because that's what his coaches told him to do.

Tebow became the fourth Florida left-hander to start regularly since Tommy Shannon took over in 1962 as starting quarterback. After him were Jackie Eckdahl in 1968 and Bobby Hewko in 1980.

Historian Norm Carlson couldn't remember any others, but did cite written references of ambidextrous Clyde "Cannonball" Crabtree using both of his arms back in 1928 when the Gators missed going undefeated after a loss to Tennessee in the final game. Throwing with both arms is something that even the wunderkind Tebow can't do—at least not yet.

Of course, no other Florida quarterbacks were gifted with the legs of Tebow, who could easily be a starting running back in most programs. Tebow looked good, but nobody could have dreamed the kind of season that was going to unfold for the left-handed sophomore.

Next up was Troy. There was concern about the Gator defense the following week when the Trojans rang up so many points in Florida's 59–31 victory as the Gators extended their home streak to seventeen—Meyer winning fifteen of those.

The Florida offense was another matter. In their first seven touches, the Gators scored seven times. After two games that was fourteen touchdowns in seventeen possessions over eighty-three-plus minutes—more than a point a minute. Tebow, though, was still a work in progress and not yet a polished quarterback.

"What we wanted to be, we could be, and that's the threat of the quarterback running the ball," Meyer said. "That's going to open up some throwing lanes. He's [Tebow] a hard guy to defend. We've just got to keep him healthy and get our line blocking."

So how was the debut of the 2007 Gators? Florida was impressive enough for losing Troy coach Larry Blakeney to say, "From an offensive standpoint, they can repeat [as national champions] and beat anybody."

In the first five and a half periods of play—remembering that the Western Kentucky game was cut 8-plus minutes short by lightning—the Gators had outscored their opponents 98–10.

After win No. 2, as the Gator players walked off Florida Field and into the rotunda to the locker room, they filed past the Gator head, most of them patting it out of a sense of obligation and not celebration. The second half hadn't been all that inspirational, as Troy outscored Florida 24–10.

What will Urban say? Once inside, Meyer herds them up. "All right, let's go, let's go, let's go! Grab a knee!

"Ballers, get up in there. Let's go!"

They gather in a circle, most on one knee.

"C.I.!" Meyer shouts, meaning it's time for Cornelius Ingram to say the post-game prayer of gratitude, which he does.

Clapping.

"OK, it's SEC time. It's time to get a little piece of Tennessee!" Meyer proclaims.

More clapping.

He knows that some players on their knees don't really grasp the significance of that.

"I was certainly proud of the way you played. I just did an interview on the field [with Steve Babik of the Gator Football Network] and was asked if I was surprised we came out [flat in the second half]. I said, 'No.' We've got a bunch of young guys who have never played football before. I look at these young faces and we were up forty-nine to seven. I'm going to tell you what—that first half! You want to win every game you play? That is the Plan To Win absolutely perfectly! That defensive performance in the first half – in my opinion . . ."

It trails off, but Meyer is almost hyper.

"I am going to tell you, I had a little bleeping knot in my stomach. I went in and watched their film. They ripped Arkansas apart in that second quarter. They ripped 'em apart! Our defensive coaches and defensive players in that first half . . . that was as good a defense—I'm not going to say it was as good as the BCS game. But I think their offense averaged about forty points a game. And we shut them completely down [in the first half]!"

Then Meyer switched gears to blocked punts. Urban is big on blocked punts and spends an inordinate time practicing them. It's a subject of great pride that Florida blocked eight punts last year. (He referred in press conference to an old coach at Montana who said that when you block a punt, you win 90 percent of your games).

"We had two blocked punts. Two blocked punts! Where's the Big Freak [Carlos Dunlap]. Where you at?"

Loud applause and whistling.

Dunlap, a freshman, is goaded into coming forward and, not sure exactly how to handle the attention, says, "I came up there and got my big ass over the line [laughter] . . . and I blocked a punt!"

Loud applause.

Meyer then turns to Brandon James, who had been suspended for the first game, but Saturday had made a 59-yard punt return.

"Here's a guy who's one of our most dynamic football players—a challenged football player [he is not on scholarship]."

Meyer doesn't even call him by name, but gives James a loving pat on the head as he moves to the center of the circle.

"I'm glad to be back," says James. "I appreciate everybody who was with me from the beginning, and I appreciate everybody who was out there with me today."

Lot of cheering. Meyer asks for Charlie Strong to come forward and recognize defense.

"After giving up seven [in the first half] we gave up twenty [in the second half]," says a disappointed Strong. "Poor performance. We have nobody, coach."

More Meyer: "Our offense was rocking and rolling in the first half. Second half we started playing sloppy. We had a guy who didn't practice much because of an injury. He had to 'War Daddy Up!' 'War Daddy Up!' That's Percy Harvin."

"Appreciate all of you . . ." Harvin says, his last words inaudible. "I'm going to come back strong. Appreciate everybody who stuck with me."

Light applause. Then it's Tebow time.

Tebow's game management was off-kilter in the second half, and the offense was often sloppy, with penalties cropping up. His coaches had told him he needed to manage the game better.

"I want to thank the defense for coming out the first half and doing a great job," Tebow says. "As for the second half, defense, I'm sorry about it. I'm embarrassed about it. We're going to get better and we don't want it ever to happen again."

Ingram had more than 100 yards receiving for the first time and gets a kudo. Then Meyer closes with a pep talk, which sounds more like wishful thinking:

"This is a good football team. We could be a great football team. Just take care of business. I know there are a bunch of others who played hard. We'll take care of you on Monday [recognition] when we've had a chance to evaluate the film. To come in here and play that game, after that s— happened in the third quarter, to come out and dominate in the fourth quarter . . . that's a good football team.

"Let's break it down right here."

Everyone comes together and shouts, "One-two-three Gators!"

They looked ready for Tennessee. So were the fans. Meyer started getting them ready on his TV show by telling the fans to avoid the orange in the Gators' color scheme and go with an all "Blue Out."

You could tell the Vols were coming just by how far the Nasty Meter was ratcheted up on talk radio and the blog sites.

Let Tennessee have its orange for a week, then, right? Not so fast, said some of the bloggers. For six pages the GatorCountry.com message boards were lit up, with the merit of the Blue Out questioned and then defended. But ultimately accepted.

I kept wondering if they were having this argument in Tuscaloosa about Crimson and White, or in Baton Rouge about purple and gold.

Urban's father, Bud, called Hiram de Fries with a concern. Urban's dad was coming to the game, but didn't have a blue Gator shirt.

Amazingly, Bud was able to land one.

18

Waltzing Past Tennessee

In a half hour, I was about to experience my dream of running through the tunnel with the Florida Gators as they were taking the field to play Tennessee. Inside the Florida locker room, you could feel the tension building.

The digital clock on the wall, right underneath the sign DO YOUR JOB, ticked off the thirty-minute countdown for the first SEC game of the season.

I noticed that instead of huddling formally for pep talks by the coach, each player had his own way of getting game-ready.

Some were shouting encouragement to others. Several players on the floor were having their hamstrings stretched by a trainer or teammate. Others, like Tebow, sat in front of their lockers, towel draped across their knees or heads, stares fixed on an inanimate object, never making eye contact or conversing unless an assistant coach happened by on a pep-talk round.

Assistant coaches prowl about on the carpeted floor, winnowing through bodies to utter instructions or encouragement. The air-conditioned room is a good thirty degrees cooler than the field they just left.

Right off, captain Tony Joiner lets everybody know what this is about with a string of epithets unsuitable for the Disney Channel: "XXXXXXXX." Joiner and return specialist Brandon James jump up and do a hip bump. James says, "XXXXXXXX."

This is going to be a big day for the Gators, and especially James, just one game back from his suspension and about to be sprung on the unsuspecting Vols.

The one common denominator in the room is the bellowing rap music, apparently considered part of the mental preparedness that builds toward that moment when they will burst out of the locker room and onto what Meyer calls "sacred ground."

With ten minutes left, Tebow is now on his back, looking at the ceiling. "Every piece of this real estate belongs to you," says assistant coach Steve Addazio, invoking the territorial imperative as he roves.

All the while, Meyer speaks only in hushed tones, if at all, moving about the room, sometimes walking out of the double doors, then back, watching his team like a nervous, expectant father.

It has been a tough week for the head coach, who admitted his nerves were frayed and that his nights were short. He would say later in his press conference that Tennessee worried him so much he resorted to taking Ambien to get to sleep—later admitting that was just a joke.

Meyer shouts, "Three and a half minutes."

Out on the field it is very, very hot, hovering around 100 degrees with high humidity and a late-summer Florida sun beating down. This sun has baked Gator football players for all these weeks, and today it is going to be their friend.

Now strength coach Mick Marotti is reinforcing the importance of good conditioning, which he had hammered home ad nauseam to the team for the past seven months.

"Are you going to melt out there? Are you going to melt down?" is the rhetorical question asked by another assistant coach.

And now the reminder from Marotti: "You train for this s—! This is what we train for. Right now there is another team over there thinking about the heat!"

"One minute!"

Now Meyer's brief pregame speech: "Take care of business. Look out for yourself. Look out for each other. C.I.!"

"C.I." leads the Lord's Prayer.

For me, the dream of running through the Florida Field tunnel is about to unfold.

The adrenaline rushes through the players as they began the trek to the field, each of them tapping the Gator head in the rotunda for good luck, some reaching up to tap the overhanging doorfame bearing the words ONLY GATORS GET OUT ALIVE.

Once at the opening of the tunnel, I can feel the heat begin to filter in and the air-conditioning subside. I have departed ahead of the team with my guide. Retired Florida Highway Patrol major Malcom Jowers takes this trek every Saturday, home or away, as sort of a personal royal honor guard for Urban Meyer, as he has been for Gator coaches for more than twenty-five seasons.

Malcom is going to coach me up on how to get in the proper lane and to stay out of the way of the trampling herd.

Even after all of these years, Jowers still gets a tingle. "It's so loud that you almost can't feel your feet hitting the ground," says Jowers, who gets about a fifteen-yard start inside the human-and-rope gauntlet, lined with cheerleaders and well-wishing ex-lettermen.

As the players line up, awaiting the signal to advance on the field, they can hear the cheer "Two Bits" thundering outside and the musical dirge signifying that the video of the attacking huge alligator is about to be unleashed.

When the jaws of the gator open on the Diamond Vision screen, the taped voice of the late Jim Finch declares, "Heeeeeeeerrrrrrrrrrrrree come the Gators!" And we are off.

As the team emerges from the tunnel, I can almost feel the g-forces of the noise on my face. The roar of the crowd is like a hundred jet planes flying overhead. I am jogging to the Gator bench—it feels like sprinting to me, because one cannot lollygag for fear of becoming a human treadmill, ground beneath the cleats of these powerful young gladiators.

Rather than reflect too much on the fact that our feet were

touching "sacred ground," we nonplayers were trying to get out of the way. Big people passed me, like I was a Volkswagen in second gear on I-75.

For one nanosecond, I allowed myself to pretend I was wearing a Gator football uniform, just as I did as a boy when I would stiff-arm chairs in my living room while listening on the radio as the team took the field. Then I pulled up at the bench and took the stairway through the stands back to the press box, back to reality.

Gator fans are invited to participate in the tunnel experience, too, providing they are willing to donate $1 million to the University of Florida.

It would almost have been worth the price for me.

As for the game against Tennessee, the last time I saw as many big plays was on Broadway in New York City, performed over five years. Rarely in a football game had I seen as many with the number of game-changing moments as Florida-Tennessee produced.

Meyer's Florida Gators smacked down Tennessee, 59–20, in their first Southeastern Conference outing of the 2007 season in what surely become known as the Blowout at the Blue Out. Plus, America was introduced to three college football stars of the future—Tim Tebow, Percy Harvin, and Brandon James. The trio was spectacular. The brilliant second-year quarterback had a hand, or leg, in much of the 556 yards of Gator offense, including 299 yards passing for two scores and 67 yards rushing for two TDs. His offense averaged 8.6 yards a play.

That sophomore triumvirate produced a whopping 748 yards and six touchdowns on some of the most exciting, circuslike playmaking in these parts since the days of the Ol' Ball Coach and even beyond.

The more venerable Gators fans were reminded of Ray Graves's "SuperSophs" team in 1969 when John Reaves, Carlos Alvarez, and Tommy Durrance roamed Florida Field before it was known as either the Swamp or Ben Hill Griffin Stadium.

Tebow laid the ball out beautifully for Riley Cooper on a 30-yard connection for Florida's first offensive touchdown. He leaped through the air to score another one from 8 yards. He made two completions on underhanded throws. He made another while falling down. From his own end zone, he lasered a perfect pass into Harvin's hands for a 49-yard gain while his receiver was on a dead run. His accuracy was remarkable.

One more time: Can Tim Tebow pass? Yes. And can Tim Tebow measure up as a starting quarterback against SEC competition? Yes.

Then there was Harvin, an athlete with so many gifts that he amazed his own coach. "I've not had one like him before," Meyer said of the playmaker his teammates call Electric.

"He is a weapon. I think you've witnessed one of the best players in college football in Percy Harvin."

Two of Harvin's plays were the most spectacular. On one, Percy took the reverse handoff from Tebow, juked once, cut back once as he sliced through two Tennesssee defenders, and doing a complete 360-degree pirouette, went darting into the end zone for a 19-yard scoring run. Writers covering the game were asking, "Could you please play that back so we can be sure what we saw, or whether it was that Reggie Bush flying through the air?"

Harvin said he was healthy for the first time all season and so were his numbers. Percy rushed for 75 yards and that balletlike score, also rolling up a career-best 120 yards on four receptions.

"I got a lot stronger and a lot bigger in the off-season," said Harvin, "and I gained twelve pounds. Last year, I just ran fast. I couldn't run a lot of the routes and stuff. This year, in the off-season and in the spring, that's all we worked on—my routes."

On another play, when Tebow's pass appeared it would be over Harvin's head, No. 1 turned on the afterburners and dove as the football bounced first off of the Vols' DeAngelo Willingham and then Harvin's face mask. While in midair, Harvin kept his concentration, pinned the ball, and came down with it.

"This offense is fun," said Harvin. "Just throw it, catch it, and run. We have so many playmakers on this team, you never know when somebody will break it open."

The 5' 6" James, still trying to get back into his teammates' and coaches' good graces after a late-summer indiscretion that got him in trouble with the law, hauled in Britton Colquitt's punt and raced 83 yards to put Florida ahead, 7–0, with key blocks by Joey Sorrentino and Butch Rowley. For the day, James had 193 yards in returns and kept his team in good field position.

"Brandon James dug himself out and continues to dig himself out," Meyer said. "This is a great night for Florida football. I took a look up there at all that blue—you can't help yourself sometimes, you just have to look—and I'm thinking how lucky I am to be coaching here."

Yes, and lucky to be coaching the likes of Tebow, Harvin, and James, too.

Tim Tebow had one semi-embarrassing moment. Tony Joiner extemporaneously kissed Tebow on the cheek, which was caught on the sidelines by the CBS cameras. Some suggested that people might begin to talk—since Joiner and Tebow had already moved in as roommates.

In three games, having scored 49, 59, and 59 points, the Gator offense began to sizzle. And college football buzzed with talk of a possible repeat national champion.

Meyer says he knew better, but many people in the program got sucked into overestimation of the team's future. However, recruiting was paying off and a depth of talent was being stockpiled, which gave Meyer enough material for the "competitive excellence" among his players.

"Bloody Tuesday," as always, would be the toughest day of weekly practice. Next was going to be a road trip to Oxford, Mississippi, never an easy place to find—and for some reason, never a place where Florida had played well at all.

19

Learning the Truth in Oxford

Deep down, Urban Meyer knew his team lacked depth and experience, but sure enough, the allure of talent and a fast 3-0 start became an aphrodisiac for fans and the media. With 25 percent of the regular season on the plus side, the Florida Gators vaulted into the national championship conversation when they suddenly found themselves ranked No. 3 in the country.

The 2007 season would prove to be almost memorable, but many of the memories were of the wrong variety. Meyer would later characterize many off-the-field player issues as "three-or-four weeks" of insanity.

The knockdowns came in various ways from an array of places and disguises. The most devastating blows were misconduct and misfortune, although most coaches will always lay it at the feet of execution—mostly poor blocking and tackling.

Good coaching cannot overcome football players acting badly off the field, the bounce of the ball, the twisting of an ankle or the bruising of a shoulder, or, worse yet, the death of a player. These were a few of the experiences of the young University of Florida football team in 2007.

Meyer's Plan to Win does not include luck, because it is designed down to every last detail, implying that proper work ethic fuels the engine that leads to success. For a moment in 2007, however, even the head coach couldn't be blamed for feeling as if maybe his Gators could be the Chosen Ones again, but he did not.

Back-to-back stellar recruiting classes produced a stockpile of underclass talent and, despite being thin on seniors, the 2007 Gators would grow up in midseason, perhaps in time for the heart of the SEC schedule. When Florida rumbled over "Rocky Top," blowing out Tennessee, it also raised false expectations. The seduction of invincibility took over. After all, the hottest athletic program in college had already shattered precedent. Who was to say it had to end?

Meyer knew trouble was around the bend at Ole Miss and kept trying to temper the optimism. While fans indulged in their fantasies about Superman playing quarterback, Meyer was grinding his teeth at the metaphor and maybe tossing and turning at night about his youthful defense.

On the heels of a national championship came the cold, blunt reality that while football was mainly about execution, like poker it is sometimes also a game of chance.

Drawing to an inside straight or bluffing with two pair might work on occasion, as it did for a while in September, but it was not a sound, long-term strategy likely to produce the desired result—and certainly not the road to national dominance.

"I even knew after the Tennessee game," Meyer said of the affliction of arrogance. "Because everybody was printing tickets to the national championship game, including, probably, members of our staff. But some of our defensive coaches—veteran coaches—knew what was in store for us."

The high-strung "playmakers," tended to prance like thoroughbreds during the good times. Truthfully, the Tennessee victory distorted the outlook of many—including those of us in the media.

"What happened is that we had some dynamic personnel making plays," Meyer said upon reflection. "That wasn't a good team, and that team that won that Tennessee game wasn't a good team. We had some great players."

The following week in practice, the Florida team was smitten with a near-epidemic of swelled heads. Some began to fall behind to a point where Meyer warned them "You may not be good enough to play here—not because of talent, but lack of effort."

Notre Dame had its "Four Horsemen." Harry Stuhldreher, Don Miller, Jim Crowley, and Elmer Layden woke up the echoes for the Fighting Irish in 1924.

Florida only needed one horse to get out of Oxford, Mississippi, alive, but Tim Tebow did the work of four. The Gators started slow and trailed 3–0 before taking command on their last two possessions, which included a 98-yard drive.

Florida led by only 14–6 at halftime as Meyer and his staff left for the locker room at Vaught-Hemingway Stadium, where the facilities were anything but state-of-the-art.

The Florida coaches reunited—those from the press box arriving on the field—and immediately began their dialogue as they walked. The defensive staff stopped just inside the door and began discussing a second-half strategy to keep the Rebels out of the end zone.

As I walked inside the locker room, I saw coaches and players jammed in three small, contiguous rooms. When the players first hit the chairs, they were immediately hydrated with Gatorade and water. They ate oranges and bananas and talked among themselves. Brandon James had a towel draped round his head like a boxer, making small talk with some of the other backs.

There were no real Win One For The Gipper speeches as the coaches conferred in clusters, formulating the plan. This was about strategy and not emotion.

"Nine minutes," announced Jon Clark, keeping time on a stopwatch.

Florida was not playing badly, but Meyer and his coaching staff had worried all week about getting the players up for the early 11:30 (12:30 EST) kickoff. They were staying in Tupelo, birthplace of Elvis Presley, which was over an hour's drive from Oxford, and they didn't want to get hung up in traffic as they had in some past road games. So they gave the players early wake up calls. Offensive line coach Steve

Addazio—they call him Vitamin A—stormed their rooms with some helpers, threw open blinds, and rousted out the players. They were fed a big breakfast early, dressed up in coats and ties, and loaded on the bus.

Now, at halftime, they were halfway through this dangerous road game against a hungry team that was trying to take the game over in the second half.

The Gators had started another flag-fest which would eventually lead to fourteen penalties—something that frequently plagued this team. After James nearly shook loose for a touchdown kick return—his first effort was 55 yards, but Florida got no points out of it—Ole Miss wisely chose to squib-kick and one of them was bobbled by James, who fell on it at the Gators' 2-yard line. Ole Miss was determined not to get beat deep and dropped as many as eight players on defense.

"Eight minutes," announced the time crier, Clark.

The player conversations sounded only like a constant buzz of nothingness—a crowd yakking at the halftime of a game, or maybe commuters awaiting a train at Grand Central Station. Finally, the first announcement. Dan Mullen emerged from a back room, where he and Meyer had been instructing Tebow and the offense, and shouted, "OK, offense! Here we go! Here we go! Right here! Right here."

Then Mullen shouted over to the wide receivers coach, Billy Gonzales, to bring his group: "Billy G.!"

The coaching clusters disassembled and information was being disseminated to the players.

Then the assessment. "They haven't challenged us or kicked our ass to make plays up front," Mullen says. "All they're doing is they're saying, 'OK, you guys have a young team and you're on the road—let's see if you can go seventeen plays every drive. That's what they want us to do . . . We've got to run hard every time we get the ball. On third down, convert it! We're going to go up and down the field on ninety-nine yard drives."

Then Meyer takes the floor. "Listen up! Nonplayers, get out of the way. Players get up here! They're playing with two deep safeties. We need to run the ball and force them to load the box and go to man coverage on the outside."

In the final two minutes, the team came together as Meyer gave them their marching orders for the second half.

Sometimes one must improvise on the road. Since they can't transport the real thing, managers do bring a Gator head, which sits by the door on top of a shelf. The DO YOUR JOB sign hangs on the far wall. A PRIDE sign is taped above the doorframe which players tap on the way out. It's the closest thing to familiar surroundings they could get in the middle of Nowhere, Mississippi.

It was a pound-it-out, hold-on-for-dear-life Gator victory, 30–24, over stubborn Ole Miss on the back and legs of their 6'3", 235-pound sophomore quarterback.

Tebow ran the ball so many times that his head coach complained about the danger of him becoming a "crutch."

Twenty-seven times No. 15 ran at the Rebel defense for a record 166 yards, breaking a forty-year-old school rushing mark set by Larry Rentz of 109 yards. It was Tebow left, Tebow right, Tebow up the middle—he carried the ball eleven times in the final period, including seven on the 61-yard drive for a field goal that gave Florida a little breathing room.

"We have to be very careful with using Tim too much," said Meyer. "He's a crutch. When things got tough, he's the horse. He carried twenty-seven times, which is far too much."

Maybe Tebow was more like a pack mule, because out of Florida's 79 plays, he either ran or passed the football 61 times. His Heisman–like total yardage was a spectacular 427. Had he not been trying to put the game away in the fourth quarter and kill the clock on the Florida final drive, he may have cracked 500 yards.

Old-school style, Tebow was more like Bronko Nagurski or Jim Brown than Peyton Manning. He wanted the ball. He wanted to win the game. And he was "always in my ear," according to Meyer.

Tebow either tried to run over tacklers at the boundary, or took the snap and patiently waited to see which way the blockers were flowing, then tip-toed into the pile before thrusting his large body into the scrum, literally carrying tacklers with him. He made coaches wonder about the myth of fragile of quarterbacks. And yes, Meyer did worry about his getting hurt.

If he was tired, Tebow didn't look or sound like it after the game. He said he really wasn't aware of how many times he was carrying the ball and wasn't sure if it was a personal record. But he knew his team needed to drive the ball as it had been doing all day and keep possession from a hot-handed Ole Miss quarterback, Seth Adams.

As Ole Miss closed the gap, there was a moment of truth for this young Gator team when some of that bad Mississippi karma came into play. Past Gator teams had been known to come unraveled in the Magnolia State, where Florida had lost three of its last four games to either the Rebels or Mississippi State. Tony Joiner's fourth-quarter interception took care of that.

Thus, out came the human battering ram, the Tebow-mobile, ramming the ball for an average of 6.1 yards per carry, including 18 carries in the second half.

Meyer later called it a "very hard day," but said he learned one very important thing about his Gator team that day in Oxford. They were not ready for prime time.

"If you had to reflect on our team now, that was who we were, especially on defense," Meyer said months later. "We had a bunch of young corners who had never played before, and they were exposed. You had a team that really didn't have to fight through adversity yet because you played at home against Western Kentucky and Troy, before beating Tennessee. And now you get hit in the face on the road, getting them up at 6:00 A.M. and dealing with all the things you have to deal with.

"Some of our players gave in that game. Later on, some of those kids gave in. And giving in is when you lose. I think there is a lot of confusion about winning and losing. Losing a game is when someone gives in. That's why I feel like football is the greatest team sport of all. You can play with ten guys going as hard as you can, and one guy gives in and you lose. And I saw guys give in. Boy, it got real hard."

The things Meyer had worried about after beating Tennessee had come to pass. Playing the fourth quarter in the Swamp was easy, he said, but "it's hard to play when you're on the road at eleven o'clock and you're not in a dynamic stadium, against a team you're supposed to beat. And you're up a little bit and all of a sudden they're starting to throw the ball on you and you've got to make a play. That's hard."

The Gators may have been 4-0 and climbing in the polls, but Meyer knew he wasn't coaching a championship-caliber team, because of the truth he had seen in Oxford.

20

Murderers' Row 2

On the last weekend of September, four weeks deep into the 2007 season, Urban Meyer faced the most difficult stretch of any college football schedule in America. After beating Ole Miss to go 2-0 in league play, now came Auburn, LSU, Kentucky, Georgia, Vanderbilt, and South Carolina—three of those games on the road.

The team began preparing to head to the Swamp, with plenty of motivation for beating the Auburn Tigers, who had ruined Florida's unbeaten season in 2006.

About 5:30 P.M. some two and a half hours prior to kickoff, players and coaches began emerging from their motel rooms. They were dressed in coat and tie, carrying overnight bags. They walked slowly and said nothing, eventually congregating in a meeting room on the south side of the building.

I was going to hitch a ride to Ben Hill Griffin on the Florida team bus, sitting near the back, to observe what this "Gator Walk" was all about.

Meyer was one of the last to emerge, and we made eye contact. "Hello, coach. So Oklahoma got beat today, huh?" I said. Urban, locked down on the task at hand, didn't respond.

He could be thinking about what he's going to say to his team in a couple of minutes. He could be thinking about one of his star wide receivers, Bubba Caldwell, who might return today from an injury suffered earlier in the year, and how much he could play him. Or he could be thinking that he doesn't want Tebow carrying twenty-seven times as he did the week before against Ole Miss. But he is so absorbed in thought about the game that he is not hearing.

In a moment, Meyer and his players would walk a few feet and board two white buses parked just a few yards away, motors running, drivers in attendance. The front of the lead bus was bearing the banner: HERE COME THE . . . with a Gator-head logo underneath the words.

"That's so our fans will know we're coming—so they won't give us the finger, thinking it's the other guys," said Malcom Jowers.

The driver of the lead Gainesville Police Department car, Johnny Horn, a big Gator fan and member of the Fightin' Gator Touchdown Club, is proud of the banner. "Our club had that made," said Horn.

Those buses will follow police escorts—two cars, about ten motorcycle cops, because those escorting the visiting team usually join up with the Gators. It is a short ten-to-twelve minute drive to Ben Hill Griffin Stadium, south on I-75, east on Archer Road, left on Gale Lemerand Drive, and stopping out front of the stadium on University Avenue where the Gator Walk will commence.

As Gator fans spot the buses, there is a sporadic Gator chomp here and chomp there, thumbs up everywhere, some raised fists. Then the frenzy breaks out as the buses pull up to unload.

"Tebow, Tebow, Tebow!" fans chant, but mostly it's yelling and screaming and whistling and clapping. "I touched him!" exclaimed a young woman.

The Gator Walk was started by Meyer to afford the fans more face time with their team and build of a sense of community. Meyer made it a point to get out of the way so the players could have the stage.

For Tebow, it could be a chore, but he was one of those rare individuals who appeared to be enjoying it at this stage of his athletic career. He usually waited to become next-to-last off the bus. Then he would take on the ceremonial responsibility of the perfect Corporate Gator, waving and high-fiving, sometimes smiling in recognition of what he considers the Gators' greatest asset: the fans. After all, he once was one.

"You've got to have enthusiasm," Tebow would later say of his interaction with the fans. "I always want to treat people on the Gator Walk just like I wanted to be treated when I was younger—shake their hands if possible. The fans have been there all day, working just like we've been working."

Today, Tebow is wearing a dark blue suit and light blue shirt, bag over his shoulder, wending his way through just in front of Louis Murphy, but stopping to make personal acknowledgements of special acquaintances, relatives, or friends. There is no time for signing autographs, but he stops and sets his bag on the pavement three times to hug the necks of three middle-aged women, as if they were aunts or next-door neighbors.

Then Tebow swings the bag back over his shoulder and assumes the position of a moving Statue of Liberty—like high five, right arm extended, slapping the flesh like Tom Sawyer running a paintbrush along the white picket fence to whitewash it.

Numerous coeds and other young, attractive women push through the five-deep gauntlet to get a look and maybe a touch.

Finally, he steps on the brick walkway that bears the names of Gator fans, living and dead, and disappears into the crowd, carrying with him a major secret about tonight's game: Offensive coordinator Dan Mullen had just checked out of the hospital that morning after an emergency appendectomy the night before, but would hopefully be in the booth to call the game.

Friday night after the quarterback walk-through, Mullen had gone to the hospital for a blood test. Just before midnight the doctors found out he had acute appendicitis and said, "You need to have surgery." To which Mullen responded, "I've gotta coach the game tomorrow!"

Mullen was told that his appendix could burst. That would not only mean leaving in the middle of the game, but that he would be out for several weeks. So doctors operated on him and he was taken to the recovery room, which he didn't leave until 3:30 A.M.

At 2:00 P.M. Mullen was signed out of the hospital and went to the hotel for the offensive meetings and team walk-through. Mullen was taking only anti-inflammatory pills. He rested for an hour before departing for the stadium. Once there, as he was walking off the field and turning a corner, Dan's wife, Megan, saw him wince, barely catching himself from falling.

So Mullen endured the pain "because I didn't want to let down the team" in an important SEC game.

At stake for Florida was a perfect 4-0 start, an 11-game winning streak, 18 straight victories at home, and of course an SEC victory (even though Auburn was in the West). Also, Meyer's personal unbeaten streak on Florida Field.

Auburn was a near forgotten enemy, a rival that had once ranked right up there with Florida State and Georgia—even ahead of Tennessee. The Tigers and the Gators had played eighty times, but in skipping three seasons, some of the heat of that rivalry had subsided. Still, Auburn was the only team to have beaten the Gators in their national championship season and had knocked off Steve Spurrier's No. 1 club at the Swamp in 1994.

There was certainly incentive enough for revenge, but the Tigers looked more as if they were playing the grudge match, because they had stumbled off to a 2-2 start. Beaten by South Florida and lightly regarded Mississippi State, the Tigers set out to regain some respect in the Swamp.

A bad moon was rising over college football that day, which was full of upsets. That equated to a bad start for the Gators.

Even though they say they didn't take Auburn lightly, Meyer's Gators must have had Georgia on their mind—or LSU or somebody else—considering the way they played for nearly three quarters.

The way the Tigers ripped through the Gator defense for 192 yards in the first two quarters, they looked more like the nation's No. 3 ranked team. Auburn went to the locker room at the half with a 14–0 lead, marking the first time since 1992 that a Gator team had been shut out in the first two quarters.

In the coaching booth, Mullen was clearly in pain. He had stopped taking pain medication for fear it would cloud his thinking, but a physician was in the booth.

Mullen's job was to pick up on the rhythm of the game, to make the snap decisions with the wisdom of a chess master, but in warp speed, and ferret out the mismatches. Tonight he was struggling. When the Florida defense was on the field and secondary coach Chuck Heater was yakking on the headset to co–defensive coordinators Greg Mattison and Charlie Strong, Mullen was slumped over, head in hands, silent.

"Dan was hurting tonight," said a fellow assistant. But not nearly as much as he was going to hurt before it was over.

When freshman safety Major Wright whacked Auburn tailback Ben Tate, causing a fumble that was recovered by Gator teammate Joe Haden, Florida began to play with some life.

On the ninth play of a 38-yard drive, Tebow hit tight end Cornelius Ingram for the Gators' first touchdown of the night, and that didn't come until the fourth period.

That was the wake-up call Florida needed, because with eleven minutes to play in the game, Percy Harvin hauled in Tebow's pass of 32 yards and took it to the Auburn 6, where in two plays Tebow plunged in for the score to tie the game at 17.

A remarkable comeback for Florida, but would it be enough?

The Gators had what they wanted: the ball in their hands and, thanks to a kick interference call against the visitors, placement at the UF 42 with 4:49 to play. With a running game, they could have eaten up the clock and negotiated better field position for a winning field goal.

Mullen went for the screen pass to Harvin, which backfired as Percy tried to cut back and lost a crucial 6 yards, creating a difficult second and 16. The second mistake was Tebow checking off the call to an option, based on what he saw the Auburn defense giving him. But the Tigers outfoxed Tebow and stuffed Kestahn Moore (it was only his third carry for the night) for no gain. On the next play, third and 16, Tebow's pass was incomplete.

The Gators had to do the unthinkable—with a tired defense, give the ball back to the visitors in the Swamp with 3:38 left. It got worse when true freshman Chas Henry shanked the punt just 25 yards, giving Auburn possession at its own 39. The Tigers began grinding away behind the running of Tate as the clock wound down to under a half a minute to play.

The answer was on the foot of Wes Byrum, a 6' 1" true freshman from Fort Lauderdale's St. Thomas Aquinas, who had to kick the winning 43-yard field goal twice—a second time because Florida had called time out to freeze him just prior to the first one. Both he nailed, albeit the winning kick was just inside the right upright.

So unranked Auburn knocked off the Gators, 20–17, in perhaps the biggest of all the upsets on "Upset Saturday."

Mullen had to suffer twice. "It was rough duty," said Mullen. "I certainly didn't call my best game."

This was the kind of game that a national champion finds a way to win, as the 2006 Gators had by blocking what could have been the winning field goal by South Carolina. This year the Gators were national champions with a target on their backs and Urban's young team seemed to lack fight.

Where would the Gators go from here—besides Baton Rouge?

Meyer took the high road, summing up the defeat thusly: "I have a lot of confidence—I love our players, I love who they are. They are family. They took a frontal blow and we will see how they come through it. Some families kind of disintegrate, and other families keep it going. That's college football. It happens each week. These guys haven't experienced that very much. There are some guys who are going to find out. So I talked to them about it. I love the guys, I really do."

He was going to have to love them, because they were about to go through some tough times together over the next four weeks.

Clearly his team had to dig itself out of a hole again to have a shot at competing for championships. The Gators were not alone in this quest, however. Five of the nation's top 10 teams lost Saturday—seven of the top 13 and nine of the top 25. Despite the loss, Florida remained in the AP top 10 at No. 9. And if somehow they could pull off a win over LSU at Baton Rouge Saturday night, they would be back in the hunt.

"When you get hit, you find out about the soul of a man and the soul of a team," Meyer said, offering the challenge to his players.

When Meyer looked back at the lost opportunity, he admitted, "That was as poor a performance offensively as I can remember having the past two years—that drive," said Meyer. "I don't want to say I was surprised, because I wasn't, but I was very disappointed."

Meyer also admitted that he should probably have taken some of the play-calling responsibilities off Mullen's back.

"I got a phone call at midnight and that kind of started us in a tailspin. I don't think he [Mullen] was the same," Meyer said, knowing that the offense was ultimately his responsibility. "I was extremely disappointed in our performance against Auburn, especially offensively. I don't think we played very well. I think defensively we did enough to hang in there. And when you hold them to seventeen, you should be able to win."

Mullen thinks he would have made the same calls on the last drive, no matter the pain.

"The first play, I wanted to get the ball to Percy Harvin," he said. "Great playmaker. Didn't want to have a negative-yardage play. So we called a quick screen to him, that I think, worst-case scenario, he gets tackled for a two-yard gain. No way we should have a bad play here—one of the safest plays we have."

As Harvin was tackled back at the Gator 36 for the loss of 6, it was the beginning of the end.

"We had gained all the momentum and all we needed was a positive play, and we didn't get it," said Mullen.

The bad moon rising had brought some more bad news with it.

First it was learned that senior starting tackle Phil Trautwein would not be able to come back this season from an injury, and that freshman tailback Chris Rainey would have season-ending surgery, but be red-shirted.

A few days later defensive captain and team leader Tony Joiner was charged with felony burglary when he attempted to pick up his girlfriend's car from Watson's Towing lot.

What did Urban Meyer have left in his arsenal of comeback

speeches? There would be no words of legends to pump the Gators back up this time.

"I have been asked how this compares to last year, and I think we are on a different planet than a year ago," Meyer said. "Our whole intent is to make sure that we get a little better. That is it. There is not going to be a big rally cry, and we're not going to have a bunch of slogans around here."

The little bit of good news was that Bubba Caldwell, who had come back from a knee injury and played sparingly, would be ready to go against LSU.

Thus began the first week of the most miserable month in Urban Meyer's coaching career.

21

Madhouse in Baton Rouge

If you're going to Baton Rouge to play LSU, no need to stir up the natives beyond their normal, everyday insanity.

Just Urban's luck, the way things were going in early October, that the Tigers moved up to No. 1 in both polls on the Sunday before. And the wackados didn't even wait for Tim Tebow to set foot on Louisiana soil before unleashing their terrorist campaign on the Florida quarterback.

Somehow they got Tebow's cell phone number, and it never stopped ringing all week.

"The whole week, in bars and all the different clubs, and everywhere at night, they were announcing my phone number in those places," Tebow said. "Starting Monday or Tuesday night, I would get a call literally ever second, every two seconds. I couldn't flip open my phone and hit anything without there being a call there. I wouldn't answer it. I just turned it on to make a call to my parents or my brothers."

They left Tebow all kinds of voice mails and text messages, some funny, but most of them crude. He and his teammates sometimes joined in the fun, laughing at most—except when a few got dark and ugly.

"There were some that were over the edge—one about killing

(my) family members in descriptive ways, ways of killing them, ways of burning them—stuff like that."

So why did he bother?

"For me to delete my voice mail, I had to go through it to hear it, at least the first few seconds," Tebow said. " 'And some of them would say, 'Hey, I'm sorry for some of the LSU people.' There would be some college kids who said, 'I'm so and so and I'm sorry.' It would be interesting to hear that, too."

By the end of the week, it was funny, and when the team took the bus ride from the Baton Rouge airport, guard Jim Tartt took over as Tebow's personal telephone operator, answering calls, by saying, " 'This is Buddy from Buddy's saloon,' " Tebow said. "And they said, 'What!? This isn't Tim Tebow?' And he just started messing with them. We had so much fun. It was hilarious."

Tebow enjoyed a measure of revenge in the game after going to the bench following his touchdown pass to Kestahn Moore for a 10–0 lead, pretending to hold a phone up to his ear and mouthing the words "Call me" to the LSU fans. So if they thought they had his number, they really didn't.

Meyer wasn't too amused about the distraction and suggested Tebow "just dump his phone." Urban had already had a tough week of dealing with Joiner's situation and had wound up stripping the captaincy from the senior safety even though the charges were dropped. But that didn't excuse Joiner's presence at the towing lot at 4:30 A.M.

The worst crime Joiner committed wasn't trespassing—it was rank stupidity and disregard for his captainship. He didn't rob a bank or assault somebody. But he did wrong, and he had to pay. But he was on the field against LSU.

There just wasn't going to be anything normal about LSU week, including my own journey to "Death Valley," which for a few scary minutes in the oppressive Louisiana heat was starting to live up to its name. I've never seen so many people outside a football arena—many without tickets and just there to party—as I did that night in Baton Rouge.

Walking to the press box, I encountered thousands of LSU fans swarming to the locker room entrance to cheer on their beloved Tigers. Suddenly I couldn't move after getting caught up in the massive pregame crowd just prior to LSU's "Tiger Walk," nearly getting pinned against the stadium in sultry, 90-degree weather. I began to sweat profusely and felt almost as if a heatstroke was coming on.

Shirt already soaked and unable to budge, I joined another sports writer in the same predicament and we squeezed our way through the crowd to a door, which we pounded on until someone answered. After we begged him, a kind LSU manager agreed to let us walk right through the locker room where Tiger players were getting dressed.

I made a note to avoid any team "walks" at SEC stadiums forevermore.

It was worth every second of the inconvenience and uneasiness to see the football game that was about to be played at Tiger Stadium.

When a team converts five fourth downs on your defense, it's a great clutch offense, poor defense, and plain out good fortune. LSU might have had all or some of all the above.

For one play shy of three quarters, Florida had its best football game of the year in Baton Rouge. The fumble by Kestahn Moore stalled a promising drive at midfield when the Gators were leading 24–14 and were about to put the dagger in the hearts of their opponents. Until then, Florida had been near flawless and Moore had played perhaps his finest game as a Gator. His value as an excellent blocker and pass receiver far offset his mistakes, which is why his coaches kept working with him on ball security.

Two subsequent events precluded Florida from pulling off one of its greatest victories of all time. A Tebow pass was intercepted when it bounced off the helmet of Cornelius Ingram, a promising young receiver learning a new position. Then the Tigers, trailing 24–21, mounted a workmanlike eight-minute, seventeen-play drive for the 28–24 win. Twice on that drive the Tigers converted fourth downs.

Some of the press box pundits wondered why, on the fourth down and 1½ at the Gator 6½ when LSU made its fifth fourth-down conversion, Meyer didn't challenge it. From the press box level, both Pat

Forde of ESPN.com and I thought Jacob Hester was short after he was hit by Ryan Stamper. So did the CBS announce crew, as well as the Sun Network's Nat Moore and David Steele.

"He didn't get it," exclaimed Moore on the Sun Network broadcast, as Stamper wrestled Hester to the ground on what looked like about a 1-yard gain. "If they give him this, the Gators ought to challenge."

Precisely my thought. Watching live, without benefit of a clear replay, you go by instincts. As I looked through my binoculars at the body language of Hester, it looked as if he came up short. If he was, the game was going to be won by Florida. But it was not.

"First down LSU!" said Steele. "Unbelievable!"

"It didn't look like he got it," added Moore. "Boy, he got a good spot."

Since then I have watched that replay a dozen times and still can't conclude if it was the right call. So with so much riding on the outcome of that spot, why didn't Meyer choose to challenge it?

Not being up to speed on the college rules for a replay challenge, I asked Urban that question in the postgame press conference. He said he felt the replay booth would "buzz down" if there had been a question and that he didn't want to risk losing a time-out.

Turns out Meyer was correct. A few days later I talked to an SEC official who had not seen the play, but spoke on the condition of anonymity.

"I was working another game, but based on what you are telling me, Coach Meyer was exactly right," he said. "You can bet that spot was looked at very carefully. We look at all those several times. And we also tell coaches not to take the chance and risk a time-out unless they are convinced it was a wrong call."

Meyer could not be sure, so he declined to use the timeout.

The official went on to say that all spots late in the game are closely scrutinized, and even though the public doesn't know it, the officials on the field are "coached up" from the booth.

"On the sidelines there is what we call the eighth official," said my source. "If the replay booth sees the spot is off, he will buzz him and he will get the word to the on-the-field officials that the ball needs to be moved up or back a few inches. We absolutely review everything."

We'll never know for sure if Hester's knee touched down before he stretched out to place the ball at the 5, as there is no video evidence to prove it one way or another.

After a second straight loss, on an LSU touchdown with 69 seconds left, there was nothing to do but "feel the sting" of defeat. That's what Meyer told his team after his Gators took the No. 1 team to the mat and couldn't keep their opponent pinned.

These were particularly bitter pills to swallow, given that both games were so close and so winnable. After rallying from a 14–0 deficit, the Gators had possession of the ball with five minutes left against Auburn and couldn't convert a scoring drive. And against LSU, they dominated the nation's No. 1 defense, only to have their hopes destroyed by two second-half turnovers.

Although unhappy about the LSU loss, Meyer would remain more disappointed about the loss to Auburn, "Because LSU was better than us, but I don't believe Auburn was."

The five fourth-down conversions were tough to swallow, but "if you sit back and look at that tape, we were playing as hard as we can. And that's really all you can ask of them."

Meyer felt his team had not made the plays on defense because nobody stepped up and some of the players weren't good enough yet.

"Auburn was a bad deal, but going to LSU was disappointing and heartbreaking. Your job as a player and coach is to play as hard as you can and try and win that game—and we went after that game, from the opening whistle. We fumbled that ball and we had an interception."

Almost lost in the defeat was the brilliance of Tebow, whose composure among hostiles was veteran-like. And his numbers weren't bad, either: 233 yards in total offense with two touchdown passes against the nation's top defense.

Painful as it was, Meyer found a silver lining—or at least pretended that he had. He referred back to the challenge he had made to his team the week before.

"I made a comment about the soul of a man and found out we have some pretty good men on our football team with strong souls," Meyer said in his LSU postgame press conference.

He even went a step further, buoying the troops as he prepared for an open date: "The future of Florida football is terrific, it really is. I guarantee we'll be back. The Florida Gators will be back. Smokin'."

Two years prior in his first season and on his first trip to LSU, Meyer had shed tears after losing to LSU. This time he was composed and emphatic that his team wasn't out of the conference race. "Every team in the [SEC] East has at least one loss and some have two," said Meyer.

A certain craziness was in the air at Death Valley, but it seemed to be pervading the SEC, if not all of college football. One SEC pundit wrote the next week, "So far, LSU beat Mississippi State, Mississippi State beat Auburn, Auburn beat Florida, Florida beat Tennessee, Tennessee beat Georgia, Georgia beat Alabama, Alabama beat Arkansas, which lost to Kentucky, which lost to South Carolina, which lost to LSU, which beat Florida."

Even if you didn't have a side in this game, it was worth watching. Kentucky coach Rich Brooks got caught up in the emotion of LSU-Florida, until he caught himself. "It was a great game, and then I had the reality check. These are the two teams I've got to play the next two weeks."

After back-to-back conference losses by the narrow margin of a combined 7 points and the disturbing off-the-field player conduct issues, the open date couldn't come fast enough for Meyer. Except when it did, the grim reaper came with it.

22

Remembering Sunshine

An old axiom among SEC fans, coaches, and players is that football is more important than life or death. The pure folly of that statement became clear the next week for the Gators when walk-on reserve Michael Guilford and a female acquaintance died in a motorcycle wreck.

On Friday before the open date, around 1:00 A.M., the nineteen-year-old freshman was killed along with Ashley Slonina when his motorcycle struck a median on campus. Police said Guilford was driving at an estimated 25-30 mph over the speed limit. Although Guilford had been attending a party with teammates, one of them said, "He was not a drinker and I know he didn't have a drink that night."

Because of his long, flowing hair and bright personality, the reserve defensive back from Quincy, Florida, had been tagged Sunshine by his teammates, after the character of quarterback Ronnie "Sunshine" Bass in the movie *Remember the Titans*.

Although the public didn't know much about him, Sunshine's teammates certainly did. Sunshine helped the Gators win a national championship without ever setting foot on the University of Phoenix

Stadium in the BCS title game, playing the role of Ohio State Heisman Trophy winner Troy Smith in the mock Buckeye offense.

On Monday, the players and coaches attended a memorial service in Gainesville, where Meyer spoke. Then a smaller group of them and their coach traveled by bus to Northwest Florida and flew back in time for practice. Meyer tried to lighten it up with an impromptu pickup game between the coaches and players, during which some of the players chided their fumbling coaches for their lack of ball security. It was their most spirited practice of the year.

Urban remembered Sunshine this way to the media: "There are certain people that have that electricity about them and a person you never forget when you meet them and that's the kind of person that Michael was. And he was valuable. He wasn't a guy that stood on the sideline and held a bag. He was a valuable member of this team."

His teammates put a Sunshine sticker on their helmets and would later add an orange bracelet with that nickname on it—plus the inscription NEVER LET YOUR TEAMMATES DOWN.

Later, Meyer sat down with a close friend for a philosophical discussion, in which they reflected on death, the purpose of life, and how a person is remembered. While Meyer grieved over Guilford's death, he took comfort in the contents of a text message Michael had sent to his father just before the wreck: "God has a plan and that plan is infallible." Urban felt Michael was OK, because "that tells you his soul is in heaven."

During these toughest two weeks of his coaching career, Urban and his players were reminded that even in the rabid Southeastern Conference, despite the mythology, football was only a game.

There is nothing like victory for a football coach to begin healing, however, and that was about to come in Lexington, where even *ESPN Game Day* was going to show up in a rare Bluegrass State appearance for a football game.

After upsetting LSU the week before, 43–37, Kentucky ranked higher than Florida—No. 7 versus No. 15 in the BCS poll—with a better record (6-1 versus 4-2).

Florida beat No. 7 Kentucky, 45–37. Tebow passed for a career high four touchdowns. The game featured spectacular play by both Tebow and Kentucky's Andre Woodson, who rolled up a combined 50 first downs, 939 yards in total offense, 9 touchdowns and a whopping 82 points. Tebow and Woodson combined for 671 yards passing.

For comparison, I harkened back to a game I covered on September 24, 1972, between Johnny Unitas and Joe Namath, played in Baltimore's old Memorial Stadium. The Jets won 44–34 as Namath and Unitas passed for a combined 872 yards.

Tebow took a firm grip on the Heisman after his 5-touchdown (four passing and one running), 340-yard day and I moved him to No. 1 on my ballot, as did a number of my press box colleagues. He would soon crack 2,000 yards total offense (2,289), and had accounted for 27 touchdowns (17 passing and 10 running).

What I liked most about Tebow, however, was his ability to stay focused through two difficult weeks, including the death of his friend, the devastating losses, and his burdened coach. He brought balance to the locker room.

I asked Meyer what he had done to hold his team together during this stressful time. The Gator coach replied, "I told those guys on Saturday night . . . When I saw LSU lose to Kentucky, I started calling the guys up, whatever time of day or night that was. I sat there for an hour just calling our guys, making sure they're, first of all, just living right.

"Nowadays it's constant motivation. Wake up in the morning and motivate them. Go to sleep at night and motivate them. Constant motivation. I think any time those kids understand that, man, there's a light at the end of the tunnel, they'll go to the wall for you. I think that's it."

Tebow always appears to be drawn to that light.

It was a nice win, but the Florida coaches weren't going to be sucked into the false read as they had been after beating Tennessee.

Meyer pointed out that Florida's defense hadn't played well and that the Gator offense had to keep matching scores by Woodson. Urban still felt somebody needed to step up and make plays on fourth down. The stats bore him out. Opponents had converted nine times in ten fourth-down attempts in the last two games, and the Gators ranked 104th nationally in fourth-down defense.

"We gave up something like four hundred yards passing. All due respect to Kentucky, Florida shouldn't do that," Meyer said.

Secondary coach Chuck Heater saw it as sort of a boot camp for his young defenders, some of whom had been toasted by Woodson.

"You don't get there unless you go through this," Heater said. "You can't in any way duplicate the process of development, and it is what it is. You've got to go out there, you've got to jump in the water, and you've got to swim and you've got to almost drown sometimes and you've got to keep going. So that's what's happening."

I suggested to Meyer that it had been a fun game for spectators, with all the offensive fireworks.

"It was probably fun to watch, but that was not a great game," Meyer said. "It was also an insight as to who we were as a team—a bunch of people who had not earned the right to be where we were."

Where they were, in fact, was on the tail end of Murderers' Row, about to face Georgia in Jacksonville. And Urban was also about to get the bad news about the injury to Tebow.

The intentionally bizarre behavior of Mark Richt and his Bulldogs would also provide Urban with one of his biggest surprises as a coach—a moment he would not soon forget.

23

The Georgia Surprise

Life is good when you own a Dawg and it's your biggest rival. But how long could the Gators keep holding off Georgia? They had beaten the Bulldogs fifteen out of the last seventeen games. And just to add insult, two Gator sports teams had hiked their leg in the Peach State and whizzed all over the state's most glamorous sports emporium.

Florida had won the 2006 SEC football championship in the Georgia Dome along with the 2007 SEC and national championships in basketball. Gator fans wanted the name changed to the Florida Dome, but they may have gotten a little too cocky for their own good.

Due to political correctness, the Florida-Georgia game was no longer called the World's Largest Outdoor Cocktail Party. Mostly over the nearly last two decades, it was the Georgia fans consuming alcohol, washing away their woe. This time, though, they would be able to hoist their glasses, bottles, or cans in celebration.

This Bulldog team brought a nasty new attitude. The latest Bad Boys of the SEC East showed their ugly intentions when, in a startling maneuver, they cleared the bench and stormed the field to celebrate

Georgia's first touchdown, intentionally drawing a personal foul (actually two).

The presence in the end zone of what looked like eighty to ninety white-jerseyed Bulldogs drew multiple yellow flags as Georgia was assessed two 15-yard penalties, forcing the Bulldogs to kick off inside their own 8-yard line. But the message was clearly sent that they were tired of being the patsy. Richt had told them if they didn't get a celebration penalty after the first score, "they would be doing morning runs."

This brought up the question of whether such an intentional act could cause Georgia to have players disqualified, because under the college rules, leaving the bench and running on the field is an ejectionable offense. And the move seemed to startle the Gators. The officials, however, saw it differently than Meyer.

Running back Knowshon Moreno, a heretofore injured redshirt tailback from Belford, New Jersey, looked like Herschel Walker reincarnated as he gashed the Florida defense for a career 188 yards rushing, which fueled Richt's offense for a 413-yard day. And the Dawgs hung the most points on an Urban Meyer Florida team ever scored in a regular season game in their 42–30 upset.

Meanwhile, Georgia's defense put a choke hold on Tim Tebow, sacking him six times and holding him to 236 yards passing and a minus-15 yards rushing.

Tebow, who grew up in Jacksonville, was already suffering from a severe shoulder bruise that limited his carries—"he wasn't as mobile," said Meyer—but was truly miserable after the loss. He choked back tears when he was asked how it felt to lose to a rival in his hometown. He said, "It hurts a lot." Then his words trailed off.

It was the third conference loss for Florida, but its first Eastern Division defeat. And while the Gators were not yet mathematically eliminated from their SEC title hopes, at 5-3 they could kiss their dreams of a major BCS bowl game good-bye. It also put a dent in Tebow's Heisman hopes, but nobody ever talks about stuff like that except writers and fans.

Depending on the outcome of Saturday night's Tennessee-South Carolina game, along with Georgia's upcoming dates with Auburn and Kentucky, the Gators retained a slim chance in the SEC—but only razor slim.

Richt was too good a football coach to be down very long and his strategy of asking his Georgia Bulldogs to "leave their hearts out on the field" worked against the Gators. Richt even called on Vince Dooley to speak to his team, saying he "really blessed us."

Looking back at the loss to Georgia, Meyer would call it "our worst effort of the year" and had not been aware of how badly Tebow was hurt at the time.

"Tim would never tell you," said Meyer. "He's saying, 'I'm fine, I'm fine, I'm fine.' You could just see his mannerisms—he just was not the same kid."

Reluctant even months later to talk about Georgia's premeditated penalty, Meyer would only say, "That wasn't right [referring to their knowingly breaking of a rule]. It was a bad deal. And it will forever be in the mind of Urban Meyer and in the mind of our football team."

Meyer has chosen not to go public with his feelings for lots of reasons, not the least of which is affording Georgia any bulletin board material to use against him.

"So we'll handle it," promised Meyer, meaning any response would be done within the rules. "And it's going to be a big deal."

Meyer took the loss to Georgia hard—his third defeat in four weeks—and had to fight off his emotions. These were tough times in the Meyer household—times when he became so upset that he feared the impact it might have on his health.

"I don't think people know, other than my wife, how much wear and tear that has on all coaches," he said.

Urban's whole family feels it, as evidenced by the letters that his two daughters wrote to him during particularly stressful times like these.

"I just want you to know how much I love you," wrote his older daughter, Nicki. *"The reason I wake up and work hard at everything every day is because I see you do that and you are the most successful person I know. Keep working hard. Every team loses. The way they handle a loss is what makes teams great. Go get LSU, take everything out on them . . . who cares about Auburn? It's in the past. Keep moving forward. Love you so much and thank you for giving me someone strong to look up to."*

His youngest daughter, Gigi, wrote:

"I was just chillin' up here, adventuring around your office. Just thought that I should let you know that I love you and that I am always thinking about you. Not only are you an amazing dad, but I have respect and look up to you so much just for the way you work and how you handle it all. It shows me that in order to be successful, you've really got to work hard in life and push to fulfill your goal. It is such an honor to have you for a dad and I couldn't imagine my life [being] any better. Live past the past, forget about those losses and just do your best. No matter what, you know that everyone will still love and respect you . . . especially the Meyer family. Keep working hard dad. I love you so much and I can't wait to sing the fight song with you and along with it get a victory hug. You are amazing at everything! Never give up. I love you."

Meyer feels the losses are on him and he bears all the responsibility, causing him to suffer. But it's something he's trying to learn to handle.

"And I worry about that and I worry about my longevity. I feel like I'm having a heart attack. Can't eat. Can't sleep. Can't do the normal functions that human beings have to do to survive. And that was as bad as I've been through, when we lost three out of four."

After the rare Georgia victory over Florida, Meyer was a little bit like Humpty Dumpty after a great fall, trying to pick up the pieces and put them together again.

Ordinarily, an invitation to Vanderbilt as homecoming guest would be a chance to get fat—except that these Commodores were nobody's patsies.

There's nothing like homecoming, however, to improve spirits. So Urban and about a dozen players rode from the team hotel to Ben Hill Griffin Stadium behind police escorts to attend "Gator Growl." The University of Florida's traditional Friday night homecoming skits lampoon the school, its presidents, the student organizations, the football team, state politicians, and the homecoming opponent.

Having missed the team bus, I flagged down one of the police escorts and rode shotgun with the officer, catching up in time to hear Meyer tell the estimated Gator Growl crowd of forty-four thousand that this was a homecoming in more ways than one.

"It has been thirty-five days since we played here in the Swamp," he said. Then he introduced eleven seniors. Captain Bubba Caldwell said of Vandy, "We're going to kick their ass!"

Urban also got a nice introduction from the emcee—it was his wife Shelley—and a lesson in Southern rock music.

Not being aware that the famous musical group Lynyrd Skynyrd had gone through literally dozens of musicians over the years, or realizing the band's name was not that of a real person, Urban asked Shelley: "Which one of them is Lynyrd Skynyrd?"

OK, so the Florida coach is a Jimmy Buffet parrothead.

Meanwhile, Meyer said at the time he was "scraping the bottom of the barrel" to find somebody to rally his team. Enter Percy Harvin, who was about to become a between-the-tackles runner in a game against an opponent that had Meyer extremely worried.

Percy put on an impressive show. On twenty touches against Vandy, Harvin produced 223 yards and two touchdowns, becoming the first player in Gator football history to both rush for (113) and receive (110) a hundred yards in the same game. He averaged more than 11 yards per touch in Florida's 49–22 homecoming victory.

Maybe to some people beating Vanderbilt wasn't a big deal, but Meyer called it "A huge win, a program win like our win against FSU our first year." And now it was time for Tebow to follow Harvin's act. Except when the Gator plane departed for Columbia, South Carolina, the next week, Percy Harvin wasn't on it.

24

The Tim Tebow Show

I arrived early in Columbia and crashed Spurrier's office without an invite. He didn't throw me out, even though the days of High Time in the Low Country were about over for the season. The Gamecocks had started out 6-1, but were now 6-4 after a three-game losing streak, in the middle of what would become a five-game slide. Unaccustomed as he was to losing three straight football games, Steve Spurrier seemed in reasonably good spirits.

On the eve of possibly his most disastrous run of an otherwise illustrious college football coaching career—if he lost to the Florida Gators, it would be the first four-game losing streak since he was at Duke— Spurrier seemed no worse for the wear.

"We had it going for a while at six and one, but really we weren't that good," Spurrier said. Not a man to lean on excuses, Spurrier did say that in the third year the transition is often difficult for coaches because of the drop-off in recruiting talent in between.

"Look at Urban," he said. "He's having to play a lot of young guys, just like we are." But Urban had one really good "young guy," who was changing the game of football with his legs and arm. Spurrier was most impressed with Tim Tebow. He would be far more impressed after Saturday night, seeing No. 15 as a one-man wrecking crew against his Gamecocks.

On Friday, some bad news had reached the hotel where the Gator team was staying.

"Percy's not here," a member of the Florida support staff told me, "and we're not sure if he's coming."

That night at the Holiday Inn in Columbia, Mickey Marotti could tell Meyer was unsettled. "All he kept saying was 'big game, big game,'" Marotti said. "We had trainers on the phone, checking on Percy. Urban had a cold and went to bed early. He was already up walking with Shelley when I got up."

Urban was not only still scratching in that proverbial barrel for a win of any kind—he was also going up against the guy with whom he would be forevermore compared. "That's always going to be here," said Meyer, realizing that since his team was probably out of the SEC East race, he was playing for pride. And he didn't want to be 1-2 against the Ol' Ball Coach.

Worse yet, he knew how fragile faltering teams could be. All he had to do was look at South Carolina, Alabama, California, etc., who had folded.

What keeps a team from folding? He remembered his 2005 club.

"Everybody says it's the coach, but, no, it's not," Meyer said. "It's the Vernell Browns, Jeremy Minceys, Jarvis Herrings.

"Those are the guys who refused to give in. Because there are other players who give in in a minute [snaps his fingers]. It's just the way life is. And if you have too many guys that give in like that, then you lose six in a row. I think Cal lost six in a row [it was actually six out of seven]. There's documentation everywhere. That was my biggest fear: If it starts doing downhill fast, how do you get it back? And do we have the guys who can?"

Deep inside, that potential for collapse worried Meyer. Now he had the additional problem of maybe not having his most versatile offensive weapons. Rumors were flying before kickoff about Harvin missing the game and possibly Tebow having a hand injury.

The rumor about Tebow was false. Right up to late Saturday at the team hotel, teammates were hoping to see Harvin walk through the front door. As he got on the team bus, Tebow turned to one of the coaches and asked, "Is Percy coming?" He was told that Harvin wouldn't be making the trip due to some kind of sinus-infection/migraine-headache combination. "And so other players will have to step up," said the coach. "Are you OK with that?"

To which Tebow added, "Yessir, I am."

As it turned out, Tebow really was Superman. Mickey Marotti suspected it all along, ever since seeing Tebow lifting weights before the 2006 season.

Marotti remembers a conversation the two of them had early in the young quarterback's development about how much he loved the weight room and lifting with the linemen.

"So I'm starting to challenge him a little bit," said Marroti, who was enjoying a hamburger with Tebow that day.

"Coach, I want to go do the leg press and see if I can beat whatever the best on the team was," Tebow responded.

So the two of them, alone in the weight room at 11:00 P.M., set out to see if the challenge could be met.

"So how many is the best?" Tebow asked, meaning, what were the most repetitions?

"Twenty-eight," Marotti said, giving a number that was at least ten higher than the best and putting on the same amount of weight that the top Gator football performer had used.

"He's grindin', grittin', bitin' his teeth, sweatin'," said Marotti.

"And that son of a gun does twenty-nine reps! And I said, 'Good job, Tim.'"

In January of 2006, as an early arriver at college, every time the quarterbacks would run the "suicide drills" from side to side of the court, Tebow did so with the same passion and emotion as when he met a linebacker head-on at the goal line.

This time, one of his competitors was Chris Leak.

"We're running the quarterbacks and running backs, down and back, halfcourt and back, foul line and back," said Marotti. "He's like in fourth place and he's running and running . . . bad form, just trying to will himself across the finish line. He goes from the foul line to the baseline and dives—midair, arms out, screeching across the floor, into the wall.

"And I'm thinking, 'He's just dislocated his shoulder, he hasn't played a down for us and he's out for the year.' He gets up. Doesn't win the race. Is pissed off like you've never seen. And I ask, 'Tim, what are you doin'?'"

Tebow replied, "I gotta win."

"And that's the way he is every day in the weight room," said Marotti. "He has to win everything. He lifts with the offensive line. He can bench-press two-hundred and twenty-five pounds, twenty-eight times. At the NFL combine, that's probably above average for an offensive and defensive lineman. He squats with five hundred pounds for reps and can do nearly six hundred."

Finally, Marotti backed Tebow off in 2007, declining to add more weights. "I would give him enough to satisfy his drive, but start developing him as a quarterback rather than a bully, or a fullback, or a linebacker."

I had been asked this question during a November 2007 practice by Carlos Alvarez, himself a Gator All American and legend: "Have you ever seen anything like Tim Tebow?" So I asked Marotti the same question and I hardly got it out of my mouth.

"Never!" he said. "Not with all the things he can do. He's almost like a fictional person. His love of the game, of being a competitor. He is a born leader and has all the leadership qualities of our greatest leaders of all time.

"And he's made me a better coach."

So you see, that Superman thing—it really was not a myth. And Tebow was going to prove it again tonight, November 10, 2007, in Columbia by answering the call of his coach with maybe the greatest offensive game ever played by a Gator.

Not even Superman could run for five touchdowns without offensive linemen. He needed people like Jim Tartt, Drew Miller, Maurkice Pouncey, Jason Watkins, and Carlton Medder. And not to slight the other blockers like Aaron Hernanez, or backs such as Kestahn Moore—and those wide receivers who are asked to block as well.

It took the stark reality of a piece of white paper bearing statistics before it sank in for Spurrier and Meyer.

Caught up in the flow of the game, both coaches had to be informed of what they had just seen—and even then they almost couldn't believe it following Florida's 51-31 victory over the Gamecocks.

"What did he get, two or three [touchdowns] running?" Spurrier commented, reluctant to patronize the opposing players too much. "I know he had a couple of long ones [passes] dropped or he'd have had more. Five? FIVE? He had five touchdowns [rushing]? Well, I saw him make a couple, but I wasn't paying that close attention or keeping count."

Translated: Either Spurrier missed it, or Tebow made it look easy, or both.

The Ol' Ball Coach wasn't the only one. Tebow's head coach was also in for a surprise as he was asked to evaluate what he called a "Heisman performance" from his quarterback.

"Five touchdowns—five touchdowns rushing, is that right? That's unbelievable," Meyer said, as the enormity of that figure finally struck him. "Wow! That's pretty good. I might buy him a sandwich tonight on the way home."

Then, walking out of the media room almost shaking his head in disbelief, the Gator coach again said to a writer, "Five touchdowns?"

Yes, five, on runs of 5, 1, 3, 2, and 5 yards.

And seven total, counting the two passing.

That number—*seven!*—was so staggering that it just didn't compute.

"We kind of made that decision to ride that horse with Tim, and he was phenomenal," Meyer said.

In fact, Tebow's totals almost caught many of the press box inhabitants off guard late in the evening. Sports writers on deadline were fiercely computing the running totals as the game wound down, hoping the math worked in the final morning edition.

Midway through the final period, with Tebow already owning six touchdowns and Florida up by a comfortable margin, most writers had their leads already written, figures to be inserted, awaiting the final gun to push the button on their computers and instantly dispatch their stories.

At that point Tebow had his five touchdowns rushing, breaking the school record for the most in a single game, also tying Wuerffel's

SEC record for most touchdowns (41) in a season by a quarterback. His one TD passing gave him a season total of 22, which equaled the conference season mark, but he was about to get another.

With just 91 seconds left, Tebow striped a 21-yard scoring pass to Bubba Caldwell for No. 7 and sent the writers scrambling back to their computers to rewrite leads and columns. His forty-second touchdown broke the record—in just ten games. In the press box there was some grumbling, a lot of typing, and there might even have been some whining accompanied by tears.

Even the local newspaper couldn't keep up. On Sunday morning, the *State* ran a photo of Tebow on one of its section fronts, going in for a score, but the caption wasn't updated and it stated Tebow "accounted for six touchdowns, five running and one passing."

Tebow makes everybody run hard, but sometimes you don't realize just how hard and high and fast he is going. He grinds toward greatness in ordinary increments that, only when added up, take on the staggering impact of the national debt.

The pure physics of this huge physical specimen hurtling through space, confronting would-be tacklers head-on, were mind-boggling. He was big. He was strong. He was fast. He was powerful. He *was* Superman. And a little bit Clark Kent.

The paradoxical profile of the 6' 3", 235-pound man-child defied the ferocity of his combative football nature. How could somebody so rugged and hard-nosed openly admit to a childlike faith in God that puts his Lord to task with prayers that somehow the Gators might still make it to the SEC championship game?

"We should have won more games," Tebow responded when asked to evaluate the year, "and we wouldn't have to pray so hard."

Tebow didn't realize what he'd done in his record-breaking performance until he was given the count by the media.

"You don't really know," Tebow said of the seven scores. "You figure it's like four or five. You don't keep track during a game." He said it was important to keep the pressure on South Carolina because "we knew with Coach Spurrier on the other side that two or three touchdowns were easy for them to make it up."

Tebow said the records would mean a lot to him one day because of the "names of guys like Danny Wuerffel and a lot of the guys who have played here. It's pretty cool to do something that like. Blessed."

Would the lag between perception and reality hurt Tebow? Having played on ESPN Saturday night, the news of his seven touchdowns would travel slowly and—as it did with Spurrier and Meyer—probably not settle into the psyche of the national media until later.

Even with such a killer performance, could Tebow overcome that age/experience bias? Odds of a sophomore on a three-loss team winning the Heisman were not strong. However, anybody with a calculator would have eventually have figured this out:

Once quantified, five touchdowns rushing, two passing and forty-two for the season—No. 1 all-time in the SEC—would certainly be enough to get him among the final four or five players to be invited for the ceremony of the Downtown Athletic Club in December.

If that didn't, then what was going to happen the next Thursday night in the Oregon-Arizona game would make it a lead-pipe cinch.

Some people expected Meyer to begin the drumbeating for Tebow's Heisman campaign right away. He was awed by his quarterback's performance against South Carolina, realizing that with Harvin out and Tebow's bruised shoulder still hurting, how badly things might have gone. Although Meyer did say Tebow gave a "Heisman performance," he purposely did not start blathering accolades because that goes contrary to his principles.

"People speak when they are uninformed—another Coaching 101 error," Meyer would explain later. "Shut your mouth until you know what you're talking about."

He did a mock interview with himself.

"'Urban do you think Tim should win the Heisman?' 'Yes, he should.' 'Why?' 'Well, I don't know. I haven't looked at his stats—I don't have time.'"

When Meyer did have time, he saw greatness.

Your eyes may see it, but often your powers of discernment just can't compute the magnitude of the accomplishment. It takes a moment to gather perspective, even when those eyes are trained in the recognition, acknowledgement and validation of athletic excellence.

Once Spurrier thought about it, he realized he had seen the future of college football. After the spectacular performance against his team, he labeled Tebow "the quarterback of the future."

Spurrier knew that the seven touchdowns easily could have been nine, even ten, if wide-open receivers had caught passes in the end zone.

"He's the type of quarterback everyone is looking for," Spurrier said after the game, noting that Tebow had an uncanny ability to hit his open receivers, "and he doesn't zing it five or ten yards over their head. And he makes some unbelievable plays when they're not open and guys are hanging all over him."

Tebow had also answered the question of his coach about whether somebody could lift the team out of its doldrums. "And Tebow could," Meyer said later in hindsight. "He pulled us right out of it with seven touchdowns."

After the tribulations of the past six weeks and concerns over whether his players could rally, Urban began to appreciate his team even more.

"And I told them at the team meeting on Monday," he said. "It was a little bit emotional. I told them that my lifestyle was going to be OK the next six months because I didn't lose that game to Coach Spurrier and South Carolina. We were not digging out—now we're moving forward. I appreciate what they did, because they played their butts off that game. That was as hard as we played in a long time. As much as I may have disliked that team at one time, that's how much like as I had for them. Because I saw them fight in a hostile environment where they could have lost that game in a minute."

Careful not to give his quarterback all the love at the expense of others, Meyer knew there had to be a delicate balance over the next few weeks as Tebow closed in on the Heisman Trophy. So he stayed true to his principles and eschewed the drumbeating role.

"I'd much rather worry about beating that School Out West. But I hear coaches do that. [They should] make an educated statement. Don't babble.' "

When the team plane arrived home from Columbia and players began gathering themselves for a wee-hours jaunt back to their rooms, Tebow hopped on the back of Tony Joiner's scooter and the two of them sped off into the night. As he watched, one of Meyer's assistants, realizing the fragility of life and perhaps thinking of the accident which took the lives of Ashley Slonina and Michael Guilford, muttered a silent prayer. "Oh, God, please watch over them."

The Superman thing could be carried just so far.

25

The First "Heisman Dinner"

The last player to arrive on Family Night was Tim Tebow. I was invited to this otherwise private meal when coaches, their wives, players, and children have dinner together after Thursday night practices—another way Meyer and his coaching staff get across the family image and role model that parents and future parents should play.

Tebow arrived a few minutes late because he'd stayed after practice to chat with a young man in a wheelchair. He hadn't just stopped to say hello and sign an autograph. He had hung out with him and his family, posed for photos, and signed autographs.

Once at the table with Hiram de Fries and me, Tebow set down his plate of chicken and pasta and bowed his head in thanks. Then he reluctantly began answering questions for the first time about the Heisman Trophy, knowing his private thoughts to me would not be made public until later.

One week before Thanksgiving 2007 and less than forty-eight hours before game No. 11 against Florida Atlantic, we were having our own little pre-Heisman Dinner to talk about his remarkable season.

I was planning to prep the young Florida quarterback with my

"Heisman Quiz"—or, as we used for the euphemism, the "H-Word Quiz." It turned out it would be useful information for him, because neither of us had a clue about what fate was about to befall him in just a few hours.

All of the unofficial weekly Heisman polls favored Oregon quarterback Dennis Dixon as the front-runner. The twenty-two-year-old Duck senior had passed for twenty touchdowns and rushed for nine in leading his team to a 9-1 record. But Dixon's statistics didn't compare with those of Tebow, who was about to become the first quarterback to have at least twenty touchdowns rushing and twenty passing.

In a bizarre turn of events, Dixon would go down with a knee injury, knocking him out of the Heisman race—putting Tebow in the pole position.

This was, in essence, going to be the night Tebow won the Heisman Trophy.

The way it had played out until then, Tebow was the next-to-last man standing. Had he chosen to sit during any of that stretch when he was injured, Tebow would most likely not have been in this position. Although only a sophomore, his durability was hard to ignore. He had declined to reveal the seriousness of his shoulder injury to his coaches just to stay on the field.

So by virtue of Dixon's fate and this new "20-20" credential Tebow was about to attain, he would take the Heisman lead. (Later, as Tebow watched the Oregon-Arizona game that night, he began to feel bad for Dixon and said, "I prayed for him.")

The H-Word is spoken in hushed tones around Meyer, who considers putting self above team both treasonous and poisonous. As much as possible, Meyer discouraged talk about the award because he gets paid to win football games, not Heismans. So he wasn't going for the hype.

Likewise, almost like fearing the chicken pox, Tebow avoided any talk about the Heisman Trophy. When he was asked if it was okay to use the H-Word in our one-on-one interview, Tebow replied with a wry grin, "You mean 'Heisman' or 'humility'?"

He already had the humility. It was taught to him by his parents as a small child. But if he could allow himself to dream for a moment, what would winning the Heisman mean to him?

"It would be awesome. It's a blessing and an honor just to be named when people talk about the Heisman. And then to mention you, it's an honor. What a prestigious event it is."

A few minutes into the interview, I administered the H-Word Quiz.

Q: *First guy to win the Heisman?*

TT: *I don't know (Sigh).*

(Jay Berwanger, he was told.)

Q: *How many guys from the state of Florida have won the Heisman?*

TT: *Seven?*

(Nah, I think it's six, right? Two, two and two—from Florida, FSU, and Miami.)

TT: *Spurrier, Wuerffel, Ward, Weinke, Testaverde.*

Q: *And the other guy from a few years ago at Miami.*

TT: *Dorsey?*

Q: *Nah, the guy from Miami . . . (Gino Torretta).*

Q: *Who was Heisman?*

TT: *(Silence)*

Q: *John Heisman.*

A: *(Silence)*

Q. *John Heisman, Georgia Tech coach.*

Tebow still had a little studying to do, but that wasn't too bad for a twenty-year-old sophomore, who would soon become "homeschooled" about the Heisman.

Tim, the fifth and youngest child and third son of Bob and Pam Tebow, was born in the Philippines, where his parents were missionaries. They had prayed for another child by the name of Timmy, but when Pam got pregnant, she found out she had contracted amoebic dysentery through the drinking water.

Doctors advised Bob and Pam to abort the fetus because they feared it had been damaged, but Pam refused because of her Christian faith. After two months of bed rest for her, Tim was born, a healthy boy whom Pam described as "skinny, but rather long," joining brothers Peter and Robby and sisters Katie and Christy.

The Tebows then moved to Jacksonville, where they lived on a forty-four-acre farm.

Like Tiger Woods, Tim had a fondness for his sport early and gravitated to it immediately. Tim has pictures of himself holding a football "at age three or four." He tossed the ball about in the yard, staging his dreams with make-believe games. His introduction to the game came through his older brothers, Peter and Robby, with Robby the first to play competitively.

Once he began competing, Tim was taught early to never, never, never take credit for anything. His fiery spirit had to be harnessed. After arriving home from a baseball game, he bragged about his accomplishments.

"Even at a young age—it started when I was in Tee Ball—I would have success in youth sports," Tebow said. "Say I would hit two or three home runs in a Tee Ball game. I wanted to *tell* everybody! 'Hey, I hit three home runs in a baseball game' . . . Or 'I ran for a touchdown.' My parents made a rule when I was young that I couldn't tell anybody what I'd done until they asked me about it. And so [I had] to work on humility."

It was the early 1990s and the Steve Spurrier era was under way, as the winning brought with it the rejuvenation of the Gator Nation. Tim's parents were both Florida grads and the family lived only sixty miles from Gainesville. They were big fans of the Gators and admirers of Danny Wuerffel, whom they would handpick as Tim's recommended role model.

Bob and Pam also pointed out Wuerffel's humility and that he always gave God the credit first and then his teammates and coaches. "For me that was huge, because sports were a lot of my world," Tim said.

At age five or six, Tim was so emotionally invested in the Gators that he'd become distraught when they didn't play well or got beat. He laughs at himself now. "I'd get so upset I'd have to leave the room. I'd get too nervous and couldn't watch the end of the game. Gator football was huge for me."

By the time he was nine, Tim was "a huge Florida fan." When his beloved Gators and Wuerffel were upset by FSU in 1996, he broke down and cried.

"I'm just sobbing—I can't stay in the room, because I'm sobbing. I was such a big fan—competitive, outgoing like that."

It was no surprise, then, when he became a high school football star. He wanted to play quarterback, so after a freshman year as a linebacker at Jacksonville Trinity Christian, he chose to play for Nease High School in Ponte Vedra, where his mother took an apartment as the rest of the family remained back on the farm.

All five of the Tebow children were homeschooled, and under a 1996 ruling by the Florida State legislature he could choose to play football anywhere in the school district.

Nease went 11-2 his junior year in the 3A Florida classification, but the Panthers moved up to 4A, where they defeated Armwood, 44–37, for the title as he was involved in six touchdowns. Heavily recruited after a career of just under 10,000 yards total offense for 95 touchdowns (he ran for 63), Tebow listed his choices as Florida, LSU, Alabama, Michigan, and Southern Cal.

It came down to Florida and Alabama, with the Gators winning out in a tight battle—perhaps due in part to his regard for Wuerffel. (Shortly thereafter, the State of Alabama passed a new law allowing homeschooled athletes to pick their athletic teams. It was called the Tim Tebow Bill.)

So widely publicized was Tebow that ESPN did a commentary on him entitled "The Chosen One," which focused on the controversy of his homeschooling.

Tim also spent three summers doing missionary work in the Philippines before enrolling in college to follow in the footsteps of his hero, Wuerffel, who has a full-time ministry called Desire Street. And Tebow continues to give back to others.

Over the spring break in 2008, while other collegians were basking on the beaches of Florida, Tebow returned to the land of his birthplace for a humane act: To perform circumcisions on impoverished children in General Santos City, the Philippines.

Of the experience, Tebow told the *Orlando Sentinel:*

"The first time, it was nerve-racking. Hands were shaking a little bit. I mean, I'm cutting somebody. You can't do those kinds of things in the United States. But those people really needed the surgeries. We needed to help them."

Tebow's acts of kindness include a regular prison ministry. Over the spring, Tebow also spoke to inmates at Lancaster Correctional Institute in nearby Trenton, Florida, walking openly among violent criminals without fear.

"No matter where I am, if I'm preaching to Muslims or in a prison, if you're in the will of God, that's safer than driving down the interstate," Tebow said to ESPN.com. "That's how I feel about it."

Though Tebow and Wuerffel are alike in competitiveness and their strong faith, that's where the similarity ends. Danny was right-handed, not a physical player, and didn't run much. He was also a more accurate passer than Tebow, but Wuerffel wasn't a full-time starter as a sophomore and didn't win the Heisman until his senior year.

The initial question about Tebow coming out of high school was whether he was going to be a proficient passer and even his Gator coaches had some questions about him.

"He's better than I thought he would be, but I was concerned a little about his throwing when we first got him," Meyer admitted. "His downfield passing has always been strong. His first spring he wasn't very good at all at his short boots [bootleg passes] and he was just dumping the ball. He'd throw it like a bad dart. He just didn't have confidence. Dan Mullen and Tim worked so hard on it. They redid his entire mechanics of throwing." As a bailout, Tebow could resort to his running.

"Obviously Tim is going to work as hard as he can at getting better. And he's a phenomenal short passer now. I was very concerned about that . . . You could tell he had zero confidence at that. He'd rather just run it," Meyer said.

Tebow said the knock on him as a passer came because of the short-yardage back role he was asked to play as a freshman.

"My role on the team last year [2006] was to go in to run the ball and get first downs," said Tebow, "and to make big plays when I was asked to. To throw play-action passes. I tried to do that role as best I could." And when Tebow got the chance as a starter to execute the whole playbook, he proved adept at dropping back and finding his receivers.

"So, because of that a lot of people all over the country would say, 'Can he throw?' I tried to use anything like that as motivation—just smile, laugh at it. And I'd just get a chance to prove people wrong. I like it like that. Situations like that I always enjoy—I don't know why, I guess it just brings out my competitive side."

That same competitive side that had ignited the spark that night in Columbia and got his Gator team rolling again. Tebow would continue his assault on the records against a Florida Atlantic team that was good enough to beat Minnesota.

Even though Tebow broke a national record, there wasn't much celebrating after Florida's 59–20 drubbing of Florida Atlantic, because the Gators had officially been eliminated from the SEC East race with Georgia's win over Kentucky. (Tennessee, the team Florida had badly flummoxed just nine weeks prior, got the dubious distinction of facing LSU, which would go on to win the SEC championship and become national champion by beating Ohio State.)

Against FAU, it was somebody else's turn for the spotlight as Bubba Caldwell hauled in a career-high 13 catches to eclipse by five the mark of 172 by Carlos Alvarez, who was on the sideline for the special occasion cheering for him. Caldwell had overcome serious injuries twice late in his career, but became a money receiver for both Chris Leak and Tebow, as well as a senior leader.

With two games still left, Tebow had become the only player in NCAA history to both pass and run for at least twenty touchdowns, as he threw for three more and posted a career-high 338 yards in the air. He also rushed for one.

There were still unresolved issues and unattained goals, such as the Heisman, beating cross-state rival Florida State, and earning a bowl bid. His finest individual plays were still to come as the team he despised most would show up the next Saturday in the Swamp.

Tebow said he had no thoughts about the Heisman, but he had plenty for FSU, the team he disliked so much.

"This is probably the greatest rivalry we have," said Tebow. "My dad would probably say Georgia, but I'd say FSU." Tim still had bad memories of that dark day in 1996 when the Seminoles mauled his hero and made Tim cry. With the mouthing off about to be done by Seminoles linebacker Geno Hayes, there would be another little score to be settled.

26

"That Was a Wow!"

There were smiles all around the football offices on Lemerand Drive because the boss was feeling pretty good. Urban's Gators were on a three-game winning streak and moving up in the rankings. They were a two-touchdown favorite over the Florida State Seminoles, whom they had beaten three years running.

"That school out west," as Urban calls FSU, was in a tailspin with a 7-4 record that would soon qualify them as "That school most likely headed south."

At 8-3 with a No. 10 BCS rating, the Gators had a decent bowl bid in play and the possibility of a ten-win season. Despite the bad news that starting cornerback Joe Haden would likely miss the final regular season game, Meyer was impressed the way his young team had been responding.

Urban was encouraged at the sight of Percy Harvin being back after a two-game layoff; thrilled about the play of punt/kick-return specialist Brandon James; happy about the conversion from offense to nose tackle by his freshman Mike Pouncey, whose brother Maurkice was starting on offense at guard; and pleased about the play of Jermaine

Cunningham, named SEC defensive lineman of the week after five tackles and a sack against Vanderbilt.

After eleven games of what would be his toughest season as a head coach, Meyer finally began to see some light, which was going to be bad news for Bobby Bowden.

Tebow was going to have a little message to deliver to Bowden's smack-talking linebacker.

As he had proven in his first year as a starter, Tebow had developed into an accurate thrower, thanks to the mechanics drilled into him by Dan Mullen. Though Tebow was as responsible for the turnaround as anybody, Meyer was always pointing out that it takes eleven men on offense.

"Now he's number one in college passing efficiency," Meyer said of Tebow. "He's got very good personnel around him. I always have to say that, because that sometimes gets overlooked. Chris Leak—and I keep going back—struggled for three games. John Elway or Johnny Unitas would have struggled for those three games. We were not very good."

Among those other ten guys, sophomore Percy Harvin was the key dynamic.

Aside from his obvious speed and receiving ability, Harvin possessed the vision and inside running acumen normally attributed to world-class running backs. That, along with the "sports-car shift" change of speeds that Mullen talked about, transformed Harvin into the go-to running back averaging more than a first down every time he touched the ball in his last three regular season games.

All of which made Harvin the perfect weapon for the Spread, designed to get the ball into the hands of the playmakers. Against FSU, Percy touched the ball 21 times for 236 yards, including the staggering 169 yards on the ground. Percy capped it off with a scintillating 24-yard run for a touchdown, which inspired CBS play-by-play announcer's Verne Lundquist's call of: "Harvin goes left. Harvin goes right. Harvin up the middle. Florida touchdown! It's just so easy . . . or looks that way."

To which Danielson added: "Fantastic! And I'm saying they're preseason number one."

That's why Meyer has said of Harvin, "He can become as good a football player as I have ever seen," and that included Meyer's prized quarterback. That's why the following season we in the media were bound to start hearing some "Percy for Heisman" whispers—not by Meyer, but by others, including Tebow.

Harvin was the crown jewel of a deep receiving corps that would lose only one senior (Bubba Caldwell) to graduation. Harvin, Caldwell, Louis Murphy, and Cornelius Ingram assaulted opponents' defenses for more than 2,500 receiving yards in 2007. The even distribution to those four was a testimony to Urban's Spread offense, with each catching 30 or more balls for an average of around 14 yards per reception.

No wonder FSU defensive coordinator Mick Andrews whined to CBS in pregame dialogue, "Most teams have one fast guy to cover—they've got *four*!"

The Seminoles were looking for anything to get their motor running before the final regular season game of 2007 for both teams. Linebacker Geno Hayes began with his mouth, declaring the 'Noles were going to hammer Tebow and deny him a Heisman Trophy: "Tim Tebow is going down. . . . That's our plan, go out there and shatter his dream for the Heisman."

Tebow said the comment by Hayes "got us motivated a little during the week—not that we needed it."

The real mistake that Hayes made was also talking trash in person during the game. Unwittingly, he was about to help fuel the engine of an eighteen-wheel semi that would soon be coming right back at him.

I've not seen every single game at Florida Field over the past fifty years, but I've probably seen as many as any sports writer. What unfolded before my trifocaled-but-still-fairly-sharp eyes were two of the finest football plays I'd ever witnessed at that stadium. And they were back-to-back. The first was inspired by Hayes's face-mask-to-face-mask confrontation and some trash talk that, Tebow said later, "kind of got me irritated and motivated."

On second down and one at the FSU 23, Tebow made Hayes pay.

Dropping back to pass and failing to find anyone open, Tebow began chugging full steam up the middle of the field, with two defenders whiffing him (one of them Hayes).

Four more gathered around the 5-yard line in hopes of stopping this 235-pound runaway freight train. The train won, as Tebow scattered several and two others hung on for dear life while he carried them across the goal line.

"Geno kind of got in my grill a little bit," Tebow explained. "And from that point on I changed from a quarterback to a football player. I just wanted to go out there and play football and hit somebody."

Tebow could beat them with his legs or, as he was about to prove on the next series, less than four minutes later, with his arm. Dropping back to pass, he looked off man coverage and laid the football into the hands of Murphy on the dead run in the corner, where only his receiver could catch it. Despite being closely guarded by the Seminole defender, Murphy's precise route was timed perfectly, and as he drew in the football, his foot slammed down inches in from the end line, like a seasoned NFL receiver.

"Wow!" Meyer said over his headset to Dan Mullen, who responded, "Wow!"

"Is he in?" Urban asked Mullen.

"Yes," said Mullen, but it was so close that it took several replays for officials to declare it a touchdown.

How was that for a statement to Heisman voters?

CBS analyst Gary Danielson called it "an absolutely perfectly thrown pass." But he also noted that most of the country had not seen Tebow's "two signature plays," because CBS was still carrying Tennessee-Kentucky in overtime to the rest of the nation. Once the Florida-FSU game went on the national feed, CBS made sure the plays were seen on replay.

(Once the season was over, Meyer would say of Tebow's two spectacular plays, "As fine a pair of football plays as maybe I've ever seen—back-to-back like that. And you can say, 'Well, that's coaching.' That ain't coaching. That's a *ballplayer*! One of the greatest players of our era, making a play. On the headsets, that was a 'Wow!' I will never forget that.")

As the Gators were killing the clock with a 45-12 domination of their cross-state rivals, Caldwell actually tried to goad Tebow into striking that famed Heisman pose, but Tebow declined. He didn't need to pose, because he looked very much like the real deal as the seventy-third Heisman winner.

The crowd was chanting, "Tebow . . . Heisman! Tebow . . . Heisman!" as the clock wound down on his five-touchdown night, sealing the Gators' fourth straight victory over Florida State.

Bowden called it his "worst ever" beating.

Meyer called it a "great team win, the finest maybe since Ohio State." Tebow was excited to "Beat a team like FSU, a team that I grew up watching play . . . Such a bitter rivalry. Georgia's a big rivalry. Tennessee is a big rivalry, but FSU . . . There's just something about that game."

In Tebow's customary victory lap after the game, as he slapped skin with the fans, he was careful to mostly use his left hand because of the severe pain in his right.

It was a Hollywood-like ending, and you almost expected the season's credits to roll behind Tebow: 51 touchdowns, 29 passing and 22 rushing, and in his first year as a starter. Tebow also tacked on 351 yards that day in total offense, which pushed him to 3,970, breaking Rex Grossman's school record of 3,904 yards in 2001 with a bowl game yet left to play.

Staggering numbers—but was it enough to make him the first sophomore ever to win college football's highest individual honor?

"If he doesn't win the Heisman, it's because of that sophomore thing," Bowden predicted. "But he might win the next two."

Once again, Meyer chose not to say much about the Heisman, but praised Tebow and said he was proud of the effort of his whole team. But Meyer knew full well he'd be going to New York the next week with his quarterback.

It may have seemed to some like a one-man band, but Superman did need blockers. The offensive line, led by Drew Miller, Jim Tartt,

Carton Medder, Maurkice Pouncey, and Jason Watkins performed solidly in a 279-yard rushing effort and allowed just one sack. An outstanding defensive performance held FSU without a touchdown and limited the 'Noles to 99 yards rushing.

The spotty defense that had been a liability all season looked to be improving. Charlie Strong's linebackers were becoming more seasoned, and although he wasn't yet at the level of Brandon Siler—the All-SEC middle linebacker before him—Brandon Spikes was beginning to make a difference. He had ten tackles against FSU, seven of them solo. Strong's promising young group of underclassmen linebackers—Spikes, Dustin Doe, A.J. Jones and Ryan Stamper—were growing up.

The Kiddie Korps on defense was a pleasant surprise as true freshman nose tackle Mike Pouncey, true freshman defensive tackle Justin Trattou, and redshirt freshman cornerback Jacques Rickerson impressed their coaches. So the future was looking better for the defense.

In 2006, the defense had carried the team to a national championship. In 2007, the strength of the team was the offense, with an average of more than 42 points and 455 yards per game—even without a true tailback.

Meyer felt that, given some of the problems on and off the field earlier in the season, 9–3 was satisfactory. "It was awful around here for three or four games," said Meyer. He did manage to win his thirty-first game in his third season at Florida and collect his seventieth victory as a head coach.

Back in contention for a year-end top 10 position, the Gators took aim on playing a January 1 bowl game. And with a large group of underclassmen (freshmen and sophomores) back, Meyer was banking on 2008 as a year to compete for the SEC title again. Plus, maybe the Heisman Trophy winner was going to be his starting quarterback when they played Michigan in the Capital One Bowl.

27

Living Large on Times Square

In late November when ballots arrived in the mail, there was still a Heisman horse race. Tim Tebow was leading by a nose, but the idle chatter on shows like ESPN's *Pardon the Interruption* and various radio programs almost seemed to cast him as a dark horse.

It was the "sophomore thing." Which was absurd. In a day when high school players jumped right to the professional leagues as stars, how could a second-year quarterback who had played on a national championship team as a freshman not be a legitimate selection?

Even with his stupendous statistics, Tebow had that stigma hanging over him. While there was no orchestrated hype from Florida, a good bit of drumbeating seemed to be coming out of other places such as Honolulu and Fayetteville, Arkansas.

Urban Meyer declined media opportunities to stump for his quarterback. He made it clear early on that he wanted no campaign for Tebow. Associate Athletics Director Steve McClain and Assistant Director of Sports Information Zack Higbee had begun their low-key approach in the summer.

"We sat down in July and mapped out a strategy for publicity for the marquee guys, which we kind of do every year," said McClain.

"Most of our strategy with Tim was to develop a presence and not make it about him. It was about our team, not just him, and the family atmosphere at the University of Florida, or the speed of the program."

Aware of the knock on Tebow that he "couldn't throw the ball," McClain and Higbee went back through the files and realized that in most every photo they had of Tebow he was running. So in the first game of the season they made it a point to get shots of him passing.

There was also a delicate balance for Meyer, who had been chastised the year before for coming out and saying his 2006 team deserved the chance over Michigan to play Ohio State for the national championship. "I was asked a question, I gave my opinion, and now I'm a lobbyist," Meyer said. So he declined to respond to the comments of Hawaii coach June Jones, who had used the old "system quarterback" tag on Tebow.

Some people worried that Meyer's reluctance to speak out on Tebow's behalf could hurt his chances in a close race. After spending a weekend of watching college football and studying Tebow's stats, Meyer finally declared: "Everybody asked my opinion and I didn't want to sound like I'm not behind Tim. I am certainly behind Tim because I do believe he should win it.

"I feel real strongly after watching the games and looking statistically at what he's done in the SEC that he should win the Heisman."

In the straw polls, Tebow had taken the lead over the injured Dennis Dixon of Oregon, but Darren McFadden's record-breaking performances were giving the Arkansas running back some late foot.

There was no need to overthink it. How could Tebow not be the slam dunk choice?

I sometimes wondered, after watching every game in person as Florida's sophomore quarterback took more than 700 of 782 snaps, if my eyes and binoculars had begun to deceive me. The Tim Tebow I saw was not only a bruising runner and a deft passer—he was the best-looking quarterback I'd ever seen at the University of Florida. Ever.

That included the two former Heisman winners, both of whom I had covered while they were Gators.

Since I had first started voting for the Heisman Trophy winner, much about the process had changed. With the speed of the Internet and the power of sports television, today you could almost have a "Heisman Trophy Favorite of the Hour."

Back in the early 1990s, sports information departments focused on telephone calls, a few film clips and mass mailings to newspapers—a practice believed to have been started by Navy in a campaign for Roger Staubach.

Florida's first Heisman Trophy winner was aided, in part, by the efforts of Assistant Athletics Director Norm Carlson sending a film clip of Steve Spurrier to five hundred television stations and dialing up various writers on Sundays to plug his candidate.

Today, with the time difference, those of us on the East Coast rarely got chances to see players such as Colt Brennan of Hawaii. Games played by Todd Reesing of Kansas and Chase Daniel of Missouri weren't exactly in the eastern time zone wheelhouse, either.

I waited until the very last play, past 3:00 A.M. Sunday, to view the Hawaii game and watch Brennan before casting my vote. Then I went online and voted my conscience electronically, fairly confident that I had voted for the winner.

Partly out of guilt, one of the late entries among the top three on my card was Brennan. His body of work was so impressive, even against lighter-weight competition. But that's also because Daniel bombed out in his big showdown with Oklahoma.

Meanwhile, at practice in Gainesville, Tebow stayed calm and kept a sense of humor about it, toying with the press one day by saying he was "practicing my McFadden moves."

Tebow was wearing an additional piece of equipment—a blue cast on his right hand—after learning that he'd fractured a bone during the FSU game. He wasn't sure when it happened, but, of course, Tebow had to keep on playing, adding to the legend.

This was the same player who stayed in the game at Nease High School with a broken leg, but still managed to score the tying touchdown on a 29-yard run in the fourth period. Nease coach Craig Howard told Robbie Andreu of the *Gainesville Sun* that he felt bad once he saw the X-ray because it showed a jagged break of Tebow's lower leg and not just a hairline fracture.

After Tebow attended the Home Depot Awards in Orlando and walked off with the Davey O'Brien Award and Maxwell Award, the reality of his likely winning the Heisman had begun to sink in.

Tebow and Zack Higbee began to think about an acceptance speech. They talked about what Wuerffel had said eleven years earlier, and Zack looked it up.

The next morning, the two of them boarded a JetBlue flight from Orlando for Tebow's first-ever trip to New York City. Tim slept all the way. He arrived to visit with his family, including his oldest missionary sister, Christy Tebow-Allen, who had flown in from South Asia.

When I arrived at the Hard Rock Cafe, where the press conference and the announcement of the Heisman winner would be held, a large contingent of Florida media was in attendance. Some of them paced about the floor, almost a little nervous about the outcome, although more so about how it might impact their stories on deadline if Tebow turned out *not* to be the winner.

Even Meyer, the reluctant "lobbyist," was a little worried because of what he called "an illogical world." He said he got a queasy feeling in his stomach.

"I got nervous about fifteen seconds before—I got that fourth-and-one feeling in my gut, like on the fifteen-yard line when I called a fake punt against Arkansas.

"I kept hearing about 'sophomore.' If we didn't make that national championship game a year ago, that's illogical . . . to have two teams play in a rematch. But it's an illogical world. I kept thinking, 'Man, this should happen, but there's some people out there that . . . who knows?'

"My biggest fear was, 'How do you deal with it?' if he didn't get it. If there was anybody who could handle it, it's Tim."

The pressure was starting to mount for Tim, too, and before he went out for the ceremony, Danny Wuerffel pulled him off to the side for a word of prayer. "And you could almost see some of the tension leave his body," said Higbee.

We watched the ceremony, which was televised from the Nokia Theater TV next door. It was an Academy Award–like moment when the Heisman Committee spokesman looked out into the crowd and announced Tim Tebow as the winner. He had received nearly half of the 925 votes and won every region, beating out McFadden by 245 points. The Arkansas running back was runner-up for the second straight year.

The youngest player to win the Heisman Trophy hugged half of New York City before thanking almost everybody in the entire Gator Nation by name—twice.

First he thanked Jesus, true to his faith and the script that Wuerffel had used before him, and then hugged childhood hero and fellow Gator Heisman-Man Wuerffel, then his competitors, his coach, his mom and dad, and even the guy handing him the trophy.

Wearing a light gray suit, blue shirt, silver tie and a big smile, Tebow accepted the trophy from Brian D. Obergfell of the Heisman Trophy Trust with his left hand, since the blue cast was still on his right.

"I want to accept this award on behalf of my coaches, teammates, and the entire Gator Nation," Tebow said. "This award is more about them than it is for me. I am very proud to represent the University of Florida."

Then he led interference for Urban and his wife, Shelley, across the street and through the masses of Times Square to the press conference in the Hard Rock Live Venue at the Hard Rock Cafe—Tebow with his arm around Meyer's neck like a high school pal—as the Big Apple parted.

"I'll never forget that moment, because that was big-time," said Meyer. "To walk out of that building, have police around you, and have people in New York City screaming, 'Tebow!' Not just Gator fans, but people. And they're pushing you along—hundreds of people—and they're recognizing Tim Tebow. I thought it was really neat for him. I loved it. I was just like a groupie. Shelley and I kept getting pushed and we kind of got whooshed behind him."

I asked Tebow that night if he felt somewhat relieved.

"You definitely do," he said. "There are so many nerves going through you—you're just anxious and excited—and then you feel a little bit relieved."

Once again, however, Tebow could not be stopped and now the legend loomed over the Big Apple like a giant Macy's Thanksgiving Day parade balloon.

Faster than a speeding bullet, accounting for 51 touchdowns in just twelve games as a starter, the twenty-year-old became the first sophomore in the nation and third quarterback at his school to win the Heisman, as well as the seventy-third overall.

How happy was Urban Meyer? "He's not my son," Meyer said, looking at Tebow, "but my son gets to go hang out with him."

Having watched all three of Florida's Heisman-Men play, I felt that Tebow could become the best of the trio, and perhaps as great a college football talent as I had ever seen.

Spurrier's guile as a play caller and consistency as a clutch performer made him the premier player of his era. Wuerffel's leadership role, poise, faith, and passing ability were the hallmarks of his national championship era. Tebow's leadership, raw talent, spirituality, ferocity as a competitor, and pure physical dominance put him in the stratosphere where maybe no player had ever gone before.

It was almost the perfect night for Tebow, except for one thing. A few days later he realized he hadn't mentioned two trainers and asked that I include them here. So Florida head athletics trainer Anthony Pass and assistant athletics trainer Kyle Johnston, take a bow.

Florida also became the only school besides Notre Dame to have three Heisman quarterbacks. The one common denominator in this trio was, as Franz Beard of Gatorcountry.com wrote, they were all sons of preachers.

"Steve Spurrier was the first Florida Heisman Trophy winner back in 1966. He was the son of a Presbyterian minister from Tennessee and 30 years later he would coach Wuerffel, the son of a Lutheran chaplain in the United States Air Force, to a national championship and a Heisman Trophy."

Some, of course, dragged out the Superman metaphors, such as: "Tim Tebow didn't have to be able to leap the tall buildings in a single bound on Saturday. They bowed at his feet as he jumped over the moon and picked his own star from the Metropolis skyline."

There was celebration everywhere in the Gator Nation. In the final round of the Merrill Lynch Shark Shootout at Tiburon in Naples that Sunday, a couple of Gators came to the final tee, hit their shots, and promptly displayed their colors. Chris DiMarco and Camilo Villegas whipped out white No. 15 Tim Tebow jerseys and walked up the eighteenth fairway wearing them, in honor of the 2007 Heisman Trophy winner.

28

In the Rearview Mirror

The one hundredth campaign of Gator football, which has been played over the last 101 years (there was no team in 1943), had been less than great—even downright agonizing at times for Urban Meyer.

The 2007 Florida Gators were too young and inexperienced on defense. There were some injuries and off-field problems and wrong-way outcomes of big plays in big games.

However, some of that was balanced off by the remarkable performance of a sophomore quarterback who fewer than ninety days prior was having his passing abilities questioned.

The outlook for Florida fans was fairly good: The Gators were on a roll, looking in their rearview mirrors at the programs of the Miami Hurricanes and Florida State Seminoles. But they were behind their curve in championships.

I did not—nor did anybody else in the universe—foresee Tim Tebow winning the Heisman Trophy. So while maybe not a memorable season, it was not without accomplishment and may yet become a harbinger for good things to come. The Tim Tebow Show story line had saved the day. At least from the writers' and fans' point of view. Not so much for Meyer, although he enjoyed it, too.

From Meyer's perspective, putting one player above the rest of the team is akin to favoring one child over others, so he shudders when too much attention is given to No. 15.

Not because Meyer doesn't appreciate and recognize Tebow's enormous talents, because nobody is a bigger fan of Tebow's than his head coach. Urban believes he needs all the playmakers he can get—Percy Harvin, Louis Murphy, Cornelius Ingram, Brandon James, Brandon Spikes, Chris Rainey, Jermaine Cunningham, Joe Haden, etc. Most of all, he is looking for leadership to enhance team chemistry. Because in 2008, the sky was going to be the limit.

The 2007 season was the year that might have been for Florida, but for a play or two against Auburn or LSU. As it was, Meyer had to dig himself out of a midseason morass to reach 9-3.

"Certainly this was not a perfect year," Meyer said. "This was an awful year for about three or four weeks—awful! Dealing with issues. This year was not Florida football at all. Defensively, offensively—there was just nonsense we were dealing with."

Beating FSU, 45–12, was more than just a victory on the scoreboard, because it resonated with the recruits and paid recruiting dividends. Four weeks ago, after the loss to Georgia and a near meltdown of the defense, things had looked pretty glum around Titletown for the 5-3 Gators. After that, Meyer's Spread offense rolled up an average of more than 50 points in a four-game win streak at the end of the season.

"To come back and play like that, and to hear what some of those kids sitting in the locker room [recruits] say . . . the future is bright. A lot of it has to do with winning that game," Meyer said.

Which, by the way, was due in no small part to the guy with the broken hand. In a year with no national championship hopes and no trip to the SEC title game, the Tim Tebow Show was grand, but the true by-product of it may not show up until the 102nd year.

Meyer looked back at the LSU game as a lost opportunity.

"If we won that game, we might have been playing in the BCS [championship] game—just like the year before, with the blocked field goal against South Carolina and the fourth and one against Tennessee," said Meyer.

What went wrong? Lack of experience, maturity, and leadership which was exposed from the Auburn to the Georgia game.

"That little stretch of games was a reflection of our team," Meyer said. "I think we were a poor team then. Auburn, the offense screws it up. LSU, a combination: On five fourth downs and you tell me we can't make a play and get off the field?

"We have two turnovers on offense at terrible times—a guy runs the wrong route and the other guy makes a noncontact fumble? That's a bad team—real bad team. It's a maturity issue. We were playing with probably five seniors, but the year before we were playing with about twenty that went through hell, and were invested and were going to find a way to win that game."

Urban classified his team early in 2007 as "a bunch of spoiled young players who got much better as the year went on, but at that point and time they never had to fight for anything yet around here.

"A lot of kids playing for us, what did they have to fight for? They had to fight for it against Auburn and they failed. They had to fight for it against LSU and they failed."

So the 2007 season was not fun—it was an albatross. "It's the hardest year I've ever had," Meyer said, "after we won the national championship."

Even if it wasn't the Sugar or the Rose or the Fiesta or the Orange, the Capital One Bowl berth was a welcome break for Florida's travel-weary fans that had been traipsing across the country, chasing dreams and collecting the booty for the past twenty-one months. While it officially ended the reign of consecutive Gator football/basketball national championships, there was certainly no whining.

The Gators made their seventeenth straight bowl appearance, which ranked first in the SEC and third in the country. Florida was making its fifth appearance in the Capital One, going into the game with a post-season record of 16 wins and 18 losses. This would be only the second time Florida and Michigan had met, with the Wolverines posting a 38–30 win over Ron Zook's club in the 2003 Outback Bowl.

There was also this matter for Meyer: If he collected his fourth straight bowl victory, he would become one of only two coaches in the nation to have accomplished that.

When he had more than a week to prepare his team, Meyer's record as a coach was 21-2—which didn't bode well for Lloyd Carr, who had resigned and would be coaching his last game for Michigan.

However, the favored Gators lost, 41–35, and dropped to a disappointing 9-4, Meyer's worst record in seven seasons. Particularly disconcerting was that, once again, they had the ball with plenty of time left and couldn't score.

With the Gators at their own 23-yard line with more than two minutes to play, Michigan poured on a strong rush with excellent secondary coverage and denied Tebow and his receivers on four straight passes. Florida, with the Heisman winner and the talented receivers, couldn't produce a single first down and the ball went over to the Wolverines.

That undid a lot of otherwise good things. Percy Harvin produced nearly 250 yards in total offense as the Gators rallied from a 14-point deficit to tie the score at 28–28 late in the third period. Tebow passed for three touchdowns and set the NCAA record for rushing touchdowns by a quarterback at twenty-three.

Despite the loss, Meyer remained optimistic about his team and he was still on pace to becoming one of the winningest college football coaches in history.

With all but nine players returning in 2008, Meyer was on schedule to approach forty wins at Florida in 2008 (he reached forty-four wins with nine losses) which would give him an average of more than ten wins in four seasons as Gator coach—the only Florida coach besides Spurrier to accomplish that.

At that pace, he also would be closing in on his eightieth victory overall in 2008, and maybe his hundredth by 2010, before he reached age forty-seven.

Meyer's 31-8 mark at Florida and overall record of 70-16 put him among the elite college coaches active through 2007, who were as follows:

1. Pete Carroll, Southern Cal	76-14 .844
2. Bob Stoops, Oklahoma	97-22 .815
3. Urban Meyer, Florida	70-16 .814
4. Mark Richt, Georgia	72-19 .791
5. Phillip Fulmer, Tennessee	147-45 .766
6. Bobby Bowden, Florida State	373-119-4 .756
7. Lloyd Carr, Michigan	122-40 .753
8. Joe Paterno, Penn State	372-125-3 .747
9. Steve Spurrier, South Carolina	163-56-2 .742
10. Jim Tressel, Ohio State	208-73-2 .739

Going into his fourth year at Florida, half of Meyer's career victories had come against a high level of competition. The Florida Gators play in the world's toughest college football league. The longevity of Bobby Bowden and Joe Paterno might have been jeopardized had they coached all those years in the SEC.

Bowden and Paterno had a thirty-one-year jump on Meyer, who by comparison is a young shaver. Just as Urban was fond of saying his young team needs to mature and "grow some whiskers," he needs a little time to grow a few himself.

Some wonder if he will be around to grow a full-length beard. If he can last, Meyer's record might rival even Spurrier's at Florida, though the Ol' Ball Coach's six SEC titles look out of reach.

No obstacle is bigger for Urban than the quality of competition he and his team must face. Like body shots in a heavyweight fight, the impact of the SEC schedule has a long-term, cumulative effect on a team.

Tennessee, Mississippi, Arkansas, LSU, Kentucky, Vanderbilt, South Carolina, and Georgia, all on Florida's 2008 schedule, averaged more than seven and a half victories each in 2007. Add state rivals Miami and Florida State to that group, and you see why there is no reason for Gator fans to apologize for the 2008 schedule's degree of difficulty.

A particularly tough time occurred in February, during the countdown for National Signing Day of 2008, when Urban and his coaches were trying to close the deal with twenty-two new players. It came to light that Urban may inadvertently and unknowingly have committed a minor violation by calling junior college wide receiver prospect Carl Moore from the Heisman Trophy ceremonies. Printed reports stated Moore somehow heard Tim Tebow screaming in the background, encouraging Moore to come to Florida.

Message boards on the sites of Florida's rivals lit up with charges of cheating by Meyer. ESPN picked up the story, raising more questions. Although the compliance department at Florida was confident there were no serious issues, it couldn't say for sure until the NCAA made a ruling.

Those close to Meyer knew this charge wouldn't hold water. Among them was his former Utah quarterback Alex Smith, who was watching TV in California when he saw the name of his former coach crawl across the bottom of the screen. Urban Meyer was being "investigated."

"I've been in the environment and know that Coach Meyer is

never going to do anything like that," Smith said from his West Coast home, where the former No. 1 pick in the NFL was rehabbing from shoulder surgery. "If anything did happen like that, obviously it got resolved and got taken care of. This is a guy of the utmost integrity."

When Meyer saw the crawl on ESPN noting that he was being "investigated," he was stunned and angry.

Smith was right. The NCAA said there were no violations. But for ten days Meyer's name had been dragged through the mud and it bothered him—mostly because he knew some of it was being used against him by rivals as a tool for negative recruiting.

Maybe at Bowling Green or Utah this wouldn't have been an ESPN story.

These were the kinds of things Urban Meyer had to learn about his visibility since he had taken over at Florida four years ago.

The most important component of Meyer's coaching schematic is how he treats and values players. As a player advocate, Meyer gives them every conceivable opportunity to succeed, which is what he means by "never giving up" on them. But it does not mean coddling them or allowing them to cut corners or cutting them slack. On the contrary, there is a Huge penance when they do wrong.

What others don't see in a player, however, Meyer can sometimes discern.

"Coach is ten times better than anybody I've ever seen," said staff member Jon Clark. "I can't do that stuff. He sees that good in a guy. He can really tell, 'Hey, great guy' or 'Maybe not so great guy.' And he's not going to give up on that great guy. He keeps fighting for him."

Urban's mentors, staff members, former players, and coaching assistants all say the same thing about him: He is passionate about the game, surrounds himself with good people, represents the players' interest in everything they do and sees to it that those who give effort are rewarded. But make no mistake: He is forceful.

Perhaps that was a gift passed along by his parents—the hammer of Bud's discipline and the velvet glove of Gisela's nurturing. In essence, by Meyer investing in his players, he is paying it forward. But what's the payoff?

It has proved to be more than just about winning football games or a ring—but, after all, that is the immediate goal at hand. And when called upon, his "invested" players were ready to pony up.

This was a testament to how resourceful Meyer was in finding, keeping, rehabilitating, and mentoring his players and teaching them how to lead. To a man, almost, they responded.

The moving parts in Meyer's program are not visible to the outsider or, at first, even those of us who were privy to peek inside. What I'd seen, heard, read, and absorbed from Meyer, his staff, and players over three years—and particularly in my role behind the scenes during 2007—was well conceived, intelligent, and plausible. But I must confess I didn't really get the big picture until much later—and then only after the tangible result became as evident as the eight-hundred-pound elephant in the room.

Looking back, I can see those yet-to-be-moving parts all on the table, like pieces to a jigsaw puzzle, waiting to be interlocked by fate—or better yet, by design. I was never really able to visualize them fitting together in a football championship mosaic until the end of Meye's second season at Florida. Then something happened that I can't really explain.

Meyer rejects the notion that his championship year was something predestined.

So why not "fate"? The Florida coach prefers to think of it as something brought about by what he terms "competitive excellence." Meyer considers himself as having sixty-six "starters," because special teams are on the same level as others—a page right out of the Plan to Win. To achieve the "competitive" part of that, he needs that depth. Eighty-five scholarships may sound like a lot, but Urban needs all of that and another twenty to twenty-five walk-ons to create the proper energy level.

A roster that large is not terribly unusual for a football program, but Meyer makes a big effort to keep all the players functional. Here is the difference: When a Florida player falls behind academically, commits a misdemeanor, breaks a team rule, becomes injured, gets homesick and wants to leave school, indulges in drugs, overindulges in alcohol, or simply has a fight and breaks up with his girlfriend, Urban Meyer or one of his assistants is there to extend a hand. Better yet, by allowing the players to be in their homes and around a family environment, the position coaches can help ward off those things.

Valuing the player and the person comes back to reward Meyer. It's not just about quantity, because Meyer is diligent about reeling in blue-chip players that are a good fit for both the Florida program and the athlete.

When Gatorade Player of the Year Johnny Brantley of Ocala's Trinity made a verbal commitment to Texas, Meyer did not give up on the spectacular young prospect whose father and uncle—John III and Scot—had both played for the Gators. Despite the presence of a Tebow with three more years of eligibility at that time, Meyer convinced young Brantley that he was needed and would be counted on in the future at Florida. As a scout team quarterback in his redshirt season in 2007, Brantley was impressive. He suffered a shoulder injury in the spring of 2008 and then broke a hand which kept him out of the spring game, but was expected to take the field behind Tebow in 2008 as a competitor of excellence.

Likewise James Wilson, a *Parade* All-American offensive lineman and former Nease teammate of Tebow's. Injured in his redshirt year and never really able to get into the flow, Wilson informed Meyer that he would like to transfer in the spring of 2008. Meyer said OK, but told Wilson to at least go through spring practice before leaving for a school yet to be named. Before the spring game, Wilson was back on the field competing, enjoying camaraderie with teammates, eventually informing Meyer he would stay a Gator.

Once in the fold, players usually become enlightened in Urban's Way and, like those before them at Florida, Utah, and Bowling Green, eventually begin to reap its dividends.

"Discipline" to Meyer is not meting out punishment after the deed is done, but rather being proactive to head off problems in the first place. "Discipline," he said, "is anticipation."

This does not equate to a free pass in life, because in all cases the players are put on track to succeed in life, not just football.

The X's and O's of Meyer's program aren't as important as the ABC's of life. People skills play an even bigger part than coaching skills, although he has plenty of both. Those people skills must extend beyond the playing field and be felt throughout the entire football organization—by players and non-players alike. Alignment with the Plan to Win is crucial for the entire group's success.

It took me a while to figure this out, but when Meyer pays it forward with his players, they want to reciprocate by giving him back their best. This is something often not detected or deciphered until after football, when the player has gone on his way. That's why we don't get to see it or hear about it as this coach-player relationship is developing—only after it has happened.

After speaking with more than forty former players at four different schools, many of them telling almost identical stories about mutual trust, I am convinced this plays a big role in the success of Meyer.

"A lot of these young players don't know it right now," said Jarvis Moss, "but Coach Meyer is teaching them things about life that they won't realize until years later."

That's the "power" of Meyer that former Utah player Bo Nagahi talks about: "He does have this power over you and I don't know how he does it or what it is. I don't know whether it's trust—that he'll sit there and give us the trust, that he brings his family before us and he has nothing to hide. All his cards are on the table. To me, if you're going to give me all your trust, I'm going to give you all my trust. And that's the way everybody felt. I wish I knew, but I haven't been able to figure it out."

Meyer motivates through momentum, both on and off the field—whether calling a surprise play to show that he's willing to be at risk with his players, or inspiring excellence through academics or athletics.

"People fail to put a price tag on momentum," Meyer said. "That's one of the higher-priority items in dealing with youth."

There is also a definite connection through commitment to a standard and a willingness to show emotion.

Tim Tebow says the first word that comes to mind to describe his coach is "passionate."

"I think Coach Meyer is passionate about everything he does," said Tebow. "He wants to be the best, to do it perfect, to do it the right way. He doesn't want to cheat it or find easy ways to do it. And he treats people the right way. He's more worried about that. I respect him more for that because he's more worried about changing guys for the better than he is about winning games.

"That's what it's all about. For me that's a coach that I can look up to for more than just calling X's and O's. I can look up to him off the field as well."

Ryan Smith says other coaches should follow Meyer's lead.

"All these players away from home are not with their parents and they don't have anybody to tell them no or 'Don't do this or that.' What coaches don't realize is you have to be that father figure—you have to be able to change somebody's life. To be able to put somebody on the right track and be their football coach at the same time.

"A lot of coaches don't want to accept that responsibility. And not only does Coach Meyer accept that responsibility, he embraces it. And that's what I loved playing under him. Because it was more than just being one of his football players. It was 'How's the family, how are the grades, is everything OK?'

"He was changing lives daily. It was just a process and it was amazing to be a part of that, to see it happen to other people around you. I saw people who were worse than I was as far as being an adolescent. And you could just see them transformed under his guidance. I think he's been a part of that his whole career. That's been his aim from the beginning, in my opinion."

The morning sun is up now at Urban's lake house, and as we finish up our coffee, we flip through the pages of *Sports Illustrated*'s commemorative issue for the Florida-Ohio State BCS title game. Each photo inspires a different memory for the proud football coach, and sometimes even the least likely photo holds a special meaning.

The traditional photo of the coach getting a Gatorade bath has, for instance, has become almost a cliché. But not to Meyer. As we turned to the page where he was getting doused by three Gators and I was about to flip past, Meyer noted something different.

"The first thing I look at," he said, "is who's doing it. To realize how far they have come."

"They" are Dallas Baker, Steve Harris, and Ray McDonald.

"These were unbelievable stories, how far they came, from one year to the other."

Baker, one of Meyer's "top five all-time favorite players," is still struggling to catch on in the NFL. "That's what I couldn't coach in the NFL," said Meyer, "because how he's not playing in the NFL I don't understand it . . . He'd be one of my high draft picks."

When we reached the photo of All-American safety Reggie Nelson, it conjured up sadness for Meyer, reminding him of the day that Reggie traveled home to Melbourne, Florida with teammates Joe Cohen and Chris Leak to give his All-American trophy to his dying mother. Three days before Christmas, Mary Lakes died of cancer.

Urban located a medal like the one he carries in memory of his mother, had the name of Mary Lakes engraved on the back and sent it to Nelson.

Urban he did the same thing for Louis Murphy upon the passing of his mother, Filomena Murphy, who also died of cancer, a little over a year later.

The photo of Tim Tebow's first touchdown, with No. 15 diving in against Southern Mississippi, inspired good thoughts.

"I call him Vitamin Tebow,'" said Meyer. "I call him about once a day if I don't see him. I may call him today. He'll pick up the phone and I'll say 'A little Vitamin Tebow.' And he'll say, 'Hey, coach, how you doing? It's a great day to be a Gator.' It makes you feel good.

"I had some friends come over the other night and I said, 'I get to wake up tomorrow and I'm still Tim Tebow's coach. Not many people can say that.' I'll tell you, a lot of people would like to coach him."

The final day of spring football for Urban on the second Saturday of April 2008 was fairly spectacular and gratifying. He found out that some of his playmakers prefer the bright lights, even in daytime.

With a spring game record crowd of sixty-one thousand and a national ESPN audience watching, 5'9", 177-pound redshirt freshman Chris Rainey from Lakeland rushed for 75 yards and made his first mark on Florida Field with a spectacular catch-and-run of 65 yards.

Meyer was impressed with Rainey, saying after the scrimmage he would start in 2008 either at tailback or at wide receiver. Urban wasn't surprised by his showing.

"I thought he would do that," said a pleased Meyer, "and he did."

I was so impressed that I gave Rainey's first big play at Ben Hill Griffin Stadium its own name: The Half-Ike-with-an-Emmitt-Cutback.

Hauling in the pass of Tim Tebow over his right shoulder at the 35-yard line, Rainey imitated the Stop-And-Go Ike Hilliard once made on a touchdown catch in the 1997 Nokia Sugar Bowl national championship win over Florida State, 52–20.

Rainey caught Tebow's pass, took seven steps, planted his left foot in a semi-stop, cut right for three steps and planted his right foot, then zagged left back to the West sideline like Emmitt Smith had done many times before him, leaving former high school teammate safety Ahmad Black with a handful of air.

As somebody in the press box pointed out—sorry about this—there were probably going to be quite a few more "Rainey Days" ahead for the Gators.

Other signs were encouraging to Meyer, including the play of defensive tackle Carlos Dunlap, who made three sacks, and the thunderous leg of freshman kicker Caleb Sturgis, who knocked in several field goals from more than fifty yards.

Then there was Tim Tebow, who played the whole game despite a high fever because redshirt freshman Johnny Brantley had suffered a broken throwing hand. Brantley, bidding for the backup job, had just begun recovering from a shoulder injury when the injury to the hand occurred while he was running the ball. Though he didn't get any reps, Brantley was expected to be competing as the No. 2 quarterback with Cam Newton. Of course, Tebow didn't have much to prove.

It was a positive spring. Meyer was able to brag about the classroom work of his players. The Gators had a team grade-point average of 2.86 for the spring, marking the seventh straight semester the football team's academic scores had improved while Urban has been coaching at Florida.

That last day of spring ball gave Meyer reason for optimism. And he was hoping that feeling rubbed off on the big contingent of recruits who were on campus.

In the locker room after the game, the halls were lined with Gator position coaches and high school football players, giving and receiving introductions and exchanging shoulder bumps.

Meyer moved about the halls with a purpose, ducking in a room with a mother and a recruit for a long conversation, working through a gauntlet of prospects with warm greetings, stepping down the hall for an extended session with a promising quarterback and offensive coordinator Dan Mullen.

I finally caught up with him in the rotunda, next to the Gator head, and asked for an assessment of the day and the future of Florida football. Eight years ago when he had come to Florida Field as a Notre Dame assistant and stood on the 50-yard line at the Swamp, Meyer was awed by the setting. I asked him to compare his feelings then and now.

"I felt like a young recruit," Meyer said of his 2000 visit to Gainesville. "It was a beautiful day and up north it was freezing cold. This was a place I dreamed of being."

Now that the dream had come true: much of the infrastructure of his program had been built—and the impact of winning a national championship had enriched the talent supply. Weren't the pieces of this puzzle coming together nicely?

"I kind of feel that way," Meyer confessed, "but I don't want to jump ahead."

If he was allowing himself to peek around the corner a little, however, Urban had to be quite pleased at what he was seeing, because there was a definite look of eagerness in his eye. I got the feeing that Meyer was just a tiny bit giddy, but his poker hand would be played with a straight face. And what a hand it turned out to be in 2008.

PART FOUR

Waking Up to the American Dream

29

The Michigan Hangover

S ometimes there's nothing like a good lickin' to set the course straight—though this notion could be considered heresy if judged by the book of Bear Bryant, or Woody Hayes, or even John Wooden.

In other words, suffering has its rewards.

No doubt the Auburn defeat in 2006 and the Mississippi loss in 2008 will be underscored as seminal moments for Urban Meyer's first two national championship teams.

As Meyer always says, it's about how a team reacts when it gets hit in the mouth. After Ole Miss sucker-punched the 2008 Florida Gators, it was either going to be all in or all down the road. In fact, the seeds for the '08 championship were planted all the way back on the first day of January of that year and linked to the agony of a bowl loss to Michigan.

There were some dark days around Gainesville following the Wolverines' 41–35 victory over Florida in the Capital One Bowl.

Having manhandled Big Ten champion Ohio State in the BCS title game the year before, surely these Gators could dust off a second-tier team like the Wolverines. Or could they?

This time they collapsed in a failed fourth-quarter comeback bid, allowing Michigan coach Lloyd Carr to close out his career at the expense of the defending national champions. Even though the Gators rallied from two touchdowns behind with a brilliant performance by Percy Harvin, who racked up nearly 250 yards in total offense, they came up short with the ball in their hands, the Heisman Trophy winner at quarterback, and failed at the mission which they had trained for all season. In two possessions over the last four minutes they failed to produce a first down.

There's nothing like a little misery to get life jump-started again. The 2008 Florida Gators didn't need the jumper cables, because there was plenty of negativity to go around for Meyer, his staff, and his players after the embarrassing post-season lapse—the kind of loss that could have set his program back years. It was the low point for a team that had already staggered through a mediocre season.

The inability to finish games had been a bugaboo that haunted Meyer's 2005 Gators from the beginning. Overcoming that barrier became a fundamental goal for the 2006 national championship team, but the problem had reared its ugly head again a year later, at the end of a most exasperating '07 season. Facing the possibility of a relapse was downright depressing.

"Our players weren't having fun, I was miserable, our coaches were miserable, all because we lost to Michigan," Meyer said. "We had changes in our staff. It was awful! It got to a point where I couldn't stand it."

Misery does not always love company—nor deserve it, at least in the case of Shelley Meyer. She goaded Urban into going on a Nike-sponsored trip for coaches.

"The only reason I went is my wife said, 'You're going!' I said, 'I'm not going on some Nike trip. We got our ass beat in a bowl game,'" Urban recalled.

Then Dwayne Wade, the Miami Heat star, came to the rescue.

While Meyer was at the Nike meeting, he and other coaches got a chance to view Wade's uplifting "American Dream" message in a commercial for Converse 3.0. It provided Urban a wake-up call for himself and his team. He recalls it this way:

"The whole theme of the commercial is, here's this young man who is living the American dream. He's an NBA player. And he comes out wearing his warm-ups. No one is there. The Miami Heat arena is empty. He's by himself and he doesn't have a ball. He comes jogging on to the court like he's being introduced. He's not. No one is there, but he's living the dream. He's having fun. Then he starts acting like he's shooting shots, basically representing the American dream.

"And then the most profound moment is when he walks up the stairs and into the public address booth, and his eyes are closed. Here's this young man with this beautiful soul, and he opens his eyes, and he's the PA announcer. And he hits the button: 'And at guard, from Robbins, Illinois, six-foot-four guard, Dwayne WAAAAAD-DDDDDDE!'"

The Wade commercial, which was inspired by a letter that the Heat star once wrote to himself, sent shivers up the spine of Urban Meyer.

"I just sat up in my chair and said, 'My God, what am I doing?' I'm sitting there feeing sorry for myself—just miserable. And then I thought: 'I'm the head coach at Florida. I've got the best job in America. I've got a healthy family. I've got great players. I've got a Heisman Trophy winner at quarterback. I've got (Brandon) Spikes at linebacker. . . .'

"So I failed to be a good leader."

At that moment Meyer began leading his team on a path toward redemption.

The Wade commercial was shown to every Gator player and even placed on a loop where it could be seen on a TV monitor throughout the spring of 2008. Every time Urban ran into a player, he'd remind them: "You guys are living a dream and everybody's miserable around here."

Drawing from a quote by Fielding Yost, the late and legendary Michigan football coach, Meyer also reminded his team of the importance of passion. "Whether you are a lawyer, doctor, businessman—whatever it is—'If you don't have love, passion, enthusiasm for whatever you do, you're not very good.'" He felt his team—and to some degree he—had lost their love, passion, and enthusiasm for what they were doing.

"And so the whole emphasis was to get that love, passion, enthusiasm back," he said.

"Love and passion" would be the motivation for getting them past one huge roadblock on the way to Miami to play for the 2008 BCS National Championship. First, though, there was hard work that had to be done a full eight months before the '08 season.

The loss to Michigan set the stage for the turnaround which would be fortified by The Promise of Tim Tebow, The Apology by Brandon Spikes, and an incredible ten-game run of victories that included the demolition of Florida's rivals.

There would be moments of serious doubt, plus a little taste of rebellion and insurrection by unruly, unhappy fans that must have felt this Gator team owed them more.

After what took place in 2008 following the 31–30 loss to Ole Miss, however, nobody was ever going to doubt Tebow again. Besides, Urban Meyer had no intentions of letting his American Dream fade again.

30

The Promise

Maybe at Auburn or Tuscaloosa or Baton Rouge—or some other SEC venue—this could have been anticipated. Certainly not at home in the Swamp against a .500 team like Ole Miss. There wasn't even a whiff. The 2–2 Rebels, with losses to Wake Forest and Vanderbilt, were not exactly striking fear into the hearts of their opponents. Most of all, not the Mighty Gators.

The polls were starting to pay attention to 3–0 Florida after victories over Hawaii, Miami, and Tennessee as the Gators moved up to No. 4 in the Associated Press rankings behind top-ranked Southern California, No. 2 Oklahoma, and No. 3 Georgia.

Under ordinary circumstances, beating Miami and Tennessee back-to-back would call for a celebration. Given the inflated egos that infected the '07 team after beating the Vols, however, there was zero chance Meyer was going to allow any of that in 2008.

With an open date after Tennessee, there was even an extra week to prepare for the Rebels. Better balance was starting to surface with an improved Gator defense and a revamped running game. Tebow wouldn't have to carry the offense on his shoulders this year. His improved throwing motion and better checkdowns were boding well for Dan Mullen's offensive unit.

To paraphrase Dickens, Gator fans were about to experience the best of times and the worst of times—in reverse order.

Florida got off to a slow start in one of those dreaded "12:30 games" that Meyer always laments and had to overcome a 7–0 deficit to Ole Miss. Tebow hit Percy Harvin on a 43-yard touchdown and then scampered over from the 1-yard line for a comfortable 17–7 halftime advantage. Surely the Rebels of Houston Nutt would pose no serious problems.

History will judge Saturday, September 27 as one of the biggest upsets in Florida football history, administered by the hand of an unranked, 23-point underdog Rebel team that pulled off the football equivalent of the Brinks heist. Certain victory looked gift-wrapped for the Gators, but they kept giving it back. Like when Rebel quarterback Jevan Snead fired an 86-yard touchdown completion to Shay Hodge with 5:26 to play, giving Mississippi a 31–24 lead. Now, indeed, the scent of upset pervaded in the air above Ben Hill Griffin Stadium.

Despite three fumbles, the only thing Florida had to do was to convert an extra-point attempt to avoid the upset—at least to send the game to overtime. Tebow brought the Gators back, driving them 78 yards in about two minutes, but the game-tying extra-point attempt by reliable Jonathan Phillips was blocked by defensive lineman Kentrell Lockett. Meyer argued, to no avail, that Lockett had illegally jumped over an offensive lineman.

Not to worry. After all, Tebow and his unit had rehearsed the two-minute drill many times since the loss to Michigan, so this would be a good test.

Zip, zip, zip. Three straight pass completions and the ball was out on the Rebel 41 with more than a minute left and time out to spare. Vintage Tebow. The Gators were nearing Phillips' kicking range. Then something went terribly wrong. Two Tebow passes fell incomplete and a rush/option pitch to Brandon James gained just nine yards.

The whole game—as well as maybe the whole season—would come down to the Florida Gators converting a fourth-and-one play at the

Rebel 32. And almost nobody thought Tebow and his mates would fail—especially Tebow.

"We felt very confident we could dominate this team because we had done it on several plays," Tebow would recall later.

Gator fans figured this was the setup for Superman: He takes the snap from the single wing, jumps behind a big body, and rides the surge for the necessary first-down yardage. So here, with the game riding on the line, was yet another chance for the reigning Heisman Trophy owner to do his thing.

If there is one play Tebow prides himself in executing, it is the short-yardage run.

There is no better power back in college football, and even when the opposition knows he's coming its way the defense can't do much about it. Tebow's brute force is so old-school, so hard-nosed, so single-wingish that coach Bobby Bowden of Florida State labeled him "Bronko" after bull-rushing Bronko Nagurski, fullback of the Chicago Bears in the 1930s.

Tebow is 245 pounds of thunder. You would have gotten long odds in Las Vegas against the Rebels stopping No. 15. Tebow moved to his right down the line, bouncing off one of his linemen, trying to squirm over the top of the bodies. But this time he came up short.

"We weren't able to get any momentum on that run and they just did a good job of stopping it," Tebow said months later upon reflection. "There was never any doubt in our minds that we were going to drive down and score and win that game. That just didn't happen. It wasn't just the frustration of the day. It was having a chance to win and not coming through. That was very frustrating. Turns out Ole Miss was a pretty good football team (the Rebels would beat Texas Tech in the Cotton Bowl). But we should have won the game."

The heartbeat of the Gator Nation skipped a beat. Some of the fans weren't just disappointed—they were distraught and incensed. Nasty diatribes originating from the stands spilled over as the Gators departed their home field, causing one assistant coach to say, "Stay close to each other."

Meanwhile, Tebow wandered back to the locker room like a broken Humpty Dumpty who had taken a great fall, collapsing in a heap of discouragement in his locker, speechless, a constant flow of tears streaming down his face. More than just an SEC loss, it did feel a lot like this was the end of his American Dream.

Such stern stuff could even challenge the faith of Tim Tebow.

"You do have to know that all things work together for the glory of the Lord," said Tebow. "But a lot of times before greatness happens, something usually has to hit bottom. Mentally. Physically. Something happens at that time. And that was the bottom for us."

Meyer took one look at the despondent Tebow at his locker and knew this was the bottom. Words would not comfort his distraught quarterback. There was really nothing he could say or do. Sitting down on the floor in front of him in total silence, Meyer leaned against the legs of Tebow.

"I just wanted him to know that I was there," Urban said.

The quarterback and the coach just sat there for about ten minutes, hurting together.

"Nobody takes it harder than Tim," Meyer said later. "Tim is like a son. Tim's just not a student-athlete. He's like a member of our family. I have as much respect and love for that guy as any player I have ever coached."

Something was said about Tebow wanting to address the media, but his coach didn't really pay that much attention.

Urban headed over to his media conference.

Sometimes Tebow clings to the pain as a memory so that it will motivate him. Six months later, he recalled the sadness of the moment. "It was terrible, coming off that field to sit in front of my locker," Tebow said. "Coach Meyer really didn't have that much to say. That's kind of how he coaches. At a time like that you really don't need to hear much."

Everything that needed to be said by Meyer on that last Saturday of September 2008 could have been reduced to one single gesture made by the Florida coach to the media. Urban held out his hands, glancing at his palms to demonstrate their closeness in proximity, like a fisherman measuring the mythical One That Got Away. Except it seemed like such a little fish—one lousy yard that nearly broke their spirit and deprived them of their championship hopes. Of course, it was more that just that. The Gators had sleepwalked through 59 minutes of football, three times losing fumbles in a misfiring offense that seemed unattached to the semblance of a game plan. The secondary gave up the home run far too often. The Florida team had been outcoached, outperformed, and outschemed.

When Meyer finished his press conference, Tebow appeared from the rear door, though the media wasn't aware of the embrace Tim had shared with his father just before entering.

"My parents were there and my dad had said something like, 'I'm proud of you as my son,' and I started crying all over again," Tebow said. "Stevie Mac (Associate Athletics Director Steve McClain) had to wait a minute to open the door to the media room so I could regain my composure."

Tebow still had one foot stuck in self-denial about not making that first down. "It's something you want as a quarterback, the opportunity with two minutes to go in the game," he said. "And you've got a shot to lead your team down to the victory. The whole time I had 100 percent trust and faith in myself and my team that we were going to drive down and score. And I still did on fourth-and-one."

The disbelief was etched on his young, ruggedly handsome face as he struggled for the words to explain what had happened:

"That's something that we very rarely do is get stopped on fourth-and-one. It's kind of been a little bit of our swagger is that we can convert, always, on fourth-and-one. We've done it the last two years. And they beat us to it. Beat us. I thought we'd get it. I thought I'd will myself to the first down. We just didn't do it."

When he had answered the last question in the press conference, Tebow tarried briefly. We in the media could sense something unusual. His eyes were misty but fiery, and his words contrite but full of grit.

"I just want to say one thing," Tebow started, taking a deep breath, "to the fans and everybody in Gator Nation. . . . You know what . . . I'm sorry. Extremely sorry. We were hoping for an undefeated season. That was my goal. It's something Florida's never done here. But I promise you one thing: A lot of good will come out of this. You've never seen any player in the entire country who will play as hard as I will play the rest of the season. And you'll never see someone push the rest of the team as hard as I will push everybody the rest of the season. And you'll never see a team play harder than we will the rest of the season. God bless."

Thus The Promise was delivered.

In all the years of interviewing athletes from baseball, basketball, football, hockey, golf, tennis, the Olympics, and even horse owners, trainers, and jockeys, I had never experienced anything like that. Sitting in the front row, just a few feet from Tebow, I turned to my colleague Franz Beard and saw the same look in his face. Together we have more than seventy years of experience in this kind of thing. Both of us were speechless at the moment. I finally came up with something prophetic like, "Wow!" And to be honest, neither one of us really realized that it was Tebow who had been the prophet.

Although he never predicted the outcome of the next ten games, Tebow had taken ownership of his shortcomings and then set the ground rules for the work ethic that would follow. He only promised effort, not results. But if Tebow didn't prophesize a championship run, he certainly implied it might be coming. And it was. His fellow players took it as the call to arms that it was.

Except for the Pouncey twins, not many of his teammates and coaches heard Tebow's Promise until nightfall. For the players it would have the desired impact.

Meyer worried that his quarterback had taken on too big a load.

"I didn't think he would do what he did," Meyer said, after seeing The Promise on TV that night. "And when I heard it, I cringed. I was wishing he hadn't done it at the time."

Once he had time to look back on it, Tebow admitted he'd had no idea of the impact made by The Promise, which has since been immortalized by a plaque on a wall outside the James W. "Bill" Heavener Football Complex. "I just wanted to apologize for the way we played," he said, "and to let the fans know something good was going to come out of this. And that maybe it was a good thing we lost this game because they were going to see a changed team, changed players, and a changed Gator football program."

The immediate response from his teammates and coaches was positive. Most wanted to get back to work immediately. Meyer changed the schedule and called for practice on Sunday, usually an off day, and Tebow addressed the same issue in the meeting.

"Not too many people said too much, but when we went out to practice you could see more focus," Tebow said. "There was definitely more hunger and an urge for greatness. That all changed."

Indeed it did. Even though tight end Aaron Hernandez feared the season may have already slipped away, when he saw the Tebow speech on TV the next day, he could tell what was coming. It was that same fiery look he sees in the huddle.

"We look in his eyes and it's business," Hernandez said. "He had that fight in his eyes and I knew he wasn't lying. That's why he's such a great quarterback. Once he said it, I knew we were going to go out there and grind because Tebow's word is his man's word. He was going to push us. It gave me chills. And once he said that, I knew we'd get back on track and have a great season."

Maurkice and Mike Pouncey had heard at least part of The Promise firsthand, as had Brandon Spikes. Maurkice was standing close by in the interview room as Tebow spoke—and they had advance notice. During his own interview, Maurkice stopped and looked up to see "a guy who wanted to take everybody on his back, a leader on the team who was really down but promised the world he and his team would rise up again." Maurkice said he knew at that moment that he and other leaders on the team had to reach down to the younger players, rally their spirits, and work much harder.

Mike Pouncey, who thought what Tebow said was "heartbreaking," was later asked by Tebow what he thought and responded, "I thought it was the right speech to give at just the right time."

The Pounceys were both on board, ready to give more and to ask their teammates to give more. And since they had such big roles as anchors of the offensive line, that would portend well.

Little by little Tebow's words caught up to his teammates. Wide receiver David Nelson had sat in his locker for ninety minutes, contemplating his own personal demons. He hadn't played in the Ole Miss game, or much over the past three seasons. He regretted that he hadn't been much help and wished he could have made a difference in "just two points against Ole Miss." He felt guilty for contributing so little in his career at Florida as a seldom-used receiver. That night as he hung out at his apartment with teammates Butch Rowley, Greg Taussig, and Rick Burgess, Nelson clicked on a Web site and punched up "The Promise by Tebow."

"It was a very powerful, powerful speech," said Nelson, "and we all were hoping his words would trickle down to the team. It was something we could all believe in and were going to ride with."

On Monday, Nelson went into wide receivers coach Billy Gonzales' office to be tutored on a special play for Arkansas. And that would be the beginning of a realization for Nelson that he needed to turn his career around—a transformation that would finally begin to take wing after the next game at Arkansas, when he would ask to be put on special teams.

Safety Major Wright called the Ole Miss loss "one of the worst experiences of my life—our defense played horrible and we let everybody down." He began to have flashbacks of the 2007 season, which was disturbing. Although he had family and friends in town, Wright didn't want socialize with them. "They're used to seeing me all happy, but I wasn't the same old Major," he said. His mother had seen Tebow's speech on TV and tried to convey the news to Major, but he wrote it off with, "Oh, Mom, what are you talking about? We just lost and Tebow's just one of those passionate guys . . . one of those guys when he says something he's gonna back it up."

When he saw it for himself on ESPN, Major exclaimed, "Oh my God! Tebow just made a promise and the team just wrote that promise down with him. I knew the whole nation was watching, so we had to back Tebow up."

For co-captain Spikes it was an extended wakeup call—one that he didn't really get until a week later. He said he was standing near Tebow when he made The Promise and knew "that he meant it."

"I couldn't sleep that night because I knew we let ourselves down, we let our families down, and we let the Gator Nation down," Spikes said. "We wanted to have an undefeated season, but Ole Miss came in our house and spoiled that. But I believe everything happens for a reason. It gave our defense a wake-up call—and it gave me a big wake-up call. I was trying to figure out what happened. Did we not play hard enough? Did we not run to the ball? What happened?"

Even though the questions were asked, it took Spikes another full week to find his own personal answers. While the alarm clock was ringing, Brandon Spikes didn't really hear it until after the Arkansas game, when he turned in one of his worst performances.

The Promise had been made. Now it was time for Brandon Spikes to stand and deliver and make amends.

31

The Apology

Losing one game was not the end of football life itself because of the possibility/probability of a one-loss team playing for the national championship. Everybody knew all roads would eventually lead through Atlanta for at least one half of the BCS matchup, despite clamoring by many national experts on behalf of Big 12 teams with glamorous quarterback stats and high-powered offenses.

At the same time, one look at the calendar revealed that the schedules of top teams were full of pitfalls and potential losses—many, in fact, would play each other. So it wasn't necessary to panic just a quarter of the way through the long season. Most likely it wasn't going to be a runaway race for the new national champion.

So how would the Florida team respond to the loss and to Tebow's call to arms? Would this loss springboard the Gators to bigger and better things the way the Auburn loss had for the Gators in 2006?

Despite The Promise, all was not well in the Gator Nation yet and the residue of nastiness still resided in pockets of cynicism among the harsher critics.

Trash talk by some fans reached a new level in the Meyer regime via the vile, vitriolic commentaries that would eventually make their way to the message boards of GatorCountry.com as well as other Web sites. At one point during the next week, so excessive became the distasteful remarks by unhappy fans that paid members were getting booted off the message boards for their negativity.

After the loss to Ole Miss, Tebow's passing ability was being called into question, as well as his judgment. After all, he had audibled in the last drive against Ole Miss on a play that didn't work. What about The Promise? Some people felt it might come up empty.

Indeed, effort was important, but talent, skill, execution of a good game plan, player intelligence, and smart coaching decisions probably counted for more. Halftime and pregame exhortations not so much. Knute Rockne's "Win One for the Gipper" speech ain't what it used to be, they said.

The most distressing aspects of the Gators' performance in the 31–30 loss to Mississippi was the failure to execute almost anything from the "Plan to Win." The Gators were 1-for-11 on third-down conversions. Mississippi dominated the field-position game, starting drives on Florida's side of the field six times. Great defense was nowhere to be found, with eleven missed tackles and blown coverages. There were three overthrows of wide-open receivers made by Tebow.

The Gators fell from No. 4 to No. 12 in the rankings on merit.

Even Meyer, when pressed about whether his team had responded to getting "hit in the mouth" said over and over, "It's too early to tell."

Judging by the Florida locker room after the Ole Miss loss, the proof would be in the doing of it.

"It wasn't like the locker room at Auburn," said Meyer, comparing the two. "Much different. That '06 team was an angry team, a violent team with a chip on its shoulder. It was so motivated to prove everybody wrong.

"This '08 team knew they had a chance to be really good. They still had a sense of entitlement because a lot of these kids hadn't earned crap around here. But the positive thing we had about this '08 team was that we had some depth. So if we weren't playing well, you started making some personnel changes, which we did."

There was still something missing, especially on defense. Changes would be in store at guard and cornerback.

Mostly, though, there needed to be a change in attitude.

"I just remember walking around here with a sick feeling in our stomach," recalled strength and conditioning coach Mickey Marotti. "And it was everybody from the training staff, to the coaches, to the players, to the managers—everyone had this sick feeling in their stomach. After what Tim said, we changed our whole schedule and practiced on Sunday."

It began with a series of meetings, which Meyer felt were needed to "get rid of the bad taste in your mouth."

Freshman Janoris Jenkins was going to get a good look at corner. There were also some offensive line issues and Carl Johnson was about to be plugged in at left guard for the Arkansas game, again one of those "12:30 games" that Meyer detested, but a game that was needed to reunite his team.

While practices that week were spirited and Meyer felt things were coming together, there was a little something lacking about the passion and joy of his two biggest team leaders. Tebow needed to work through some of the negative vibes that had been directed toward him. And Spikes just didn't seem to have a sense of urgency. Defensive coordinator Charlie Strong could tell that about his star middle linebacker the morning he entered the hotel room of Spikes and fellow linebacker Ryan Stamper to awaken them before the game in Fayetteville, Arkansas.

Spikes was moving slowly and almost lethargic.

Strong told him, " 'Spikes, you're not going to have a good day today. I can just tell by your mood and your attitude right now.' And he just went out there and played so . . . well, he didn't play the way Brandon Spikes plays."

Spikes wasn't the only one with a problem. At the half there was so much bad karma among the players that their coach was beginning to fear a serious breach in team comradeship. "I wasn't sure we were even going to come out for the second half," said Meyer. "There was no energy. It wasn't a great environment. We had gotten our ass kicked the week before. We started to question each other. The players questioned themselves. That was the worst locker room I've ever been a part of in twenty years."

Back on the field, special teams finally came alive and, after a slow start, the Gator offense rallied on the strength of a huge day by freshmen running backs Chris Rainey and Jeffrey Demps, both of whom rolled up over 100 yards each and scored on big plays—Rainey going for 75 yards and Demps for 48.

Despite what looked to be an easy win, with 512 yards total offense, half of that didn't come until the fourth period. And Arkansas hung around for three quarters, trailing 17–7.

You could tell Tebow was not at his best mentally. His throws were not really as authoritative and crisp. The Promise had been made, but the delivery had not, so the weight of the universe seemed on his broad shoulders. Meyer could also see an absence of the joy that had always radiated from his quarterback's face.

It was time to go, as Meyer likes to say, and with the ball at his own 17, Tebow set out on an 83-yard drive to bust the game open in the final period. At the Arkansas 21, he faded back and threw a high, hard fastball—what baseball people like to call "high heat"—and stuck it in the hands of Percy Harvin for the touchdown. Some of the frustration, disappointment, and even anger were expunged by Tebow with that one throw. It was cathartic.

Instead of that traditional fist-pumping, energetic trot off the field, however, Tebow sauntered back to the bench, head slightly down. Seeing this, Meyer immediately met him at the sideline for a chest bump, just to get Tebow's motor running. "And he crushed me," Meyer said, later thinking the better of having taken the equivalent of an 18-wheeler head on.

"I really felt bad," Tebow said of the blow to his coach. It wasn't nearly as painful to Meyer as the loss to Ole Miss. And his coach knew that there had been a message in that pass that Tebow was back and open for business. Meyer wanted to see his quarterback's passion return, almost at any cost—even badly bruised ribs.

While there were some big plays on defense, too, including a drive-killing interception by cornerback Joe Haden, none were made by Spikes. As Strong had predicted, the middle linebacker did not have a good day, even in a 38–7 victory. Spikes rarely seemed in the right place, whether a receiver was making a catch in front of him or a blocker was knocking him off a ball carrier. He was far from dominant—and sometimes was just barely present. And he knew it.

"That we won the game was almost a sense of relief as opposed to excitement," said Meyer. "But when we got back, I saw the old Tim Tebow."

Spikes was yet another matter. He had some scores to settle with himself and his teammates.

"We knew we were a better team with better athletes," Spikes said, looking back on the Arkansas game. "It was a gloomy day and we were just going through the motions, relying on our athletic ability to get the job done. We didn't have that spark that a Florida defense usually has. We're a team that needs an edge and we have to play with a lot of passion and energy. That day I didn't feel like I brought that to the team."

The Gators arrived back in Gainesville late Saturday. That Sunday, Spikes called a defensive meeting because he felt just getting people together would help clear the air. He told his defensive teammates he was sorry and that he would play harder, he would play smarter, he would devote himself to becoming a student of the game, and he would improve every day. And he would also ask them to do the same.

He did, and they did.

"When we didn't line up right or pay attention," said free safety Major Wright, "Spikes would get all over us."

The leadership didn't end on the field. Spikes took it to the film room, where he studied tapes and showed others how to do the same. One of the things Major Wright learned from him was how to read the opposing quarterback—something that would later pay Wright dividends in the national championship game.

"I felt like it was on me to get guys to play a little big harder," Spikes said later. "I just tried to get them to play a little above their ability, to be their leader. And if they weren't giving full effort, it was my job to get after them. I found a way to lead them. They let me in and let me coach 'em up."

It was enough of an incentive to light the spark again.

Tebow wasn't there at the defensive meeting, but felt it helped because it showed "guys just being honest with each other and seeing how much each other cared."

This was just the kind of leadership Charlie Strong had been looking for from No. 51. And it all began by Spikes stepping up to apologize for letting his teammates down.

"He is a guy on our football team that our players follow," Strong said. "When you talk about your leader on defense everyone talks about the middle linebacker. The guys know that our defense is going to go as Brandon Spikes goes."

The engines were running and momentum was just beginning to build in perhaps the greatest ten-game run in the history of Gator football. Starting with LSU, Spikes was about to solidify his place among the elite players in Florida's 100-plus years of football.

32

The Championship Run

It was a slow crawl, but the bandwagon jumpers were making their way back to the station. They didn't quite realize yet that the train was already pulling out for the promised land and the remaining nine games of the ten-game quest for the crystal football. Some of the fair-weather ones would not have been welcomed aboard if Urban Meyer had his way.

In defiance of that school covenant immortalized by the song "We Are The Boys From Old Florida"—in particular, the line "In all kinds of weather we all stick together"—a hard-core group of fans went to the dark side. Some were still taking potshots on talk radio and Internet message boards. Even a few former Gator players from other coaching regimes were casting doubt.

For those who like to use the line from *The Godfather*—"It's not personal . . ."—you had better check with Meyer and offensive line coach Steve Addazio before you say it around them. Taking shots at their players is very, very personal—especially when those taking them are blood brothers of the Gator Nation.

Meyer didn't notice all the "noise"—he just kept his head down, kept coaching and grinding toward the next opponent, 2007 national champion LSU. The Tigers had wrested victory from Meyer's Gators the year before in a wild finish.

Now they were ranked No. 4 in the nation.

Perhaps lost in all the glitter of a championship run was the fact that some writers, talk show hosts, and Internet bloggers still didn't consider Meyer's Florida team very physical. In fact, the label "soft" was implied about the offensive and defensive lines. Around the SEC, LSU was considered physically superior.

Addazio was furious at that suggestion that his offensive linemen weren't tough and let them know they were being disrespected.

Once Meyer reflected on what was said about the "soft" offensive line, he, too, was miffed—and even more so at the critics.

"You hear people say, 'Don't take it personal,'" Meyer said. "You're out of your mind if you don't think people take it personal. What are you talking about? We spend more time with the players than we do our families.

"Don't take it personal? What the hell do you think we do for twelve to fourteen hours a day? We're giving our soul to these kids and have somebody write that you're not playing very well or you're a disappointment. What would you do if someone said that about your child? I know what I would do. We're going to go and have a fight. Because that's what you're supposed to do to protect your people."

Addazio was even more steamed. His anger fueled his linemen— Phil Trautwein, Carl Johnson, Maurkice Pouncey, Mike Pouncey, and Jason Watkins, along with their backups.

Meyer said he never seen his offensive line coach so ticked.

"I've known Steve Addazio for a long time and I've never seen a guy come out of his skin more than him," Meyer said. "Because he loved those kids. And those kids had a great love and respect for him. And that group, from that point forward, was the best offensive line in college football."

Beginning with LSU and the world-class reputation of its defensive front seven, Florida's offensive line outplayed everybody on its schedule. And Addazio's linemen took pride in the physical conditioning that allowed them to finish the job in the fourth quarter of big games.

Finally, Addazio got the precision he was looking for. "Five guys firing on all cylinders and getting their assignments right. If four guys hit perfect and one guy doesn't and that one guy is at the POA—point of attack—you've got a problem," said Addazio. "So you want to get as many plays as you can with five guys executing at a high level. That's called consistency and that's what I wanted to see."

With the nickname "Captain Panic," Addazio may be a very animated and fiery coach who doesn't hold back his emotions, but he is also a very steadying influence. As Marotti noted, it was the philosophy of Addazio that kept the Gators cruising down the interstate toward Miami in moments when a few players tended to stray.

If Addazio is "Captain Panic," then Marotti is "Captain Pain" because he's the taskmaster who puts Gator players through the rigors of off-season drills that propel their energetic fourth-quarter thrusts. Marotti and Meyer always emphasize the benefits off-seasoning drills that pay big dividends in the crunch time of big games. Great teams are not built in fall practice or forged by big plays in a game, they say, but rather built on preparation and work.

"It takes hours and hours and hours and days and days you go through after a bowl game until the bowl game the next January," Marotti said. "It's a 365-day process, and there's a lot of ups and a lot of downs—you've just got to keep fighting. Steve Addazio makes a great analogy when he says, 'Steady in the boat, steady in the boat.' And if somebody veers off an exit, just grab 'em and get 'em back on I-75. And if you're going north, you stay north. You just try to bring as many guys as you can. A lot of times throughout the year guys aren't sure they're cut out for this, but you've just got to keep them around and on board."

Keeping those strays rounded up can be a huge task, which was the biggest challenge for coaches in the Michigan aftermath. That's when they came up with "The Power of the Unit." There is a certain philosophy of some organizations, churches, and in businesses that small groups, or cells, are the infrastructure held together by chemistry and commitment. The 2008 Gators found strength in individual groups with divided responsibility—offensive line, defensive line, special teams, wide receivers, etc.—that were hinged together by purpose.

There was something happening to Urban Meyer's team, in a good way, and the full impact of it started to show up.

"The week of the LSU game you could see the biggest change," Tebow said. "We really stepped up our practice, our preparation, and our determination. We were becoming the team that we were always aspiring to be because we really made a big jump."

"The Power of the Unit" began to jell the team, the result, perhaps, of a challenged defensive leader, a quarterback with revived enthusiasm, and offensive and defensive lines on a mission. With it came better special teams, alert secondary play, emerging receivers, and a rushing attack with a game-breaking threat. Now the team was becoming one big unit as the LSU Tigers arrived in Gainesville. The level of football played from that game forward surprised even the head coach.

"It was foot-on-the-accelerator for the next ten weeks," Meyer said. "I didn't see the ten-game streak coming. That kind of shocked me. I thought our offense would be pretty good. I had no idea how good."

Much of the credit he laid at the feet of his longtime assistant coaches. Addazio, Strong, Gonzales, Marotti, and Chuck Heater have been with Meyer since he came to Florida, as were Dan Mullen (offensive coordinator) and John Hevesy (tight ends), though both of the latter would leave for Mississippi State at the end of the '08 season. Newcomers Dan McCarney (defensive line), Kenny Carter (running backs), and Vance Bedford (cornerbacks) fit in nicely. (In the spring, Meyer added Brian White in place of Hevesy and quarterback coach Scot Loeffler to replace Mullen, whose coordinator responsibility went to Addazio.)

As usual, Chuck Heater had come up with another surprise, a fact that no longer surprises Meyer. Safety Ahmad Black developed into a first-rate strong safety whose seven interceptions—one of them at a critical point in the BCS title game—would tie for the nation's best.

Starting with Arkansas, Florida outscored teams 469 to 131 and would end the season beating the nation's No. 1 teams—Alabama and Oklahoma—back-to-back.

Among those ten wins were a lesson in scoreboard decorum for the tail-tucking Georgia Bulldogs; an evening of *Dancing in the Rain* and Tebow's *Braveheart* Face in Tallahassee; and the best fourth quarters ever played by an Urban Meyer–coached team against Alabama and Oklahoma.

Against LSU, Spikes and his defense suffocated the Tiger offense and Brandon returned an interception 52 yards for a touchdown as the Gators announced they were back with a lopsided 51–21 victory.

The SEC's leading rusher, Charles Scott, wound up with Spikes marks up his back, courtesy of Strong's defense. Spikes and his defensive mates held Scott to just 35 yards rushing—half of that on the game's last play. Spikes played his career-best game against LSU, picking off two passes, returning the second one for a touchdown that put the game out of reach as the slaughter of the nation's No. 4 team ensued.

And then there was this extracurricular activity after the touchdown pick: In perhaps the most unusual end-zone celebration, Spikes stopped and punted the ball into the night sky toward the fans in the south end zone.

Sorry, he said, something just came over him.

"Aw, man, I never took a pick to the house in my life and it was sort of the passion of the game that took over," Spikes pleaded.

Meyer muttered under his breath, "I'm going to kill him . . . but that's all right."

From there, the victory march rolled on and Spikes was the co-bandleader—"rolled" being the operative word, because the Gators flattened a pretty good Kentucky team the following week, 63–5. It was homecoming and Tim Tebow treated the alums to a record-tying performance before more than 90,000 with two rushing touchdowns, tying the career mark of 36 held by Emmitt Smith. His teammates tied another record with a little block party with three blocked kicks.

That's the same Emmitt Smith, by the way, who set the record for most career touchdowns in the NFL.

The afterglow of the 63–5 victory over Kentucky lasted all of five minutes. With Georgia up next there was no time for celebration. There was an immediate uptick in practice. It was about then that Meyer noticed something special about his team. During Tuesday and Wednesday practice sessions for the Georgia game, the coach could see routines beginning to emerge.

"After the win over Kentucky, I noticed they were playing with much more confidence," Meyer said. "We preach this to our players all the time: All great players, all great teams have a routine. And I saw our kids starting to believe that how we practice on Tuesday—which we had been preaching all those years, everybody does—they actually started listening.

"Now you get these premier athletes in the seventh week of the season to come out and practice like maniacs on Tuesday. They must know that's going to help them on Saturday or they're not going to do it. That's the first thing I noticed. That's why I talked about the professionals on our team. Those sons of guns came out to work every Tuesday and Wednesday and went to work—as good as any team I have ever been around."

Perhaps that had something to do with the team Florida was playing.

Meyer's assessment was about to be proven true the following Saturday. He played it down, but there would be a little something special coming up for Georgia the next Saturday in Jacksonville. The Bulldogs would be put on notice to never try and embarrass a Meyer team again.

Brandon Spikes sent a message on the opening series when he unloaded on Georgia's Knowshon Moreno, locking him in his sights on Moreno's first carry. "Our whole off-season was Georgia, Georgia, Georgia," said Spikes. "I got so sick of hearing that, so the first chance I had to make a big play I wanted to set the tone and get the job done."

After taking a handoff from quarterback Matthew Stafford, Moreno was greeted square-on with a Spikes smackdown, after which Brandon just lay there on top of him, face mask to face mask, in total domination. Once he had the attention of the Georgia running back, Spikes let him know there was more of the same coming.

"I figured I stuck him and let them know how it was going to be the whole game," said Spikes.

Round One went to the Gators as they set out to gain redemption for "The Incident" the season before. The knockout was on the way.

"I don't know if they thought they could tackle Knowshon—maybe just control him for the day," said Strong. "But when Spikes made that hit, those guys kinda realized they can hit him, they can tackle him . . . and that hit just shot so much juice through the whole defense."

Brandon Spikes led by example and his teammates followed.

In addition to a 49–10 drubbing of Mark Richt's team, Meyer prolonged the agony in the final minutes by calling his last two time-outs in the final minute as backup quarterback Johnny Brantley kept handing off the ball to tailback Emmanuel Moody. The Gators weren't even trying to score. Meyer just wanted the Bulldogs to get a good look at the Jacksonville Municipal Stadium scoreboard.

The mystery of how Meyer would answer Georgia's excessive celebration turned out to be the 49 points on the scoreboard.

Meyer wasn't about to let his players storm the end zone, even after the game. He said he had too much respect for college football.

So, in theory, Meyer was saying, "Take a look at those forty-nine points, Bulldog Nation."

That was Urban Meyer's answer.

Meyer said over and over that showing disrespect to anybody was not nice.

"It's all how you are raised and how you are brought up through the ranks," Meyer finally said in the spring of 2009. "I was always raised that you never say something about an opposing coach or an opposing team. You just don't do that. You don't ever do anything to disrespect that organization. Certainly not in public. You can use your little foxhole mentality to get the point across. But you certainly never call somebody out or put them in a position where you question their manhood or who they are. Because what are you gaining?"

It has been written and said that in 2007 when the Bulldogs virtually emptied their bench after their first touchdown that it provided an impetus for the victory. Meyer doesn't agree.

"You embarrassed a program," Meyer said. "You embarrassed the families of a program. You did something illegal. That's all over. There's certainly no more of that. That's why we did not come out publicly, because we don't do that. That's none of our business. Internally, it is. Certainly not on a national level."

Meyer says he'll never say anything untoward about an opposing coach. "Talk about an opposing coach? No, they're all fine coaches. They're all good people. But the focus needs to be on your team. The focus was on our team and getting our respect back. Because we felt like we lost respect in that game."

That having been said, Meyer admitted it was "the most satisfying win of my career" and he made sure the players knew it—including Percy Harvin, who was standing by him on the sideline. And not just because he was able to gain back respect—also because this was Florida's last remaining major hurdle on the path to Atlanta.

"I got kind of emotional after the game. And Percy was standing right there. And I said, 'From the bottom of the hearts of our coaching staff, we love you guys. Appreciate what you just did. You don't know how badly we wanted this one.' And my voice was kinda cracking. And Percy said, 'Yeah, man, I could see in your eyes that was a gratifying win for a group of coaches and players to experience that. Plus it's a great rivalry.'"

That moment for Meyer brought recollection of Vince Lombardi's speech about "Man's finest hour . . . when he . . . in a good cause . . . lies exhausted on the field of battle—victorious."

It was a night Urban wanted to never end. Although he'd never own up to the "payback"—in the press conference he said he just wanted to (wink-wink) get Moody some work—the fact is that he always likes answering criticism on the field and not in the media.

But a friend of Urban ratted on him, saying, "Probably if they would have had ten time-outs left, Urban would have used them all." Florida State on November 29 was the next big hurdle. Meanwhile, the Gators dusted off a decent bowl-bound Vanderbilt team, 42–14, to clinch the SEC East, and crushed a defensively competent South Carolina, 56–6, pausing to hammer The Citadel, 70–19, on Senior Day as Meyer said good-bye to eleven seniors. Many thought others would be joining those eleven as playing their last home game—notably Harvin, Tebow, and Spikes.

Next the Gators went *Dancing in the Rain* in Tallahassee.

33

Dancing in the Rain

Of all the games and all the nights and all the stadiums where he has coached his teams, there has never been a more surreal moment than what Urban Meyer experienced during a downpour in Tallahassee prior to Florida's regular-season finale against a revived 8–4 Florida State.

His football team literally danced its way into his heart.

With torrents of rain falling before and during the game, sloppy conditions seemed to be playing right into the hands of the Seminoles, who weren't prone to pass nearly as much as Florida and relied mostly on defense.

This was the 53rd meeting with the "school out West." Though never having lost to FSU and being favored by two touchdowns on the road, there would always be angst for Meyer, Tebow, and those who still consider the Seminoles right there with Georgia as the Gators' most hated rival. Now would not be a good time for that to change.

Marching along toward a date with Alabama for the SEC title and a chance to vault themselves into the BCS title game, they all knew that the Seminoles could ambush them and salvage a mediocre season by upsetting the 11–1, No. 2-ranked Gators.

And now this quagmire on Bobby Bowden Field—a major cause for Meyer's concern.

The water was almost ankle-deep and the sheets of rain were near blinding in pregame warm-ups. Meyer wondered if they should even play the game.

"The rain was coming down so hard that you couldn't see your hand in front of your face," Meyer said. "I am watching the water on that field start to swell up. And I am starting to think, 'Maybe they should delay this.' Because I'm beginning to wonder how our kids are going to play in this stuff."

He also worried about ball security. Since FSU's offense had been struggling and Florida's defense was on a roll, Meyer suggested to offensive coordinator Dan Mullen, "Let's make this a field-position game and hang on to the ball." Mullen looked at his boss and said with semi-defiance, "We'll be fine." Meyer firmly repeated his suggestion just before kickoff: "Let's get our single-wing stuff ready, because we are *not* throwing the ball in this stuff."

Usually at the end of warm-ups when Gator players at both ends of the field respond to Mickey Marotti's whistle, they converge to the middle for one final play after Urban has given him the signal. With sightlines impaired and the noise of the rain falling on their headgear, the players could hardly hear the whistle or see the coaches. So Marotti never got the signal. Suddenly, as if they were programmed to react autonomously, the players responded on their own in what Meyer called "one of those magical moments" as they played like Gene Kelly—literally dancing in the rain.

Meyer looked up to see players running toward each other. "The offensive linemen and defensive linemen are all dancing around, chest bumping and you still can't see in front of your face. They just all seemed to bond right there in the rain, as if to say 'Nothing can stop us.' I could not believe it."

Marotti saw the same thing from a different vantage point.

"They were jumping up and down," Marotti said, "and they just seem to come together as a team at that moment."

Tebow remembers Meyer waving his hands and "going around getting crazy—and when he did that, he made the whole team go nuts. And he won the game when he did it. We had more juice than FSU. And we went out there and hit them in the mouth."

To the coaches, this was an example of the bond that the players had created, which was now beginning to take hold.

On the other side of the field, the Seminole players stood and watched almost in awe without response.

This was when Urban realized he was coaching a special football team—one ticketed for greatness.

"It hit me that they would go down as one of the greatest college football teams in history," he said. And perhaps that portended of things to come, like beating No. 1 teams back to back in the post-season. (Alabama was No. 1 in the AP poll, Oklahoma No. 1 in the BCS.)

Although Meyer's confidence soared, he still worried about the conditions causing turnovers. Florida returned to the locker room. Mullen insisted to him, "We're fine—we're going to let the offense go. This is Tim Tebow's kind of night."

To which Urban retorted, "You'd better be right, big boy."

And he was.

First, however, there was some splish-splashing to do on the way to an impressive 45–15 win for the Gators' fifth straight victory over FSU.

The drama heightened in the second quarter when Percy Harvin suffered a high ankle sprain with Florida holding a narrow lead. It proved to be a costly injury.

ABC color analyst Bob Griese was right on with two predictions just seconds after the injury:

1) **Harvin probably wouldn't be able to play against Alabama the following week;**
2) **The Gators would be OK without him because of so much speedy talent like Chris Rainey and Jeffrey Demps.**

Correct and correct.

Tebow has always responded with an uncanny sense of urgency in moments like this, just as he did the night in 2007 when Percy was a late scratch in Columbia, South Carolina. Tebow took a firm grip on the 2007 Heisman Trophy as he scored seven touchdowns against the Ol' Ball Coach, Steve Spurrier.

With the Florida State game still very much in question at just under ten minutes before the half, Harvin already gone and the Seminoles just having cut the margin to 14–6, the Gators faced a third-and-one play at the FSU 4-yard line. There was no big surprise about what was coming.

These are the moments when Tebow's will seems to ignite his teammates. Aaron Hernandez has seen it before. "It's like coach Mick (Marotti) says," Hernandez said. "You can just look in his (Tebow's) eyes and you can just tell he's ready to go, and you feed off of it. And when Tebow is ready, everybody is ready."

Taking the direct snap and immersing himself inside a cordon of big bodies, Tebow seemingly propelled the whole pile, mushing in the mud toward the goal line face-first. As the pile of bodies unfolded, all you knew was that Tebow was somewhere at the bottom. Until the official touchdown was signaled and Tebow came up with garnet paint smeared across his face, it seemed uncertain as to whether he had made the first down, let alone scored.

Tebow emerged from that scrum with what will forever be known as the *Braveheart* look, akin to Mel Gibson's war-painted face from the movie of the same name—Tim's favorite film. That image of Tebow happens to be one of the coaching staff's favorite symbols of competitive fire and heroic effort. If it needed another caption, surely it would have to be "Fire and Rain."

At first glance, the "*Braveheart* Face" looked almost like the bloody, pummeled mug of a boxer. Until ABC announcer Brad Nessler assured viewers that that was just end-zone paint on Tebow's face and not blood, there were a few anxious moments for Gator fans. The TV cameras zoomed in on Tebow's garnet mask as he walked helmetless back to the sideline, capturing the image in Emmy-worthy fashion. This was high theater at its best and Tebow played the part magnificently. And he was enjoying the part for many reasons.

"That will definitely go down as one of my favorite games to ever play in," said Tebow, "and one of my favorite moments . . . the weather . . . the win . . . and that also sparked us for the next two games, which was pretty cool."

Tebow's mom wasn't too crazy about the look, but heck, it was just a boy playing in the mud.

"She liked it, but she'd rather have me all clean-cut," said Tim. "That's a mother, you know."

Football was fun again and a far cry from that glum day in Fayetteville, Arkansas, when his coach had to chest-bump him to start a fire in his belly. Fun. And that's how it went for all the Gators as they danced the night away, completely dismantling their cross-state rivals with 502 total offensive yards. Dan Mullen had been right.

Many Gator fans pirated a still photo from the TV screen and it soon became one of the most popular in Florida football lore. Some bloggers use it as their avatar. Tebow even has a copy "around." Urban, who admits to having the photo hanging on his office wall, said Tebow's performance will be remembered as "one of the greatest ever by a quarterback."

As colorful a moment as it was, and as symbolic as the "Braveheart Face" may have been, Meyer was equally as impressed with a Louis Murphy catch and Tebow throw right before the first half because of what it represented: It was an NFL-caliber play.

"I loved our performance when we called the speed post to Murphy in the rain on the two-minute drill," said Meyer. "For people who say Tim might struggle in the NFL: I can count on one hand the number of people who can make that play and probably have a couple of fingers left over. In a driving rainstorm where you can barely see, Tim throws a speed post on time—which is hard to do on dry surface. And (he) hits Murphy right between the numbers in a two-minute drill against a good defense. Hit him right in stride! And Murph slid. And two plays later he throws to Aaron Hernandez for a touchdown. I sat back and watched that play and I was amazed."

With just under ten minutes to play, Florida led 45–15 when Johnny Brantley came in for mop-up duty but never threw a pass on the final two possessions.

Game, set, match—on to the Georgia Dome for an SEC ring in what Urban Meyer will always remember as a classic.

34

Driving Toward History

Reaching Atlanta was rewarding, but arriving at the Georgia Dome was not the desired final destination for Urban Meyer and his Gators, who were eventually hoping to land 660 miles to the south. There could be no Miami, however, if they didn't get out of Atlanta alive.

For that to happen, the No. 2 Associated Press–ranked school would have to beat the nation's No. 1 team in the SEC title game.

For the first time in any league championship game, the AP No. 1 team was pitted against No. 2.

Only fifteen times in forty previous meetings nationally had the second-ranked team won—one being Meyer's 2006 Gators beating Ohio State and another when Steve Spurrier's 1996 team defeated top-ranked Florida State, both with the national title on the line.

Yet the betting lines favored the Gators by nine points, even though the Alabama Crimson Tide boasted the nation's No. 3 defense and one of the best offensive lines in America and was considered physically superior to the Gators by most. Also Nick Saban was regarded as one of best in the business—highly respected by Meyer.

Meanwhile, Meyer's sixty fellow coaches didn't give his team much respect, because the *USA Today* poll had the Gators at No. 4, as did the BCS standings. This poll snub was starting to sound like a familiar tune, but Meyer's teams seem to relish that underdog role.

If there were any flaws in Florida's team they would surface against the unbeaten Tide, with its dominating offensive line, senior quarterback, and strong running attack that averaged 200 yards per game. Just how the Gator offense would fare without Percy Harvin remained to be seen.

Florida's offense was smoking hot and, while only ranked No. 17 nationally, was just four points shy of the school record 660 points. They were beating up on teams in the first quarter, 136–3, and had only trailed once all year, for a total of just over 15 minutes out of 720. But would this Gator offense be at its best? Would the potential loss of Harvin cost Florida a chance at another SEC title and BCS national championship?

In past years when Harvin was out, sometimes his absence sparked the team and brought it together on another level of competitive excellence. Meyer had seen other players step up big in Harvin's absence. Unbeknownst to Urban, he was about to see it again.

"When Percy went down, I felt the energy all along our team," Meyer would say later. "Because Percy has come a long way now. Percy was not a team player at first, which today a lot of these players are not. But he improved in that department little by little and by the time he left Florida, he was all about the team. It was one of the biggest transitions I've ever seen."

Hernandez had developed into a weapon, as proven the previous week with two touchdown receptions against FSU—his second and third in two games. And Meyer was about to see the highest level of play in the fourth quarter by any team he had ever coached: A shutdown defense and two textbook drives when they were needed most.

Finally this Florida team had jelled, with every player buying in. If their coach loved these Gators after the Tallahassee rain dance, he was going to be ecstatic about them after what they would do in the final quarter against Alabama.

Harvin or no Harvin, however, the Gator defenders had their work cut out for them. Though their pass defense had developed into a force

and they had tied a record for most touchdowns scored off of interceptions (five), there was still some question if the front seven could man
up against the Tide's stout offensive line.

The tone was set early as both teams scored. Alabama fired the first
volley and took the lead on a Leigh Tiffin field goal and the 10–7 margin lasted for 9:29 until Jonathan Phillips tied the score at 10–10. Remember wide receiver David Nelson lamenting the fact that he had not
even gotten in the game against Ole Miss? He was being reborn, starting the week before on a huge special teams play when he fell on an
onside kick of the Seminoles. Now Nelson was stepping into the line of
fire against Alabama with the reception of Tim Tebow's go-ahead
touchdown pass of five yards, which put the Gators in command at the
half, 17–10.

But trouble was looming. Just as Meyer had predicted, Alabama
came storming back after the half, tied the game, and took control for
the whole third period, making a powerful statement.

Alabama's massive offensive line, anchored by All-American center Antoine Caldwell and All-American tackle Andre Smith, was rip-
ping holes in Florida's defense as the Crimson Tide running backs
Glen Coffee and Mark Ingram came thundering through them. This
was becoming a game that Alabama seemed able to control.

John Parker Wilson put together an impressive 91-yard, 15-play
scoring drive that took nearly seven minutes off the clock in the third
quarter. Resorting to the ground attack, the Tide ran the ball five
straight times and tied the score at 17-all on Ingram's two-yard trip.
Then they went ahead 20–17 on Tiffin's field goal and began to swagger
like the No. 1 team they were, perhaps creasing the Gators' confidence
with doubt.

"We saw this thing coming down the road," Meyer said. "All you
have to do is watch it on videotape. . . . We knew it would come down
to the fourth quarter to win it."

Could his Gators reverse the momentum?

Though Saban had the game where he wanted it, up by three going into the last period, the Gators had prepared for this occasion,
physically and mentally.

There were many key stretches and big plays in the Southeastern

Conference Championship Game, but none that will live longer or bigger in Gator football history than the journey Tim Tebow took his team on with fifteen minutes of football left to play. Though this Florida football team had been playing at a peak for eight games, nothing could ever come of it unless this drive was successful and the task was accomplished.

With Dan Mullen mixing up the offensive repertoire, plus the aid of a 15-yard penalty on Dont'a Hightower for yanking on Jeffrey Demps' face mask, Tebow took the Gators on a 63-yard march with an array of touches by everybody from Emmanuel Moody to Demps to David Nelson to Aaron Hernandez. The latter came on a shovel pass that surprised even Tebow, "because we hadn't been talking about it."

Tebow came to the huddle after he got the play from the coaches and he blinked at Hernandez. "And I knew it was the shovel pass, because he knows that it is my favorite play," said Hernandez. "I had my family with me at the game. And it gave me chills. I just knew I had to get this first down. . . . Like it always happens: Tebow drew the defensive end in and gave me the ball. I had to make one person miss and get the first down."

The tight end hammered it down to the 3-yard line on a 6-yard gain and from there Demps hopped over bodies as he was sprung by Tate Casey's block to score and put Florida up 24–20.

There could not be letup by Florida, however, not even with a lead, because with Alabama's display of muscle and firepower, surely the Tide would come rolling back.

Somebody on defense had to make a stop and then the Gators needed a long drive to put the game away. Florida defensive end Jermaine Cunningham answered the call this time, coming from the outside on third down to sack Wilson and force an Alabama punt.

Now for the finish. No. 15 knew what had to be done: He needed to deliver the knockout blow.

"We've got a chance to go win it here," Tebow told his offensive teammates.

Seven minutes, twenty-seven seconds remained. I wrote down on my yellow notepad: "The whole season is riding on this drive."

On the sidelines, Meyer called his team together and positioned himself almost nose-to-nose with the offensive lineman—"right there in the face of the Pounceys."

Go win the game here, he said. This is the reason you ran those stadium steps in January, February, and March, why you did those midnight lifts, why you took and delivered all those blows on "Bloody Tuesday" practices. The Pounceys led the sprint, with the confidence that the hard work they'd put in would make them stronger and fresher.

"We trained harder than anybody in the country and we really believe that," said Tebow.

Hernandez remembers, "The coach said, 'Take the field with a lot of energy and intimidate the defense.' Because if we ran out there and they're tired, we knew we were going to walk over them. It wasn't easy, but we had to keep fighting. Alabama was a great team. We just drove it down the field."

"We were very excited," Tebow said later. "We had a lot of momentum and we said 'Let's just go win it here—no reason not to.' So we just said throw it on our shoulders and let's go get it. We were able to put that drive in."

The 65-yard closing drive was something to behold and, once again, Tebow knocked it out of the park. First he rammed for a yard and a first down. On the next play, he stepped up and then back and laid a beautiful strike into the hands of Louis Murphy for 33 yards to the Alabama 31. A play later Tebow completed a 15-yarder to Hernandez, who carried it down to the six from where Tim bulled his way to the one on the next play.

Then something shocking, if not outrageous, happened when officials flagged Meyer for "sideline interference." The actual call was listed as being against a player, Roderick Blackett, for some inexplicable reason. And the penalty moved the ball back to the Alabama 6 where Demps was stopped cold. Meyer had gone to the field to get the attention of his players, because some didn't realize the twenty-five-second clock was running after the previous inadvertent whistle. Without discussion, he was hit with a 5-yard penalty, which moved the ball back from the 1 to the 6-yard line.

Meyer was fuming, so mad in the press conference later that he had to count backwards and bite his tongue to keep from saying something to get himself in trouble. It frightened him that he feared he might have cost his team the game.

"I wasn't saying anything to the official. I was simply trying to get the team back because it was an inadvertent whistle and our kids were walking back because they thought it was a time-out," Meyer eventually explained. "I was out there telling them to stay. I thought that for a second that I had lost the game for Florida. Because now it's second down and six and then it's third down and six. And that's when Tim and (Riley) Cooper score. And it's Tim's third read. Cooper made a great play, too."

Another big play by a seldom-used receiver saved the day and the season. This one was a low liner from Tebow to Riley Cooper, the football/baseball player who reached down to dig one off the grass and cradled the low pass like the precious cargo that it was. Florida 31, Alabama 20.

As the legend of Tim Tebow grows over generations to come, they will talk about this night. Meyer certainly won't forget.

"I don't know the entire history of the University of Florida," Meyer would say, "but I can imagine that drive and that fourth quarter will go down as one of the greatest."

Tebow was named the game's MVP, with three touchdown passes. Despite all that, his stats—40 touchdowns, 12 running, and 28 passing . . . 564 yards rushing, 2,515 passing with only two interceptions—wouldn't be enough to win him a second Heisman Trophy ahead of Oklahoma's Sam Bradford.

Of course it's not about statistics, except the size of Tebow's heart.

"I've had some great players, and I've got some great players on this team," Meyer said. "But I've never had one like this. Tim's got something special inside him. I'm not talking about throwing. I'm not talking about running. I'm talking about making everyone around him better. That fourth quarter was vintage Tim Tebow."

The historical significance of the drive was not lost on Meyer, nor was Tebow's tenacity lost on Saban.

"He's a great competitor. He takes his teammates on his shoulders a lot," Saban said. "They have a lot of confidence he's going to make plays, and they play that way. They scored two touchdowns where we had them covered about as well as we could cover them."

Alabama's fourth-quarter offensive total was one yard of offense on eight plays with no points.

Meanwhile, all the buzz seemed to be around the Big 12. Oklahoma crushed Missouri 62–21 in the championship game and would be rewarded with the other berth in the national championship game.

As it did two years prior, Meyer's team appeared to have peaked at just the right time. Florida's coach would lay it at the feet of Mickey Marotti's off-season conditioning program and what the two of them call "Fourth Quarter Domination." They would get to prove it four weeks later in Miami against Bobby Stoops' Sooners.

35

Later for the Sooners

This habit of Ohio coaches winding up in the national championship game was getting to be old hat. Once again, Urban Meyer (Ashtabula) was taking on another member of the Buckeye State coaching fraternity: Oklahoma's Bob Stoops (Youngstown). Between the two of them they already owned 191 career wins and a pair of national titles. Urban was about to notch his eighty-third and stay a couple of percentage points ahead of Stoops for the No. 2 spot among all-time winningest active college football coaches with at least five years on the job.

Stoops was coach of the No. 1-ranked BCS team and AP's No. 2. The reverse order was true for Meyer. While the two men could not be classified as close friends, they were more than acquaintances and mutually admired each other. About the only real similarity, aside from home state, was they both were a touch old-school. In that vernacular, the Gator coach was going to "dance with the one that brung you." Which meant Meyer would be harkening back to his tried-and-true Plan to Win: Playing great defense, winning the turnover battle and concentrating on field position. Special teams had been the key to his success since his Bowling Green days and it would be the same in the

BCS title game at the Orange Bowl. If Meyer was going to become the first coach to win two BCS titles, he was going to do it his way.

Stoops, although a former defensive coordinator under Steve Spurrier on the 1996 national champion Gators, preferred offensive firepower.

Florida was a three-point favorite to win its second national title in three seasons. Meyer felt his No. 9-ranked defense had to neutralize Heisman Trophy winner Sam Bradford's No. 1–rated hurry-up offense. The Gators had some pretty impressive stats of their own: A plus-22 in turnover margin (No. 1 in the nation), 24 interceptions, and a school-record five returned for touchdowns.

The X factor for the Gators was the quick, aggressive young secondary, which reacted to the thrown football with precision. And that was going to pay dividends. Cornerbacks Joe Haden and Janoris Jenkins could man up and play on an island, which would allow safeties Major Wright and Ahmad Black, as well as nickelback Will Hill, to roam. If Oklahoma thought it could fool these players because they were all sophomores or freshmen, it would be making a huge mistake.

The Sooners were a bit cocky, however, and eventually that surfaced in pregame interviews—something that did not exactly have Bob Stoops doing backflips with pom-poms. Before he could stop Dominique Franks from spouting off, however, the sophomore cornerback had the audacity to trash Tim Tebow.

"If you look at the three best quarterbacks in the country, they came from the Big 12," Franks said in one of the media conferences for all to hear.

Stoops just cringed and put a muzzle on his sophomore cornerback the next day.

Meyer's team made that kind of guy pay. (See Geno Hayes of FSU, the Georgia Bulldogs, Ricky Jean-Francois of LSU, etc.)

Urban would take that low-hanging fruit for his imaginary bulletin board. (There was apparently no real bulletin board in Miami.) Meyer had played the propaganda card with the "ten feet of nonsense" wall of bulletin board clippings that was exploited before the 41–14 victory over Ohio State in the 2006 BCS National Championship Game at Glendale, Arizona.

Tebow hardly needed another kick in the groin about not winning his second Heisman Trophy, despite getting the most first-place votes. The fact that the Heisman went to the quarterback on the opposing team wasn't exactly lost on Tim.

"Don't wake up a sleeping giant," warned Percy Harvin.

Too late. The giant was awakened. I could see it in his eyes. I could see it in the nervous leg shake as he was being grilled over and over and over by the media about the Franks comment. It's like a torture chamber when they release several hundred media members on you about three times a week.

"Obviously I'm competitive and I want to win at everything I do, so there was a little bit of extra emotion in me and I definitely wanted to prove something," Tebow said later. "It's not all about statistics, but the league that you play in, the difference you make on a team, and the player that you are. It was about my teammates who got behind me and all the text messages I got from them after I lost (the Heisman)—probably a hundred of them from guys saying they were behind me. Our team was very fired up for the game. And I wouldn't change a thing of how that happened."

So Tebow was sick of hearing it and somebody was just going to have to pay. After all, Florida's offense wasn't exactly small potatoes, have sparked a nine-game streak that had seen the Gators put up an average of 49.4 points per game.

Deep down the Gator coaches knew their offense could move the ball against the Sooners. Meyer and offensive coordinator Dan Mullen, who was already hired as coach of Mississippi State, were fully aware that OU was No. 63 nationally in total defense and No. 98 in pass defense.

And then there was the secret weapon: If the game got to the fourth quarter fairly even, Meyer, his coaches, and his players knew that it belonged to them. They relied on the commitment of Fourth Quarter Domination, as had been proven against Alabama. Meyer lays the credit for that directly at the feet of strength and conditioning coach Mickey Marotti and his staff. "The best in the country," said Meyer. The work these Gators put in had actually begun the year before. So, both mentally and physically, they were ready to go.

Surprisingly, though these two teams averaged 100 points a game between them, defense ruled the night. Florida got big interceptions by Major Wright and Ahmad Black and key stops on the goal line by soon-to-be departed Torrey Davis. And the Gators would dominate the fourth quarter. Oklahoma, one of the most potent offenses in college football history, could only muster twenty-one yards on eight plays in the final twelve minutes of the game.

The first period wound up in a tie. Harvin finally got into the flow, but uncharacteristically Tebow got picked twice by the Sooners. Considering he had thrown fewer interceptions per season than any starting Gator quarterback in history (1.62) that was a rarity. On the second one, Oklahoma reached the Florida 1 but couldn't score—stymied by Davis, who after two big plays in the national championship would drop out of the program. It was defense that kept Florida in the game as the Gators put on a virtual clinic in the tipped pass drill to once again stop Oklahoma just before the half.

A Bradford pass to Manny Johnson was broken up by Joe Haden and then tipped three more times—by Black, Wright, and Ryan Stamper—before falling into the hands of Wright, who was having a huge night. Earlier in the first quarter, Wright had lowered the boom on Johnson, who looked as if he had possession of a pass behind Haden. Wright's ferocious hit jarred the ball loose and it fell to the turf on the Florida sideline. Clearly, Wright had timed his hit by not going for Bradford's pump fake. Wright's dedication to watching film earlier in the season had made a difference.

By the middle of the game it looked like old-fashioned SEC defensive smashmouth football, tied at 7. Then Tebow muscled up and made his move, hammering the Sooners to the ground with relentless effort and power. On the drive for the go-ahead score, Tebow carried six times for 38 yards of some determined running, including a gallant effort for a 12-yard run on third-and-10. Harvin took it in for the score from two yards out. That propelled the Gators to a 14–7 lead with a little over four minutes left in the third.

Now came the fourth quarter the Gators had talked about so much.

"Oklahoma's style of offense was very challenging," Meyer said, "Up-tempo, the fast plays, the fast alignment, and then they go. I'm glad we had a month to prepare for it." In the process, Florida coaches had a chance to borrow from the technique and use it on the Sooners.

"In the fourth quarter against Oklahoma we went to no-huddle," said Meyer. "The negatives of the no-huddle are that it limits your substitution and your motions. The advantages are that you wear out a defense and you limit their calls and defensive substitution."

A blocked field-goal attempt by Dunlap—the Gators' ninth blocked kick and Dunlap's third of the season—proved a big momentum changer.

In the fourth, the skillful Bradford brought his team back for a 14–14 deadlock with a 77-yard drive. Florida countered with Phillips' field goal to go back on top, 17–14, with just under 11 minutes left in the game.

Would the Gators, indeed, dominate? Would the Plan to Win work again? Would Meyer's coaching technique of counting on less-than-marquee players to come through big in key situations hold true? What about the young secondary coached by Chuck Heater and Vance Bedford—could it stand up under the assault of the reigning Heisman Trophy winner?

Here came Oklahoma, quickly advancing to midfield, where Ahmad Black was about to register one of the biggest plays in the history of Florida football. Ahmad Black of Lakeland, Florida, who had gotten lost in the shuffle and didn't seem to fit the profile of Chuck Heater's elite athletes—"too small, too slow, too everything," Heater would say.

Some of those so-called marginal players of the past who may not have been noticed or been major contributors to the program were about to blossom into key performers. Coaching deep in the roster and not giving up on players would, once again, prove to be an asset to Meyer.

From the sideline where Meyer watched, from the press box and even on the Fox telecast, for all the world it looked like Bradford, despite heat from Dunlap, had just connected with Juaquin Iglesias at the Florida 24 on what would have been a backbreaking play for the Sooners.

But wait! Somehow Black, trailing the play, lunged toward Iglesias as the receiver was turning to pull down the ball, and took it away. Or did he? Instant replay would show that Black, indeed, stripped it from the hands of a falling Iglesias and, as he spun to the ground like a helicopter, managed to hold on. Interception number twenty-six of the season for these ball-hawking Gators (Black's seventh) and one that couldn't have come at a better time.

Black still isn't sure how he did it. "If I had to do it again I couldn't," he said months later. "It was probably a one-of-a-kind play. I don't even know how I did it myself. You do a lot of drills where you put your arm in there and rip the ball out. And I always kid around and try to catch it in practice. And I guess I did it in the game—I don't know.

"I stuck my arm through there and pulled it out. He didn't have it tight—he didn't catch it all the way. Coach told me it was one of the biggest plays of the game, but I just think it was one of the big plays our team made to win. We had a lot of big plays."

Meyer thinks it was a little bigger of a play than that. "They were driving the ball," said the Florida coach. "We were up by three (17–14). It was one of the greatest plays in Florida football history."

If that didn't slam the door, Tebow would with the help of an unlikely hero: David Nelson. There was one tick under ten minutes left when Tim took his team on an 11-play, 76-yard drive, which was helped along by a clutch catch from his roommate, the seldom-used Riley Cooper, on third down and 12. It appeared stalled briefly again on third down and six at the OU 11 after a false start by the Gators until Hernandez hauled in another shovel pass over the middle.

This was the moment of David Nelson's football life—David Nelson, who had never even gotten on the field in the loss to Ole Miss. Second down and goal at the Oklahoma 4.

"Coach Meyer looked at me and said, 'Go win the game,'" Nelson said. "And I jogged out. I swear it was the longest jog from the sideline to the huddle that I've ever done. I was running in slow motion. My heart was beating a million times a minute. I didn't even listen to Tebow call the play. The whole time he was calling it I was saying to myself: 'You have to get off the line scrimmage and you have to catch this ball—even if he's holding both of your hands, you have to find some way to catch this ball.'"

It was time for the jump pass and Nelson knew, once he saw the alignment, that it was coming to him.

"I acted like I was going to block my man and when he peeked inside, he turned his eyes to Tebow and he lost sight of me, so I slipped inside of him," said Nelson. "Tebow just jumped up and put the ball in a place where if I didn't catch it, nobody would have caught it."

Touchdown Florida, and Nelson just kept on running with the football, like he wanted the moment to never end.

"I honestly don't remember the next thirty minutes of what happened," he said. What happened was that Nelson and his teammates would be conducting interviews and celebrating their second national title in three years.

One moment Tebow won't forget: He actually got an unsportsmanlike conduct penalty for doing a Gator chomp in front of defensive back Nic Harris—the first of his football career, and shocking behavior for the otherwise nearly perfect twenty-one-year-old. But Tebow would take it because OU had been trashing him as the "fourth best quarterback in the Big 12."

"I just wanted to do something (to Harris) that that would say 'It's not about you or me—it's about the Gators!'" Tebow would explain later. "It was for the Gators fans. They all loved it. I probably got a thousand people telling me how much they loved that stuff. It was just kinda in the heat of the moment—probably not the right thing to do, but it worked out pretty good."

Meyer feigned anger at Tebow's penalty, but looking back on it had to laugh. "It was funny," Urban said. "I didn't think so at the time because I am so paranoid and I'm such a maniac I started yelling at Tim. And he gave me that look like, 'Hey coach, c'mon . . .' It was all good. I made the comment after the game, 'He's going to be running at 6:30 tomorrow morning. . . .'"

Tebow didn't run and Urban didn't get upset, of course. Nor had he taken umbrage at either the Gatorade dunking—he was snookered by Louis Murphy and Javier Estopinan—or the butt slap from Harvin late in the game. While Percy's gesture may have been a little weird, it didn't bother his coach. "I gave him a look," said Meyer, "but he didn't mean anything by it. He was just kidding around."

Perhaps it was Percy's way of saying good-bye in his final game. Would Meyer also be saying *sayonara* to his best players on offense and defense, Tebow and Spikes? In a few days the Gator Nation would know the answer to that, during the victory celebration at Ben Hill Griffin Stadium. Tebow came to the podium, said what appeared to sound like his last good-bye, and as he walked off to the chants of "One more year, one more year," turned and said, "And one more thing. I'm coming back!" The fans erupted. A few days later Spikes announced he would forgo the NFL draft as well. That meant Florida would have most of its team intact the following season with eighteen of twenty-two starters returning.

In Meyer's office a few months later, as we talked about the upcoming season, I pointed out that November 28, 2009, was going to be a special day: Senior Day, possibly the last game Florida State's Bobby Bowden would coach against Florida, Tim Tebow's last game at Ben Hill Griffin Stadium, and the final home game for a special group to Meyer as well, he pointed out. (He is always quick not to separate Tebow from the rest of the team.)

"There will be a whole bunch of those guys, too," he said. "It will be the first time I've ever been with a program from start to finish. Every kid now who walks on that field, we recruited and brought here. We know his family inside and out. We've grown with them."

There is no denying how he feels about Tebow, however, and it was in that interview that he revealed just how much. As we discussed Tim's role as a leader, how he had mentored his successor, Johnny Brantley, Urban saw a future for Tebow after his NFL career is over: coaching.

At Florida maybe?

"I foresee that someday Tim Tebow is going to be a head football coach. Maybe at Florida," he said. "I told him that."

What did Tebow say?

"He didn't dispel it. He doesn't say no. I think he's that talented. I think he commands that much respect. I think he understands the game very well. I think his work ethic is impeccable. I think his whole mission in life is to be on a grand stage and change people's lives.

"Name a better opportunity than that—to sit in this office and be a head coach. At first I was joking around with him. And then I got serious and said, 'You need to do this. Go play and have your stuff going on, but also go coach.' He'd go up through the ranks fast."

No doubt this would trigger the "Urban Meyer is leaving Florida for _____" stories again, just as the remarks earlier in this book about Notre Dame once being his "dream job" did. Headline: Tim Tebow to succeed Meyer, who's going to Notre Dame!

You just knew it would.

For being honest with people, including Miami sports talk host Jim Mandich in 2008, Meyer has had that "dream job" tape replayed over and over, no matter how many times he says he doesn't want the job. He wouldn't care, except that it's simply not true and he doesn't want young recruits to believe that. No matter, one Florida East Coast columnist and a Birmingham, Alabama, talk show host/writer keep making up his mind for him. The Alabama guy fabricated a story that Meyer would be leaving for South Bend after the 2009 season.

Finally when he had enough, Meyer sent me a text in July saying, "I am NOT leaving Florida. My family and I are honored to have the best coaching job in America." Translated by the guy in Birmingham: He's lying. I know he's lying because his lips are moving. Of course, the lips of the talk show host/writer were moving when he said that.

Sorry to disappoint those who said otherwise, but on August 3, 2009, Urban Meyer signed a new contract through 2013, making him the first $4 million coach in the SEC—which I guess means he won't be going to South Bend despite those reports.

Then there was Lane Kiffin, who targeted Florida and Meyer as Tennessee's nemesis, managed to take away one of Meyer's wide receiver commitments from South Florida, and then accused Meyer (wrongly) of violating NCAA recruiting rules. Meyer's response: Just don't respond. The most he could conjure up about Tennessee's renegade coach was: "People say, 'Coach, why didn't you respond?' The fans enjoy a little sparring back and forth.' I just don't believe in that."

What Urban does believe in, strongly, is that his players not only need motivation, but love. Yes, that's right—love. It's something he learned about human behavior while he was a college student. He was reading a book called *Motivation* in a course for a group project that had set out to discover the strongest forms of it. The group came up with love, fear, hate, and survival.

And actually, a little bit of all that is rolled into Meyer's coaching style—especially love. "I remember sitting in a big classroom with four people. And groups of four people with two weeks to work on it— Summer A, Cincinnati, 1984. Our group came up with those four motivations. First we came up with love, fear, and hate, and we added survival later."

They use the "love" word quite a bit around the Florida football program. Urban uses it when talking to Shelley about the group of players he's coaching. "Every once in a while I'll call her during the day and I will tell her, 'I love this team.' I love being around these guys. And she's used to me whining and complaining a lot."

One thing he loves most is the work ethic. In an effort to take their minds off all those No. 1 preseason rankings, Meyer promised the most grueling off-season and prefall workouts in the history of the program.

"The days of 'rah rah' and having to motivate them are over," said Meyer. "Our guys are down there working. And we've just got to keep the pedal to the metal. You've always got to worry that if you sit back and reflect and think how great things are, somebody's going to catch you. History shows that after the '96 team, somebody caught Florida. As a matter of fact, they got passed. And we can't let that happen. You don't have time to sit back and reflect. I want to make sure our guys enjoy it here. I want to make sure our players are taken care of . . . our coaches are taken care of. But we're working as hard as we ever have to make sure nobody's catching us."

One wonders when, if ever, Meyer has had a chance to enjoy his success, because he rarely takes time off except to go to his lake home nearby. As Satchel Paige once said, he doesn't want to look back "(because) something might be gaining on you." On one occasion over the spring, he did take a day or two with most of his coaching staff and their wives to relax at the Longboat Key Resort near Sarasota. Billy Gonzales and his wife were away, as was his wife, Shelley. But there was just a moment when he relaxed while he and the staff were onboard the *Entrepreneur,* a 110-foot yacht belonging to Congressman Vern Buchanan—a longtime friend of Urban's. As the *Entrepreneur* pulled up to the edge of Tampa Bay, the coaches and their wives shaded their eyes from the searing Gulf of Mexico sunset to view the porpoises jumping around the boat—all the while enjoying a little wine, beer, or champagne in a rare relaxed moment. Urban was chatting with Congressman Buchanan as well as friends John Alvarez, Thad Boyd, and singer Mel Tillis.

This was how national championships were supposed to be celebrated, but it was only a snapshot of the good life, however long it lasted. Turns out it would only be for a few hours before it was back to work. But it was a few hours to gain peace of mind.

"The new guys don't know," Urban said of his journey at Florida. "But there are a few top-end coaches on our staff who have a very good idea—and they were there from the beginning—what 'peace of mind' means. And that means we have depth now in the offensive line. We have tough guys who love football. We have the quarterback we want and we have the backup who is going to be a very good player. We have six corners who can play major college football. When is the last time Florida had that?"

Of course, there was much work to be done. There was the matter of the number of players who have been arrested over four-plus years that critics like to throw up in his face (estimates run between twenty-five and twenty-eight), for which Meyer takes ownership, but he never apologizes for his effort to straighten out lives. He does say he and his staff are doing more thorough screening of conduct among recruits and that the quality of the players is first-rate. He likes to brag about Florida's 100 percent graduation rate after 2008. But after all, as Tebow points out, part of the mission is helping young men get their lives on track. One of those most appreciative is Aaron Hernandez, who came to Florida in January 2006, just after his father had died. He was feeling lost and drifting, "headed down the wrong path," according to Hernandez.

"I had a little emptiness in me. He kind of filled it—a father figure, someone I could look up to," said the junior tight end from Connecticut. "He was always there for me. Even when I made bad decisions, he always took me through them and taught me the right direction. And he showed me the love I needed at the right time."

Only now has Hernandez come to understand why Urban Meyer was so hard on him for not paying attention to studies, or doing the wrong things off the field.

"He always wants the best for his players. Sometimes it seems like he doesn't like you. He knows how to play mind games with you to make you reach your potential. Not many coaches in this world really care about their players. He cares about his players. Wants the best for them. Wants them to have a great education. Wants them to do stuff out of football once they're done. He and I have a bond. I love him as a father figure as well as a coach."

By late spring Meyer was still trying to find time for a championship dinner but there was one event he wasn't going to put off: Presenting his father, Bud, with another championship ring. His sister Erika Jones, who was there, recalled the evening with Urban, her father, and Earle Bruce. (Urban also was going to be inducted into the Lou Holtz Hall of Fame in East Liverpool, Ohio.)

Wrote Erika: "Urban was especially excited about this evening because he had ordered Bud his second national championship ring and was planning to present it to Bud that night. It was a beautiful, sunny summer evening at Buckhead Mountain Grill in Newport. As we were enjoying nachos on the Ohio River, Urban had privately planned a ring delivery with our waiter.

"The waiter came to the table asking for Bud Meyer. He said there had been a special delivery for him and then surprised Bud with the ring driven down from Columbus. When Bud opened the box, the entire patio was taken back by the massive No. 1 'bling' sparkling in the sun. Bud, in his standard demeanor, accepted the ring in silent pride. As always, Earle and Bud spent the evening exchanging stories about the good ol' days. My daughter, Aidan, who is in awe of Coach Bruce, asked him in detail about his coaching career. The entire evening was filled with great old football stories surrounded by a rotation of wonderful courses and patrons paying their respects to the table of talented coaches."

It was a way, Urban said, of showing Bud appreciation for all those laps he was made to run, for all the discipline he was tendered, and for teaching him about life's core values. It was a son's way of saying thank you and I love you to his father and, yes, stopping to smell the roses.

In the life of Urban Meyer, smelling the roses just doesn't usually make it onto his calendar very often.

It just wouldn't be Urban's way.

INDEX